POLITICAL LEGITIMACY IN MIDDLE AFRICA

POLITICAL LEGITIMACY IN MIDDLE AFRICA

FATHER, FAMILY, FOOD

Michael G. Schatzberg

INDIANA UNIVERSITY PRESS   BLOOMINGTON AND INDIANAPOLIS

This book is a publication of

Indiana University Press
601 North Morton Street
Bloomington, IN 47404-3797 USA

http://iupress.indiana.edu

Telephone orders   800-842-6796
Fax orders   812-855-7931
Orders by e-mail   iuporder@indiana.edu

The paper used in this publication meets the minimum
requirements of American National Standard for Information
Sciences—Permanence of Paper for Printed Library Materials,
ANSI Z39.48-1984.

Manufactured in the United States of America

Library of Congress Cataloging-in-Publication Data

Schatzberg, Michael G.
Political legitimacy in Middle Africa : father, family, food /
Michael G. Schatzberg.
p.   cm.
Includes bibliographical references and index.
ISBN 0-253-33992-8 (cloth) — ISBN 0-253-21482-3 (pbk.)
1.   Political culture—Africa.   2.   Political socialization—Africa.
3.   Legitimacy of governments—Africa.   4.   Family—Africa.
I. Title.
JQ1879.A15 S32 2001
306.2'0967—dc21   2001002060

1 2 3 4 5   06 05 04 03 02 01

For Elisabeth

CONTENTS

ACKNOWLEDGMENTS

Had I known this book was going to take so long to complete, I might not have had the resolve to begin it. Over the past twelve years it has occupied too many of my thoughts and has consumed too much of my life. Frankly, I am happy and relieved it's finally done. Now I can move on to other long-deferred research ventures, and I am at last able to express my profound gratitude to those people and institutions who have supported me both intellectually and financially throughout the life of this project.

I first conceived this study while plying my trade at the Johns Hopkins University School of Advanced International Studies (SAIS) in Washington, D.C. SAIS generously provided a sabbatical leave during the 1988–1989 academic year that permitted me to do some preliminary research in West and Central Africa, as well as to do some initial writing without the usual daily distractions. The project was further aided by a fellowship at the Woodrow Wilson International Center for Scholars in Washington, D.C., where I blissfully spent 1990–1991. I am deeply indebted to the Wilson Center, its energetic staff, and the other fellows I encountered for a most productive and stimulating year. A truly remarkable institution, the Wilson Center graciously provided me with a haven, as well as the time and freedom to wander down intellectual pathways that I might never have discovered otherwise.

Since then, I have hung my hat at the University of Wisconsin-Madison— another remarkable institution. The Graduate School furnished me with summer salary support that facilitated my research, as well as a Vilas Associates Award that enabled me to do field research for this project in Brussels and Senegal during the summers of 1993 and 1994. The College of Letters and Science generously provided a sabbatical leave during the 1998–1999 academic year. It was during this time, liberated from courses and committees, that I was finally able to bring the research to closure and draft most of the manuscript. My intellectual homes at the

Acknowledgments

university, the Department of Political Science and the African Studies Program, helped in ways too numerous to mention. I extend my heartfelt appreciation to all these nooks and crannies of a great university.

While such institutional support is always crucial, all authors know that the most profound debts we incur are to the friends and colleagues who touch us along the way. I have been more fortunate than most in this regard, and I am pleased to record my gratitude to all of these individuals. Crawford Young, Jan Vansina, Thomas Spear, Aili Tripp, Richard Merelman, René Lemarchand, and anonymous readers for Indiana University Press all read the entire manuscript. Although they did not always agree with me, and still don't, their criticisms and arguments have made this a much better book. Other friendly critics who generously offered constructive comments on earlier papers, ideas, articles, and presentations include Atieno-Odhiambo, Linda Beck, Florence Bernault, Diane Ciekawy, Donald Emmerson, Pierre Englebert, Jo Ellen Fair, Edward Friedman, Jeremy Liebowitz, Wyatt MacGaffey, Gregory Maddox, Jean-François Médard, Kathleen Mulligan-Hansel, Stephen Ndegwa, Marion Smiley, and Michael Williams.

I am also grateful to the following colleagues and institutions for inviting me to share early versions and portions of this work with a wider audience. Atieno-Odhiambo and Gregory Maddox (Rice University and Texas Southern University); Achille Mbembe (Columbia University); Pierre Englebert (Pomona College); Jean-François Médard (Université de Bordeaux); the Centre de Recherches Entreprises et Sociétés (CRES) and Espace Afrique in Geneva; and Babacar Kanté and Babaly Sall (Université Gaston Berger, Saint-Louis, Senegal) all provided venues for me to speak. They, and the audiences they assembled, listened and then gently pointed out where and how my work might be improved. They were usually right.

Several superb research assistants also helped me. Gilbert Khadiagala (then a student and now a colleague) at SAIS, Anne LeMay at the Wilson Center, and Andrew Sessions and Lynda Kellam at the University of Wisconsin all contributed. In addition, my students—graduate and undergraduate—at the University of Wisconsin-Madison politely considered my occasionally bizarre ideas with good cheer and engaged intellects. They persistently demanded that my ideas be comprehensible. This had the happy (though often painful) effect of forcing me to formulate them more clearly in the first place.

Janet Rabinowitch and Dee Mortensen at Indiana University Press have been wonderfully patient editors and were always understanding when deadlines arrived but the manuscript did not. I am also grateful to Edinburgh University Press for permission to use portions of my previous analysis contained in "Power, Legitimacy, and 'Democratisation' in Africa," *Africa* 63, no 4 (1993): 445–461; and to Editions Karthala for permission to use parts of my previous analysis contained in "La sorcellerie comme mode de causalité politique," *Politique africaine* 79 (October 2000): 33–47.

Over the years I have had so much help that I am sorely tempted to withhold the customary absolution. I can't do that, however, because on more than one occasion I stubbornly chose not to follow all this excellent advice. Responsibility for any remaining errors of fact or interpretation, analytical shortcomings, or other deficiencies is, therefore, mine alone.

Finally, my companion, Elisabeth Karpov, also contributed. She always seemed to know when I needed to be alone with my thoughts, but still conspired to drag me away from this book whenever she could. Her gentle distractions encouraged me to raise my head from the manuscript to appreciate life's finer moments. For this, as well as for providing substantial doses of balance and sanity in my life, I am extremely thankful. Her love, friendship, support, and soothing presence have been sweet anchors.

Michael G. Schatzberg
Madison, Wisconsin
2 March 2001

POLITICAL LEGITIMACY IN MIDDLE AFRICA

1. | Metaphor and Matrix

This book is about the cultural logic of legitimacy in middle Africa. It argues that political legitimacy in this corner of the globe rests on the tacit normative idea that government stands in the same relationship to its citizens that a father does to his children. In turn, this normative idea ultimately derives from a pervasive, yet largely unarticulated, conceptual understanding of the distribution of rights and responsibilities within a highly idealized family. This implicit conceptual vision of a family, moreover, is a major component of what I call the moral matrix of legitimate governance. Moral matrices are present in all societies, and they change across both time and space. They form a culturally rooted template against which people come to understand the political legitimacy, or "thinkability," of institutions, ideas, policies, and procedures. This is also a book about how people shape the parameters of their political universe; how they define key political concepts; and how they understand and act on alternative notions of political causality. Contrary to widely held Western social scientific assumptions, the contours of the political realm, definitions of key political concepts, and comprehension of causality all vary according to culture and context. Assumptions of universality in these matters are largely misplaced. Social and political scientists must demonstrate the universality of their core notions rather than simply assuming them.

This position is both consistent with, and a response to, the challenge of David Sills and Robert Merton, who have lamented the dearth of social science materials from non-Western cultures. "The social sciences themselves," they write, "are primarily products of Western civilization, and Africans, Asians, and other non-Westerners who work in the social sciences generally use the theory and methods of the Western social sciences as their framework. . . . Certainly a major challenge for the social sciences—if not for all the sciences—is to find ways of incorporating the basic ideas of African, Asian, and other non-Western thought into the Western paradigm."[1] To this, however, I would add that the Western paradigm of the social sciences might well need to transform itself as it absorbs these disparate understandings of the political universe from other portions of the globe. As we shall eventually see, the theoretical and epistemological consequences of this are large and warrant attention. Many such observations lie scattered along the route of this intellectual journey but are more properly discussed at its end.

The original "puzzle" that set me down this path presented itself in the mid-1970s. While doing field research in Mobutu's Zaïre, I noticed that local verbalizations of an ideal administrative role model, as well as a more generalized political discourse, often referred to a *"bon père de famille* [good father and family man]" as a model worth emulating in other political or social arenas. The more I spoke to people, the more I read the normal administrative correspondence in the archives, the more it became clear to me that there was something going on that I did not understand. To be sure, there was the example of Mobutu's cult of personality and its incessant propaganda that painted him as the "Father of the National Family." But there was also a replication of this imagery and metaphor at other levels throughout the state machinery and in other segments of society. Where did this notion of *bon père de famille* come from, and why was it so widespread? What did it mean? What sorts of assumptions went along with it? Why was it so diffused? Since I was then more interested in the political dynamics of social class formation and how social class identity varied according to context, I did not try to unravel these questions but filed them away for later attention.[2]

Some years afterward I returned to the puzzle of the "good father and family man"—this time pursuing my investigations of it as a manifestation of Mobutist ideology and political thought in the context of an oppressive Zaïrian state in uneven decline.[3] The present work, however, pursues two additional parallel tracks of inquiry. The first concerns the diffusion of paternal and familial language in other states and is thus broadly comparative. An initial investigation of Cameroon—prodded by the stimulating works of Jean-François Bayart and Achille Mbembe—persuaded me that such language was not uniquely Zaïrian, and I began to think of this as a more general pattern of political language that might carry with it a set of assumptions that were somehow related to questions of political legitimacy.[4] Virtually all students of politics in Africa, Westerners as well as Africans trained in the prevailing paradigms and approaches of Western empirical social science, have misunderstood the nature of political legitimacy in African regimes. More specifically, there has been an unfortunate tendency to confuse longevity with legitimacy, or the absence of coups with both stability and legitimacy.[5] Furthermore, at least since the worldwide movement toward political liberalization gave birth to a new literature on democratization starting in the early 1990s, there also seems to be an unstated assumption in many of these works that democracy, at least in its most commonly analyzed Western electoral form, is by definition politically legitimate. Sadly, this is not always the case. Two underlying reasons help to explain this confusion: first, in our attention to political economy and other theoretical models derived primarily from the experience of the West, we have tended to underestimate the enduring importance of political culture; and second, political scientists have tended to ignore the significant body of clues provided by both political thought and political language.

The second track, therefore, was focused on political thought and the way political language and political perceptions help to shape it. Let me emphasize that political thought, here, does *not* refer exclusively to the speeches and writings of the "great men" temporarily occupying the region's State Houses and presidential palaces. In restricting their attention to the substantive content of the speeches and writings of major politicians and pan-Africanist figures, scholars writing in a sterile, static, and narrowly exegetical Afro-Saxon tradition have usually emphasized formal ideologies and proceeded along predictable paths of inquiry. Some have described and explained the writer's main political themes;[6] others have preferred a biographical approach, tracing the evolution of their subject's thoughts and the key political influences on them.[7] A third strategy has evaluated how these political ideas have, or have not, been translated into policy.[8]

Although occasionally valuable in providing a top-down, state-centered picture of African political thought, such investigations have missed the dispersion of political ideas in ostensibly nonpolitical arenas such as economics, religion, social and family relationships, sports, art, and literature. Equally missing from this roll call is the politically important world of sorcery and the occult. These missing domains are crucial because, the political openings of the 1990s notwithstanding, the unfettered expression of overtly political ideas remains tentative in many African states. To understand the full range of political thought in this part of the world, then, we must examine the diverse means by which people voice political ideas indirectly. In other words, political thought in middle Africa must be redefined to include the works of novelists, dramatists, poets, musicians, journalists, theologians, philosophers, and social scientists, as well as proverbs, fables, and oral literature. Attention to these apparently nonpolitical spheres is also important because large numbers of middle Africans do not necessarily share Western assumptions concerning the normative and empirical relationships between politics and the larger social environment.[9] Furthermore, as we shall see, the inclusion of these sources becomes all the more critical because middle Africans inhabit a political realm whose boundaries can differ substantially from those prevalent in parts of the West.

The phenomenology of Alfred Schutz, Peter Berger and Thomas Luckmann, Nelson Goodman, and Jerome Bruner has greatly influenced my orientation to the subject of political language and perceptions.[10] In short, and at the risk of a vast oversimplification, people can and do construct and then structure their social worlds. If they perceive a phenomenon, believe in its existence, and then act on their perceptions and beliefs, then—at least for them—the phenomenon in question is very much a reality. In addition, Clifford Geertz's "thick description" and the careful attention to language of George Orwell, Murray Edelman, Kenneth Burke, and Jan Vansina have also been sources of much stimulation and inspiration in their intelligent approach to a culturally sensitive analysis of texts.[11]

Ronald Inglehart has argued that the time has come to redress the balance in social analysis between economics and culture, and that cultural variables have been deemphasized to an unrealistic degree. He also maintained that different societies are characterized by a specific syndrome of political-cultural attitudes and that such attitudes are enduring but not immutable.[12] I agree, although my methodological predispositions run in a direction rather different than Inglehart's careful analysis of Western European and international survey data. My own inclinations, both epistemological and methodological, lead me more toward Clifford Geertz, who sees culture as "the structures of meaning" through which people "give shape to their experience."[13]

Careful attention to political language, which is certainly able to enlighten us about the cultural components of political legitimacy, can help us to elucidate these "structures of meaning." Since notions of political legitimacy, in middle Africa as elsewhere, are communicated in linguistic exchanges between those who have power and those who do not, it is vital to examine the specific language, metaphors, and other images used to transmit thoughts about politics. Moreover, the approaches and insights of both Michel Foucault and Michel de Certeau are also relevant, since notions of political legitimacy are communicated in this daily discourse.[14] Both the powerful and powerless participate in this, and the specific expressions used to fashion, transmit, and then refashion thoughts and perceptions about politics and political legitimacy thus assume a critical importance. The ordinary and unremarkable events of daily life themselves provide landmarks giving shape and structure to this political discourse. Only in undertaking the analysis of these metaphors and imagery will we begin to appreciate the conflict for this terrain of the mind occurring between those who control the state, on the one hand, and the powerless, on the other. The struggle is real; the interaction, dialectical.[15]

This chapter begins with a brief examination of the methodology employed and the methodological issues raised in this study. I then detail the pervasive prevalence of paternal and familial metaphors in various facets of middle African political life. In turn, this leads to a statement of the four premises of the moral matrix of legitimate governance, as well as to an examination of the some of the theoretical and epistemological assumptions pertaining to the concepts of legitimacy, political subjacency, and the idea of political "thinkability." The chapter concludes with a brief plan of the rest of the work.

Methods

The methodological core of this research project is a close, interpretive reading of either daily newspapers or weekly news magazines in eight African states, supplemented, of course, by other primary sources drawn from different domains such as presidential speeches and interviews, party manifestoes and policy statements, memoirs, theology, philosophy, popular literature, and interviews—both formal and informal—with as many people of all walks of life as possible when I was fortunate enough to be in the field. Throughout, my focus is as much on how things are said as on what is said. In short, what words, images, and metaphors are employed by those who have the power to present their actions and policies to the wider public? How do the media present the banalities of daily life? Are there linguistic phrases which recur? What are their cultural connotations? How does the citizenry react both to the content and to the linguistic style? Does public reaction manifest itself through newspaper columns or letters to the editors, for example? Do the powerless use the same metaphors and imagery as the powerful? Do they use them in the same way, or are there important differences? The focus, in other words, is on the political language found in primary source materials.

The countries in question are (moving from west to east) Senegal, Côte d'Ivoire, Ghana, Nigeria, Cameroon, Democratic Republic of the Congo (from 1972 to 1997 known as Zaïre, and I tend to use the two names interchangeably), Tanzania, and Kenya. Why these particular states? Cameroon, Congo, and Kenya were choices that came easily because I had lived and worked in all three countries.[16] In addition, the basic model of the moral matrix of legitimate governance was first elaborated in the context of the Congo, then applied to Cameroon, and I was reasonably certain that some parts of it would make sense in Kenya as well. Tanzania and Senegal were included because I wished to examine at least two states where I anticipated that some of the more extreme paternal aspects of the matrix would either not fit at all or would display substantial variation. In general, I was wrong about this, and the fit was in some regards far better than I had anticipated, but such was my original intent. I was also able to spend several months in Senegal in 1988 and 1994, and that also made me anxious to include that country because I felt that an Islamic dimension might be important. Côte d'Ivoire seemed to fit the basic model of the moral matrix that I was elaborating; Nigeria is too large and important to ignore; and, finally, I had hoped that Ghana—especially under J. J. Rawlings—would also provide some variation because Rawlings' initial radicalism made it seem as though a different type of regime and political experience was in the offing. With the exceptions of Nigeria and Tanzania, I was at least able to visit briefly all of these states at one time or another to conduct informal interviews and to collect locally published materials such as political pamphlets and sermons.

In some ways these eight states provide an ample range of variation according to colonial heritage (British, French, Belgian); official languages (English, French, Swahili); geographic location (West, Central, and East Africa); formal religions (Catholic, Protestant, Islamic); and regime type (semi-democratic through blatantly authoritarian). The majority of people in these countries are poor, and the World Bank classifies all eight states as low-income economies.[17] Insofar as the study of politics in sub-Saharan Africa goes, like Claude Raines in the movie *Casablanca,* I have rounded up the usual suspects. Most of the references and citations contained in this book refer to these specific countries. In general, I feel quite confident applying the line of analysis elaborated here to these eight states, although there is a range of variation among them. I am also reasonably comfortable applying the broad thrust of the analysis to other states in West, Central, and East Africa, and from time to time I have done just that. But I do not attempt to extend this analysis to either the North African tier of states, the Horn of Africa, or most of southern Africa. Certain aspects of governance in those areas may, or may not, reflect some of the premises of the moral matrix, but I refrain from speculating about this. Other scholars, if they wish, may perform that labor. The usual constraints of time, money, and the unfortunately painful limitations of my own expertise also played a role in limiting my specific focus to these eight states.

Given the complexities and variations of politics in all areas of the African continent, I am hesitant to generalize my findings and analysis to "Africa" as a whole. But since my selection of states spans the usual regionally germane geographic divisions, it would be inappropriate to use those as a shorthand way of referring the eight states in question. And, as I am unable to discern another characteristic that might unite these eight states under a commonly used rubric, I have resorted to the phrase "middle Africa" to designate these particular states collectively because they stretch across the vast middle portion of the continent.

The book was originally planned to cover the 1980s, but the research and reading took far longer than anticipated. Where possible, therefore, I have extended the analysis well into the 1990s. As mentioned, the major primary sources for this study are newspapers and news magazines. The publications' names, the location published, and the dates consulted follow immediately: *Le Soleil,* Dakar, Senegal, 1980–1989, 1991; *Fraternité Matin,* Abidjan, Côte d'Ivoire, 1980–1989; *Daily Graphic* and *People's Daily Graphic,* Accra, Ghana, 1980–1989; *Daily Times,* Lagos, Nigeria, 1980–1989; *Cameroon Tribune,* Yaoundé, Cameroon, 1980–1989; *Elima,* Kinshasa, Zaïre, 1980–1990; *Daily News* and *Sunday News,* Dar es Salaam, Tanzania, 1980–1990; and *Weekly Review,* Nairobi, Kenya, 1983–1996. In addition, I also consulted *West Africa* magazine (1983–1996), a London-based weekly newsmagazine that generally reflected Nigerian interests and perspectives. All of these publications were read regularly either in the field or at the Library of Congress, or were obtained on microfilm through interlibrary loan. To my pleasant surprise, the microfilm collections were reasonably complete and did not contain too many missing issues. I also subscribed to both *West Africa* and *Weekly Review* during the years in question. Finally, an exceptionally able research assistant carefully read, took notes on, and photocopied for me the daily compilations of press, radio, and television transcriptions that the Foreign Broadcast Information Service (FBIS) put together on all of these states from 1980 through 1994.[18]

Why newspapers, and why state-controlled newspapers at that? First, my intent was never to read them for an idea of what was actually occurring in any of these countries. Especially during the 1980s, and even to a great extent after the various political liberalizations and shifts to competitive, multiparty elections occurred during the 1990s, these papers were not terribly good guides to actual events. They were either state-controlled, or at the least heavily state-influenced, and even if some of them occasionally wished to demonstrate independence, they were subject to severe constraints in all authoritarian and single party–dominant regimes. But because the states did so heavily dominate them, reading them became useful as I tried to discern the acceptable state line and, importantly for this study, the preferred metaphors and images that kept recurring. Second, they also tended to cover the vagaries of daily life reasonably well, and accounts of local court cases, sports pages, and coverage of the banal events of the state administration such as retirement parties, educational seminars, normal bureaucratic rotations, and the like were sources of enlightenment once I had figured out what the predominant metaphors and images actually were. Third, the papers also reprinted the texts of speeches by the various presidents as well as other high-ranking politicians of a particular regime. Editorials and opinion-editorials were also most useful. Moreover, and from different corners of the social spectrum, letters to the editor concerning apparently mundane matters were also useful in my efforts to determine just how far the regime's preferred imagery had spread throughout the society. Inevitably, however, the editorial selection of these writings skewed the "sample" in favor of those who were literate, better educated, and, in some places, wealthier. Photographs and cartoons also helped to unravel the importance of certain underlying political images and metaphors.[19]

My aim has been to discern threads of a common discourse that appear consistently in all eight states at different times, locations, political spheres, and social arenas. In seeking these common discursive threads, I assume that if they appear widely, in an array of social, political, geographic, and temporal contexts, then in some ways they may be taken to reflect, or be seen as indicators of, certain unarticulated assumptions about political life. For example, if a certain form of paternal imagery appears systematically in different countries; in different social strata; and in domains as diverse as the policy positions of political parties, presidential speeches and statements, state administration, education, formal religion, labor, and sports, we may assume that this persistent and pervasive imagery reflects certain patterns of thought that have important consequences in structuring how people approach and understand political legitimacy. Similarly, if discussions of the relationship between success at soccer and the prevalence of sorcery in the locker rooms appear consistently in the sports pages and popular literature of different countries at different times, we may assume that this reflects a certain diffused understanding of causality. I also assume and expect that the intensity of any particular discursive strand will vary according to differing contexts. In one sense my methodological demarche thus derives partially from Foucault's approach to intellectual archaeology.[20] Since this study is based on an interpretive reading of the data, my analytical judgment inevitably comes into play. Equational precision through quantitative analysis is neither a possibility nor a goal in these circumstances.

Paternal and Familial Metaphors

Presidential Fathers

Paternal and familial metaphors and imagery are pervasive throughout middle Africa. They are found in far too many venues for this to be the result of mere co-incidence. Let us begin at the center, with the president of the republic and how the press often presents and portrays him. Virtually all heads of state in middle Africa have wanted the press to view them as kind, loving, solicitous individuals who were the fathers of their nation. To be sure, however, some portraits were more detailed than others. In this latter category, Côte d'Ivoire's Félix Houphouet-Boigny (1960–1993) stands out. For example, on President Houphouet's seventy-sixth birthday a front-page editorial in the state-party's daily newspaper presented the regime's preferred political imagery:

> At each of these steps in our History . . . Houphouet-Boigny and his People were inseparable. They remain so. For married to the latter, for better or worse, he carries with him the aspirations of his brothers and sisters, the children of this country. And they manifest toward him admiration and affection for his wisdom, his pragmatism, and his sense of tolerance and forgiveness, and his love of dia-logue.
>
> To convince oneself of this, . . . [we have] that phrase of an elderly seller of spices . . . regarding the Head of State: ". . . He is the papa of us all. Thanks to him we have found liberty. . . ."
>
> "Papa of us all": what a magnificent definition of the role of the "Old Man" at the head of our country! "Papa" knows how to be available for each of us; he knows how to listen to us; he knows how to dress our wounds; comfort us in our efforts; stimulate us when we are asleep, and call us to more solidarity and to the union of us all.[21]

The same language and imagery could have been found in the Ivoirian press on any of Houphouet's birthdays. The following year, for example, a front-page edi-torial in *Fraternité Matin* noted: "There is no need at our level, to return to what Ivoirians owe him, to the attachment and affection that they hold for him." Simi-larly, on the same page there was a huge photograph of Houphouet, with a cap-tion reading: "An international stature, foundation of the confidence that investors dedicate to him, a well known realism favoring the cooperation between our coun-try and the rest of the world, and an almost divine respect for his given word make of Félix Houphouet-Boigny the serious partner from whom one will always find a solution and a response to the preoccupations of each instant."[22]

Houphouet always appeared to revel in his image as the father of the Ivoirian national family. He was often photographed with children, giving them gifts and showering affection on them. The press coverage of the twentieth anniversary of independence described one scene this way: "At the end of the spectacle of the dance . . . the Head of State accomplished another gesture. He summoned all the small dancers. He even took some of them in his arms. . . . And as he certainly does with his own grandchildren when they are good [*sage*], he gave these anonymous children, by way of presents, several envelopes containing bank notes."[23] He was the generous, kind, and giving father and grandfather who rewarded his offspring when they were "good." The children, to be sure, were always fulsome in their praise of their political "father" and never lacked any opportunity to demonstrate their gratitude for all the president-father had done for them. One thing this meant was voting for Houphouet whenever there were elections. In 1980, when Houphouet was reelected with 99.99 percent of the vote, the state-controlled daily laconically reported that "Ivoirians manifested on Sunday their fidelity and their gratitude to their 'Old Man.'"[24] Similarly, whenever any semi-official gathering concluded, there would usually be the formulaic motion of thanks to the president. At the end of a training seminar for prefects, sub-prefects, and mayors, the concluding motion noted that the participants "thanked filially their 'Old Man' for his total availability in the service of his children in their apprenticeship of communal life."[25]

Houphouet, moreover, was not shy about invoking the paternal metaphor himself, even in settings where it might well have been inappropriate and perhaps even resented. So after the conclusion of a 1985 seminar on justice, the participants—mostly magistrates and other ranking officials of the justice department—paid a courtesy call on Houphouet at his home in Yamoussoukro. The president greeted them as "my dear sons, my dear grandsons."[26] It is certainly conceivable that the use of such familiar and paternal language to mature and educated adults might have rankled more than a few of the distinguished jurists present.

These paternal and familial metaphors permeated the state's mass media on a daily basis while the "Old Man" was alive. Moreover, the example of a certain type of language promulgated from above could also be parroted from below. When a prefect arrived at a new assignment, he used the occasion, as was customary, to present to the absent president "his infinite gratitude and also a big thank you."[27] A letter to the editor of the daily newspaper entitled "Thanks to the Father of the Nation" demonstrated the same point even further down the political and social hierarchy: "By my voice, all of the young people of my age more particularly the transporters . . . of Yopougon thank you with all our heart, Papa Houphouet, for so appreciable a gift that you have offered to us in opening the autoroute . . . [to] our neighborhood. . . . May the All-Powerful preserve you still longer for the happiness of all the sons of this country who owe you so much!"[28]

The imagery held even in death. When the then prime minister, Alassane Ouattara, announced Houphouet's passing in late 1993, he could state simply, "My dear Ivoirian sisters and brothers: Côte d'Ivoire has become an orphan. The one who has embodied our people for almost half a century—the father of the nation, President Félix Houphouet-Boigny—passed away. . . ."[29] This announcement not only underscored the regime's preferred paternal and familial metaphors, it also recalled for the Ivoirian Francophile elite Georges Pompidou's announcement of the death of Charles de Gaulle, France is widowed ("*La France est veuve*").

Houphouet, of course, was not alone in his predilection for paternal imagery. Both of Kenya's post-independence heads of state, Jomo Kenyatta (1963–1978) and Daniel arap Moi (1978–), have also found it most congenial. A June 1968 editorial in the *Kenya Mirror,* for example, noted:

> For Kenyatta is Kenya and Kenya is Kenyatta. This fact will remain a historic pronouncement for many generations to come.
>
> Mzee Kenyatta is the father of every family in Kenya—he is just not only the father of the Kenya nation.
>
> Not many leaders and statesmen have been so loved, adored and revered as much as Mzee Kenyatta.
>
> That's why we are grateful that Mzee Kenyatta who fought for Kenya's freedom for almost all his life will lead the nation in the Madaraka Day celebrations.
>
> The importance of Mzee Kenyatta is reflected in a statement made by a former Senator when he declared that "Mzee" is Kenya's saviour and liberator. Another former senator stated: "Jomo Kenyatta is not only our political saviour but also our Messiah."[30]

Not to be outdone by his illustrious predecessor, President Moi also styled himself as the father of the nation. Speaking in the context of a veiled warning to certain Kikuyu oppositional interests in 1990 and referring to Kikuyu children, Moi noted: "I want the people of Kenya to understand that I am not a tribalist. These children are my children, and I am a Kenyan citizen."[31]

Similarly, in February 1990 after the still unexplained murder of Kenya's foreign minister, Robert Ouko, his widow delivered a moving eulogy. With President Moi present, and speaking directly to him, Christabel Ouko said: "Lastly, I would like to thank most sincerely Your Excellency for the help you have given to us as a family. In the Ouko family, we know you as our special father. . . . I know we are not alone. You are still our father. You will still be there to help us."[32] Although under the tragic circumstances it was quite possible that Mrs. Ouko and her audience infused the imagery with a cynically ambiguous hidden transcript that called attention to Moi's paternal shortcomings, it is nonetheless striking that she still employed the paternal metaphor.[33]

Unsurprisingly, given the cults of personality that flourished while they were in power, both Zaïre's Mobutu Sese Seko (1965–1997) and Cameroon's Ahmadou Ahidjo (1960–1982) also presented themselves as loving, caring, solicitous national fathers. A few samples should suffice. A 1981 editorial noted Mobutu's action on behalf of an ailing Zaïrian musician in these terms:

> One of the greatest Zaïrian artist-musicians, Kabasele Tchamala, who was admitted to the university clinic several weeks ago, and whose state of health has already inspired much worry, has been, since Friday evening, transferred to Europe. There he will be treated at [*suivre les soins*] a specialized clinic. It is the Father of the Nation who decided this while putting at the disposal of the sick musician the financial means necessary. This gesture of General Mobutu Sese Seko proves that he is always attentive to everything that touches the life of each son and daughter of this country.[34]

Similarly, when visiting his home province of Equateur after the 1984 election, Mobutu attended a ceremony of the pioneers (the regime's equivalent of boy and girl scouts) so that the youth could congratulate him on his electoral victory. In this context, one pioneer greeted Mobutu in these paternal terms: "Citizen President-Founder of the MPR [Mouvement Populaire de la Révolution], and dear Papa. . . ."[35]

Even though Mobutu's public relations apparatus was usually more active than Ahidjo's, the latter still had no trouble conveying the paternal message to his people. The third Union Nationale Camerounaise (UNC) party congress in 1980 declared, for example, that Ahidjo was the "TRUE AND AUTHENTIC UNIFIER AND FATHER OF THE NATION."[36] In a similar vein, paternal imagery also peppers the following account of one of Ahidjo's visits to Bertoua:

> Three young kindergarten girls had the fresh [honor] to express to the Father of the Nation the message of welcome in offering him a flamboyant bouquet of flowers just as he got off the airplane.
>
> The city, which already had a great ambiance, tripled its effervescence. President Ahidjo, seated in his Mercedes 600, did not tire of raising his arms to the people who could not contain themselves, [and were] no longer were able to control themselves. One would have even believed that the people wanted the head of state to stop at each meter of the trajectory. . . .
>
> Everywhere there was a holiday; children, adults, old people, everybody was mixed up in the irresistible manifestation of this joy. What could be more legitimate when these populations do not cease saying out loud that: President Ahidjo, in deciding to hold the agricultural show at Bertoua had wanted to offer us a gift of the century. . . .[37]

Even Ahidjo's successor, Paul Biya (1982–), for a brief moment after the transition following Ahidjo's retirement from the state presidency, mentioned that his predecessor "remains the father of the Cameroonian nation, as well as the artisan of its unity and development."[38]

Middle Africa's philosopher-kings, Tanzania's Julius Nyerere (1961–1985) and Senegal's Léopold Senghor (1960–1980), were occasionally seen in this way, although neither one indulged in the cult of personality so characteristic of their fellow heads of state. When Senghor voluntarily relinquished office at the end of 1980, the president of the Supreme Court evoked the paternal theme in his remarks for the annual presentation of New Year's good wishes to the president. This would be the last time that he would address Senghor in this role. "You have manifested your intention to leave us soon," he said. "Your political comrades feel orphaned and your friends are sad."[39] Similarly, the director of the national drama company wrote that "Léopold Sédar Senghor is leaving. In effect, since the announcement of the departure of the President of the Republic, the Lion, the Father of the Senegalese Nation, does not cease to astonish us. . . . In regretting the departure of Senghor whom we have so loved, respected, for having given to our country its pride in the world, we can only greet the arrival in power of his dauphin whom we will back up to permit him to continue the line traced by the Father of the Senegalese

Nation."[40] Seven years after his departure, Cardinal Thiandoum continued to respect and admire Senghor because he was the "Father of the Nation."[41]

And while Senghor's chosen successor as president, Abdou Diouf (1981–2000), did not succeed him as the father of the nation, the media and his ministers never hesitated to paint him as a father figure. In 1985 the then minister of education, Iba Der Thiam, delivered a speech evoking the theme:

> Mr. President, your presence here this morning honors us and constitutes a powerful encouragement to refine our reflection. Especially in having just said in front of the pupils who represent all their comrades, how you envisage moral and civic education, you yourself are even the incarnation of how African society practices that education: you are the father who comes to encourage his children, his nephews, to pursue their effort and to lead always a straighter life devoted to the community. . . . Model that you are for all Senegalese who rightly congratulate themselves for having carried you to the supreme magistrature; model, you are one in particular for the children and adolescents of this country who find in you the accomplished example of the man that each one desires to become.[42]

The Tanzanian press never participated in a cult of personality for Julius Nyerere. Furthermore, one could often go several consecutive days without any reference to the president in the *Daily News*. Yet one may speculate that some of those feelings might have been buried beneath the surface, for when Nyerere finally retired completely from public life in 1990, he was widely praised as the father of the nation. One radio report noted that the chairman of the Chama Cha Mapinduzi (CCM), Nyerere's successor Ali Hassan Mwinyi, "asked the leaders and all the Tanzanian people to give him every assistance so that he could steer the ship bequeathed to us by the father of the nation, Mwalimu Nyerere."[43]

Mwinyi (1985–1995) also avoided the perils of a personality cult and never really adopted the paternal imagery as his own. He would, however, still resort to certain aspects of familial imagery in different contexts. For example, when speaking to a meeting of elders and veterans in 1987, he thanked the elders for their cooperation and for their contribution to the nation during the independence struggle and during the first government of President Nyerere. He told them "I am your second child. . . . I need your care, cooperation and assistance."[44] This reversal of roles, with the president placing himself in the position of child vis-à-vis the elders, is most unusual in middle Africa, and it is perhaps not surprising that the only two instances of it I have thus far been able to find are Mwinyi and Diouf, who followed "fathers" who did not let the cult of personality flourish. (Parenthetically, Diouf, as we see presently in the context of Islam, would also initiate this role reversal when interacting with the heads of Senegal's major Islamic brotherhoods.)

Nation as Family and as Growing Child

One of the most consistent themes across time and space is the explicit comparison between nation and family. A variant of the nation-building rhetoric of the

1960s that, at least on one level, seeks to eliminate or reduce the political salience of subnational or ethnic identities, the comparison between the nation and a family writ large appears virtually everywhere in middle Africa. President Moi is a case in point: "I already said we in the Republic of Kenya must completely wipe out tribalism so that we can live as a people in one family. I will not turn my back on my struggle to combat and eradicate anything to do with tribalism. We must all speak with one voice."[45] Ten years later, after the introduction of multiparty politics, the refrain remained unaltered: "You have to believe in your country Kenya. Kenya is your mother, Kenya is your father."[46] This parental and familial imagery strikes responsive chords among the population. After all, most people understand what a family is and what a father is supposed to do, and this is reflected in letters to the editor in which, for the most part, the metaphor of nation as family is accepted. One man put it this way: "President Moi has been busy spreading the gospel. He has told us we are all Kenyans. We are one big family." Or, in a different letter, "Kanu (Kenya African National Union) leaders should behave as a parent who shuns any activities that can instil fear in the family."[47] So powerful, so pervasive is this image that even hardened members of the political opposition find themselves using it—albeit with a rather different emphasis. Novelist and long-time political opponent, Ngugi wa Thiong'o, put it this way in response to a question concerning the workability of the concept of democracy in Africa: "Even in a family, people have different opinions, they have to debate on what is going on; then what about a nation or a huge family, a continental family or a national family? We must be able to express ourselves. Nobody should ever be penalised in Africa for having a different idea from another person."[48] For both the state and the opposition, in other words, the notion of a large "national family" is quite thinkable and thus legitimate. At issue is what occurs inside that family and how the national "kinfolk" treat each other.

Another major theme of this discourse is to compare the growth of the nation with the growth of a child. Senghor's elegant prose nicely captured this in his radio address to the nation on the eve of Senegal's tenth anniversary of independence. "In a planetary civilization in becoming," he said, "ten years is still the very first childhood since nations, in the past, took centuries to be formed. But for us, Senegalese, this tenth year of our emancipation must be the age of weaning. . . . We must adopt, together, a single resolution, affirming our firm and constant will to leave economic childhood."[49] And when Senghor stepped aside ten years later, one commentator cast his evaluation of the succession in similar terms: "Simply, the Senegalese State and first and foremost its chief, find themselves today in the situation of a father of a family reinforcing his advice directed to his children who have finally reached a mature age, that is to say, to those in whom any absence of lucidity becomes culpable."[50]

In a like manner, the Rawlings regime, which generally resorted to paternal and familial imagery far less often than Kenya, Zaïre, or Côte d'Ivoire, employed the same analogy of human growth and developing maturity when Ghana turned twenty-seven in 1984. A front-page editorial in the *People's Daily Graphic* put it this way:

> At the Independence Square on March 6, Flt-Lt Rawlings likened Ghana to a man of twenty-seven years old.
>
> He said that at the age of 25, every thinking young person begins to look at life and redefine his or her priorities in the light of past experience and a deeper understanding of his or her circumstances and environment. At this stage in life, he said, the needs and values imposed by others are examined, and to see which are found to be irrelevant are discarded. That is what Ghana did on 31st December [the date of Rawlings' second coup], nine weeks before she was twenty-five years old.
>
> The Leader of the Revolution continued that a man of 27 is different from a man of 25. By this time he will probably have a family, and he must shoulder his own responsibilities. He can no longer put the blame for the inadequacies of his life on his parents or teachers. He has reached an age where his immature characteristics should have given way to a mature realisation of his own obligations and where he should be headed in order to fulfil them.[51]

Once a child, Ghana had now developed into an adult. As in other parts of middle Africa, the imagery is so strong that even Rawlings (1981–2001) in his younger and more radical phase was wont to pull it out of his rhetorical kit bag. Speaking before the National House of Chiefs, Chairman Rawlings mentioned that the stores were empty and that people lacked basic items such as oil, sugar, soap, kerosene, cloth, and hoes. "Some of our citizens," he stated, "think that it is because the Government is so wicked that is why things are in such a state. We do not blame them. Which child has not felt that way before as regards its parents? But at least you and I know that it is not so."[52] Even a left-wing populist like Rawlings had trouble avoiding the imagery.

To be sure, this comparison between nation and family—both implicit and explicit—is widespread throughout middle Africa. It surfaces habitually on anniversaries of independence, New Year's Day, election day, on the occasion of ministerial reshuffles, changes in political regime, or other such events when either the chief of state, other politicians, editorialists, or commentators feel the need to mark the passage of time in the nation's trajectory.[53] So when Ali Hassan Mwinyi accepted the CCM nomination for the presidency of Tanzania in 1985, he paid glowing tribute to his predecessor in these terms: "You have brought us [up] like the way a parent brings up his or her children and now that you want to rest we must all of us thank you for your great work."[54]

Nigerians, too, share the notion of a national family, debating its meaning at length and with enthusiasm. One 1980 letter to the editor advanced the idea that Nigeria should have a new name. The correspondent argued: "In the first place the name is a foreign name coined by a foreigner Mrs. Lugard. It is only a mother that gives names to her children. We are not the children of Mrs. Lugard."[55] Presumably, however, Nigerians are someone's offspring even if Mrs. Lugard's maternity is in doubt, and this is readily apparent in any number of different sources. Reflecting on the short-lived democratically elected administration of Shehu Shagari (1979–1983), one reasonably prominent politician wrote: "We have not achieved the union of souls and spirit which alone can make us feel like inseparable parts of the same organism. We do not act and behave toward others from outside our ethnic group as if we are brothers from the real blood flowing from our mother Nigeria. . . . We must accept that we share one great mother—Nigeria—and that we are siblings of that enormous monument of motherhood which nature so benevolently gave to Africa and the world."[56] And some years later, a newspaper report picked up on the family metaphor in an administrative setting. Commenting on the administrative style of one of Nigeria's military governors, the article extolled the virtues of Naval Captain Mohammed Lawal, the then governor of Ogun State. The Captain had a quiet but firm disposition, handling matters gently but forthrightly. A pregnant woman praised him, saying: "This governor is advising us like a mother advises her children."[57] Although it has been convenient to use Nigerian examples here, the maternal slant on the family metaphor recurs periodically throughout middle Africa and receives more attention in Chapter 6.

Although there are obviously variations, the notion of political fathers (or mothers) at the head of a national family is durable and seems to travel well in time and space. Now war-torn and ravaged, Sierra Leone has had a succession of political fathers. The long-ruling "Pa" Siaka Stevens gave way to General Joseph Momoh, his handpicked successor in 1985. When *West Africa* asked how he envisaged his role as executive president of the republic, General Momoh replied with splendidly mixed metaphors. "Not much different from that exercised by any head of state from any other country. You look upon yourself as the father of the nation, it is a ship of state, and you are at the helm: you make sure you direct it safely as much as possible, but I think that my greatest desire will be to see that we are able to bring the greatest good to the greatest number of people in the country."[58] Some months after this interview appeared, the same magazine published a letter to the editor praising General Momoh for being "so imaginative," and asking him to consider the following proposal:

> We have, since colonial rule, let Western and Eastern ideologies influence our development. If the president can now consider scrapping any form of political party and develop a "family union" in which we are all brothers and sisters belonging to the same fold, there will then emerge a new form of African ideology and at the top will be a "family head" instead of a president.
>
> So this is the beginning. Sierra Leone will not only unite by this form of family ideology, but the whole of Africa will really start the march towards a firm unity. . . .[59]

After a military coup had brought Captain Valentine Strasser to power several years later, another letter commended Strasser for his actions: "He is now effectively 'father of the nation' and we urge him to be as rigorous and meticulous in this capacity as a true soldier should."[60] The political contexts may change, but the notion of a political father at the head of a large national family endures.

The State

As one might expect, the state is both a major purveyor of the prevalent paternal and familial metaphors as well as one of the major sites where these images are found and manipulated. This is readily apparent in the rhetoric surrounding political parties. In 1982, for example, Côte d'Ivoire's state-party, the Parti Démocratique de la Côte d'Ivoire–Rassemblement Démocratique Africain (PDCI-RDA), held a five-day conclave at Yamoussoukro that brought together 590 cadres and party militants including members of the executive committee, general secretaries of the various party sections, prefects, sub-prefects, and mayors. Its aim was "a general reconciliation," but to achieve this a good deal of dirty laundry had to be washed "inside the family." Houphouet, of course, confidently predicted a happy outcome. In his plenary address, the president stated, "We are not judges, we are brothers— Spare the rod and spoil the child ["*Qui aime bien, châtie bien*"]—brothers who must attempt the impossible to save their sick mother. And Côte d'Ivoire is sick from the division of her children."[61] Or, in the words of another high-ranking party official in 1984, Denis Bra Kanon, "As you know, our party, the Democratic Party of the Ivory Coast-African Democratic Rally (PDCI-RDA) is first of all a family, a very big family within which all Ivoirians are born, grow up, and thrive. And, as in any family, the members ought to meet as often as possible to discuss common problems and together seek solutions to their everyday difficulties, share their joys, their hopes, and their sufferings. We are not here to perform miracles, but we are here to call for your vigilance to fight troublemakers."[62]

The death of Houphouet, the head of the family, in 1993 did not diminish the importance of the familial metaphor. In a 1994 interview Houphouet's successor, President Henri Konan Bédié (1993–1999), noted the following in response to a query concerning a faction within the PDCI who were claiming to be "younger brothers": "Yes. If they claim to be President Houphouet-Boigny's followers, I believe they are men of conviction, they are PDCI-RDA activists. . . . These problems should be solved within the family because the PDCI-RDA is one big family, a home that is being thoroughly renovated since its major change." Continuing, Bédié added that "big families are even more close knit when they endure a loss. . . . I am determined to work toward the unity of the family."[63]

My focus on the PDCI is merely illustrative, for one finds virtually the same language and imagery present in political parties throughout middle Africa. A letter to the editor of *West Africa* from a Ghanaian, for example, argued that "all Nkrumahists [should] consider the question of appointing a true leader or 'father' to act as a guardian of Nkrumah's ideology."[64] Similarly, industrialist Alhaji Asuma Banda, someone working to bring about unity in the reborn version of Kwame Nkrumah's Convention People's Party (CPP), was also concerned about finding a "father." In response to a query concerning the role of former president Hilla Limann in the CPP, Banda responded, "By virtue of the office that Dr Limann held, as a former President of this country, on the CPP ticket, he holds a very unique position in the CPP family." When asked what Limann's position in the party was, he replied, "He's our father. In the absence of Kwame Nkrumah, it's Limann."[65] One final note on political parties: In 1995 a Nigerian politician, Sarah Jubril, formed her own political party and called it the "National Family of Nigeria."[66]

The armed services also receive their share of familial attention. Early in his presidency, Paul Biya instituted an annual pilgrimage to the Cameroonian military academy to preside over the graduation exercise of each new class of young officers. In 1983 Biya noted that this particular ceremony was special for him because "it gives me, in effect, the occasion, since my accession to the Supreme Magistrature, to have, in my role as President of the Republic, Chief of the Government and Supreme Chief of the Armed Forces, my first direct contact with the grand corps of the State that is the large family of the National Armed Forces." Several years later, after the army had played a key role in supporting his troubled transition to the presidency, at the same event Biya noted: "I thus intend, by seizing this exceptional occasion, to give evidence to these young officers, and beyond, to the large family of the Cameroonian armed forces, of all my attention and my constant solicitude."[67] Like Biya, Mobutu also had a keen sense of the army's political importance and would, therefore, usually take care to present diplomas to newly commissioned officers in the Zaïrian army. On these occasions the "Father of the Nation" would demonstrate his "solicitude" to his state's forces of coercion.[68]

Paternal and familial metaphors also extend into the domain of international relations and foreign policy. The press, at least in the French-speaking portion of middle Africa, typically presents the annual summit meeting of the Franco-African heads of state as a family reunion of the "large French-African family."[69] The same imagery also permeates descriptions of various sets of bilateral relations. For example, on the fourth anniversary of the ultimately ill-fated Confederation of Senegambia (1981–1989), Senegalese President Abdou Diouf addressed the people of both nations. "As you can see," he reminded them, "in addition to major affective reasons for the natural union between Senegalese and Gambians like the members of one and the same family, there are objective and rational motives militating for the rapid edification of a strong and united—thus operational— Senegambia."[70]

Commentators and editorialists also describe bilateral and international disputes in this language. One front-page editorial in the Ghanaian press mourned the loss of forty-six Ghanaians in the Côte d'Ivoire in these terms:

> We are mourning not because we love doing so, but the thought of the incident sends torrents of blood through our dilated arteries and veins.
>
> It is unbelievable; yes, it is, that, a member of our own extended family—in a sister state to be precise—should stab us in the back! . . .
>
> How could Ghanaians be "happy" when 46 of us have been thrown into a small Ivorian Police Cell built for Six people, and left to die from want of food, water and air. Among them were children between the ages of 10 and 13!
>
> Ghana's first President, . . . Nkrumah, had intended an Organisation of African

Unity (OAU) of African states that would take the nationals of each other state as members of a large family—one people with one common destiny. . . .

One basic insurance any family has is the extension of assistance, aid and support to any of its members who finds himself or herself in a crisis. Ghana expected her brothers and sisters in the extended African family to come to her aid now that she finds herself unable to make ends meet.

One thought moral support would not have been denied Ghana if material assistance was not available. But instead of material or moral support she has persecution as her reward from those she had helped to wean. . . .[71]

The sense of betrayal is all the more palpable because a "sister" state and a member of the "extended family" has been responsible for delivering this evil stroke. It is even harder to accept because Nkrumah's Pan-Africanist vision, to a certain extent institutionalized in the Organization of African Unity (OAU), saw each member nation as part of a "large family." Moreover, given Ghana's early role in promoting African independence, there is bitterness at the betrayal of those whom she helped "to wean."

There is, in addition, a sense in which the generalized trait of great respect for age that is so characteristic of many African societies is also at work in the conduct of international diplomacy. Not too long after succeeding Senghor, for example, Abdou Diouf made a pilgrimage to Yamoussoukro to pay his respects to Houphouet-Boigny. Diouf's speech upon arrival gave the usual diplomatic niceties a paternal and familial emphasis. "My first words," he said, "are to express my respectful gratitude to my elder, to my father, President Félix Houphouet-Boigny, who has had the great amiability, the great gentility to invite me. . . . And the principal goal of my visit is to drink deeply at the source of wisdom, political courage, lucidity and determination that [is] President Félix Houphouet-Boigny. . . ."[72] When Sékou Touré visited Houphouet, the language was similar. As he was leaving, the Guinean president described the happiness he felt while being at the side of his "older brother." Several years later, in 1984, after Touré's death had paved the way for a military coup, the new Guinean prime minister, Colonel Diarra Traoré, visited Abidjan. When asked the reason, Colonel Traoré replied that he wanted to see President Houphouet "whom we consider like a dean, a sage, even a father. . . . What is sure is that our conversation occurred in a relaxed atmosphere, and as the President himself specified, in a purely familial framework."[73] This general respect for age and the wisdom born of experience appears elsewhere, too. When Kenneth Kaunda visited Ghana in 1987, a page-one editorial lauded "Big Brother Kaunda and his comrades at the Frontline" for their commitment to the ideals of the liberation of the continent from white minority rule. "Ghana welcomes Big Brother Kaunda to share his wide experience with the revolutionary leadership," the editorial continued.[74] No Orwellian double entendre was intended.

Paternal metaphors also enter the realm of international relations when middle Africans criticize their international dependency, or perhaps just their relative powerlessness, in relation to the stronger states of the West. In 1991, for example, the Kenyan government arrested political activist Gitobu Imanyara. The action came at a time when the Moi regime was under intense external pressure to institute both political and economic reforms—including multiparty elections. The United States government objected and issued a press release calling for Imanyara's immediate release. An editorial in *The Standard* put it this way:

> We similarly abhor the remaining part of the United States demand which seems to revive the cause of the old misunderstanding between Washington and Nairobi. The United States must cease its paternalistic attitude towards other nations, *constantly pointing the finger at them like the father towards a miscreant child.* It must be stressed without reservation that Kenya is a sovereign country, and its government has the full right to act within the confines of the country's laws.[75]

Members of a political opposition can also use the same paternal imagery to accuse the West of paternalism. Adopting the format of the Lord's Prayer, in 1991 a Zaïrian newspaper ran a poem that castigated the West for having supported Mobutu for so long: "Our Father who is in the West / Let your reign never again come nor that of your creature Mobutu Sese Seko, whom we forever disavow. / Let your will be done no more here, like that of your pawn that you have just rejected, we hope, sincerely and definitively. / Give us this day our daily bread, and that which we need to rebuild the country laid low by the incapacity and bad faith of he in whom you have erroneously had confidence. . . ."[76]

Social Institutions

By no stretch of the imagination restricted to the state, paternal and familial metaphors permeate all areas of social life. The realm of formal religion is a case in point. When the Archbishop of Paris visited Dakar, for example, the local press described the event in these terms: "Mgr Lustiger declared himself impressed. If it is important for a grandfather to see how his grandsons have inherited the family heritage, the Archbishop of Paris will return happy."[77] Of importance here is not whether the archbishop himself employed this familial metaphor, but that a Senegalese journalist thought it an appropriate way to frame a relationship, thus imbuing it with a meaning that most of his readers would surely understand.

Certain aspects of the complex world of Senegalese Islam occupy our attention in Chapter 3. For the moment, however, let us simply note that high-ranking officials of the Senegalese state often invoke the paternal metaphor when trying to honor, show respect, or pay deference to the leaders of the more important Sufi brotherhoods. In 1981 then Prime Minister Habib Thiam traveled to Touba, home of the Mouride order, to celebrate the brotherhood's annual festival. In addressing the Mouride's Khalife-General, the prime minister noted: "You are our father and we come to ask your advice for we know that the ultimate goal of your work aims less at your own person than at the collective happiness of the nation. . . . We reaffirm our availability and remind you that we are only your children and nothing but your children."[78]

The political, economic, and social importance of the large brotherhoods is such that Diouf always solicited the endorsement of their leaders before elections and, more generally, throughout the course of his presidency. In the period prior to the 1983 elections, to cite one instance, the Khalife-General of the Tidiane order invited his religious followers to support President Diouf, noting that "first of all, he is received as a son, as a full member of the large family and as a disciple of the brotherhood."[79] Before the 1988 elections, both the procedures and the language used to describe it was identical. When the marabout of Ndiassane endorsed the president, Diouf declared that he had come "to pay a courtesy visit to his father and his brother disciples [*talibés*]." "This demarche," the president continued, "is not political, but is that of a son towards his father . . . to take advice and to solicit prayers."[80] Two points are worth making at this juncture. First, the obvious flattery aside, both the Senegalese religious elite and the ruling politicians seemed to find the familial language and paternal metaphors comfortable forms of expression. Second, the specific phrasing effectively enabled a common language for both electoral and religious affairs.

The imagery of father and family finds its way into other corners of daily life as well. Ndongola Mavakala, president of Zaïre's Imana Football Club, referred to the "green and white family" (Imana's team colors) in a 1986 interview.[81] Similarly, after an excellent showing by the national soccer team, Houphouet declared himself to be the team's captain. In commenting on this, an editorialist noted: "This particular mark of attention, the Chief of State extended to all sporting disciplines in our country. Thus will he conduct himself and bring his paternal solicitude to all our national teams [*formations*] with a view toward raising them to the highest step on the podium."[82]

If there is a prevalent and almost unthinking level of comfort in the use of these terms and images in middle Africa, this does not necessarily indicate agreement over who is to be the father and who are the members of the family. In polities riven by ethnic and communal divisions such as Kenya, Cameroon, and Nigeria, this is often an emotionally potent political issue. During portions of the 1980s and with increasing frequency during the 1990s, much of national political life in these states could be viewed as a struggle over political "paternity"—who, in other words, was going to be the "father" of the large national family? Nigeria comes readily and dramatically to mind. Until his death in 1987, Obafemi Awolowo was the most prominent Yoruba politician and, in some quarters, their "father." When he died, the coverage of the event liberally, particularly in the southern press, referred to him as "Pa" or "Papa."[83] Approximately a year after his death, one columnist noted, "In his own tribute to you, the naval chieftain, Vice-Admiral Augustus Aikhomu said Nigeria will miss your fatherly advice. That statement has since proved prophetic."[84] Although in his later years Awolowo could offer "fatherly advice," he was never able to become Nigeria's political "father," much to the distress of his many supporters.

When Nnamdi Azikiwe, another ultimately unsuccessful giant of Nigerian politics, passed away some years later, many praised him in similarly glowing paternal terms. Ambassador Mahmud Yahaya, a national election commissioner, said that Azikiwe's death had removed "a great father to us all."[85] But like his Yoruba adversary and life-long rival Awolowo, Azikiwe could never transcend his Igbo ethnic base. In death these men might well have become political fathers of the nation, but in life their paternity remained restricted to the confines of their respective ethnic groups. The stature of both men was such that others viewed them largely through the familiar paternal and familial lenses. Ola Rotimi described them both:

> Zik can be likened to a father who, having nurtured his children into adolescence, is chary of taking actions that might agitate the joys of that state. Consequently, he might, simply but firmly, ask a son to remove an ash-tray filled with cigarette butts from the living room. Benignly expecting compliance, he might leave the scene after the instruction.
>
> By contrast, Awolowo, more like a mother, is finical about the process as about the result of a domestic assignment. He would not only tell you to throw out the ashes, but would also make sure that you didn't throw them in the face of the wind only to have the same ashes blown right back to mess up the entire living room.[86]

In Kenya the issues, and the rhetoric, are similar. President Moi quite actively presents himself as the father of the nation. During the 1980s, on national holidays and during electoral campaigns, Moi's supporters would place full-page advertisements in the press. A typical one showed Moi addressing a crowd at a rally. The cropped photograph assumed the shape of the map of Kenya in silhouette. The question in the headline asked, "Which Leader Is Closest To His People?" The subheading, and of course the response, was "The Father of the Nation." Nowhere on the page is Moi mentioned by name, although there was no ambiguity as to who wore the paternal mantle.[87] For many years until his death, Moi's main rival was Oginga Odinga, once Kenya's vice-president under Kenyatta and the generally accepted "leader" of the Luo. Odinga's stature was such that he was seen as "the venerable father of opposition politics," but like Awolowo, he never achieved the top position.[88]

Family Festivals and Family Photographs

Common familial language permeates public and private sectors. Businesses and the state throughout middle Africa, but especially in Senegal, Cameroon, Zaïre, and Côte d'Ivoire, use these terms regularly and have crafted a series of ceremonial occasions that reinforce them in the consciousness of both management and labor. At these events, whether in the public or private sector, management decides to honor its workers with medals for longevity on the job or exceptional productivity, or to pay homage to someone who is retiring. On such occasions there is usually a set-piece speech from one of the workers praising the paternal leadership and family atmosphere of the company or the state office; in turn, the leaders acclaim the workers for their devotion to the larger goals of the administrative or business "family." Private firms often purchase space in the newspaper, providing a "news" article to mark the occasion of the formal ceremony and speeches and to present the "family festival" (*fête de famille*) to the general public.[89] The state, how-ever, does not need to buy space to publicize its family festivals, for the press cov-ers such events regularly and considers them to be news. Furthermore, virtually any ceremonial event—a graduation, the end of a training seminar, the arrival of a new administrative superior, an administrative transfer, or any sort of an an-niversary or special occasion—may easily be described in this way.

Several examples should suffice. When seven bureaucrats of the Senegalese treasury stationed in Ziguinchor retired, when a Senegalese postmaster decided to leave the service, when a Zaïrian bureaucrat departed after having served the coun-try for thirty years, the relevant ceremonies were all described as "family festivals" or as "small, intimate and familial manifestations."[90] Routine bureaucratic trans-fers also occasion "family" festivals. Such festivals occurred when a Senegalese official moved from a prefecture to a sub-prefecture; when a police commissioner was asked to take up a new post; when a bureaucrat in the Ministry of Urbanism was promoted to a new assignment; when two bureaucrats attached to the Sene-galese École Nationale d'Administration et de Magistrature [National School of Ad-ministration and Magistracy] moved on to other tasks; and when a regional gov-ernor was transferred to a different region.[91] Educational settings regularly feature family festivals and familial language on the appropriate occasions. The end of the school year at a kindergarten, a conference at Senegal's École Nationale Supérieure, the annual distribution of academic prizes at year's end, and the twenty-fifth an-niversary of a school's founding all stand as illustrations.[92]

Of course, some family festivals are restricted to a particular society's best, bright-est, and wealthiest. For example, family festivals were held to mark the following occasions: a grand ball in honor of the Ivoirian École Nationale d'Administration and its famous and well-placed alumni, the opening of Zaïre's fifth legislature at the Palace of the People in Kinshasa, and the annual presentation of New Year's wishes and greetings to Jeanne Biya, the First Lady of Cameroon. Each year Mme Biya would receive the wives of the members of the party's central committee, the national office of the Women's Organization of the UNC, the wives of cabinet min-isters, and the spouses of all President Biya's other immediate collaborators in the presidential couple's private quarters. In the words of one press account, "Mme Biya then waded into the crowd for about fifteen minutes, moving with grace and delicacy between groups, lavishing kind words and congratulations. Here, she in-quires about news of the family, later, it will be a joke, all in a climate of serenity particular to family reunions. For it is really all about a veritable festival within the family."[93]

Photographs also furnish evidence of the diffusion of this imagery. In Côte d'Ivoire, Senegal, and Cameroon (but only rarely in Zaïre) the newspapers regu-larly reproduce a "family photograph." At the end of certain training seminars, diplo-matic meetings, administrative or political occasions such as the arrival of a new administrator or a party meeting, educational gatherings, awards ceremonies, and the like there is a photograph attached to the article describing the conference or meeting. The picture is invariably a formal pose of the different participants, and the caption almost always reads something like "gathered for the traditional family photograph are. . . ."[94]

The Moral Matrix of Legitimate Governance

It seems apparent, in other words, that the language and imagery of father and family are widespread throughout middle Africa. They are easily found in any number of different domains, in both public and private sectors. In one sense, such language and imagery are "natural." Most people do not even stop to think about them, much less question them. They just unthinkingly accept the metaphors and the images they conjure up as a normal mode of communication, for they are also part of an easily grasped mental template. In this regard, they are part of the diffused understanding of common sense and are thus hegemonic.[95] To be sure, some of the examples cited above are part of carefully orchestrated cults of personality, but there is more to it than that, for even a cynic would have to ask why, among all possible metaphors and images, the propagandists selected these particular ones. The imagery and language of father and family are pervasive in middle Africa because they strike a resonant and deeply embedded cultural chord. They form part of a culturally valid and mostly implicit comprehension of the limits of political legitimacy based on a complex and generally unarticulated moral matrix of legitimate governance derived from an idealized vision of patterns of authority and behavior within the family. And because this imagery is so consistent across time and space, I would submit that the notions of "political fathers" and "political families" also form part of a discourse that has important consequences for an understanding of the cultural logic of political legitimacy. Moreover, this discourse and this language both reflect and contribute to the further consolidation of an implicit notion of what constitutes a legitimate form of governance. This is generally accomplished first through an idealization of the implicit model of the family and then through its extrapolation and projection to other spheres of life, including the political domain.

Obafemi Awolowo provides an unusually clear statement of this idealized model of the family:

> The FAMILY has an unwritten constitution which is essentially the same for any family in any part of the world. Under this constitution, the affairs of the family are presided over and administered by the *paterfamilias, materfamilias* or both of them in some sort of esoteric partnership. Here in Nigeria, it is the *paterfamilias,* advised and assisted by the *materfamilias* and the other adult members of the family, who keeps the reins of the family in his firm control. He combines in himself legislative, executive, judicial, and administrative functions. Because of his inherent affection for them, the paterfamilias does everything in his power to cater to the nurture, welfare, and happiness of all the members of the family without dis-

crimination. The affection, however, is mutual between the paterfamilias and the other members of the family. Because of this, these other members trust the paterfamilias completely in all he does with the affairs of the family.[96]

Although there are some variations according to specific contexts, Awolowo's articulation of his idea of a family points us in the right direction.

In one sense, the moral matrix is similar to what Victor Turner has called a "root paradigm," or "certain consciously recognized (though not consciously grasped) cultural models in the heads of the main actors."[97] But it should be emphasized that these are not paradigms in Thomas Kuhn's sense of the term, for they are allusive, implicit, and metaphoric; they are mental and often emotional images and understandings rather than coherent intellectual boundaries for scholarly reflection and debate. The available data have permitted me to formulate four premises of the matrix. Since I treat them at greater length in Chapters 5 and 6, here I introduce them only briefly.

Premises of the Matrix

Premise 1: The Father-Chief

There are two sides to this particular coin. On the first side there is the loving, kind, understanding, always solicitous, and caring paternal—and occasionally maternal—figure. Contained within the imagery of father and family and the moral matrix on which it is based, there is an implicit promise of nurture and paternal care. Fathers in middle Africa are providers, nourishers, and protectors; people expect fathers to fulfill these roles. Parenthetically, the "father" does not necessarily have to be the biological sire but is usually he who nourishes and protects. In this context, parts of Claude Meillassoux's model are relevant. The father "feeds," "marries," and is thus entitled to "eat" part of the children's labor or the product of their labor. In exchange, the children receive protection, care, and security.[98] A Swahili praise poem in honor of Nyerere and the Arusha Declaration appearing in the newspaper *Uhuru* in 1970 put it another way. Discussing the Arusha Declaration using images of food, the poet stated that before the declaration there was less to eat. People could then eat only basic foods like porridge and greens (*ugali na sukuma wiki*). But now, when Tanzanians put the declaration in their hearts, they are fatter than before; they eat rice and fish (*wali na samaki*).[99]

Clearly, therefore, an important economic dimension is contained in this premise of the moral matrix. When political fathers care for, nurture, and provide wealth for their children, their political legitimacy is enhanced. When, on the other hand, economic conditions deteriorate and they are no longer able to nurture the population in this way, their political legitimacy will decline markedly. When the harvests are poor, when the rains fail, when the livestock dies, when the state's revenues are not themselves used in creatively productive economic ventures, then political legitimacy will diminish. In other words, when political fathers see to it that their children have the resources to "eat" (both literally and figuratively), their political legitimacy tends to remain strong. Ironically, just as paternalistic personality cults were reaching their apogees at various times in the 1970s and 1980s, the ability, and often desire, of leaders to care for their political children was receding dramatically.

The second side of the coin is less loving, less nurturing, and less paternal. If the father smiles and forgives, the chief snarls and punishes. This harsh and repressive visage has confronted many middle Africans when they have protested their lot. Occasional and "necessary" parental discipline—of course undertaken only with the good of the child in mind—can be transformed into vicious and nasty repression when the political "children" repeatedly fail to toe the political line or are insufficiently grateful for all that their father-chief does, and has done, for them. The benevolent father thus gives way to the malevolent chief whom people expect to command both the forces of coercion and the forces of the occult, deploying them as arms of governance. These are part of his strength, power, and legitimacy. The occult is the focal point of Chapter 4.

The unstated yet potent political logic of this rhetoric is insidious. In the first place, even if the political opposition places an altogether different accent on the paternal and familial language, they have still let the state dictate the ideological terrain of the political debate. Furthermore, if Presidents Moi, Mobutu, Biya, or Houphouet are (or were) the "fathers" of their respective national "family," their people are reduced to the role of his children. The regimes can present, therefore, any political protest as the work of "ungrateful" or "misguided" or "wayward" children. They are all brothers and sisters, and like siblings who squabble over inconsequential matters, citizens do also. Important political questions, such as ethnic competition for scarce resources, may thus be presented as the petty sibling rivalries of those lacking in maturity. And, as Chapter 5 shows, the "father" must occasionally "discipline" naughty and immature children for their own good. The political consequences of framing the political discussion in this manner are important as the metaphors contribute to an implicit "infantilization" of the population.

But while the chief disciplines and punishes, the father forgives and pardons. Chapter 5 also indicates that the presidential pardon, a common constitutional power in most states, is presented and understood in a special way in middle Africa. For example, in 1986 Cameroon's Paul Biya "magnanimously" pardoned fourteen "political agitators." A front-page editorial in the local press noted that those pardoned were grateful to the "Father of the Renewal [renouveau] and to the humanistic tolerance he incarnates." Biya thus demonstrated that although vengeance is human, the pardon is divine. The columnist also reported that those released had promised not to take up their political activities again, and that this would be "sage" or wise.[100] There were two implications: first, that Biya had a "divine" quality, and second, that when commenting on the wisdom that the pardoned Cameroonians would demonstrate were they to refrain from resuming their political agitations, there occurred an implicit infantilization of the population.

Premise 2: The Limits of Consumption

As Chapter 2 shows, power in middle Africa has much to do with "eating" (in both literal and figurative senses) as well as with other forms of consumption. The second premise of the moral matrix thus indicates that while the father-chief may "eat," and even eat well, there are nevertheless limits placed on how much he can and should consume. In a sense, this premise deals with the imprecise frontier between an acceptable appetite and political corruption. In a rough-and-ready calculus of legitimacy, the first and second premises will probably vary directly most of the time. In other words, the more the people have to eat (the better are the general economic conditions), the larger will be the permissible range of chiefly or presidential appetite. But if the people begin to go hungry, if economic conditions deteriorate, then appetites the citizenry might once have tolerated in good times will no longer be perceived as falling within the prerogative of the father-chief. Similarly, the longer the father-chief has been in power and the more he has eaten, the less likely people will be to accept continued presidential gluttony. For example, I would argue that Houphouet's decline in legitimacy coincided with increasing economic difficulties, a tenure in office that—at least to some—was beginning to seem eternal, and the fact that certain of the "Old Man's" more grandiose and expensive projects (e.g., the basilica at Yamoussoukro) were perceived as the fruits of corruption.

Moreover, when external forces beyond the direct control of the father-chief—whether in the form of falling commodity prices or the rigors of a Structural Adjustment Program—cause the population to suffer economic deprivation and hardship, to maintain their level of legitimacy political father-chiefs must demonstrate that they, too, are no longer "eating" as they once did and that their portions have also been reduced. In this regard Abdou Diouf's decision at the end of 1983 to renounce two months of his official salary in solidarity with Senegalese peasants struck by a severe Sahelian drought is instructive.[101] Was there an element of political cynicism at play here? I am unable to say. But even if there was, we nevertheless need to inquire as to why it took this particular form. In addition, an editorial commenting on what it called a "presidential road show" in Hilla Limann's Ghana, acidly noted: "Customarily, presentation of gifts to visiting dignitaries is perfectly regular. But what is the objective of loading the President with tons of food when in fact, their prices are so prohibitive that ordinary folks in the villages are having problem [sic] feeding themselves and their families[?] . . ."[102]

It is also worth noting that throughout middle Africa the language of corruption is often related to the language of food: *madesu ya bana* (beans for the children), and *un petit quelque chose à manger* (a little something to eat) in Zaïre; as well as the ubiquitous East African equivalent, *chai* (tea). Similarly, in Tanzania during the 1980s, bribery became known as obtaining a bit of *mchuzi* (gravy).[103] During the 1980s and 1990s many folks came to believe that their leaders had "eaten" too much, and there was a consequent corollary that their legitimacy had declined apace. Before they died, the widespread sentiment was that the personal wealth of Mobutu, Houphouet, and Nigeria's last military strongman, General Sani Abacha, had gotten entirely out of hand. The same can still be said of Moi and Biya. The popular resentment against Houphouet's hometown basilica (reportedly the world's biggest church), ostensibly paid for from *Le Vieux's* personal funds, is but one example. As popular Kenyan author David Maillu once wrote, assuming the voice of a desperate, down-and-out alcoholic, "I want to meet my MP, / he must show me the way out; / but my MP is always surrounded / by men with big tummies / and thin people like me / have no chance of seeing him."[104] The "men with big tummies" have eaten too much, and throughout the past two decades countless ordinary middle Africans, the "thin people," have increasingly demonstrated that they have had enough.

Premise 3: Inclusion and Exclusion

The third premise of the moral matrix concerns the treatment of women and has two aspects. The first notes how significant portions of the dominant discourse tend to define them as being somehow beyond the parameters of the political kingdom. Often consigned by the discourse to the home, the familial foyer, the farm, or development projects, women are thus defined out of the political realm. In Ghana after the second coup of J. J. Rawlings, a female member of the Provisional National Defence Council (PNDC), Aanaa Enin, urged women, as the journalistic account had it, "to shed their apathetic attitude towards developmental activities in the country since it is only by getting involved that they can be a force to fight against their harassment."[105] The message was clear. One ends harassment (she was speaking of the harassment of market women, who were often seen as price gougers) not through politics, but through participation in development activities and projects.[106] One consequence is that their voices are not heard. Put briefly, the rights of women (and by extension I also intend women to stand for other marginalized groups in society) may not be abused, and, importantly, the political father-chiefs must willingly hear their voices and take advice from them.

The dominant discourse permits women an advisory role but does not often speak of equality, except perhaps to deny the possibility. One Nigerian male put it this way:

> In recent years, women all over the world have been fighting for equality with men. And they claim that what a man can do a woman can do, even better. But I think that what the women are asking for is not equality with men but equal rights and opportunities for both men and women. Biblically, God made a woman as a helper to man but not man's equal. It is just like an adviser to a governor or a president. As an adviser you cannot claim to be equal to the governor or the president. But you as a human being like the governor or the president, have your own right to live, express your mind and exercise your legal right to freedom of speech and worship and to do things the way you like within the law. And if your master should try to deny you these rights, you have the option of fighting for them within the law. I think this is what the women are doing and we have come to agree with them in their struggle for equal rights or what they term women [sic] liberation.[107]

With but few exceptions, articulate and overtly political voices of women in many middle African societies usually tend to be heard only when their societies are in crisis. Prior to those key junctures, however, shrewd political father-chiefs may seek their counsel and listen to it quietly, in the background. But the deeper a society plunges into economic, social, or political crisis, the more likely it becomes that quiet advice will become public outrage. In one sense, the fact that women are increasingly vocal and prominent in various forms of protest activities should be taken as a measure that a regime's political legitimacy is declining markedly. This is perhaps best seen by juxtaposing two Zaïrian incidents. The first occurred in 1975, the United Nations' International Year of the Woman. Never ones to miss a public relations opportunity, Zaïrian leaders hastily organized a national conference on the subject. State-party officials from all subregions were instructed to dispatch worthy female representatives from their districts to the national capital. Assembled quickly, the women discussed various topics for several days prior to the appearance of President Mobutu. After Mobutu's speech to the delegates, he agreed to answer questions. An elderly Ngbandi woman (and thus a member of Mobutu's own ethnic group) arose and stated publicly that women had had enough and that Mobutu should relinquish power and go. As an old woman, she did not fear the president's wrath and declared that he could do whatever he wanted to her. Although visibly angered, Mobutu neither responded nor retaliated.

The second incident took place in Kinshasa in late April 1988, when women gathered to protest the high rate of infant mortality, the excessive cost of food, and the general conditions of misery prevailing in the country. They carried photos of Patrice Lumumba, Joseph Kasavubu, and Etienne Tshisekedi, the leader of the Union pour la Démocratie et le Progrès Social—a major, although then illegal, opposition party. Soldiers and secret police intervened quickly and arrested 60–200 of the demonstrators. Twelve of them remained in custody of the military security service, whose agents repeatedly raped them. Reports indicated that some of those responsible for these atrocities were HIV positive.

Mobutu's response was extraordinary. Several days later he delivered an address in Lingala to thousands of Kinshasa's youth. During this speech (which was subsequently rebroadcast on radio and television) he told his audience:

> When . . . I was still at Gbadolite I heard that a dozen women . . . had demonstrated. . . . You see a demonstration. What do you do, you, JMPR [party youth]? What do you do, you, CADER [party youth disciplinary brigade]? You are not going to wait for the gendarmes, you are not going to wait for the soldiers or the JMPR. You know the meaning of our dearly acquired peace. You have shoes, kick them. I'm not saying disorder, but kick them. I'll say it again, kick them. You have hands, hit them. You have a head: *KAMO!* [violent head butt] You remove them from the road in the name of peace.[108]

Between these two incidents something had clearly changed. Laughter coupled with the observation that Mobutu had behaved correctly (i.e., had done nothing) after the first incident was replaced by shock and revulsion after the second. Popular reaction to Mobutu's cavalier assessment of the plight of the captured demonstrators showed that he and his regime had violated a deep-seated moral tenet concerning the role and treatment of women in society.

In August 1990 President Moi phrased at least part of this premise of the moral matrix more positively. Telling government officials to mind their manners at all times, he continued: "You government officials, do justice to everyone wherever you are. Show the people a good image of the government. Show them how the government works. Serve the people properly. *If you are approached by an elderly woman, talk to her properly.* . . . See to it that the citizens feel protected. Do not allow anyone to feel desperate."[109]

Relevant evidence also comes from other sources. David Maillu, referring to a fictional Akamba village, phrases it this way:

> Being afraid of such public ridicule by women at communal work, every sensible husband had to exercise great discipline in all his movements and in handling the affairs of his home and marriage. There were women composers to "cut" songs about the bad man to be ridiculed. Such songs would be sung openly and loudly at communal works by the women jointly with the intention that the man should hear them together with his comrades and the public. The victim could do nothing to the women. He was forced to mend his ways of life. Thus women exercised some power in ensuring good behaviour.[110]

In other words, the key formulation would be a realization that the rights of women and other marginalized individuals may not be abused and, importantly, that political leaders must willingly hear their voices and take advice from them. Good husbands and fathers, after all, accept counsel from their wives and treat them with respect. Within the matrix there is an awareness that the voices of women and adult children have a place and must be heard. The last point is especially critical in understanding the juxtaposition of the two Zaïrian incidents. The father's willingness to listen to advice, however painful, from an elderly woman in 1975 had by 1988 given way to the chief's fury that women would dare to support his opponents openly.

Premise 4: The Alternation of Power

The fourth premise of the moral matrix is that political fathers, and elders, have to permit their children to grow up, take on increasing degrees of responsibility and influence, and eventually succeed them in power. Permanent power is thus illegitimate, as are all "presidents-for-life." A letter to the editor of *West Africa* is also germane here and probably reflects a widespread popular sentiment: "Today, Togo is in deep trouble because Eyadema is clinging to power after 26 years of being at the top. Enough is enough. It is time for Eyadema to go."[111] But since that letter in March 1993 Eyadema has not gone, and that is a major part of the problem.

In a curious way the rhetoric surrounding military coups in much of Africa underscores the illegitimacy of permanent power. After all, why else do the soldiers invariably say, either in their first speech or in their first interview, that once they have accomplished their mission of setting the polity on a sound course, of ending corruption and economic mismanagement, of improving the lot of the ordinary citizen, that they will willingly return to the barracks and that their regime will be a temporary one? The 1994 coup in the Gambia provides a case in point. In its aftermath the coup's leader, Lt. Yaya Jammeh, claimed that his would be a "coup with a difference," and he vowed that he and his fellow soldiers were "not here to perpetuate ourselves" and that they would return to the barracks "as soon as we have set things right."[112] When asked how soon the ordinary Gambian could look forward to free and fair elections, Jammeh replied: "Well, we are not giving any timetable for free and fair elections. That does not mean that we are here to stay too long. We are not here for that."[113] Jammeh is still in power, albeit at the head of a civilianized multiparty regime after elections in September 1996. Most observers found these neither free nor fair.

Similarly, when General Ibrahim Babangida seized power in Nigeria, one relevant headline in the *Daily Times* read, "We Won't Overstay—IBB," and the article went on to state that the general had assured all concerned, "The present military leadership won't stay in office a day longer than necessary."[114] It was not until fourteen years later, at the end of May 1999, that the Nigerian military finally returned to the barracks. The soldiers (Buhari, Babangida, and then Abacha) had been in power continuously since 1983. The point here is that with the possible exception of J. J. Rawlings' second coup in Ghana, virtually all soldiers have proclaimed that their regimes would be temporary rather than permanent. Early in his regime Rawlings admitted that unlike 1979, when he handed back the reigns of government after three months, this time would be different. He told the BBC: "In other words, I want us to understand something about the conception of power. Any man who talks about the handover of power through the ballot box or through whatever means supposes that power is not at the right place, because power is not transferable. Power must lie in the roots, with the people. The people must be part of the decision-making process and this is precisely what we want to achieve."[115]

In this regard—Rawlings excepted—the vast majority of the soldiers' statements upon seizing power both reflect and affirm the provision of the moral matrix indicating that permanent power is illegitimate power. Even if they have absolutely no intention of honoring this premise of the matrix, they still feel obligated to recite the usual mantra about their "temporary" regimes. In other words, one key to maintaining political legitimacy is the rejection of permanent authority, a point that is underscored by the often joyous popular reactions to some military coups. Rotation of elites is thus crucial. The mistake many observers make, however, is in believing that this rotation, this *alternance,* must be accomplished by an exchange of power among two or more political parties. That is but one possibility. Another possibility—that of rotation among different political generations within the same political party—was amply demonstrated by the political transition in Senegal between President Léopold Senghor and his successor, Abdou Diouf, at the start of

1981. This transition, as well as those which occurred in Tanzania and Cameroon, commands our attention in Chapter 6.

I should like to add one final word concerning the middle African moral matrix presented here. These four premises certainly do not exhaust the number of premises possible and worthy of examination. References to communalism and the communal aspects of middle African life, for example, appear frequently throughout the discourse and would thus constitute a valid subject of further study and a potential fifth premise. I have selected these four premises because of the frequency, intensity, and centrality of their place in the discourse, and because of my own prior interest in these subjects.

Subjacency, Legitimacy, and the "Unthinkable"

Since so much of the matrix is based upon our usually unarticulated assumptions and understandings of what is acceptable in political life and political behavior, seeking to understand its contours and their consequences drives us toward an appreciation of those phenomena which might be either politically thinkable or politically unthinkable. It points us, in other words, toward an awareness of the realm of "subjacent politics." The politically subjacent arena contains those pre-theoretical notions and assumptions which, while not predicting or determining our political thoughts or behaviors, nevertheless tend to structure them within a range of politically thinkable possibilities. In approaching the subject this way, the work of George Lakoff, a cognitive scientist who has written elegantly of both the importance of metaphor and the role of implicit models of political behavior, provides certain guidelines. Lakoff tells us, "One of the most fundamental results in cognitive science, one that comes from the study of commonsense reasoning, is that most of our thought is unconscious—not unconscious in the Freudian sense of being repressed, but unconscious simply in that we are not aware of it." Put slightly differently, people have an unconscious system of concepts. "A conceptual metaphor," according to Lakoff, "is a conventional way of conceptualizing one domain of experience in terms of another, often unconsciously."[116] The studies of Denis-Constant Martin, a French political scientist, emphasize the importance of a sensitive reading and understanding of the language of politics, as well as the necessity of seeking out unidentified political objects (*objets politiques non identifiés*).[117] This, too, has suggested several worthwhile research orientations.

To make both the discussion in this chapter and the analysis in subsequent chapters as clear as possible, it is necessary to detail some of this study's more important assumptions. The first major assumption is that all societies have a moral matrix of legitimate governance. This matrix shifts and changes over time, albeit sometimes slowly, and is certainly influenced by the diffusion of external events and ideas. A timeless, ahistorical "ethnographic present," in other words, would be most misleading. Equally misleading would be an essentialist argument seeking to isolate the uniquely or authentically middle African aspects of the matrix, for such a procedure would be impossible. Paternal and familial imagery, for example, has been important in other societies, both past and present—in seventeenth-century England, in the early days of the American Republic, and in various contemporary Asian societies.[118] Founding fathers, national fathers, have also appeared elsewhere, as the cult surrounding George Washington should remind us.[119] But the precise configuration of any moral matrix will differ from place to place, from time to time, from context to context. Depending on time, place, and context, it is quite conceivable that some societies will share certain premises of a matrix while not sharing others. Furthermore, within any society there is likely to be subcultural variation, often substantial, in the degree to which certain premises of the matrix are shared. Not all premises of the matrix will hold equally in all cases. There is a range of variation, and in some instances the "fit" will clearly be better than in others. There will be, moreover, different mixtures of the premises, as well as different weightings given to them depending on the context.[120] Logical consistency is not a requirement of any matrix, and there may well be premises of a matrix that are contradictory. Indeed, such contradictions are common and a source of political competition and conflict in all societies.

Were I interested in studying the moral matrix of the United States, for example, I might well be looking at the "sacred" nexus of law, contract, and market—all undergirded by an assumption of the sovereignty of the individual.[121] In this regard, it might be useful to envisage an inverted three-dimensional triangle with individualism resting on the bottom and law, contract, and market as the three sides. The degree of legitimacy of any given political action, political orientation, political thought, or idea will be contingent on the extent to which it is able to tap into the underlying and politically subjacent premises of the moral matrix. Consider Newt Gingrich's "Contract with America" during the 1994 congressional elections. On one level this might have been nothing more than a brilliant public relations ploy, but part of the reason it was so successful in helping the Republicans to gain control of the House of Representatives was that it effectively tapped into certain culturally resonant subjacent notions of the sanctity of contract.

A second critical assumption is that in all societies some things are politically thinkable while others are politically unthinkable. Throughout this study I define political legitimacy as that which is politically thinkable. Moreover, the best way to gauge thinkability is by examining mainstream political discourse. What is thinkable in one place and time may not be thinkable in another. Let me emphasize that in using the terms "thinkable" and "unthinkable" I am being literal: Can we, do we, think these thoughts? This is not to be confused with normative orientations, preferences, or points of view. Questions of normative desirability, of morality and immorality, need to be considered on an axis separate from one dealing with questions of thinkability and legitimacy. Unfortunately, therefore, in all societies some normatively reprehensible actions and ideas are quite thinkable politically. To provide but one example, disastrously, it is quite "thinkable" for Hutu and Tutsi to slaughter each other in Rwanda and Burundi.

Similarly, in some times and places, certain political actions and ideas might simultaneously be both morally desirable and politically unthinkable and illegitimate. The progressive extension of the franchise in U.S. history comes readily to mind as a case in point. At the Republic's founding it might well have been normatively desirable to extend the vote to African Americans or women, but those options were—literally—quite unthinkable for the vast majority of the population and its political leaders and were thus illegitimate. The political struggles for civil rights, as well as the quest for gender equity, also demonstrate that changing notions of thinkability can result in political conflict. For example, at least on the level of discourse, there were for a time serious regional variations in the thinkability of integration and racial equality. Gradually, however, as these concepts became increasingly thinkable, the locus of political conflict shifted from whether to achieve them to how best they could be realized. A new, thinkable, hegemonic discursive order emerged that valued racial equality. It became unthinkable to oppose it, and those who did were shunned and ridiculed. Political legitimacy, thinkability, thus excludes neither conflict nor—in extreme cases—instability. It merely provides a central portion of the intellectual and cognitive terrain on which such conflict is played out.

Let us consider another example. In 1998 the U.S. Department of Justice filed an antitrust action against computing giant Microsoft. As of this writing, *United States v. Microsoft* is still *sub judice*. Regardless of the eventual outcome, however, the breakup of Microsoft is thinkable, and thus legitimate, because it would reaffirm or re-enable the market while punishing violations of the law against monopolistic business practices. At the same time, however, the retention of Microsoft as it is would also be thinkable, and thus legitimate, because it would reaffirm market success. There is, however, a third policy option. To the best of my knowledge, no major U.S. politician or political pundit is discussing the nationalization of Microsoft. Why not? No one is exploring this policy option, or even speaking about it, because—quite simply—in the American political context it is unthinkable and illegitimate. At present in the United States the nationalization of Microsoft is not an option. It is not even considered; it is not on the policy agenda; it is not thinkable and is, therefore, illegitimate because such an action would deny and invalidate the politically subjacent concept of the market.

The political fate of the first surgeon general in the Clinton administration, Dr. Joycelyn Elders, is also relevant and instructive. A controversial and outspoken figure, Elders initially created a stir in late 1993 and early 1994 when she argued that the legalization of drugs was a serious policy option and ought to be considered. She further stirred the roiled political waters when she endorsed gay and lesbian adoption and argued that the Boy and Girl Scouts should admit homosexuals. On 1 December 1994 Elders delivered a speech at a World AIDS Day conference at the United Nations. During a question-and-answer session, and in the general context of AIDS breaking down many old taboos concerning discussions about sex, psychotherapist Robert Clark asked her what she thought were "the prospects of a more explicit discussion and promotion of masturbation." Elders' carefully worded response was the following: "As per your specific question in regard to masturbation, I think that it is something that is a part of human sexuality and it's a part of something that perhaps should be taught. But we've not even taught our children the very basics. And I feel that we have tried ignorance for a very long time, and it's time we try education." The White House, the incoming Republican-controlled Congress, and the media interpreted her remarks as an open advocacy of teaching schoolchildren about masturbation, and Bill Clinton fired her.[122] Regardless of what she actually said, regardless of the context in which she said it, what matters here is people believed that she had uttered a thought that was completely unthinkable, completely illegitimate.

Finally, let me suggest a counterfactual thought experiment. Imagine President George H. W. Bush phoning up the chairman of the Joint Chiefs of Staff after the November 1992 presidential elections and ordering General Colin Powell to call out the troops, seize all federal buildings, and shut down all mass media. Then imagine Bush delivering a national television address declaring the election null and void. Once again, to the best of my knowledge, none of the news-oriented talk shows, no learned commentator, no syndicated newspaper columnist ever even considered this possibility. Yet those of us who study politics in Africa and other areas of the globe know that such things often occur. In the American context, however, such a thought is utterly unthinkable and illegitimate.

For an idea to cross the frontier from unthinkable to thinkable, it would first have to link to a politically valid subjacent concept. In other words, it would have to speak to a premise of the moral matrix of legitimate governance. For example, if for some it was unthinkable to impeach Bill Clinton for narrowly partisan reasons or because he lied about a sexual relationship, for others it would become politically thinkable to impeach William Jefferson Clinton for the violation of his oath in court and his violation of the "contract" he entered with the American people when he swore to preserve, protect, and defend the Constitution of the United States. The second set of phrasings link to two of the three politically legitimate subjacent notions: the sanctity of contract and the rule of law. The more an idea or action can be linked to, or tap into, the politically subjacent notions which form the premises of the moral matrix of legitimate governance, the higher the degree of political legitimacy it will be likely to achieve.

The third major assumption of the study is that moral matrices do not, in and of themselves, explain anything. Nor, for that matter, does a culturally sensitive comprehension of key political concepts, an accurate mapping of the parameters of the political, or an understanding of alternative causalities. A working knowledge of all of these ideas is critical to both theory and explanation, however, and should precede them because they enable us to see and understand the intuitively grasped cognitive and intellectual terrain on which politics occurs. Moreover, the moral matrix of legitimate governance, as well as these other critical cultural factors, will enable us to generate hypotheses and approaches rooted in endogenous knowledge and understanding that will add richness and focus to already existing conceptual orientations. Social scientists studying their own societies, or those quite like them, often take factors such as moral matrices for granted. Those of us who study societies that are, in significant ways, culturally different from our own, cannot afford to do this and must become cognizant of these matrices.

The moral matrix of legitimate governance is simply an implicit cultural and cognitive template encompassing the sum of tacit understandings of how key political concepts, such as power, are intuitively and implicitly defined; of what constitutes the parameters of the political kingdom; and of how individuals comprehend the forces of political causality. These topics constitute the bases of Chapters 2, 3, and 4. Contained within the matrix is also a set of general and imprecise understandings of the rights and responsibilities of political office, of who shall be included or excluded from the political realm, and for how long one may hold political office. I treat these ideas in Chapters 5 and 6. The matrix also provides a sense of what is or is not politically thinkable and thus legitimate. Legitimacy, as well as the question of how its cultural logic might be connected to democracy in middle Africa, forms the core of the seventh and concluding chapter.

2. | Representations of Power

Although in some ways the special province of political scientists, the concept of power belongs to all the social and human sciences. Scholars working in a variety of academic disciplines (political science, sociology, anthropology, and philosophy among them) have shaped our views of power in ways that have not always proved helpful in the study of politics in middle Africa. This is because they have combined deductive theorizing and generalization from predominantly Western, secularized cases to explain political phenomena, behaviors, and data drawn from empirically oriented African fieldwork. Regardless of the specific proportions of theory and data involved in this mixture, their definitions of power—whether stated or not—structure inquiries into politics in the direction of certain empirical phenomena that are common and easily recognizable in the West.

In terms of the argument expressed in Chapter 1, these definitions contain assumptions that make it thinkable both to include and to focus attention on those empirical political phenomena that have readily observable Western counterparts. Unfortunately, while this procedure facilitates relatively easy comparison across national and cultural boundaries, it also has a serious disadvantage in that it often excludes, unknowingly and unthinkingly, other relevant local phenomena that may be every bit as germane to our understanding of power and politics in various parts of the world. It then becomes, quite literally, unthinkable to include these phenomena in our analyses because definitions of power aspiring to universal applicability do not always lead us to recognize them as politically important, and even less to give them the attention they deserve. To be sure, all societies have such political phenomena that occasionally assume a surprising and unexpected importance in the local context. Furthermore, in some cases these may be quite important to our understanding of certain forms of political behavior. In this regard, middle African societies are no different than any others. In all cases, there is thus a danger that a "one-size-fits-all" definition of power (or any other concept) may obscure more than it illuminates. This unfortunate outcome is even more likely when definitions of power and other key ideas in the social sciences are generated in societies with other cultural understandings. When these concepts are then applied in different cultural regions where the initial assumptions guiding their formulation might hold only in part or, in some cases, not at all, the result is often a distorted or skewed representation of political reality.[1]

This chapter argues that many "standard" Western definitions of power miss the mark when applied to politics in middle Africa because they do not always lead researchers in the direction of certain contextually defined political factors. Moreover, these factors—not always obvious to the naked eye—are crucial in any attempt to understand the nature of power in many middle African settings. Power has locally relevant meanings that vary in both time and space. It is not that "standard" definitions of power are always "wrong"; they are not. It is simply that they are often incomplete or inapt when applied to political settings outside those of their initial formulation.[2] The result is often a picture that is out of focus because it misses those elements of power that political actors simply take for granted and assume to be important without ever really thinking explicitly or systematically about them. These elements of power remain, for the most part, unarticulated. But that does not mean they lack importance.

This examination of power in middle Africa begins with an overview of some of these influential, Western, definitions that have achieved near canonical status. They are frequently cited and frequently taught. Yet, in some ways, we would all be better advised to seek locally relevant meanings of power through an examination of sources that reflect perceptions and understandings indigenous to the areas we study. Power, like any other concept, is most immediately and passionately understood through the eyes of those who experience it. In addition to the speeches and texts of various middle African politicians, I present evidence drawn from sources that political scientists tend to ignore such as letters to the editor of various newspapers, novels and other forms of literature, as well as the works of popular writers and intellectuals such as the Kenyan David Maillu and the Congolese Zamenga Batukezanga. By probing these sources for their hidden assumptions and meanings, I aim to present an understanding of power consistent with middle African assumptions. I argue that power has three additional faces in this part of the globe that orthodox definitions often miss. The first of these is eating, or consumption; the second face is spirituality—broadly defined to include formal world religions (e.g., Christianity and Islam), the cosmological world view containing the abode of the spirits and ancestors, and sorcery; the third face of power is its unity and indivisibility.

Two caveats are in order. First, although I present evidence drawn from a variety of literary sources, my aim is to examine literary texts as sources of data about political perceptions and political behavior, and as indicators of usually unarticulated political assumptions. That is, I wish to plumb literary texts for what they might tell us about politics. As a political scientist I pretend neither to be able to contribute to an understanding of various forms of African literature nor to make a contribution to literary theory. I leave those tasks to more qualified scholars.[3] My methodological intent is simply to explore the theoretical uses to which political and other social scientists might put such literary sources of data and perceptions about politics. Second, although I argue that these additional faces of power are important for a fuller understanding of politics in middle Africa, they are not unique to this part of the world. Middle Africa's contacts with other regions have been so pervasive and important that any attempt to construct an essentialist argument emphasizing this area's unique specificity would be futile.[4]

Power Defined

Prevalent notions of power in the West are both transformative and Newtonian. That is, they assume that power is designed to induce changes in behavior and that it is often met with resistance. Max Weber, for example, defined power as "the probability that one actor within a social relationship will be in a position to carry out his own will despite resistance, regardless of the basis on which this probability rests."[5] Bertrand Russell defined power as "the production of intended effects. . . . A has more power than B, if A achieves many intended effects and B only a few."[6]

Robert Dahl sees power as a subset of influence, and his often-cited definition of influence displays the same assumptions and has had an enormous influence on contemporary American political science. "A influences B," he writes, "to the extent that A gets B to do something that B might not otherwise do."[7] In a slightly later formulation, Dahl advanced the notion that "power terms in modern social science refer to *subsets of relations among social units such that the behaviors of one or more units depend in some circumstances on the behavior of other units.*"[8] Reacting against Dahl's work, Peter Bachrach and Morton Baratz advanced the notion of nondecision-making, arguing that "power is also exercised when A devotes his energies to creating or reinforcing social and political values and institutional practices that limit the scope of the political process to public consideration of only those issues which are comparatively innocuous to A. To the extent that A succeeds in doing this, B is prevented, for all practical purposes, from bringing to the fore any issues that might in their resolution be seriously detrimental to A's set of preferences."[9] Building on the insights of both of these schools of thought, Steven Lukes defines "the concept of power by saying that A exercises power over B when A affects B in a manner contrary to B's interests."[10]

In a similar vein, but this time further elaborating on Russell's definition, Dennis Wrong defines power "*as the capacity of some persons to produce intended and foreseen effects on others.*"[11] More recently, Kenneth Boulding has advanced the notion that there are three major categories of power: threat power, economic power, and integrative power, which are "closely related to another tripartite division: the power to destroy, the power to produce and exchange, and the power to integrate, that is, the power to create relationships such as love, respect, friendship, legitimacy, and so on."[12]

Michel Foucault's works have also attracted much attention, but like several other seminal figures in the social sciences, his definitions lack clarity and appear to change over time. There is, however, a structural element in that he sees power as the ability to "structure the possible field of action of others."[13] Moreover, this is partially accomplished through the production of reality. In his own words, "We must cease once and for all to describe the effects of power in negative terms: it 'excludes,' it 'represses,' it 'censors,' it 'abstracts,' it 'masks,' it 'conceals.' In fact, power produces; it produces reality; it produces domains of objects, rituals of truth. The individual and the knowledge that may be gained of him belong to this production."[14]

It is not my intention to provide an extended critical discussion of any of these definitions. This sampling is meant to be indicative and representative of major themes and trends, not exhaustive. In virtually all of the definitions cited above, power works to transform either one's behavior or the structures that shape it. And with the possible exception of Foucault, there is an assumption that one will, to the extent possible, resist such a transformation if one is aware of it and perceives it to be contrary to one's own interests. Even Africanist anthropologists such as W. Arens and Ivan Karp, who cite only Weber and Lukes among the social scientists I have listed above, argue, "Transformation is the key to understanding concepts of power in African societies."[15] These transformative and Newtonian assumptions are perhaps best expressed in James G. March's seminal essay, "The Power of Power." In a discussion of the influential school of community power studies in the United States, March notes that "social choice will be a predictable extension of past choices unless power is exerted on that choice"; and "when power is exerted, the modification of the choice will be proportional to the power."[16]

When contemporary political scientists write about politics outside the West, they usually assume two things: first, that definitions and assumptions about power generated in the West will be applicable; and second, that power will be visible and thus subject to empirical observation and measurement, Bachrach and Baratz notwithstanding. Furthermore, political scientists also usually assume implicitly that the power will be most apparent when located in its "proper" place, the state.[17] But in much of Africa, Western concepts of power cannot be simply applied without considering contextual variations in the local political arena. Without attention to context, the treatment of power will at best be only partially valid.

Let me be clear. My intent is not to suggest a wholesale rejection of Western notions of power, for in certain African contexts they can be quite illuminating. Various aspects of power do have universal applications and are well understood in most African settings. When, for example, a platoon of well-armed soldiers terrorizes a village, people know that their weapons give them the power to pillage, loot, and rape despite any resistance that might occur. But to the readily recognizable transformative and Newtonian aspects of power we must add those locally important and contextually understood representations of power that I believe the vast majority of middle Africans understand intuitively and implicitly. Power must be related both to its locally relevant, physically observable manifestations and to its origins in the cosmological world view of its inhabitants. A more complete understanding of power in this part of the world requires that we discuss three additional faces of power in many middle African societies. I consider each in turn.

Local Faces of Power

Eating

Power and politics in African societies often have more to do with consumption than transformation. Power frequently concerns the capacity to consume, or the ability "to eat" as expressed both literally and figuratively in many African languages. Moreover, and following logically, if power and "eating" are related, then it is reasonable to expect that one possible and observable manifestation of power will be ample girth. In other words, the anthropological notion of "big man" often has a quite literal meaning. And while it might be objected that consumption is, in fact, but one type of transformation, this type of consumption goes well beyond standard ideas of transformation.

During the transition to the Second Republic in Nigeria, for example, one of the political parties that sprung up unabashedly called itself the "I Chop, You Chop Party." In West African Pidgin *chop* means both "food" and "to eat." The implication was that if you voted for this party you would eat—not only in the literal sense, but also in the widely understood figurative sense of being able to "eat" a slice of the well-understood and often invoked "national cake."[18] Nigerian writer Kole Omotoso puts it this way: "The control of central government has been in Nigeria, the sumptuous pot of soup with mixed meat and fish which all nationalities have always wanted to corner and if possible eat alone. All the conflicts in the history of the country have been over this pot of sumptuous soup."[19] Or, to use a metaphor prevalent in Kenya that dates from after independence (*Uhuru*), especially among those in the political grouping around Jomo Kenyatta, the "fruits of *Uhuru* [*matunda ya Uhuru*]" grew in the state. As one notoriously sticky-fingered Kenyan politician put it in 1982, "*Uhuru* is sweet!"[20] The metaphor has remained in common usage since then.[21]

Similarly, Jean-François Bayart reminds us that in Cameroonian French when someone either obtains or loses a position in the state the usual expressions are either "*On lui a donné la bouffe* [They have been given something to eat]" or "*On lui a enlevé la bouffe* [They have had the right to eat taken away]."[22] There is, as well, the Cameroonian proverb, "*La chèvre broute là où elle est attachée* [The goat grazes where it is tethered]." More specifically, in 1982 one Cameroonian commentator noted that this particular expression, already commonly used, had had its meaning transformed substantially. Where originally the phrase had connoted that workers should enjoy all of the legal benefits that came along with their positions, increasingly it had come to mean that those who occupy positions of responsibility in management should enjoy and consume, as much as they are able, the very public goods that they have the responsibility to preserve or administer.[23] A Tanzanian columnist, resorting to the relevant Swahili phrase where appropriate, noted the same phenomenon in these terms:

> . . . Upon appointment or election, leaders attract general congratulations for a start. These are simultaneously reinforced by a remark that sounds like a joke but is quite instructive.
>
> The lucky man or woman is "bombarded" with hearty *hongera* [congratulations], followed by a suggestion that *umeula* [you have eaten it], advanced by closely familiar well-wishers with whom one may be on joking terms.
>
> Those not so close stop at *hongera* and reserve the other part for indirect chats in which they observe that so-and-so *ameula* or *kaula* [he ate it].
>
> The key word here is *kula* [to eat], implying that the person graced with a post or promoted to a higher one has been exposed to opportunities for *eating*.
>
> Eating does not in this context relate to the conventional practice of taking food, but making money—much money—and thus securing a means to consolidate oneself economically.
>
> And money here is not supposed to represent extra income derived from higher pay and allowances attendant to the lucrative post. It is presumed to be money acquired through dubious means. . . .
>
> Practically therefore, leadership positions are for some synonymous with "licences to eat." . . .[24]

In other words, one is powerful if one can "eat"; the more one eats, the more powerful one becomes. There is thus a close correlation between the language of food and the language of corruption in many middle African states. Several examples should suffice. In a 1982 newspaper commentary on life in Kinshasa, one journalist noted that Zaïre's capital was infested with "vultures." Referring specifically to the traffic police, he noted that they take up positions along the road to intercept and harass motorists on the pretext of inspecting their papers. But even when the papers prove to be completely in order, they still say, "Give some money, it isn't your papers that we are going to eat."[25] In the run-up to the elections in Kenya in late 1992, many opposition candidates and their prominent backers were invited to "eat *ugali* [porridge]" or take bribes, with senior officials of Kenya's state-party. And when Kenya's vice-president and minister for planning, George Saitoti, came under political attack in 1993, the thrusts and parries were occasionally expressed in similar metaphors. In defending his collaborator against these attacks, President Daniel arap Moi noted in Swahili: "*Saitoti amekula kitu gani ya mtu?* [What has Saitoti eaten that belongs to anyone?]"[26] Similarly, Nigerian elections through the 1980s and 1990s have witnessed the introduction of a new culinary delight, the *naira* sandwich.[27] Voters standing on line to cast their ballots were tempted with two slices of bread surrounding several "tasty" banknotes if they agreed to vote the right way. In this context, Samuel Doe's remarks to students in 1989, before the Liberian horror began, are also germane: "If you mind us politicians, we will leave you all. All we want are your votes, and finish with you; that's all we do. We play with the people's brains, convince them and confuse them. After we've finished talking politics, you know what we look for? We want to eat."[28]

Food is obviously related to this capacity "to eat." David William Cohen and Atieno-Odhiambo note that in Siaya, a rural community in Western Kenya, "food is, pre-eminently, about power; and discussion among the folk of Siaya about scarcity. . . . Diet and taste and food colour . . . are in a very fundamental sense about the distribution of power and rights in the wider society."[29] Similarly, and by extension, there is a sense in which much of the incessant discourse of the various states around the question of dependency on external sources of food, increasing agricultural production, the seemingly never-ending quest for self-sufficiency in food, and the ability to feed oneself, is also about power. Simply put, a state that cannot feed its population is potentially vulnerable to the dictates of others, remaining dependent and thus relatively powerless. This notion was long a staple of political discourse in Tanzania because of Julius Nyerere's ideological doctrine of *Ujamaa* socialism and self-reliance, and similar themes appeared regularly in the discourses of other countries as well.[30]

Kenya's Moi, for example, has noted: "A nation that cannot feed itself is a nation that cannot claim to be truly independent."[31] Similarly, a Ghanaian editorial used the anniversary of national independence to remark, "Most readers would expect us to comment again on Ghana's twenty-seventh independence anniversary which fell yesterday. But we are not going to do that. Instead we are going to concern ourselves with food production, because without enough food to eat, our independence will remain but a flag and an anthem. . . ."[32] Along these same lines, a Ghanaian politician and one-time member of J. J. Rawlings' PNDC, General Arnold Quainoo, explicitly drew the analogy between personal freedom and national independence. The account of his speech in the daily press noted that "no nation can have her peace or ask other nations to leave it alone to manage her own affairs if she cannot feed herself. Similarly, an individual who cannot feed himself and yet demands to be left alone to have his peace of mind is deceiving himself. Thus the ability to feed oneself is the foundation of freedom."[33] A comparable Nigerian comment made essentially the same larger point while phrasing things in the current domestic idiom of food: "President Ibrahim Babangida . . . will want Nigerians to think more about baking rather than sharing the cake. . . . If these countries today in their 'friendship' give us the loans with strings attached, that, unfortunately, is the price we pay for having not baked our cake in the first place."[34]

Images of food, eating, and the metaphor of bigness due to overeating are widespread throughout middle Africa, occurring even in an ostensibly nonpolitical arena such as soccer. Noting that soccer (football) is an excellent way for members of Nigeria's wealthy elite to launch a political career, one commentator somewhat cynically described these would-be sportsmen as follows: "Although they themselves are never involved in physical sporting events due, most probably to their heavy build-up and protruding stomachs, they loved and married sports because of fame and perhaps, as a result of the penchant to shed their excess naira vaults."[35] Indeed, after then President Shehu Shagari chose to reward the members of Nigeria's team with a house and a car after a victory, there was speculation that henceforth—and largely because of this act of generosity—future membership on the national team would be less a matter of skill than of ethnic and regional origin. Eating "national cake" had also become part of the national pastime.[36]

Different variations of this imagery also occur frequently in presidential statements, the speeches of many politicians, and the press coverage of daily life. The metaphor of eating is so pervasive that is has become a shorthand frequently used to translate complex political thoughts and ideas to a simple and easily manipulable set of images and phrases. For example, in a 1981 May Day speech exhorting both the Tanzanian population, and especially Chama Cha Mapinduzi (CCM, the then single state party), to reflect better the ideals of socialism and self-reliance which—he then claimed—were permanent features of Tanzanian politics, President Nyerere noted, "Some leaders, including party cadres, think that they have been given positions of responsibility to merely sit down and eat. We have no business with such weak and opportunistic minds."[37]

Similarly, in 1991, Kenya's President Moi spoke to a political rally in Murang'a. Commenting in both general and specific terms of the detention of one of his political rivals, Kenneth Matiba, Moi noted:

> If you want to see rich people in Nyeri, you will find them—the big people and a very small number of small people. Big people are rich even in Kiambu. . . . Despite everything that happened last year, others still say: Moi will release Matiba, or why is Matiba being detained? I am not after anybody. I do not provoke anyone. What do I want from anybody? It is my duty to protect the citizens' lives. . . . I will take my time deciding when Matiba should be released from jail. He is being protected and fed, and he has even gained weight. [laughter] When I am convinced that he should come back and live peacefully with the citizens, I shall set him free. I have no scores to settle with him. My responsibility is to protect the citizens' lives, and I have no desire to lie.[38]

His use of the imagery includes references to "big people" and the distribution of resources among regions, as well as a cynical, laughter-provoking remark that his imprisoned opponent, Matiba, was doing well in confinement because he had "even gained weight" and that, therefore, Moi could not be accused of abusing him. So flexible is the imagery of food and eating that it can be used both metaphorically ("Big people are rich") and literally (Matiba has gained weight).

We have already noted in reference to Nigerian soccer that complicated matters of ethnicity and ethnic balancing are often expressed through the use of these images. The same often occurs in Kenya. In 1994 Elijah Mwangale, a prominent politician, declared that he would contest the vice-presidency of the ruling majority party, the Kenyan African National Union (KANU). Mwangale, a Luhya, emphasized one of his pet themes, the idea of a Luhya presidency. Mwangale, *Weekly Review* noted, said that "it was their turn to lead and 'eat' just as the Kikuyus 'ate' in the days of the late president Mzee Jomo Kenyatta who was from their community and the

Kalenjin who were 'eating' from the current leadership of President Daniel arap Moi. '*Bubwami kimiandu* [Power is wealth],' Mwangale declared and called on the Luhya to seek ways of getting to power if they hoped to get rich."[39] In a like manner, in late 1993 a veteran Luo politician, Achieng' Oneko, phrased his opposition to a unitary system of government in terms of food. "The unitary system," he maintained, "took away powers from the local governments to institutions. Development came to be based on political considerations. If one region was considered not to be in good books, the region did not enjoy its fair share of the national cake."[40]

Eating and power go together throughout middle Africa in ways both obvious and subtle. At the end of 1984, the state-controlled Senegalese daily, *Le Soleil,* featured an article on a lunch that was held at the Institut de Technologie Alimentaire (ITA, Institute of Dietary Technology) with the aim of encouraging people to consume local products so as to reduce dependency on foreign foodstuffs. The elegant meal featured appetizers such as stuffed millet pancakes, quiche Mary, beef sausages, bread with paté and tongue; main courses of well-known Senegalese fish dishes and local juices; and, finally, cakes for dessert. It was described as a *"pantagruelesque* [Pantagruelian; huge]" lunch that the institute offered in honor of the government, and the article listed an impressive array of cabinet ministers in attendance. There was also a photograph showing the government dignitaries in correct attire, at the table, eating. The caption read: "The ministers at table. They were all appreciative."[41] In an impoverished country beset by economic crisis, where many people can only afford to eat one meal daily, the detailed description of a menu well beyond the financial reach of the vast majority of the population, the ministerial roster of the rich and powerful, and the photograph of the members of the government at table certainly presents a message that goes beyond the necessity of reducing dependence on foreign foods. Here there is a direct link between the almost incessant discourse concerning food and self-sufficiency in food, on the one hand, and the more subtle and often unstated notions relating food, eating, and power in the popular consciousness. Consumption, especially in *"pantagruelesque"* quantities which will, of course, inevitably produce obese physiques, is implicitly understood to be about power, wealth, and the distribution of resources.[42] The commissioner for education of Imo State, Nigeria, phrased this slightly differently in the mid-1980s under the Buhari military regime. While trying to suggest how the Nigerian work ethic might be improved, he noted that gluttons do not obey what he called the law of give and take. "Knowledge of this law," he wrote,

> will therefore compel us to contribute to the restoration of Creation's stock of these sustainers of the link between the body and the soul, and the way to do that is to work hard. Even a glutton should appreciate this point since the harder he works, the more he prepares his body to absorb more and more of these "goodies" of nature—i.e., air, drink and food—in which he finds his delight. Unfortunately many of them do not. They want to take without giving and thus often grow obese.[43]

The powers that be certainly do not enjoy a monopoly on the use of this imagery. It long ago passed into the domain of popular discourse. Even those who criticize what "eating" has come to represent usually do so in terms that may ultimately reinforce the strength and pervasiveness of the metaphors involved. Columnists and other popular commentators on current affairs occasionally poke cynical fun at those ministers who eat so well for lunch. During the administration of Hilla Limann in the late 1970s and early 1980s, one Ghanaian observer, Elizabeth Ohene, penned a tongue-in-cheek lament on just how "tough" life was for the ministers, managing directors, and the other big men of the regime. In her words,

> Luckily for him, he does not have to buy lunch on this particular day because there is an official lunch for one reason or another. So you see where the excess weight comes from. Here is somebody whose normal fare used to be boiled green plantain with kontomire (or whatever the equivalent is in other parts of the country) and he finds himself eating a three course meal with how many martinis and liquor to push it down. Oh the things that big people will put up with for the country's sake! . . . In other words the next time you see a fat Minister or Managing Director, don't forget that it could mean overwork. . . .[44]

It would appear that well-fed ministers trying to cope with three-course lunches are not unusual in this part of the world.

In another column she reflected:

> Every time somebody mounts a podium, the talk is about the SHARING OF THE NATIONAL CAKE, anytime somebody takes a pen, we are sharing the national cake, every resolution is calling upon the government to give some group or area, their share of the national cake.
>
> It is obvious therefore that everybody believes that there is some cake with frosting and all sitting some place—at the Castle Osu most probably—waiting to be shared and the knife to do the slicing appears to be in the hands of the government of the day.
>
> In our present circumstances the people have voluntarily given the knife to Dr. . . . Hilla Limann to undertake the sharing and the knife being rather massive and almost impossible to be manipulated by one person, the President has chosen a team to help with the knife. Every once in a while, of course some people seize the knife without our consent and with it the cake also, I presume and arrogate to themselves complete control over the sharing.
>
> So completely have we taken this saying into our national vocabulary that everybody appears to have forgotten that there is a process to be gone through before a cake arrives.[45]

It is worth noting once again that these images are so flexible, evocative, and rich that they easily lend themselves to the discussion and description of some of the complexities of democracy and economic production in terms that most ordinary citizens readily understand and identify.

In an essay on why certain African politicians seem to love power so much that they are unwilling to relinquish it, one commentator noted sweepingly that "the African loves power, and those who bathe in the sunshine of that power love power more than he does. So, to be able to eat from the crumbs that fall from his table, they dance around him, tell tales, manufacture enemies just as fast as they manufacture titles."[46] In a book of social commentary published during the latter part of Ibrahim Babangida's military regime, Niyi Oniororo, national chairman of the Nigerian Council for National Awareness, wrote a series of essays in the form of open letters addressed to specific portions of Nigerian society. In his letter to the Nigerian military, Oniororo accused the soldiers in these terms: "No sooner you get power than you start displaying bigman-nism [sic] and you also start treating the common people as beasts of burden. You get so drunk in power that you also see yourselves as tin gods and the rest of the society are simply regarded as lesser beings who deserve only tiny crumbs from your tables."[47] Who gets to sit at the table, how many places are set, and who gets to eat the crumbs are key political issues in middle Africa.

While it is difficult to judge precisely, my impression is that even private citizens resort frequently to the metaphor of eating. Even though the sample is skewed because of literacy, one way to gauge this is through a close reading of the letters to the editor in most daily newspapers. In Nigeria in the early 1980s, one correspondent railed against a local television program, wondering whether it served any useful purpose. The particular program, produced by the Nigerian Television Authority (NTA), was "Cooking Time," and the writer lamented that the majority of Nigerians "are not financially solvent as to be able to prepare most of the foods been taught [sic] them during the programme. 80 per cent of Nigerians do not have their kitchens so well equipped like that one used by the N.T.A. during the programme. With ₦100.00 a month, how can Nigerians be able to prepare meals with ingredients running up to ₦15.00. Some families do not even find it easy to prepare common 'eba' and okro soup to feed on. Since the majority of Nigerians are in this class and the aim of the N.T.A. is to serve the masses, they should replace the programme 'cooking time' with a programme that will teach our women how to economise the sum of ₦100.00 a month being paid to their husbands."[48] This letter, although nominally about a television program, was also about eating, power, wealth, and social class.

Nigerians who pen such letters to the editor also adopt variants of these images. People use the idiom of the "national cake," for example, in a wide range of circumstances. One writer used his letter to the editor to protest the 1981 Oyo State budget because his town, Ikire, had no powerful godfathers "at the corridor of power like other towns that received more than what they bargained for in the 1981 budget. . . . It appears that all towns fully represented in the Government were being given priorities at the expense of the others. . . . I am therefore appealing to the Oyo State Government to please give us our fair share of the cake. We cannot continue suffering while others enjoy."[49] As we have seen, questions of revenue allocation in Nigeria are usually understood and expressed as being about a share of the cake. Another letter writer noted that discussions of revenue allocation were not productive. "Rather than battering ourselves over revenue allocation and issues connected with sharing our national cake, let us collectively bake a larger size of national cake," he wrote.[50] Or, in the context of a different political situation after the aborted election of June 12, 1993, a Nigerian living abroad was moved to write to *West Africa* about his thoughts on the new constitution. In his words, that "the concept of rotational Presidency as a means of power-sharing should evoke such passion is perhaps understandable, because it never has been difficult to show that politics in Nigeria is more about 'cake-sharing' than giving the people a chance."[51]

In late 1982 the Tanzanian Ministry of Health held a conference on obesity among executives and senior civil servants. This conference received some attention in the press and subsequently attracted a series of lively letters to the editor. Some correspondents were quite angry about what they deemed the misuse of government funds for such an event. One of them put it this way: "Recently the public through the Ministry of Health showed signs of concern about our Executives and other senior officers' health. The worries stemmed from their over-weight and the resultant medical complications. Some readers of this paper wrote a lot on how to trim and keep down our Executives' big bellies. Apart from physical exercises, the Executives should learn how to live ONLY on their official incomes. That is the best medicine."[52] Indeed, an article appearing some months later again took up the question of obesity, noting that "unfortunately, obesity is not seen as a health hazard by most people simply because there seem [sic] to be a tendency of associating it with wealth and personality. This makes some women prefer obese husbands (or boyfriends) while men would go for obese women saying that the thin skinned are not good. Some women believe that you are more 'secure' when you have an obese husband."[53] The article might well have added, although it did not, that the reason for this preference was a culturally diffused awareness that obesity is the sign of someone who has eaten, and eaten well, both literally and figuratively.

At least in the popular view, politicians and bureaucrats "eat." Two Kenyan letters capture this nicely. The first, written in 1991 while KANU's political monopoly was still in effect, praised President Moi but criticized the party leaders. "They are overworking him! Today he is at State House, Nairobi, received [sic] a VIP from foreign country, tomorrow in the countryside officiating at a Harambee meeting, the following day at the coast on a meet-the-people tour, and our so-called leaders are in Nairobi feasting on roasted goat and calling for beer."[54] The second, written five years later, was clearly a product of political liberalization. It argued that "Kanu has failed to implement its policies and had bred and perfected the art of 'eating and political manipulation.'"[55]

The meaning and message of the metaphor is also reinforced by popular literature. One Tanzanian short story, appropriately entitled "Eating the Country," tells the story of a man living in Dodoma, who is having the usual troubles making ends meet when an old classmate contacts him. His old friend is a free-spirited high roller who holds a top post in a regional branch of a parastatal organization. They meet for lunch, and the wealthy visitor says: "'We are eating the country, Joseph, *kula nchi* [eating the country,] this is the ripe time and don't waste it because nobody will show you how to do it—*shauri yako* (It's up to you),' he said fondling his big belly and continued. 'You see, with me never has a month passed without travelling out of my working station and of course you know what that means—

IMPREST' [a per diem for professionally related travel]. He washed down the potatoes with wine and laughed in his usual oily tone. . . ."[56]

The imagery of food, eating, and size appears quite often in the works of David Maillu, one of Kenya's most prolific authors. Moreover, there is at least some evidence that Maillu is also one of Kenya's most widely read authors, even though the East African literary establishment deems his work undeserving of serious critical attention.[57] In *My Dear Bottle* Maillu adopts the voice of an alcoholic to make disparaging analytical points about Kenyan society. Speaking of his member of Parliament (MP), the narrator notes that many MPs never sat for their school examinations, and yet "you should hear them / coughing out power."[58] Power, in other words, is something to be eaten or consumed, and then coughed out. Similarly, when the down-and-out narrator dreams of becoming an MP, he phrases part of his reverie this way: "I would keep a big lump of money / for use during elections / because a big politician without money / is like a dog without teeth." When he comments on his boss, the imagery reappears: "My big boss got this job / straight from jail / where the Government had thrown him / You see, for many years / he had been working for the Government / as a big man."[59] In this imagery, and especially in Maillu's repeated use of the word "big," we see that size and power are closely related.

Maillu's epic, *the kommon man,* more explicitly relates consumption to physical size and power. The poor man who narrates this tale has been cuckolded by a member of the wealthy elite. His bitter invective is worth citing at some length. Talking of his diet, the man relates: "The food I eat is the common diet / of others like me / who are supposed to keep silent about it / by doing the unwritten law of my country. / They don't want me to say I'm hungry / and they don't want me to say what I think / about them. / They want me to keep silent / and smile always like people / who have enough to eat and who are free / to say what they think about everything. . . . And as they eat you / they say and believe that / things are meant to be that way."[60] Here, the ability to consume both food and people is a sign of power. Furthermore, in some contexts it also pertains to witchcraft, as we see later in this chapter.

Describing his wife's wealthy lover, Makoka, Maillu's narrator recounts that

> He works in the city, Nairobi / as a big man, an executive who combines / business execution / with executing people's wives. / He goes home for lunch / to eat wives of the city workers / who don't have cars to go home / for lunch.
>
> The Jolly Man has a big tummy. / One wonders how he does it with women. / My wife knows about it but would she tell me how?
>
> *Uhuru* is good! / It is here to stay, and / the times are gone when all Kenyans / looked so thin / like the country dwellers one sees / during election campaigns. / When you see our nationals / in big conferences / you can't miss being impressed. . . . / There is always something interesting / common to them: / they shine / and they are all jolly like Makoka. / They have thick necks, / fat and round heads / with nice folds of fat / round their necks.
>
> When they sit / our nationals and people of money / have to position their

stomachs. / When they walk, they do so elegantly / arching their elbows / as their imported expensive shoes / sound on the floor heavily. / When they knock at your door and you say / Come in! / You see the tummy first / then the owner of the tummy follows. / And they usually knock at the door proudly / and arrogantly / like the police.

One wonders why they are so fat and round / and what they actually eat. / But I have an idea. / In Makoka's house I saw how they eat. / They eat soft food and drink / either beer or milk / or honey / or anything they wish. / When they belch, you get an idea / of the virtues of being a man of money. / They belch so richly, so impressively!

When the driver opens the car door for them, / they get out or in with difficulty / because of the fat. / And when they sit / the car sinks on their side. / Big people usually sit in the rear seat / to read a paper / or to have a nap / as the expensive prominent car / swallows the road.[61]

Once again, the ability to eat both food and people results in physical corpulence. Big men are always eating something (or someone). Even their material possessions get into the act as their "expensive prominent," and most probably big, cars are "swallowing" the road.

In addition, although I do not dwell on it, there is also within Maillu's works a close relationship between sexual activity, food, size, and power that often takes the form of a sad commentary on some of the more grotesque and excessive aspects of contemporary life. As he writes, "Then my brother pointed out that / men who seem to be most active / in making school girls pregnant / are the so-called big men. / The men with money / the men in high authority / the law-makers / the headmasters / the big administrators / the big politicians / the big police officers / and their lineage."[62] Indeed, Maillu's writings, some of which border on the pornographic, and which Bernth Lindfors labels "venereal verse," add weight to Achille Mbembe's analysis of the banality of power in contemporary Africa. Maillu's imagery parallels Mbembe's attention to the Rabelaisian excesses of the elites, and the defensive and cynical ribaldry of the powerless.[63] Indeed, it cannot be entirely accidental that some African politicians find it expedient to identify themselves in one way or another with the power and sexual potency of a rooster. When, for example, Joseph Désiré Mobutu became Mobutu Sese Seko Kuku Ngbendu wa za Banga as part of Zaïre's campaign for cultural authenticity in the early 1970s, the quasi-official translation of the name was understood to mean something roughly like "the all conquering warrior who triumphs over all obstacles." But many ordinary citizens preferred a different translation—"the cock who leaves no hen intact." In 1994 President Moi told his supporters that henceforth he should be hailed and praised as Moi jogoo, or Moi the cock, which was also KANU's symbol.[64]

This reading of Maillu's use of imagery concerning food, political power, and physical size also parallels Willy Umezinwa's analysis of certain selected novels of Chinua Achebe, Nuruddin Farah, Ahmadou Kourouma, Ezekiel Mphahlele, Ngugi wa Thiong'o, and Nkem Nwankwo.[65] Umezinwa argues that expressions such as "fat meat" or "mammoth mercedes" when used by politicians in these novels refers to "the notion of immeasurable and limitless qualities and quantities."[66] In the political arena, when "national cakes" are at stake, eating, the profligate and conspicuous consumption of resources, and even gluttony may be among the most visible outward manifestations of political power. Stated another way, there may be an awareness among African novelists and other political thinkers that political power confers the ability to consume and is most easily observed in both the sheer physical size and other excesses of consumption of many politicians and "big men."[67]

As we have seen, images of food and the metaphor of eating pervade political discourse throughout middle Africa. One last set of examples will further demonstrate the point, while leading us to an examination of the second face of power. In a televised press conference in August 1990, the Ivoirian defense minister reflected in these terms on the government's decision to permit multiparty elections:

> We have decided to behave according to the wishes of the Westerners. I think that since we have learned to eat wheat bread and we believe that in saying our morning prayers, we think only of our daily bread, we forget that yams and fufu are also our daily bread. And here too, when it comes to meeting essential needs for man's survival, opinions also differ even if it is interpreted otherwise. I apologize for using such down-to-earth imagery, but I have intentionally chosen my words to show that there are undoubtedly diverse ways to go about interpreting reality.[68]

Indeed there are, as a voice from the lower end of the Ivoirian political hierarchy, a teacher, made clear in a poem published in what was then Côte d'Ivoire's lone daily newspaper, *Fraternité Matin,* ten years before the minister's address: "Our Father who art in heaven / Give us this day / Rice / Yams / Bananas / For / We are dying / All / Of Hunger / And my God! / We haven't even / The right / To say / That we are dying / Of hunger."[69]

As we can see in the two Ivoirian passages with the mention of "daily bread" and the use of the format of the Lord's Prayer, images of food and eating can often be related to broadly religious, spiritual, or otherworldly concerns. In fact, "eating" is a profoundly ambiguous notion. On the one hand, there is a widespread recognition that not only is the father-chief entitled to eat, he has to eat well (in a material sense). On the other hand, however, we must realize that "eating" often refers to the occult arts of witchcraft and sorcery, which are firmly rooted in local cosmologies. For sorcerers, too, often "eat" their victims (in a figurative sense), and the ability to eat, in the first sense, is often confused with eating in the second. In other words, the assumption is often that those who can "eat" materially are able to do this because they can "eat" their victims spiritually.[70] Powerful politicians often deliberately confuse the two meanings, and stories usually circulate about the spiritual and magical prowess of various political leaders. Eating and food are both symbols, and, as is true everywhere, symbols are ambiguous and multivocal.[71]

Spirituality

Although there are three distinguishable manifestations of this second face of power, in point of fact the fine distinctions I draw between formal religion, local cosmologies and belief systems, and sorcery are just that—they are analytic categories that order information. In daily life people may only rarely recognize such distinctions, and I suspect that many ordinary individuals would understand that these categories are quite ambiguous and that there is considerable overlap between them. Shrewd politicians certainly understand this and make use of it.

Formal Religion

Formal religion in middle Africa is part of the spiritual face of power. Or, as Anglican Bishop Henry Okullu, one of Kenya's most politically contentious clergymen, once put it, "Politics and religion are the same thing, for clergymen are concerned with the entire development of human beings."[72] Zaïre's late president, Mobutu Sese Seko, was masterful in his use of religious symbolism and imagery. Until the political liberalization of the 1990s, the state-controlled press presented Mobutu and his regime using the overtones of Christian imagery. For example, one year the annual celebration of Mobutu's seizure of power in 1965 was presented as the "Feast of the Resurrection":

> Thanks to the Mobutist Revolution, Zaïre has again found peace and unity. The Zaïrian has become a new man, reconciled with himself. He has again found his identity and his soul. He has undergone a complete metamorphosis. That is why we say that the holiday of 24 November is that of the Resurrection. In effect, . . . Marshal Mobutu Sese Seko has genuinely resuscitated Zaïrian man who was politically immature, unconscious, dead. . . . For this gigantic revolutionary work, it is a great pleasure for us to thank the Father of the Nation and to send him our filial congratulations on the occasion of the twenty-second anniversary of the Second Republic.[73]

Of interest here is the combination of Christian, familial, and paternal imagery. In the act of political resurrection, of course, God the Father is subtly confused with Mobutu, father of the national family. And because Mobutu is the father who resurrects Zaïre from the chaos of the First Republic and all of its ills, Zaïrians owe him filial thanks and devotion.

In a similar vein, Mobutu's opening speech to the fourth regular session of the Central Committee of the Mouvement Populaire de la Révolution (MPR) in 1982 also emphasized his ability to bring about political resurrection: "As soon as a Zaïrian citizen is deprived of his civic and political rights for five years, as is the case of the 13 former parliamentarians, he must be considered as politically dead. And as long as there is not a measure of grace from the head of state, he remains dead during all this time. And the dead don't speak."[74] The spiritual symbolism is obvious: In political terms Mobutu has the power of life, death, and resurrection. In addition, and to anticipate Chapter 5's attention to the father-chief's right to pardon, such imagery is almost sure to confuse an ordinary, secular judicial power (the extension of executive clemency) with the world of the supernatural in the minds of many listeners. Mobutu's political adversaries were certainly aware of this, for at the end of August 1990, the then recently legalized opposition parties met in Kinshasa to condemn, among other things, "the harmful influence of the marabouts and other occult, destructive practices that govern us through the MPR."[75]

Earlier in the Second Zaïrian Republic, the hints of Mobutu's divinity were even less subtle. At the apogee of Mobutu's cultural revolution in 1974, Interior Minister Engulu declared:

> In our religion, we have our own theologians. In all religions, and at all times, there are prophets. Why not today? God has sent a great prophet, our prestigious Guide Mobutu—this prophet is our liberator, our Messiah. Our Church is the MPR. Its chief is Mobutu, we respect him like one respects a Pope. Our gospel is Mobutism. This is why the crucifixes must be replaced by the image of our Messiah. And party militants will want to place at its side his glorious mother, Mama Yemo, who gave birth to such a son.[76]

Kenya also has its share of ambiguous permeabilities between the spiritual and the political. In 1990, and in the context of the debate then raging over the number of political parties the country should have, a controversy arose over the correct form of polite address to use in reference to President Moi. Some of the president's critics, both secular and clerical, objected to the title *Mtukufu,* or exalted one. Since the title has a distinctly religious connotation, secular critics might well have objected to the eventual possibility of running an election against an opposition candidate known at *Mtukufu.* For their part, some members of the clergy might have found this particular title blasphemous when applied to someone other than Jesus Christ. Addressing this matter directly, and speaking in Swahili, President Moi announced: "I said in 1981 that I did not want to be called *Mtukufu* [exalted] because this applies to God. Look for another appellation that can be used instead. These government officials have not given me an answer to this task of rendering 'the term excellency, your excellency' into 'something else.' I am satisfied if they just call me Moi. . . . If you say President Moi, that is enough."[77] Kenyans, of course, were not deceived by his false modesty, and the term has remained in use for both KANU and official government functions.[78]

And while this general topic receives greater attention in the next chapter, for the moment suffice it to say that neither politicians nor clergymen are inclined to deny God an important role in political life. At a Harambee meeting in 1990, Elijah Mwangale, then a minister in the KANU government, declared that President Moi's accession to the presidency in 1978 was not an accident, but rather the reflection of God's wish that he lead Kenyans. And, from the more explicitly clerical side of the polity, in that same year, the Anglican Archbishop, Manassas Kuria, claimed that all of the Church's statements on national policy had been inspired by the Holy Spirit of God.[79]

Moi, and while he was alive, Mobutu, were not the only heads of state whose sycophantic supporters reveled in comparing them to the Christian deity. Cameroon's Paul Biya tried on the divine mantle in 1985. The occasion was the metamorphosis of Ahmadou Ahidjo's single party, the UNC, into Biya's own creation, the Rassemblement Démocratique du Peuple Camerounais (RDPC), at the Fourth Ordinary Party Congress held in Bamenda at the end of March 1985. Some weeks later an article in the national press drew the explicit comparison by calling attention to the signs that party militants held aloft at a public rally: "Finally a liberating party"; "Henceforth our militancy will be without reserve"; and "President Paul Biya is the Messiah."[80]

Even heads of state who avoid such comparisons, however, will nevertheless go out of their way to mingle with those who possess spiritual power. During Félix Houphouet-Boigny's presidency (1960–1993), the Ivoirian regime took special care to see that the country's Catholic hierarchy and the comparable Islamic dignitaries received glowing press coverage in the state-controlled media. These articles invariably associated the president and other key members of the Ivoirian government with the relevant clergy. For example, when two new Catholic bishops were consecrated in 1982, the news article noted, "Two new dioceses, two new Bishops, a rich harvest for the Catholic Church of the Côte d'Ivoire which has been on holiday since Saturday."[81] Two things are worth noting here. The first is the use of language pertaining to food (harvest) to describe the augmentation in the number of bishops. Presumably this relates to the increased power, presence, and prestige of the Church because of the two new bishops. The second is that this front-page story features a photograph of the twenty-three Ivoirian bishops—all dressed in white, wearing their mitres—surrounding President Houphouet dressed in a black suit. Such events, numerous throughout middle Africa, are only partially about religion. They are also about power. More specifically, both the article and the photograph indicate that there is obviously mutual respect, even admiration, between those who hold one form of power (President Houphouet) and those who hold another (the Catholic bishops). In effect, and to anticipate a later argument, Houphouet's presence at this event reflected far more than his own personal brand of Catholicism—however devout he might have been. It was also a tacit recognition that respect is due to other forms of political power.

Local Cosmologies

While consumption produces corpulence, an important and visible indicator of power in many African societies, there is also a far less visible side of the equation. The cosmologies of countless African societies divide the world into two spheres: the visible and the invisible, or the material and the spiritual, and there is no inviolable boundary line separating them.[82] Mbembe demonstrates this in an essay in which he analyses transcriptions of some of the dreams of Ruben Um Nyobè, the assassinated leader of the Union des Populations du Cameroun. He argues that for Um Nyobè and other southern Cameroonians there was a "paradigm of the night" pertaining to the invisible world that was every bit as important and real as the conventionally studied and quite visible "domain of the day" that the colonial power dominated. Um Nyobè, and presumably others, believed that what happened in one domain could and did influence what took place in the other.[83]

Other evidence concerning both the political reality of the spirit world as well as the importance it holds in the lives of ordinary individuals may be culled from many disparate sources. Simon Bockie, for example, provides a noteworthy internal perspective on how the visible and invisible worlds interact among the Bakongo (Manianga) people of Lower Congo. He details both the qualification for election as a chief, as well as the procedures involved. In a sense, the chief of the *kanda* (a small section of a clan) is the embodiment of ancestral power. It is incumbent upon him to understand and interpret the ancestors' wishes, for he is in a real sense the link between the ancestors and the world of the living. The ancestors, for their part, are instrumental in the process of selecting a chief and are rarely shy about making their wishes and desires known. These are usually transmitted to living family members through dreams and other signs. In addition, to this particular responsibility, the ancestors also select the individual who is to become a healer, or *nganga*.[84] More recently, during the 1998 presidential elections in Gabon, the chairman of the superior council of the Bwiti cult declared his support for one of the major opposition candidates running against President Omar Bongo. The chairman stated: "The elders have said: the spirit of complacency is to be eradicated from the institutions of the republic," and he added that he was speaking on behalf of the order's most senior adherents who, in turn, were in direct contact with the divinities. Bongo was nonetheless reelected, but the spiritual dimension of politics was clearly an issue even if the ancestors and cult elders proved themselves wanting as political prognosticators.[85]

During the Zimbabwean war for independence, anthropologist David Lan studied the role of the Shona spirit mediums in the guerrilla warfare and showed how they came to play an important role in the struggle. The mediums eventually lined up behind the guerrillas because the chiefs had been thoroughly discredited in the eyes of the population and the guerrillas pledged to return alienated land to the peasant farmers. One of Lan's underlying arguments is that the guerrillas received political legitimacy in the eyes of the villagers through the intermediaries of the spirit mediums.[86] While I cannot speak to this point with absolute certainty, to the best of my knowledge political theorists have yet to begin accounting for the political role of ancestral spirits in either democracy or revolutionary warfare.

Calculating politicians understand this spiritual face of power and consciously make use of it. When one of President Mobutu's close collaborators, Nzondomyo A'Dopke Lingo, died in 1984, Sakombi Inongo, the regime's information minister and longtime praise-singer, wrote:

> No, militants do not die. Through their faith in the revolution, through their patriotic engagement, through their fidelity to the Chief of the Party-State and to the people . . . [they] are always, although dead, living among us. Their fate is in-

divisibly sealed with the revolution in the triple cadre of a political-spiritual marriage, a social alliance and a community of interests.

Militants do not die. They are immortal for the example of their life will forever guide the steps of future generations and the memory of their exploits is im-
perishable within us. . . .

Bantu cosmogony discerns, moreover, three entities in society: the dead, the
living, and God. These three entities are indissoluble and it is to the dead which
falls the task of watching over society and, in case of need, of interceding on its
behalf with the Creator.

The immortality of man is thus inscribed in our ancestral conception of the
world and of human destiny. . . .

The certainty of living—like Nzondomyo—immortally at the interior of the
revolution . . . to shine there indefinitely with a thousand fires like the stars . . .
to thus light the religion of some and to guide the conscience of others, this certainty therefore can only comfort the militants of the MPR in the justice of the options of the Party-State and in their determination to confront the forces of evil. . . .

The militant does not die. He can lose a battle but never the war for his faith
is an impassable rampart. An impregnable fortress.[87]

The juxtaposition of appeals to both Christian theology—eternal life through politically militant loyalty to Mobutu—and to beliefs in Bantu cosmology—ancestral
militants of the state-party watching over us and interceding for us—is striking.
The spiritual world is, therefore, also a world of power and politics and, as Chapter 3 demonstrates, the West's usual binary opposition between church and state
holds little water in middle Africa.

Sporting events are often sites where the spirits and ancestors play an important role. One such case occurred in Zaïre in 1987, when the minister of sports
found it necessary to intervene with Batéké chiefs on behalf of the national football team, the Leopards. The problem arose because during the run up to the 1974
World Cup, corrupt officials of the party-state had used the excuse of backing the
Leopards to levy a national tax ostensibly to support and equip the team. This surprised the population because even though copper prices had plummeted in April
1974, the regime was still engaging in grandiose expenditures, and it seemed to
most Zaïrians as though the state had money. Although this supplementary collection went well at first, eventually things got out of hand, and the agents in charge
of assessing the tax became known as the "invaders." Cutting a wide swath through
the villages, they took whatever was not nailed down. People complained, and were
ignored. Village elders placed curses on the Leopards, who were subsequently hu-
miliated and lost all of their matches without scoring a single goal. Remembering
all this with great bitterness, some Batéké village elders placed another curse on
the Leopards so as to hurt their chances in a current match against Angola. Their
perfectly logical reasoning was that if the Leopards were unsuccessful, the "invaders"
would not descend on their villages as they had in the past. In consequence, the
minister decided to do something about the rumors that were circulating, so he
invited some Batéké chiefs to his residence so that they might conduct a ceremony
to exorcise these evil influences from the Leopards. The chiefs conducted their cer-

emony, blessed the team, and predicted a three-goals-to-none victory—which did happen. The ancestors, it would appear, can have an effect not only on the actual outcome of the match, but also on the adherence of the population to certain symbols of national unity.[88]

Sorcery

The spiritual face of power in middle Africa also has a dark side—sorcery. Although I address sorcery at greater length in Chapter 4, this dimension of power warrants some preliminary attention now. The phenomenon is captured nicely in some of the writings of Zamenga Batukezanga. Although Zamenga has denied that he is a "popular" author, he readily admits to being the Congolese writer who is the most widely read. What counts most for him is the "message that I address to the world, that of an African, a Zaïrian who lives with the mass and who tries to loyally transpose its aspirations, its joys, its pains, etc."[89]

Set in Bas-Zaïre, his novel *Bandoki (les sorciers)* relates the story of a series of terrible deaths that befall a village and tells of how the villagers seek to end the deaths and understand why this situation has occurred. When a villager discovers evil-thinking *bandoki* (sorcerers) among them, the cry goes up: "Imbeciles, / Idiots, / It isn't true / That you sleep. / You are only horrible ndoki / That you hide in / Owls / Partridges / Monkeys / Eagles / Jackals / Bats / To capture / Everyone's children and / Eat them or sell them in the market. / Stop, / Stop / Coming to my brother's. / During the day, / Yes / But not at night!"[90]

It is worth remarking that the power of sorcery is often expressed using the same metaphors of food, eating, and consumption—but this time they are applied to the domain of the night and the world of the spirits. Certainly, anthropologists have confirmed in a wide range of settings and contexts that many people believe that sorcerers figuratively "eat" their victims. It seems most unlikely that the appearance of this imagery in relation to both the material and spiritual domains of life is purely coincidental, and I think it is safe to say that sorcery is another manifestation of power.[91]

Although anthropologists working at the village level have long provided us with studies of sorcery in various locales, belief in sorcery is by no means restricted to the villages and rural populations. During the summer of 1980, for example, a front-page story appeared in the Kinshasa daily, *Elima,* relating the findings of an Argentine astrologer. Basing his work on an Aztec horoscope, he predicted that Ronald Reagan would win the U.S. presidential elections later that year.[92] This forecast was taken seriously in Zaïre, and its placement on page one of the major newspaper was certainly no accident. Had the editors failed to appreciate its importance to their readership, it either would not have made the front page or would have been consigned to the comics (which is usually the case in the United States, for example). Furthermore, it is perhaps also significant that with a simple phone call or visit to the U.S. Cultural Center, where newspaper accounts of current U.S. polling data were easily available, the editors could have based their story on a different source of data. Consider as well the frequent use of magical charms and potions by success-seeking characters in *La vie est belle* (Life is beautiful), the 1987 film of Zairian musician, Papa Wemba, that is set largely in Kinshasa.

In another of his urban novels, *Mille kilomètres à pied* (A thousand kilometers on foot), Zamenga tells the story of Ikel and his family. The protagonist moves from being a student in Europe and then a bureaucrat, to taxi driver, to a collector and seller of glass fragments, thus exemplifying the volatility of Zaïre's social class hierarchy. One of the other taxi drivers Ikel meets is an old hand at the trade who assures him that it is practically impossible to succeed in the business without making use of occult and supernatural forces. This older driver assures Ikel that on more than one occasion he has been spared the fate of crashing his vehicle or hitting pedestrians while driving at great speed only because of his magical charms (*fétiches*).[93]

Nor are these beliefs in the domain of the invisible restricted to those without much formal education. In *Chérie Basso,* a book-length letter to his wife which tells her of his journeys abroad, Zamenga relates his trip to attend a scientific conference at the University of Manitoba. Although visiting between terms, he is astonished to find that professors are still at work in the labs and libraries, and he contrasts this to Zaïre, where "a good number of ours spend the length of the day running behind the politicians, businessmen and sorcerers [*féticheurs*] in order to actively solicit nomination to a political post."[94]

Indeed, Zamenga sees the world of politics as an arena in which occult forces operate with varying degrees of success. *Mon mari en grève* (My husband on strike) tells the story of a bourgeois Brazzaville couple, Laurent and Alice, who are among Congo-Brazzaville's upwardly mobile "beautiful people." This novel follows the couple through their difficulties in dealing with the husband's extended family, their failure to win money on a television quiz show, and their experience with a false prophet. Along the way, Laurent tries to rise within the political party, making full use of sorcerers to purify him and make him attractive to the political kingmakers within the party, but he is unsuccessful in this.[95]

This interaction of politics, eating, and sorcery is also a theme which appears occasionally in Maillu's work. In *the kommon man* Maillu tells of an ex-minister: "Oh, I pity the ex-Honourable Choyo / These days, I hear, he's so thin / and he's always locked up in his house. / One of his wives has left him / and I hear he's facing serious cases / over some Harambee money / which he ate. People says that he's looking / for a powerful wizard / to eliminate his opponent. / His opponent is a young dynamic politician / dedicated to serve his people."[96] There is, in addition, Maillu's book-length poem, *After 4:30*, whose imagery also indicates a relationship between eating, sorcery, and the dark powers of the night. The poem is narrated by a single mother, bitter about how men have treated her, who has given birth to a son and been left by the boy's father. Displaying a gender consciousness that is years ahead of its time, she notes all of the inequalities and double standards that women endure, and weeps: "Child, it's not my wish to be / what I am; / I didn't tell your father / any bitter word; / I never abused him / only that I was too ignorant /

of what truth is to a criminal. / He left me and followed another woman / like a hungry dog; / now he barks in the house of someone else / away from his children, where / he eats his fill. / I hear that / that woman made your father nice food / cooked in the same pot / with her own knickers!"[97]

To reiterate, "eating"—in the understood and accepted political sense in which I have been using the term—is charged with ambiguity. More than just a physical activity, at the same time it often connotes the use of sorcery and an attempt to bring the occult powers of the invisible world to bear on political contests and other struggles in the material world. In the mid-1990s an unsuccessful Kenyan election candidate protested his loss before the courts on the grounds that the successful opposition MP had won the seat because of a powerful oathing ceremony called *Khulia Shilulu,* or eating the bitter thing. According to the sorcerer's testimony, the MP's own blood was mixed with herbs and the meat of a ram. After having eaten a portion of this potent concoction, the candidate solemnly swore that he would always oppose President Moi. The meat was then passed around to supporters who, on tasting the meat, swore to vote for the eventual MP or accept death if they did not.[98]

Other examples of sorcery abound throughout middle Africa. In Tanzania during the mid-1980s there was a *mumiani* scare that terrorized parents and children for a while. This was a fear of criminals who kidnap people, drink their blood, and then abandon them to die. In Senegal national passions were aroused in 1983 when one of the premier first-division football teams lost to a Ghanaian club, in Ghana, after psychological harassment at the airport where their "amulets" were confiscated. And, most recently, in 1997 a fear spread throughout portions of West Africa that certain individuals had the power to drain one's virility with a touch, or even a simple handshake. Sorcery, the dark side of power, is an important part of the political terrain in middle Africa.[99]

Indivisibility

The third face of power in middle Africa is its unity and indivisibility. Contrary to the historically recent Western experience, power in middle Africa cannot easily be divided or shared, a usually implicit understanding and assumption that is nicely captured in the Zaïrian/Congolese cultural axiom, "*Le pouvoir se mange entier* [Power is eaten whole]," which is dispersed throughout a wide range of current Zaïrian/Congolese discourse.[100] For more than three decades Zaïre's Mobutu articulated the indivisibility of power in both word and deed. Addressing a distinguished gathering of Belgians in Brussels in 1980, Mobutu argued that power in Africa was an individual notion of authority and that whoever holds power "intends to exercise it in its plenitude." Continuing the analysis, he maintained that "in all circumstances there must be a chief, guarantor of the good functioning of all institutions and capable of making himself heard and of reestablishing [a] threatened order."[101] And, in a speech some years later dealing with the party: "On many occasions, I have already said this to you, I repeat it today, publicly, without detours and with force: Zaïre is a unitary State, and it shall remain unitary. Our national party is the Mouvement Populaire de la Révolution and it is the only one. As long as I shall live, it will always be thus. It is clear, and that shall not be discussed."[102] Mobutu's centralizing and unitary political will was incarnated in the MPR, which was, in the words of the catechism of the party's central committee, "the unique source of power and legitimacy in Zaïre."[103]

In this regard, as in so many others, Zaïre might well have been an extreme case. It was not, however, a deviant one. In general, and precisely because Zaïre's exaggerations permit stark clarity, one can easily recognize in what Basil Davidson has termed the "Mobutist paradigm" many of the broad features of political thought and practice in middle Africa.[104] One may discern in the daily discourse in most middle African countries two general categories of phenomena that speak to the unity and indivisibility of power. The first concerns the inability, or unwillingness, of many heads of state and other politicians to share either power itself or, perhaps even more tellingly, the symbols and rituals of power. The second, a more subtle manifestation, emerges from an examination of some of the symbolic interactions between the different institutional bases of power in middle Africa, and especially some of the interactions between civil and spiritual power. These interactions ultimately indicate that seemingly different manifestations of power in this part of the world are cut from the same cloth. Those who can command formal religious power, as well those who are masters of the forces of the night, are "players" on a continuous field of power that they share with politicians, bureaucrats, and others whom political scientists conventionally view as power holders.

Sharing the Symbols?

Several examples drawn from Kenyan politics speak directly to the unwillingness of politicians to share even the symbolic aspects of their power. In 1981 President Moi sternly warned the late Oginga Odinga, then a former vice-president and a potential rival, "I am the only 'father,' the only head of government of this country."[105] Some years later, Odinga claimed that in that same year (1981) he had agreed to work with President Moi, Jomo Kenyatta's successor, because, according to Odinga's version of the story, "the president had begged Odinga like a son going down to his knees before a father. According to Odinga, President Moi had told Odinga: 'Come *Baba* [father]; join me and let us work together for this country.'" Moi, however, categorically denied the assertion that he had referred to Odinga in this way, as *Baba,* and maintained that the only man he had ever called *Baba* was Kenyatta—the founding father of the Kenyan nation to whom all owed gratitude for the country's stability and prosperity. In addition, in 1994 one of President Moi's sycophantic courtiers claimed that he had never referred to the late Odinga as *mzee* (elderly wise man) because he reserved that term exclusively for the president. Similarly, in 1995 another opposition MP, George Anyona, asked to know why in Parliament others could not address him as the "president" of his party. The attorney general explained to him that, by law, the title of president is reserved exclusively for the head of state.[106]

At stake here is control over several symbolic dimensions of politics, with Odinga and other members of the opposition laying claim to certain key symbolic titles. Who is to be the political father, Moi or Odinga? Who is *mzee,* a respected and learned elder, Moi or Odinga? Who is Mr. President, Moi or Anyona? Moi and his supporters vigorously rejected all such claims because they implicitly understood that power is divided only with difficulty, even on the symbolic level. Odinga and the political opposition, of course, understood the importance of these symbols— especially the metaphor of political fatherhood—and tried to seize this symbolic high ground. Political opposition and conflict were thus partially channeled into a struggle for control of politically resonant cultural symbols that Moi was most unwilling to share.

It is also worth noting a minor political flap in early 1990. When one of Moi's ministers objected publicly to seeing a portrait of Jomo Kenyatta placed along side that of Moi because the latter was, after all, the head of state, an outcry ensued. Moi later resolved the issue by stating that it was fine to hang Kenyatta's portrait at home, but not in public places.[107] Although Kenya was still a one-party state at the time the affair of the presidential photograph arose, precisely the same issue occupied Nigerians for a while under the multiparty regime of Shehu Shagari in the early 1980s. Rumors had circulated that some states were refusing to display portraits of President Shagari in their public offices. Upon hearing this, one federal senator intoned that it was an act of disrespect to the president. When, several days later, the Bendel State House of Assembly threw out a motion asking that the president's portrait be displayed in all offices of the state government, a *Daily Times* editorialist argued, "To refuse to display the portrait of the President, is, we assume, to refuse to acknowledge his existence. But it just so happens that the President does exist and he has existed since September 26, 1979; and some 80 million people in this country are aware of that." One columnist went even further, likening the act of refusing to display the presidential portrait to Ojukwu's act of rebellion in leading the Biafran secession: "Some states in Nigeria by their refusal to put up President Shagari's photographs are behaving in a way not too different from that of Ojukwu because the failure to observe that symbolic act is a statement such that President Shagari's position as President of the country is not recognised in those areas. . . ."[108] I suspect that what lay behind these comments over the president's portrait—in Nigeria as in Kenya—was an unstated recognition and understanding that power is eaten whole and cannot be divided easily.

Political authorities express the same point in slightly different ways elsewhere in middle Africa. While serving under the late Houphouet-Boigny, the "Old Man's" eventual successor, Henri Konan Bédié, was elected president of the national assembly. On taking office, he addressed his legislative colleagues in these terms: "Permit me here, dear colleagues, to address my very sincere and very deferential thanks to the President of the Republic, to the uncontested Father of the Nation, His Excellency Félix Houphouet-Boigny, to whom we owe so much. In effect, President Félix Houphouet-Boigny remains the inestimable source and the essential and unique inspiration [*inspirateur*] of all political action of our country."[109] Or, in the words of a columnist who could usually be counted on to dispense the approved political line, "We have become a nation. And this [nation] has only one father, only one: Houphouet-Boigny."[110]

Throughout middle Africa the imagery of the unity and indivisibility of power is closely and complexly related to questions of national unity. In Cameroon, where, according to Bayart, there has been a particularly persistent ethic of unity, this relationship emerged clearly after Ahidjo's initial resignation from office and his subsequent efforts to reclaim his power from Biya.[111] When Ahidjo stepped down from the presidency in November 1982, he at first retained his position as head of the sole political party, the UNC. But the question existed, at least in the minds of some—and perhaps eventually in Ahidjo's mind as well—as to just how complete his withdrawal from power was to be. With Biya running the state and Ahidjo in charge of the party, the situation was politically unstable. Egos and protocol became involved; conflict resulted. A major cabinet reshuffle in June 1983 saw the departure of several of Ahidjo's lieutenants, and the former president reacted angrily—not only because they were removed, but because Biya had not even consulted him. Ahidjo left the country in July, and in August Biya announced the existence of a plot against the security of the state implicating Ahidjo and two of his military aides. Several days later, from France, Ahidjo resigned as national president of the UNC.

Trying to consolidate his hold on power, Biya moved quickly to take over the reins of the party as well as those of the state. One authoritative editorialist, Henri Bandolo, put it this way:

> Paul Biya at the head of the party, as at the head of the State, thus will be fulfilled the wish of Cameroonians to see the man who has their total support enjoy the plenitude of powers. . . .
>
> It must be that, from an authority suffering from no ambiguity, and henceforth he has all our confidence and our total support, Paul Biya assures the Nation of the certainties that he carries for better tomorrows. . . .
>
> And because it is President Biya who symbolizes the unity of the Cameroonian Nation, it must be clear once and for all that he is the sole and unique symbol of it, dazzling and radiant, any cloud thrust aside and dissipated. National unity cannot be cut into small slices certain of which may be confiscated by individuals. The authority of he who is the guarantor of this unity would no less be able to be cut into small slices [*ne saurait non plus être coupé en rondelles*].[112]

In early September 1983 the UNC Central Committee elected Biya as national president of the party, thus ending an unhappy period of formal executive bicephalism. The political conflict between the two men endured, however. The conspirators, including Ahidjo, were charged with subversion, found guilty, and sentenced to death. Although Biya commuted the sentence to life imprisonment, an abortive military coup in April 1984 failed in its aim of removing Biya from power.[113]

Similar discussions of national unity, of nation-building, of creating a sense of national identity are not restricted to Cameroon, for these have all been common themes in daily political discourse throughout middle Africa. Nyerere, for example, could usually be counted on to stress that Tanzanians were one people and that neither the CCM nor the government would tolerate "tribalism" of any sort. In his words, "Tanzania is one and it is for all Tanzanians. Our religion is CCM and the Party will not tolerate tribalism."[114] Nation-building, creating a sense of national identity, maintaining national unity, containing politicized ethnicity all went together and were woven into the same political and discursive fabric. Lost from sight, however, is the fact that all these usually quite laudable goals were based on an implicit understanding of the indivisibility of power.

Although in Cameroon there was briefly a duality in the exercise of power, the arrangement was unstable and did not last long. While personal ambition, thirst for power, psychological insecurity, and all such explanations cannot be dismissed, they can only take us so far without an appreciation of the cultural connotations of power. Put simply, one of the reasons the bifurcation of power did not work is because power, as we have seen, is not easily divided in this part of the world. But even when power was divided, tacit cultural understandings and assumptions concerning the unity of power made admitting and openly recognizing the fact of executive duality awkward and uncomfortable. For example, in early 1983, shortly after Ahidjo had resigned the presidency, he undertook a national tour to reinvigorate the local party organs. In an interview after his return to Yaoundé, he noted:

> I remain, naturally, national president of the UNC in conformity to the wishes of the militants. There is not, however, any dualism or bicephalism in the exercise of power. The party and the government have, each one, a well defined and distinct domain of responsibility. The party, I have said, defines the orientations of national politics. The government applies these taking into account our possibilities and the fittings [aménagements] which concrete realities and circumstances call for. If each one plays his role in the framework of the collaboration implied by our regime of governing democracy, there would not be any ambiguity.
>
> To answer your question I shall say that M. Biya is entirely the chief of state and that there would not be any duality, but a complementarity, between his action and mine and there exists no dissension between us.[115]

Some months later, of course, two-headed power generated confusion and uncertainty, and provided fertile ground for Ahidjo's political maneuvers. Once the two positions, chief of state and head of the party, were again held by one person, President Biya did not hesitate in recognizing the division of power as a serious problem.[116]

A comparable duality of power in Tanzania did not provoke a succession crisis, and, for a time after Ali Hassan Mwinyi became president in 1985, Nyerere remained chairman of the CCM. But in this case, it should be noted, the decision to separate the two hats of party chairman and president of the republic was justified, at least in part, on the grounds that the resulting bifurcation of power would only be temporary. When, in 1987, Nyerere accepted the nomination for another term as CCM chairman, he stated that President Mwinyi wanted him to do the party work and that it was not yet the right time to recombine the two posts. When he finally did retire completely in 1990, Nyerere referred to the anxiety that accompanied his resignation of the state presidency, noting "we thought it was logical to separate them [the two offices, party and state] *for a time* to lessen the anxiety of the transition."[117] The unstated assumption, of course, was that this separation was strictly temporary. No explanation was needed as to why it was necessary to justify the impermanent nature of the bifurcation because all understood, implicitly, that except under special circumstances divided power could be dangerous because power is eaten whole.

Power is not easily relinquished. As we see in Chapter 6, one of the few to have done it successfully was the first president of Senegal, Léopold Sédar Senghor. After Senghor left the presidency in January 1981, one commentator in the local press moved to reassure his readers that the new president and Senghor's designated successor and longtime *dauphin*, Abdou Diouf, really was in control. His analysis of these events categorically rejected even the remotest possibility that Senghor had, in effect, decided to retire in name only and that he was really going to remain in power by pulling strings and influencing the course of political events from the background. His conclusion reaffirmed the major point: "Here, therefore, is Abdou Diouf the only master on board the great ship P. S. [Parti Socialiste]."[118]

Power is indivisible, and political leaders jealously guard as their exclusive prerogative even the symbolic nomenclature associated with power. In other words, by definition, there can only be one father of the large national family, and the presently serving political "father," the president of the republic in most cases, is unlikely to be willing to share his paternal rights and responsibilities with any of his political "children." Families, so the refrain goes, can have only one father. Or, put in terms of the incessant Lingala chant heard on radio and television in Zaïre during the last fifteen years of the Mobutu regime: "*Tata ko? Moko. Mama ko? Moko. Mboka ko? Moko. Mokonzi ko? Moko* [One father, one mother, one country, one chief]."

Finally, let us conclude this section with the following tale. In May 1992 the respected Nigerian-controlled newsmagazine, *West Africa,* reported that the leader of the Independent National Patriotic Front of Liberia, Prince Yormie Johnson, had exhumed the body of Liberia's former president, Samuel Doe. Although Johnson had killed Doe in September 1990, he now claimed that Doe's remains had to be dug up "to prevent his spirit from dividing the country." Moreover, Johnson stated that unless Doe's body were exhumed and cremated, and its ashes sent to Mecca, peace would be slow in coming to Liberia. By way of an explanation for these actions, the report noted that Johnson was supposed to have told witnesses that he had "had a vision of a ring in Doe's stomach whose power continued to divide Liberians."[119] If we consider these three faces of power, the reasons behind the exhumation of Samuel Doe become clearer. Johnson's vision told him that Doe, his old adversary, had literally "eaten" a ring and that this ring, located in his stomach, had the power to divide Liberians. To reassert the unity and indivisibility of power in a divided land, Johnson needed to exhume Doe, destroy his remains, and literally export them so that Doe's shade would no longer be present. Presumably, once Johnson had the ring and Doe's spirit was gone, power would again be unified and indivisible. Johnson could not accept only a portion of power; he had to have it all. Since others in Liberia have also believed that power is eaten whole, the consequences for the people of that troubled land have been catastrophic. Put starkly, if Johnson could not share power—even in a dream—with the spiritual presence of a man whom he had killed, how then could he share it with those who are still living?

Players on a Field

The daily press in middle Africa devotes much attention to matters of religion. Although the degree and depth of coverage vary from country to country, those who control the various media seem to take matters of formal religion seriously. National, state-controlled daily newspapers, as well as independently owned media, often devote many column inches reporting on the minutia of religious life in ways that occasionally surprise those reared in a different tradition. For example, when the city of Douala received two new Catholic bishops in 1987, the guest list read like a *Who's Who* of the Cameroonian elite. The ceremony occurred

> in the presence of M. Joseph-Charles Doumba, the minister in charge of missions attached to the Presidency of the Republic and personal representative of the Chief of State. Other personalities present at the ceremony: Ministers Léonard-Claude Mpouma of Posts and Telegraph, George Ngango of National Education, Adolphe Moudiki of Labor and Social Providence, the first vice president of the National Assembly, M. Théodore Mayi Matip, the secretary of State at Information and Culture, M. Raphaël Onambélé Ela, the governor of Littoral Province, M. Luc Loé, the chancellor of the University, M. Laurent Esso and many other officials [*responsables*] of the administrative and political apparatus. All the bishops of Cameroon and the archbishop of Libreville were equally in attendance at the episcopal consecration.[120]

Similarly, even though it pertained to a much smaller religious grouping, the *Cameroon Tribune* nevertheless also noted the consecration of a Presbyterian pastor. The story covering the event noted that "M. Anyong Davis, 34 years old, married, was consecrated a Pastor of the Presbyterian Church of Cameroon on 2 December 1984 in the village of Demk (Bafia). The chapel of this locality showed itself to be too small to contain the thousands of guests, priests, relatives, and friends who were there . . . [for the occasion]. The ceremony was also enhanced by the presence of administrative authorities, [and] some political, municipal, and law enforcement officials of the arondissement of Bafia."[121]

In Senegal, where at least 90 percent of the population is Muslim, Islamic holidays and events receive comparable attention. For example, in the words of one dispatch:

> The Muslim community celebrated yesterday in communion and contemplation Aid-El Adha, or Tabaski, which commemorates the perpetuation of the

sacrifice of Abraham. The President of the Republic attended the ritual prayer of the grand mosque of Dakar presided by the Imam Ratib, El Hadj Mawdo Sylla.

It was in a totally pious atmosphere with the diffusion of verses of the Koran that the Head of State made his entrance into the grand mosque in the company of the Prime Minister. The Presidents of the National Assembly, the Economic and Social Council, and several members of the government, of Parliament, [and] the diplomatic representatives of Muslim countries had already taken their place in the building. Several minutes later it was the Imam's turn to make his entrance. . . .[122]

Similar ceremonies are replicated throughout the country on the relevant holy occasions. They usually feature the visit of a high-ranking delegation from the state to the imam or, in the case of the Sufi brotherhoods, the Khalife; an exchange of warm, familial greetings; several speeches with the Muslim dignitaries praising the state officials and vice versa; pledges of mutual loyalty and support; and, of course, prayers for the head of state and other political leaders.[123] To be sure, although we see in Chapter 3 that authorities of the Senegalese state devote special care and attention to the larger Sufi brotherhoods such as the Mourides and the Tidjianes, something else is occurring here.

In Côte d'Ivoire, press coverage of the Roman Catholic Church is particularly extensive. Ordinations of priests are presented in great detail, and the articles are often accompanied by photographs. An account of one such event described matters this way:

> The Lord has just given a new priest to the Catholic Church of Côte d'Ivoire in the person of Aka Kouassi Nkruma Pierre. His ordination was done yesterday in his native village by Monseigneur Bruno Kouamé of Abengourou in the presence of the bishop of Bouaké Monseigneur Vital Yao and an important delegation of monks and sisters.
>
> It was for the Christian community of the diocese of Abengourou a moment of intense emotion on the occasion of this sacerdotal ordination of one of theirs who, despite the thousand temptations of our current society[,] chose to place himself in the service of God, thus becoming the 10th priest of this diocese.
>
> Let us indicate that the ceremony was marked by the presence of the Prefect of Abengourou, M. Philippe Coffi Béhibro, [and] the Ministers Amoakon Thiémélé and Emile Brou, sons of the region. . . .[124]

A previous article had made it clear that Father Nkruma was not only the tenth Ivoirian from the diocese of Abengourou to become a priest, he was the third from the Canton Feyassé and even the second from his village of Yakassé. So the event, while certainly noteworthy in the life of a man and his family, could scarcely have been considered a "first." Why, then, was this event—like so many others of its kind—given extensive coverage in a section of the newspaper usually reserved for political news? Why, then, was the local political authority in attendance as an honored guest? Why, then, did national ministers from the locality return for the event?

Why did one of them even go so far as to mark the day with a special "gesture"—presumably a substantial financial gift—that would enable the newly ordained priest to purchase a car?[125]

Since the similarities in these events transcend both national borders and religious divides, we can ask the same questions posed immediately above of all such events in middle Africa, regardless of location or religious tradition. First, the press coverage. My initial inclination was to dismiss the extensive coverage of ordinations, consecrations, religious festivals, and religious affairs in general as being due to specific contextual characteristics (e.g., Houphouet's devout Catholicism or the political and economic importance of the Sufi brotherhoods in Senegal). But prominent attention was also given to such matters in Cameroon, Zaïre, and Nigeria, with progressively lesser attention being offered in Kenya, Ghana, and especially Tanzania. In other words, when viewed in comparative perspective, contextual specificities seemed unpersuasive as an explanation. Perhaps, then, we could explain the attention devoted to the religious sector by the fact that in most of these societies the state controlled the media. And with but the brief exceptions of Ghana under Limann, Nigeria under Shagari, and perhaps—with some qualification—Senegal, these societies during the 1980s could scarcely be called democratic. So perhaps there was no "political news," or at least none the regime wanted exposed, and the state needed to fill the pages of the national press with something. Or since ministers and other high-ranking dignitaries of the state were almost always present at such events, perhaps the prominent press coverage was simply another way of publicizing the luminaries of the regime.

While some of these explanations are partially valid, there is more to it than that. Neither the extensive press coverage nor the well-documented presence of high-ranking state officials can be understood only as the tools of a political class intent on maintaining its control. And although I agree with Bayart that this pattern could also be a manifestation of what he calls the "reciprocal assimilation of elites," that, too, is only part of the puzzle.[126] Put simply and directly, both the extensive press coverage and the usual ministerial-level presence at events such as the simple ordination of village priests also signify something else. These events should be understood as recognitions being extended from the holders of one form of power to those who can command a different form of power. They are signs of respect, not necessarily for the specific individual or for the specific religion (although I do not exclude that), but for a new "player" on the field of power. Extensive attention to a new priest or bishop, to an imam or a Khalife, thus mark and celebrate the arrival of a new participant in the power game. There is also a sense in which power holders may use these events to associate—or even fuse—their power with another's. These rites of passage and rituals of belief are also about power and who has it.

Unless there was a serious political crisis within one of the major congregations, the Ghanaian press tended not to devote extraordinary attention to things like ordinations and the daily life of the various formal religious establishments. On one such occasion, however, one of very the few that I came across, it is worth noting that the ceremony was described in much the same way as were similar ceremonies elsewhere in middle Africa. The induction of the Reverend Stephens as the sixth president of the Methodist Conference of Ghana was noteworthy because it resolved a political division within the church, and an impressive roster of governmental authorities attended the event. In the words of the front-page article, "The solemn ceremony attracted some dignitaries and Secretaries of State, including Mr Justice D. F. Annan, Mrs Susan Al-Hassan, Members of the PNDC, Dr Ben Abdullah, Secretary for Culture and Tourism and Nii Abeo Kyerekuandah IV, Greater Accra Regional Secretary. The rest are Mr. S. S. Omane, the Inspector General of Police, Mr. George Quaynor-Mettle, Greater Accra Under Regional Secretary, Members of the Diplomatic Corps. . . ."[127] They attended to celebrate the unity of power within the church and to honor and respect a new player on the field of power.

In a sense, even where the press does not always cover assiduously nominally religious activities such as ordinations, it still provides extensive coverage of other "players" who enter the game. Ghana under J. J. Rawlings and, to a certain extent, Nigeria would be examples. In both of these societies, as in Cameroon, the coverage of customary rulers is extensive. This, I would submit, is neither because of an infatuation with the survival of "quaint" customs inherited from the days before the colonialists, nor out of a more contemporary sense of cultural pride, but is instead due to the fact that certain chiefs, emirs, fons, and lamidos were able to retain or, in many cases, recreate some degree of power and legitimacy over time.

There is, therefore, substantial coverage of the country's chiefs, and articles about various enstoolments regularly appear, as do photographs of the newly enstooled chiefs and other customary officeholders. For example, the extended caption to one photograph noted the higher chief seated shaking hands with the newly enstooled chief inclining slightly towards him, which is always a sign of respect. Both are wearing Ashanti attire. The caption reads: "Mr. Kwaku Amofa (right) [standing], Managing Director of Amofa and Sons Limited, in Kumasi, at the week-end, swore the oath of allegiance to Barima Kofi Adu II (seated left), Omanhene of the Kokofu Traditional Area as the Anantahene of the paramountcy in the Ashanti Region under the stool name of Nana Amofa Odaatu I. Picture shows Barima Kofi Adu II (left), Omanhene of the area, congratulating Nana Odaatu I (right), after he had been sworn in as Anantahene of the area."[128] Once again, the reason for this sort of an article is most probably the same as that for the articles detailing the ordinations of clergy in other states: to recognize and honor a different form of power and a new player on the field of power.

In Ghana, as elsewhere, political leaders often like to associate themselves with the symbolic trappings and legitimacy of chiefly authority and power. One article in the *Daily Graphic* showed the paramount Ga chieftain, Ga Mantse, Nii Amugi II, presenting a stool—a symbol of chiefly authority—to President Hilla Limann, who was represented at the ceremony by his vice-president.[129] Similarly, in 1980 on the occasion of his fiftieth birthday, Mobutu traveled to Lisala, where after three days of festivities he was installed as the grand customary chief of the Bangala.[130] And in 1984 the fons of the Northwest Province installed Paul Biya as the Supreme

Fon. This report also noted that President Biya was scarcely an initiate in these customary matters, for the previous year, fifteen Douala chiefs had interceded with their ancestors so that they would view the president as their son, as one of their own.[131] Ordinarily analysts might view such events as attempts to manage politicized ethnicity in culturally plural societies by trying to foster a greater sense of identity between specific ethnic groups and the national state and its president. Depending on the circumstances, close observers of political life could also view such ceremonies as cynical attempts to induce political quiescence by trying to convince various populations that they now share a kinship with the president and that, therefore, "one of their own" is now in power at the center.

There is much merit in these analyses, and I do not dispute them. But such analyses implicitly operate from the top down. That is, they either look at the needs of the national "system" for continued stability and the consequent necessity of containing ethnic conflict, or they tacitly adopt the perspective of the head of state who needs to be able to "manage" conflict or "create" identity to remain in power. Given the preceding analysis, however, it is also possible to argue that the various heads of state who associate themselves in this way with some of the ethnic groups in their respective countries are also seeking to identify themselves and associate with a different form of power. The ambiguity that results from having access to different sources of power (i.e., the state, formal religion, the ancestors, sorcery) can only aid them and provide them with a certain political comfort. In addition, if we assume that most heads of state have the desire, regardless of the source of their motivation, to maintain the unity and indivisibility of power, it is possible to understand that such ceremonies are also a means of making sure that power continues to be eaten whole. Moreover, if we further assume that most people in the society also share the desire to maintain the unity and indivisibility of power, it then becomes possible to view the importance of these ceremonies from the bottom up. Certainly, analysts may not err in ascribing a somewhat cynical motivation to the customary chiefs and fons, who may let themselves be manipulated by the national powers. It is, in fact, likely that they wish to gain something from the transaction: perhaps a monetary payoff, or a subsequent favor, or even to create the sense on the part of the national "father" that he also has "children" in a particular locality. Without dissenting from this line of argument, I would submit that people in the periphery, both fons and farmers, may well share sentiments underscoring the appropriateness of the unity and indivisibility of power. This means that in some cases they might understand that power should be eaten whole and that this cannot happen unless they are able to establish a fictive ethnic bond with the head of state, who would thus become a son of the soil.

As we have seen, players on the field of power appear periodically. They also disappear. This means we should understand that obituaries and death notices are often more than a simple announcement of the passing of a loved one, a national figure, or someone who has touched various lives while alive. They are also indications that another player on the field of power will no longer be part of the game except, perhaps, as an ancestor.[132]

Conclusion

First, let us return to the definition of power. Standard definitions stressing the transformative and Newtonian aspects of power miss three crucial faces of power in a wide range of middle African contexts. These faces, the material, the spiritual, and the unitary, may be discerned in the use of imagery concerning food, eating, and size. Such metaphors, moreover, are related to both the visible and invisible worlds of power. "Big men" eat not only food, as Maillu remarks, but people as well; sorcerers "eat" their victims in the dead of night. Political struggles thus ensue between those powerful enough to eat and those who find themselves located in a lower position in the political food chain. To better account for these dimensions of power in many middle African contexts, I would define this omnipresent yet often ungraspable concept simply as the ability to control and consume both resources and individuals.

Second, there is the question of sources. It is regrettably unusual for political scientists to integrate literary sources into their scholarly analyses, although there is one partial exception—the widespread use of novels in undergraduate courses.[133] Chinua Achebe's *Things Fall Apart, Man of the People, No Longer at Ease,* and *Anthills of the Savanna* have introduced generations of students to many intricacies of politics in Africa. But why is it that what is so useful for undergraduate teaching is not recognized as a valid source of data for research? Why is it that when campuses across the country are debating the inclusion of the Achebes and Soyinkas within the so-called canon, political scientists seem reluctant to probe their works, as well as those of other writers and thinkers, for insights into the nature of politics, society, and culture in Africa? Michel de Certeau's observation that the novel (and I would add other forms of literature, journalism, and popular discourse) has "become the zoo of quotidian practices since the existence of modern science" is certainly apposite here.[134] Such sources can provide us with vibrant, living representations of the world of politics in many settings, and scholars who ignore these endogenous perceptions and perspectives in the construction of their theories do so at their own risk.

Denis-Constant Martin's call to seek out "unidentified political objects" is relevant here. Referring to verbal expressions, he identifies three discourses worthy of attention in this search: the discourse of politicians themselves; the discourse of ordinary citizens about politics; and the discourse of indigenous observers (which is often the closest we can come to capturing the expressions, imagery, and metaphors of the populace).[135] This chapter, and indeed this book, tries to take seriously and, where possible, integrate sources drawn from all three discourses: the first discourse, the words of those in power (their speeches, for example); the second, the quotidian expressions of common citizens (such as letters to the editor); and the third, the writings of perceptive and knowledgeable indigenous observers such as Maillu and Zamenga. The combination of all three discourses will eventually enrich our conceptual appreciation of both the structural and contextual complexities of politics in middle African settings.

Third, and obviously related to the second point, there is the question of perceptions and perspective. We have either misunderstood, or perhaps forgotten, that varying contexts may induce peoples to perceive and construct their political worlds in many ways. In this regard middle Africans are no different than West Europeans or North Americans. Occasionally, however, these differences are important, as Valentin Mudimbé has reminded us. "Until now," he writes, "Western interpreters as well as African analysts have been using categories and conceptual systems which depend on a Western epistemological order."[136] The application to middle African politics of various concepts of power derived from Western experiences is a case in point. None of the definitions emphasizing the transformation of behavior because of the actions of another individual would necessarily lead us to explore, however tentatively and cautiously, the spiritual realm or the forces of the night. To be sure, although anthropologists have done so with some success at the local level, I suspect that this results more from their immersion in fieldwork and their focus on village micropolities rather than from a theoretical armory pointing them in the right direction. Unless we begin to take indigenous understandings of concepts and categories more seriously than we do currently, we shall continue to miss vital and living elements of politics in this part of the world. Just as people in middle Africa have perceptions of power that differ from our own in certain key respects, they also have implicit understandings of the contours of the political realm that do not completely overlap those prevalent elsewhere. It is to this subject, the parameters of the political, that we now turn our attention.

3. Parameters of the Political

Until quite recently many political scientists tended to assume that the search for Kwame Nkrumah's oft-heralded political kingdom ("Seek ye first the political kingdom") was best conducted within the state. Politics was, of course, to be found there, so they were not wrong in this assumption. But this understanding of the contours of the political kingdom narrowly focused the scope of "politics" on those institutions such as political parties, or various portions of the state, that could readily be observed interacting with ethnic groups, social classes, and other political phenomena that had easily identifiable Western counterparts. Nkrumah's famous injunction coupled with intuitive and usually unstated Western understandings of the parameters of the political thus short-circuited the search for politics in other spheres of life. One aim of this chapter is to chart some of the parameters of the political in middle Africa by seeking the political in spheres of life such as religion, as well as sports and business (including labor-management relations), which the majority of political scientists do not usually view as being part of the political realm. For example, empirical political scientists are more than occasionally uncomfortable dealing with any spiritual phenomena in their analyses for these are, by definition, "other"-worldly, "super"-natural, or "para"-normal and thus cannot be observed directly. But as we have already seen, in middle Africa there is no "other" world where the spirits, ancestors, and mystical forces reside. They are in our world, the real world, the natural world, and they form an integral part of it while playing a role in politics and in shaping political perceptions. They also have a great deal to do with power and are directly relevant to the definition of the frontiers of the political kingdom.

The first large section of this chapter treats formal religion and argues that the classic, secular notion of separation of church and state is a poor guide to understanding either politics or religion in this part of the world. Instead, I take up the analytical thread introduced in Chapter 2 and argue that we may also understand and appreciate those who command various forms of spiritual power as "players" on a political field. And while this field certainly includes the state and politics as conventionally defined, its parameters need to be broadened to include a role for the spiritual world. Throughout middle Africa there is an elision of spirituality and state, of politics and religion, and we shall see that these analytic distinctions merge and overlap in so many ways that segregating them becomes all but impossible. In its broadest form, this is obviously a universal phenomenon. There are, for example, traces of similar elisions throughout the Islamic world. Dale Eickelman and James Piscatori remind us that although there is within Islam a widely shared tradition of ideas and practice, there is no single Muslim view on the relationship between religion and politics. There are, instead, a variety of Muslim views, and an understanding of the widely differing local contexts—political, economic, and cultural—thus becomes important.[1] In the United States, although constitutionally a secular society, the presidential candidacies of well-known religious figures such as Jesse Jackson and Pat Robertson need no comment. Moreover, the political skill of certain Popes is legendary. In other words, the variance in local reflections of these elisions is substantial. In the middle African context more specifically, this chapter examines procedural commonalities between church and state; how certain policy doctrines and theology occasionally overlap; and how some individuals operate comfortably as both preacher and politician.

In the second section I shift gears and examine the frontiers between state and sports, and state and business. My argument here is similar: namely, that common Western categories of analysis—in this case the fashionable binary opposition between state and civil society—have little practical meaning in much of middle Africa because the parameters of the political in this area of the globe are rather different. Both sports and business, like religion, are areas that political science tends to see as being outside its proper purview. In middle Africa, however, they are part of the political kingdom and occupy sites on the region's continuous political field.

Once again, let me state as precisely as possible the argument of this chapter. Standard dichotomies and binary oppositions (such as church-state and state–civil society) that help frame our implicit appreciation of the parameters of the political realm tend to exclude significant portions of daily life that are—at least in middle Africa—very political. Nkrumah's political kingdom includes the state, but it also contains territory that, at least for many political scientists, remains largely uncharted. Moreover, one way to increase our understanding of political phenomena is to seek out previously undefined domains of political life. As in previous chapters, much of the evidentiary basis for this argument is gathered from a disparate array of sources, and my procedure is to glean indications of the parameters of the political from an examination of the relevant discourse. The body of evidence is substantial, albeit at times indirect.

The work of other scholars has guided my thinking in some of these matters. Bayart, for example, has argued convincingly that the study of politics and religion in Africa is poorly formulated and suffers from two illusions. The first is that both politics and religion constitute homogeneous domains when, in fact, neither realm is uniform. The second is that despite the facile and often unthinking secular conceptualizations of both "church" and "state" now prevalent in Western social science, these domains are not independent of each other.[2]

Such misconceptions usually lead to fairly predictable analyses of relations between church and state in any particular country. David Throup's essay on conflict between church and state in Kenya is a case in point.[3] Typically for such analyses in Africa, the historical trajectory traces the movement from subservience of church to state under colonial rule, to a period of respectful cooperation between the two entities during the early years of independence, and then on to a period of increasingly open conflict between church and state as the excesses of the single-party regime became more and more obvious. Moreover, in this—as in similar treatments—the often implicit assumption is that confrontation between church and state results because the state, particularly in its single-party guise, is a monolithic organization with a totalizing vision of its role. Its manifest destiny is to occupy all political, ideological, and organizational space, and any organization outside its boundaries thus constitutes a threat. Unsurprisingly, therefore, Throup argues that in the face of the "demands of a hostile secular authority" Kenya's various churches have been led to formulate a single "indigenous theology of resistance."[4] Ultimately the analysis boils down to two monolithic entities, church and state, which interact dialectically. In addition, although his treatment of the subject does make some attempt to differentiate between the various Christian denominations, he analyzes their interactions with the state only at the elite level of the various political and religious hierarchies, not recognizing the possibility that interactions at the local level might be considerably different.[5]

G. P. Benson's essay in the same volume, however, provides a subtler look at the question, and goes well beyond Throup's straightforward analysis.[6] Based on a close reading of the works of both President Daniel arap Moi and Anglican Bishop David Gitari, Benson sees the clash between church and state not so much in the state's expansionist tendencies, but rather in the theological tradition of scriptural hermeneutics. He argues that from their reading of the Bible, the churches were committed to justice, equity, and freedom, feeling the obligation to confront a state established by God when it had gone astray in these matters.[7] According to this interpretation, conflict results because of the uneasy coexistence of two incompatible ideologies: President Moi's *Nyayo* and the churches' Biblical hermeneutics. Taking a step in the right direction, Benson's essay comes close to assuming that church and state exist in a single field of power, arguing correctly that Moi sees church leaders as indistinct from other leaders of Kenyan society. The president thus implicitly absorbs them into the "national leadership, bound by the same requirements of [political] loyalty . . . that apply to other leaders."[8] Unfortunately, Benson's analysis does not go far enough in this direction because, unlike Moi, he does not assume the indivisibility of power in Kenya and Africa.[9]

In addition, Stephen Ellis and Gerrie Ter Haar have recently noted that both political science and economics contain disciplinary assumptions that are simply not prepared to deal with the importance of the invisible spiritual world and its effects on political life. Power, they maintain, has roots in the invisible world.[10] To these useful notions I would add the elaboration that "politics" and "religion" have roots in both the visible and invisible worlds, and that power flows between them without regard for the sanctity of disciplinary categories of analysis. Most middle Africans understand that "politics" and "religion" are parts of the same terrain; that power flows between the visible material world and the invisible spiritual world; and that the political kingdom contains a politically significant spiritual terrain. Moreover, intelligent and gifted politicians know the contours of this terrain and are comfortable traversing it in either its material or spiritual manifestations. They understand that in their culture power is unitary and cannot be divided into separate boxes.

The Elision of Church and State

Although the contemporary discourse concerning religion and politics is complex and often contradictory, it nevertheless contains a persistent strand of thought that assumes a certain commonality of ground and ordinary permeability between politics and religion. One dissection of the flaws of Nigeria's political class during the Buhari regime in the mid-1980s put it this way: "One most unfortunate aspect about Nigerian politicians is that they regard politics as a matter of life and death. Anybody who shared different view from theirs or belong to other opposing camp is seen as an enemy. Any criticism of their action is tagged confrontation. The Nigerian politician would go to any length to see that such person who shared a different view or belong to opposing camp or criticise him must be destroyed [sic]. Our politicians see themselves as tin-gods as soon as they get power forgetting that power belongs to God and no condition in this world is permanent."[11] Here we have the frequently expressed notion that power derives ultimately from God and that, therefore, it would be rather difficult to divorce the spiritual from the political. Similarly, in an address marking the start of the 1981 legal year, the Catholic bishop of Enugu, Dr. Michael Eneja, urged the magistrates to improve their performance during the coming year. The bishop reminded the judges that, in the words of the article, "law functionaries were servants of God the Supreme Law-Maker. . . . The Catholic Bishop observed that citizens who failed to abide by the law of the land extended their disrespect to God. . . ."[12] Even those of an explicitly left-wing persuasion who are intent on citing Lenin and view politics as "the continuation of economic war on a higher plane" nonetheless formally define politics so that it includes a spiritual dimension. "Politics," according to one Ghanaian observer, "in fact, should be seen as the art by which people or class of people using a set of guiding principles try to direct and guarantee their material, social and spiritual interests and exert their influence and dominance over the society."[13]

Chapter 2 examined some of the events surrounding the transition between Ahidjo and Biya in Cameroon. After the violence ended in April 1984, Monseigneur

Jean Zoa, the Catholic Archbishop of Yaoundé, celebrated a High Mass. At this well-attended service, and in the presence of several cabinet ministers and other political personalities, Zoa delivered a homily in which he compared the events of the protracted political transition to a superhuman battle between life and death. He presented the events that had occurred as "diabolical," designed to divert Cameroonians from "the essential." And, according to the archbishop, this "essential" was the societal project that President Biya had elaborated. He further noted that Biya's project was one that made Christians feel at ease because it was inscribed in the domain of the Holy Spirit and it seemed to draw its inspiration from the human preoccupations of Vatican II. The prelate also underlined the need for an individual and collective renewal which, he thought, should transcend ethnicity and lead to effective action. More precisely, he advanced the notion that there should be "intermediate bodies" such as apostolic movements, unions, professional associations, and a political party that would be "veritable schools of discipline and responsibility." To those who would accuse the Cameroonian church of meddling in politics, the archbishop retorted that "the Christian faith is not a flight from terrestrial realities, but on the contrary, an invitation to place ourselves decisively in the service of our neighbor and of the community. We are the sons of Cameroon," he added, "and we must in the face of history, regenerate a new Cameroon."[14]

Zoa's remarks, and indeed the service itself, point toward several things worth noting. First, and on the most basic level, the archbishop refers to the actions of those plotting against the government as "diabolical." This should be understood literally, not figuratively, as a reference to the devil and his works.[15] That the devil would intervene in the political arena and have a role in such tumultuous political events only reinforces the permeability of the boundary between church and state, and between public and private realms. Second, Zoa sees a near-complete association between Paul Biya's political project, on the one hand, and the Holy Spirit and the humanistic orientations of Vatican II, on the other. The third point worth retaining is that Zoa finds an answer to certain problems in institutional structures, "intermediate bodies," which closely resemble civil society, although he also includes the political party in his plan. In the archbishop's thinking, therefore, an entirely clear-cut distinction between political, civil, and religious spheres of action might not exist. Finally, the absence of an unambiguous boundary between the political and the religious is also apparent in Zoa's explicit rejection of the notion that the church is meddling in politics, and that the very Christian faith he professes, in a sense, invites involvement in worldly affairs.

Throughout his career, the now retired bishop of the Church of the Province of Kenya (Anglican), Henry Okullu, has been one of that country's most outspoken, and politically contentious clergymen. Echoes of Monseigneur Zoa's rejection of "meddling" in politics are also present in Okullu's thought, and some of his texts are instructive in this regard. Writing in 1974, Okullu noted that the church and its councils in East Africa then had "a very comfortable relationship with the State and tend in some areas at least to be a mere government department with the responsibility of offering prayers for the leaders."[16] And although Okullu's arguments at times do seem to assume that church and state are separate and discrete spheres, he maintains simultaneously that there may not be a clear-cut distinction between that which is Caesar's and that which is God's. The following passage is illustrative: "The Church claims no temporal power over men but appeals to their hearts and consciences. It is given the right to correct, admonish, censure. *Therefore it is no interference in politics* for the Church to warn the State that unrighteousness on public matters will bring calamity to the people."[17] Politics, in other words, is not a separate portion of the terrain demarcated by a gate through which religious thinkers and spiritual leaders can, and should, pass freely. Because politics would seem to be part of the terrain on which religious thinkers and spiritual leaders already exist, there is no sense of violating a territorial frontier. Throughout this work Okullu ranges over a host of "political" topics without the slightest self-consciousness or sense of trespass. He speaks comfortably of the church's role in curbing corruption, takes a position against the notion that the single-party conforms to African traditions, and argues that "a system which gives the elector the impression that he can change his leader when in fact he has not the remotest chance to do so is bound to breed frustration that sooner or later must express itself in undesirable methods of opposition."[18]

Twenty years later, and after his retirement from the pulpit, Bishop Okullu replied to a question on whether he aspired to a position of national leadership. "I want to refrain from declaring anything in that kind of direction," he answered. "I will respond to the people's call. The people's voice is God's voice. I am still listening. But I am not afraid to respond to people's desire."[19] In this slightly mixed imagery we find an easy elision of a popular political draft and a religious calling. Two years later, in 1996, *Weekly Review*—in an article that was at times snidely critical of the bishop's penchant for politics—reported that Okullu was not one to hide behind his pulpit and that, in fact, he was quite proud of his political record. He was cited as saying, "I have participated in politics since my heyday as the provost of Nairobi's All Saints' Cathedral and as Bishop of the Maseno South Diocese I participated in calling for the re-introduction of multipartyism. . . . I am a politician and will die a politician."[20] For Okullu and Zoa, politics and religion coexist on a single plane where the analytical frontiers between them have become increasingly indistinct.

The elision of church and state is also apparent when viewed from the perspective of practicing politicians. In 1984, during his annual speech marking the formal opening of the judicial year, Senegal's President Abdou Diouf, one of the region's more articulate political leaders, enunciated his views on the meaning of a secular state. Speaking on the general theme of freedom of opinion and expression, Diouf divided his remarks along two axes: respect for others and safeguarding democracy. Under the first rubric Diouf conveyed his understanding of secularity:

> Secularity can also be a manifestation of the respect for others. It is a question, of course, of a well understood and well practiced secularity.
> This secularity would not know how to be anti-religious: that would no longer be, moreover, a true secularity; that would be, alas, as in certain countries, to institute atheism as the state religion.

I will go further in saying that a secular state cannot be unaware of either religion or religious institutions. Seeing that citizens embrace a religion, it falls to the state to facilitate the practice of this religion, as [it does] the other vital activities of the citizens.

It also falls to those who govern to educate themselves to decide and, therefore, to listen to and consult with the religious authorities. And the statesman who would not do it would not be behaving secularly, but blindly and deafly: to be clear, he would not be behaving as a statesman and he would not be respecting his fellow citizens.

In return, each one, whatever his religion and the favor which it enjoys in his country, has to respect whoever does not share his faith or who has chosen to express it differently. . . .[21]

For Diouf, then, the truly secular state should facilitate the religious practice of its citizens while consulting regularly with the relevant religious authorities. In this regard, for as long as he remained in power, Diouf practiced what he preached.[22]

Procedural Commonalities

Throughout middle Africa there is an almost constant, and quite banal, round of courtesy visits that occurs between holders of power. These tend to follow similar patterns regardless of country, the type of state, the level of administration within the state, the nation's dominant religion, or the confessional beliefs of the particular head of state. The occasions may be ordinary or unusual, but these events seem to follow a conventional and well-understood script. There is also, at events that occur regularly such as ordinations, certain rites of attendance and deference that participants customarily follow. And, lastly, at times the congruence of various procedures between the ostensibly religious world and the domain of the state is so marked that ordinary citizens comprehend and react to nominally religious contexts in much the same manner that they do to the ostensibly political sphere.[23]

Courtesy Visits and Acts of Presence

In 1989, when the elderly Khalife-General of the Mouride Brotherhood, Abdoul Ahad Mbacké, passed away, President Abdou Diouf and a high-powered ministerial delegation were quick to appear at Touba to pay homage to the deceased and, most respectfully, to greet and thus "recognize" his successor. In the words of one observer, "Sadness could be read on the face of the chief of state. . . . The son had just lost his father. President Abdou Diouf recognized the brutality of the loss in presenting to Serigne Abdoul Khadre Mbacké the condolences of his government and of all the Senegalese people. . . . In a response designed to be brief because of the painful circumstances, the new Khalife-General of the Mourides assured President Diouf of the continuity of the excellent relations that have always existed between the government and the Mouride community. 'We will never cease praying for you,' . . . said the new Khalife-General."[24] The Mouride succession, even though nominally an event of only religious significance, was nevertheless seen to be (as it was) a political occasion of prime importance. Unity through the invocation of the deceased's paternal filiation to the president, an exchange of brief speeches pledging the continuity of mutual support, the presence of an impressive collection of cabinet ministers following in Diouf's wake, all were ordinary and often-used procedures even though this particular event was itself extraordinary.

On an equally special although far more joyous occasion in 1983, Bernard Cardinal Yago, newly consecrated and fresh from the ceremony at the Vatican, returned home to Abidjan to attend a thanksgiving mass in his honor. The cardinal noted that the great honor done him easily transcended his person and reflected on the entire nation. "That is why you are here," he said, "Christians and non-Christians, for the thanksgiving mass. Thanks for your fraternal presence. Many of you have come, led by the President of the Republic, whom I would like to thank particularly. Mr. President . . . I keep alive the emotional memory of the warm embrace that translated your joy and pride at the same time as your affection for the servant that I am."[25] Here, too, even though the event was uncommon, an ordinary procedure—the courtesy visit—extended recognition to a newly empowered player on the field of power.

Although a devout Catholic, Houphouet-Boigny did not limit his attention only to the events marking the life of that particular church. When a new president of the Methodist Church of the Côte d'Ivoire was installed, Houphouet was there with an important governmental delegation.[26] When Ivoirian Muslims celebrated their important regular holidays such as Tabaski, a festival commemorating Abraham's sacrifice and marking the end of pilgrimage to Mecca, the religious ceremony was invariably an occasion for an important ministerial delegation, of the Muslim faith, to render honor to the spiritual powers with their act of presence.[27] Such events almost always featured an exchange of respectful greetings, blessings, and prayers for the continued prosperity of the nation and the continued good health and presence of President Houphouet at the head of the nation. Comparable manifestations and ceremonies occur regularly not only in Côte d'Ivoire, but throughout middle Africa.[28]

The act of presence by political authorities at religious ceremonies is both ordinary and ostentatious. Such events are covered extensively in the local media, no doubt reinforcing a general impression that—in some unspecified way—the head of state and his political minions are privy to, or are perhaps touching, a rather different form of power. There is also on such occasions an almost seamless elision between submission and fidelity to God and then the ritual thanks to the head of state for all he has done for the particular community of believers that is celebrating its festival. In one case, Cardinal Hyacinthe Thiandoum, head of the Senegalese Catholic Church, told four new priests at their ordination that henceforth they would have new powers. He enumerated these as the power to consecrate the bread and the wine to bless the people, to proclaim the Good News and to dispense the word of salvation, and to be the eyes and the ears of Christ to see and understand the needs of his people. The new priests would follow their program, which consisted of "a double fidelity to the country and to God."[29] In a like manner, while it is possible to understand and interpret the juxtaposing of two press photographs—of then President Ahidjo casting his ballot in municipal elections and the other of Catholic Bishop Ama doing the same—as a simple and straightforward "endorsement" of the regime, it also could be understood as the bishop's act of presence and deference to a different form of power.[30]

Acts of presence and courtesy visits are important throughout middle Africa. In Chapter 2 we noted that ordinations of priests, consecrations of bishops, and enstoolments of chiefs are all occasions that need to be marked and honored.[31] To be sure, there are national variations in these patterns. In general, acts of presence at ordinations and other ostensibly religious events seem most frequent and marked in Côte d'Ivoire, Senegal, Cameroon, and to a slightly lesser extent in Zaïre/Congo. Although in Nigeria and Ghana the "political" presence at these events—as well as the attention the press devoted to them—was weaker, it was counterbalanced by a large and visible political presence at enstoolments and ceremonies awarding various customary titles.[32] In Kenya press coverage revolved around issues of disagreement and contention between clerics and representatives of the KANU state, while in Tanzania the press almost never paid attention to such matters.

Senegal, however, stands out among even those states where this pattern of behavior is frequent and noticeable. Given the political and economic weight of the Sufi brotherhoods, this is unsurprising, and Senegalese politicians probably spend more time and expend more effort on these matters than do their counterparts elsewhere in the region. Leonardo Villalón's study of Fatick argues that the strength of the brotherhoods has meant that the state has had to seek an accommodation with the religious infrastructure and organizations that lie outside its boundaries.[33] Although there is much merit in this analysis, I should like to note that both the marabouts and the politicians occupy sites on the same field of power and that, in fact, there may be more of an elision and overlap of rites, rituals, and procedures than Villalón indicates. For example, each brotherhood has its annual festivals, usually commemorating the anniversary of its founder, or the accession of its current leader, or the birth of the Prophet Mohammed—the list of relevant and important occasions is quite long. At such events the relevant politicians will be there to honor the power of the marabouts with an act of presence and the ritual exchange of prayers and pledges of mutual admiration and support.[34] In one such instance, Habib Thiam, then Diouf's prime minister, visited the notable marabout Serigne Moustapha Bassirou Mbacké at Prophane. Thiam and his delegation were there to honor the marabout, as well as to convey the president's greetings to the marabout and his family. The prime minister's speech underscored the religious importance of Prophane's annual festival, while the marabout responded in kind by thanking the government for its material support. Then, speaking of the national elections, the marabout—implicitly adopting a very narrow definition that equated partisanship with politics—denied that he interfered in politics because, as he put it, his disciples (talibés) worked for several different parties. At the same time, of course, he was thanking the government for its financial help, expressing his desire to collaborate closely with national authorities, and praising the availability of President Diouf for consultations.[35]

The Routinization of Elision

Other forms of elision even appear to have become bureaucratized and ritualized. The huge annual festival of the Mouride brotherhood, the Grand Magal of Touba, is prepared jointly by both the brotherhood and the state. The minister of the interior chairs an annual committee, composed of both bureaucrats and marabouts, to plan the great event. And in many of these cases of religious commemoration, the state extends important material and financial support to the religious festivities.[36] To anticipate a later theme, at the very least one can say that such joint participation in the planning of a religious event calls into question the status of the boundary line separating the state from civil society.

Administrative tours of the "bush" are a staple of the daily life of the state in middle Africa. In most cases a vestige of colonial administrative policies and practice, such travels occur at all administrative levels, with representatives from the "higher" level making inspections and visiting their subordinates throughout their administrative circumscriptions.[37] If the visitor is important enough, and if transportation conditions permit it, it is customary for the administrative subordinates to meet the visiting dignitary when she or he first sets foot on the local soil. This is often at an airport, but if the visitor is traveling by car or rail, it could also be elsewhere. In 1981 Prime Minister Thiam visited the northern Region of the Fleuve. Accompanied by his spouse, the minister of rural development, and the secretary of state for human promotion, Thiam was met at the frontier of the region by the governor, the mayor of the commune of Saint-Louis, and the marabout of Mpal. Of importance here is that the local authorities would include the marabout in the official delegation assigned to meet the prime minister as a matter of course. The account of the event simply listed his name and position along with the others, drawing no special attention to it. It was a completely routinized matter of courtesy extended to the visiting power.[38]

Although this can only be conjectural, I suspect that had the marabout, or a similar religious figure, not been there to greet the prime minister, the latter would have observed it and inquired about it. The marabout's absence, in other words, would have been dazzling and noticeably out of the ordinary. A small digression emphasizes the point. In 1975 Zaïrian President Mobutu visited the upcountry town of Lisala. As was customary there, too, when Mobutu's yacht docked at the river pier, he was immediately met by the local members of the subregional committee of the MPR. Once in private, the president wanted to know why the local Catholic bishop had not been invited to join the official delegation. Mobutu was reportedly angered by this slight to the local clergy, and he insisted that the state-party's representatives do everything possible to get along with the bishop. Since there was then considerable tension between Mobutu and the Catholic Church, his reaction could thus be seen as somewhat surprising. When initially relating this episode, I thought it showed that Mobutu was still concerned about maintaining cordial, working-level relations with the Catholic Church. That interpretation only went so far. On reflection, it now appears to me that Mobutu's anger was also an indication that the bishop, as a recognized holder of a certain and real form of spiritual power, had to be part of the official delegation because to do otherwise would be to fail to acknowledge and respect the unity and indivisibility of power. Mobutu thus understood the bishop's absence as something out of the ordinary and, perhaps for him, worrisome.[39]

Local marabouts and imams are usually in attendance at ceremonial occasions marking the arrival of a new representative of the state in Senegal. Typically, for example, when a new prefect takes office, there is a higher administrative official present to perform the ceremony, and other representatives of the administration, the judiciary, the state-party, trade union leaders, and religious authorities also attend. In one case, the incoming prefect appealed to all of these individuals—including the religious authorities—to help him work toward the eventual success of the state's administrative reform.[40] In other words, asking the marabouts for assistance and support on an administrative matter, to facilitate success in the realm of politics, did not raise any eyebrows and was not unusual. Such acts of presence have become regular and routinized in Senegal and elsewhere. Representatives of the state call on the spiritual powers, while the marabouts and priests return the gesture on the relevant state occasions.

At certain moments it even appears as though the marabouts are imitating administrative procedures that the state has long employed. There are times, for example, when the local press describes the travels of the marabouts to visit their followers much as it would describe an administrative trip to the "bush."[41] When this occurs, the local officials of the state return the favor, and the honor, with an act of presence. Both the nominally temporal and the nominally religious powers are seen to be doing the same things: They visit and tour their respective administrative and religious circumscriptions, they make contact with citizens and religious followers, they exchange courtesy calls and acts of presence with each other, they heap each other with praise and visible and vocal signs of respect, and they pray for each other and for the head of state. In other words, the various rituals present both sets of authorities as players who occupy a recognized place on the field of power.

Routinization of elision appears in other ways as well. As is customary in both state and church, when a powerful player departs for another posting, a ceremony usually marks the occasion. As is often the case, state authorities are invited to religious occasions and vice versa. When one of Yaoundé's auxiliary bishops was transferred to his own see at Sangmélima, the church authorities organized a solemn mass in his honor. Major political figures from the government attended and were prominently visible in the front pews. After the ceremony there was a reception, on church grounds, at which time the minister of defense elevated Monseigneur Zoa, the bishop of Yaoundé, to the rank of Grand Officer of the Order of Value. Although the newspaper headline proclaimed that this ceremony was about "religion," the elision between the realm of the political and the domain of the spiritual is still striking. This emerges not so much in the quite normal act of presence of an important ministerial delegation at a solemn mass, although this argument could be made, but rather more overtly in the use of a "religious" occasion to present Monseigneur Zoa with a state decoration.[42]

Reflections of the Society

Unsurprisingly, many formal religious establishments mirror certain problems afflicting the larger society. In Zaïre/Congo, for example, one press account detailed the malaise besetting the clergy in Kenge Diocese in Bandundu Region, where the northern parts of the diocese were far more developed economically than the south. The Zaïrian bishop who succeeded the last European to hold the post hailed from the south; according to certain sources, once in power he slighted other parts of his circumscription. According to the report, the bishop transferred material goods from the north to the southern portions of the diocese. In addition, he was also reputed to have favored the education of young priests from his own ethnic group (Yaka) without worrying overly much about others in his region. Of the ten students the church sent to Europe from this diocese, seven were from the south. Similar figures were also common in the diocese's administrative and educational services. As a result, the clergy in the northern part of the diocese sent a report to Pope John Paul II asking for the division of the diocese into two separate entities.[43] Although I do not have the necessary information either to conclude or to verify this particular story, it is nonetheless worth noting that this specific tale could have been told of many of the MPR's subregional commissioners. The issues (ethnicity and the distribution of material resources) were the same, the uses of power were similar, and the recourse to higher outside authority (the Pope as opposed to President Mobutu) were all strikingly alike. Zaïrians reading this story, or hearing of it, would not have been surprised, because whether it is exercised within church or state, power is eaten whole. Players on the field of power react in certain ways, and the story of the divisions within this particular diocese certainly would not have shocked most people.

One can also discern reflections of societal ills in the following report on the Ghanaian religious establishment. On Palm Sunday in 1980, priests and members of the congregation of the Sea Cathedral of the Catholic Church in Takoradi locked the doors and boycotted the service. They later held a four-hour demonstration in the city against the bishop, whom they accused of ethnic favoritism; refusing to lead development projects within the diocese; refusing to let women read the lesson during mass; and downplaying the importance of prayer meetings, ecumenism, and the adoption of local culture into the church. In a memo submitted to the Vatican through the local nuncio, the dissident priests maintained that the diocese was plagued by "paternalism, autocracy, tribalism and apathy." They further alleged that the bishop lacked leadership skills, and, in consequence, the clergy and the laity were frustrated because the result was "straight-jacket bureaucracy at the expense of Christian charity."[44] It would appear that even the sins of the church resemble those of the state, as do the appropriate methods of "political" protest.

Over the past fifteen years Kenya's President Moi has often vocalized his concern about the "intrusions" of various religious organizations and members of the clergy into the political realm. When, for example, the National Council of Churches of Kenya (NCCK) annoyed the government, the president quickly labeled the council's activities as "subversive." At a Harambee meeting Moi questioned the organization's Christian ideals and wondered why the NCCK had dropped the word "Christian" from its name. (It was formerly the National Christian Council of Kenya.) He warned Kenyans to be cautious of the NCCK's activities, accusing its voter education seminars of subversion and instructing civil servants to keep their distance from this troublesome organization.[45] This was but one more salvo in the ongoing struggle between Moi and the Kenyan clerics, whom the president repeatedly criticized for involving themselves in politics. This, however, is one of the few things that both Moi and the clerics actually agreed on: namely, that the clergy were involved in the political realm. Why this occurs, and how priests and politicians understand the parameters of the political kingdom, may become clearer after examining the occasional convergences between certain strands of policy and theology.

Policy and Theology

Defining the parameters of politics in middle Africa is not nearly as easy as the classic "Render unto Caesar" injunction would have it. A Ghanaian commentator put it this way:

> There are some people who think religion and politics must so rigidly maintain their separate identities that the "twain shall never meet." They argue that if the church concentrates on the area of morality and spiritual upliftment, the other area, that is, the materialistic world would take care of itself.
>
> The opponents of this view who are in the majority say the churches cannot sit idly by while their flock are subjected to injustices and buffeted by the harsh realities of present day world economy.
>
> The latter view appears to hold away [sic, sway] among [the] modern generation of priesthood. In recent times, Bishops and priests of all shades and religious persuasions and convictions seem to be worried about the quality of life of their congregations in particular and the world in general.
>
> While this country is very far from having a Bishop Abel Muzorewa to lead a political party, our local priests are never short of ideas or tongue-tied when it comes to politics—by which I mean speaking out on national issues which may help make life a bit more tolerable before we all make our final exit to meet our Maker and account for our lives on earth. . . .[46]

Clergy are, of course, concerned with morality. Increasingly, however, and especially during the past twenty years, as many African societies have traversed periods of declining or stagnant economies coupled with turbulent polities, clergy of many denominations have taken to speaking out on national policy issues. At times—for example, when considering corruption within a society—it is most difficult to determine where politics ends and religion begins.

But in a real sense, this formulates the problem badly. When one of Monseigneur Zoa's pastoral letters, read from the pulpit in the presence of nine cabinet members, pointedly reminds both his clergy and the lay faithful that "their duty is to pray every day for the chief of state, for his collaborators and for the peace of the country," the boundary line between politics and religion becomes obscure. Similarly, when—in a different context—Zoa underlines that there is a convergence between the official doctrine of the government and that of the local church, it becomes difficult to sustain the perspective that Caesar and God are operating in different spheres.[47] When the clergy and the formal religious establishments of their respective countries support their policies and pray for their continued good health and long-lived political rule, the ruling politicians are, of course, delighted, and there is no talk of "rendering unto Caesar." President Moi, for example, presumably had no objection to an NCCK publication that appeared in the aftermath of the abortive coup d'état of August 1982. It stated: "The Church is the Body of Christ. The leaders of the Church have a duty to assist, to guide, and to encourage the President, so that he can fulfill his duty of being a good imitator of Christ. In that way his *nyayo* will always be as a good and healthy path for both Christians and other citizens to follow."[48] On the other hand, and equally predictably, when clergy are critical, politicians take offense and accuse them of meddling in politics where, to be sure, they do not belong. As one Kenyan journalist put it, "At the heart of the matter has been a question of the definition of just what constitutes political activity in which the church may indulge. Church leaders have repeatedly stated that pointing out and criticising politicians' mistakes is part of their pastoral duty."[49] Defining political activity certainly is the heart of the matter, as is recognizing that in middle Africa the parameters of the political enclose a significant spiritual terrain.

President Moi is quite correct to view Kenyan clergymen such as Bishop Okullu as national leaders who are engaging in politics. Moreover, the clergy know and understand this, often arguing that their political involvement is legitimate because it springs ultimately from their theological beliefs and spiritual calling. Engaging in politics to alleviate the plight of their flock, they argue, is precisely what they are supposed to be doing. The rancor comes from the fact that since power is indivisible, heads of state are quite content to have them involved in politics when their positions support the government, but less than overjoyed with them when they point out that the government is failing to meet its responsibilities to the population. In other words, the difference in Kenya, and other comparable cases, is not over where to draw the line between the realm of politics and the realm of religion, because implicitly for some, and explicitly for others, no line is recognized. Mwai Kibaki, one of Kenya's former vice-presidents, expressed it this way: "Politics and religion are inseparable. To suggest that politics should be left to the politicians and religion to the clergy, is a terrible intellectual arrogance. . . . This way tends to suggest that through some mysterious magical process, some politicians have become specially qualified as to be the only ones to pronounce on political issues."[50] All power holders—be they professional politicians or professional clergy—understand that they occupy a common terrain. At issue are policy differences that are very political.

Clergy of many countries and faiths openly and candidly embrace their political role. In 1993, for example, the Catholic archbishop of Kisangani, Monseigneur Laurent Monsengwo Pasinya, traveled to Leuven, where he received an honorary degree. At that time he explained, "The role played by the Church in Zaïre in political matters is comprised of three rubrics [volets]. In effect, first there exist the interventions which are the outcome and the consequence of its prophetic mission *in the service of the world*. Next come a series of actions which are the result of *pastoral options* decreed by the Episcopal Conference of Zaïre (CEZ). Finally we find the positions taken by the Episcopate in the framework of the *Magisterium,* in order to enlighten the choices of the faithful in the political domain."[51] Enlightening the choices of the faithful in the political domain can lead to contentious policy differences, as well as political conflict with the other powers that be. Some of these disputes we examine later. For the moment, however, let us explore some of the more tranquil interactions in which both politicians and priests agree and assume that they have common goals and aims.

Common Goals

Although the Mobutu regime had numerous points of policy contention with the Catholic Church over the years, it nevertheless usually maintained cordial relations with the Protestants. In 1985 the then prime minister, Kengo wa Dondo, appeared at the Protestant Church of Lisala in Kinshasa's Kasa-Vubu Zone as Mobutu's personal representative. He was there to attend the opening of the eighth ordinary session of the National Synod of the Church of Christ in Zaïre (ECZ), the national umbrella organization grouping all recognized Protestant churches. In the course of his remarks, Kengo noted that the churches and the state were in the service of the same cause. He further stated that their common objectives invited a fruitful collaboration to achieve the advent of a better social order. "'We must harness ourselves to the consolidation of this collaboration in such a way as to insert our diverse development projects into a socially integrated comprehensive plan,' the Prime Minister specified."[52] Given the history and context of the Mobutist state, there could be little doubt that Kengo's natural assumption would have been that the state was to play the dominant role in this collaboration. That could go without saying. Nonetheless, his speech still called attention to the fact that, at least from his perspective, both church and state had the common goal to develop a better a better social order.

The notion that church and state have certain mutual goals transcends considerations of regime type and specific denomination. In Tanzania from time to time, some of Nyerere's remarks would tend to obscure the differences between church and state while assuming that the two do, or perhaps ought to have, common objectives. For example, in 1981, while addressing the 550 clergymen of the Evangelical Lutheran Church, Nyerere maintained that pastors should organize their followers for self-improvement here on earth rather than in the afterlife and sharply criticized those clerics who preached to their congregations that Tanzania's lack of development was ordained by God. The president argued that they should help their faithful to solve daily problems. Religion, like socialism, sought to establish justice in human society, he reasoned.[53] Similarly, several years after Nyerere had relinquished the national presidency, the president of Zanzibar and thus the union's second vice-president, Idris Abdul Wakil, made a comparable argument while addressing Islamic leaders at the opening of a conference of the Islamic Councils for East, Central, and Southern Africa in Dar es Salaam. "We should not confine our energies and thinking to the preaching of Islam only," he advised. He maintained that religious leaders had often exempted themselves from working for development because it was, in their view, the responsibility of the politicians. To Wakil this was improper because all religions advocated the well-being of man, and to think otherwise was an incorrect interpretation of the Koran. Once again, although this time to an Islamic audience, we have a politician arguing not only that the state and the church have common goals, but that a contrary interpretation of the Koran would be incorrect.[54]

The same assumption of common goals could even be discerned beneath the revolutionary rhetoric in Ghana after the second coming of J. J. Rawlings in early 1982. Speaking before the World Methodist Council's first West African seminar on evangelism, Chairman Rawlings argued that the church has an obligation to make people aware of their civic duties. In his words, "Any real religion imposes a heavy responsibility on the individual, not for the sake of his or her soul, to merely win some heavenly personal commendation, but to contribute to the upliftment of the whole society in which one finds oneself."[55] In the regime's early days, the state was not the only party assuming that there was a unity of common goals. Various church establishments also articulated much the same thoughts. Presbyterians wanted to cooperate with the state to build a new scale of values for Ghanaians, while the Catholic bishops wished the Rawlings government to see them as "friends and collaborators in helping the poor and ordinary people in this country." The bishops, however, were not in agreement with the state on other important matters. They clearly wanted the people to be able to select the way they wished to be governed, a suggestion the Rawlings regime was certainly not willing to countenance in the early years of its rule.[56] In general, however, at least in the official and semi-official discourse, there was usually not much doubt as to which institution was to be in the driver's seat in achieving these common goals. Rawlings, like Mobutu, usually insisted that the church was there to assist the government in carrying out these common goals rather than vice versa. From the perspective of both the Castle and Mt. Ngaliéma, there was no question as to who was the senior partner in this collaboration.[57]

The Kenyan Clerics

I have already alluded to the thought and career of Bishop Henry Okullu as illustrative of the difficulties involved in drawing even an analytic line between the political kingdom and the spiritual world.[58] In the next several pages I examine some of his theological writings, as well as those of Timothy Njoya and David Gitari, quoting liberally from them to preserve—to the extent possible—each author's voice and perhaps his intentions as well. My intent here is not to examine these writings as theology, even less to evaluate them as original contributions to a theological discourse, something I am assuredly not qualified to do. Rather, my aim is far more limited: to extract from their writings the clerics' perceptions and understandings of politics and, by inference, their views on where the parameters of the political may be found. In this regard, the methodological procedure closely resembles my use of African popular literature in Chapter 2. I am simply reading theology closely in the hopes that it will shed light on important political questions, while trying to furnish enough extracts from the primary materials to permit readers to form judgments of the positions of all three political thinkers that are independent of my own.

Although Okullu would like to restrict the usage of the term "political priest" to those clergy who actively seek electoral office, such as the late Archbishop Makarios of Cyprus or Zimbabwe's Bishop Abel Muzorewa, he understands that the term has a wider and more colloquial usage. In other words, for many "if a preacher refers to suffering, the poor or an unjust social order which gives birth to and sustains that suffering, he is deviating from his duty and involving himself in 'politics'. That is why, according to some people in Kenya, I am a 'politician.'"[59] Ultimately, however, for Okullu the fact that priests are "political" in this wider sense stems directly from the act of baptism. He notes that in baptismal vows people promise to fight against sin, the world, and the devil. As far as the fight against the world is concerned, Okullu elaborates using Zambia as an example:

> When we see one section of Zambia with fewer roads, school teachers and medical facilities than the rest of the country, this is not an economic accident [sic] but a result of unjust economic planning which leaves one part of society poor and the other rich. Christians pledge themselves at baptism to fight against this and to seek to demolish those structures of oppression and injustice. So Christians must involve themselves in the fight against oppressive states, exemplified by South Africa. This is the struggle against the world.[60]

Or, phrased in a slightly different manner, "Churchmen may not have the expertise to reform an economic system. But they have the duty to say that a system which leaves the majority of our people poor and jobless and without proper housing is immoral and unjust, and should be corrected by the appropriate specialists. Our prophetic role requires us to ask moral questions concerned with national projects and demand answers from political leaders."[61] For Okullu, therefore, "politics" and the necessity of political practice and involvement are built into the theological foundation of his religious beliefs.

Okullu is certainly not the only Kenyan clergyman who demonstrates the point. In this regard, the theology of the Reverend Timothy Njoya, for many years the rector of St. Andrew's Presbyterian Church in Nairobi, also merits reflection. By virtue of his courage, intellect, and attention-commanding pulpit in Nairobi, Njoya has been of Kenya's more politically engaged and visible clergymen. In his early writings he is also quite critical of Okullu on several points.

Njoya defended his doctoral dissertation at Princeton Theological Seminary in 1976. In general terms, his work, "Dynamics of Change in African Christianity: African Theology through Historical and Socio-Political Change," sees the unity of colonialism and missionary Christianity in Africa and makes a sustained argument in favor of a continuous conversion that destroys all traditions, even those theological traditions brought by the missionary churches. He understands conversion in this sense as a liberating experience that is both religious and political. Some of the origins of these positions may be found in the experiences of his early years:

> When I went to St. Paul's United Theological College in 1964 I found the systematic and dogmatic theology that missionaries were teaching Africans too anachronistic and petrified to be of any earthly use. I worked in opposition to that theology until I left college and worked for the Presbyterian Church of East Africa, in the rural parishes. The people of Mwimbi and Chuka with whom I worked proved to me that even poor and oppressed people are capable of generating their own theology. I found my life caught between the spiritual movement of the people and the systematic and dogmatic theology which missionaries had taught me. I decided to stop reacting to Missionary Christianity and to devote all my energies listening to the problems Christians were facing. . . .[62]

Using the experience of conversion as a focus, Njoya argues that "the liberation of a Kenyan, spiritual as well as material, is as much a political salvation as it is a religious matter."[63] More specifically, Njoya argues that the transformation of East Africa from "tribal and feudal politics to colonial and neo-colonial politics" owed a great deal to conversion from Paganism (his term) to Christianity. In his own words, "Politics as a social system continued to affect Christianity by offering opportunities for elites educated in missionary schools to rule other Christians and dominate the non-Christian population. The conversion experience was therefore at once a political experience and religious experience, and was also a capitalist value. In other words, to be Christian was during the Advent to be an employee or potential employee of Church or state and therefore a member of a special class." Put slightly differently, Njoya maintains that Africans became Christians to be transformed so that they would eventually become capitalists and the rulers of an independent state.[64]

Njoya also has much to say concerning aspects of organization and democracy within the church. Commenting in specific reference to Tanzania, he notes:

> The Church contradicts itself when it adopts socialist rhetoric while in fact it feels threatened by it. A Christian bishop knows only too well that he acquired his po-

sition by nomination from the top and not by popular election. He may call his followers "Ndugu" (comrades) but in his mind he understands he is an autocrat with his bishop's council performing the role of lieutenants (oligarchy). No bishop can relate to other Christians as brothers while they as sheep have no power to vote him out of his shepherdhood but relate to him as sheep to a shepherd. Hence, the pretext of the Church to play a social and popular role in a democratic socialist republic contradicts the very essence of Church hierarchy as a feudal, patriarchical and inaccessible system. While the Church in Tanzania may speak the language of African socialism as a survival tactic, it would be very presumptuous for us to credit such a Church with the qualities of critical consciousness unless such self-awareness reflects itself in changes within the life of the Church.[65]

Worthy of emphasis here is Njoya's observation that the hierarchical daily life of the church may not be entirely congruent with certain church doctrines, and his glimmer of a suggestion that both socialism and democracy might well require changes in the church's organizational structures.

In one of the dissertation's concluding passages, he notes: "The self-liberating character of the Church requires liberation throughout the society. The Church's struggle takes place through the identification of the self with Christ the Messiah, the divine object, who sensitizes us to respond to the needs of others as subjects in God's kingdom, not as objects of exploitation."[66] Throughout Njoya's analysis, in other words, the realm of the political and the realm of the spiritual seem hopelessly confounded, thoroughly interpenetrated, and thus generally quite difficult to disentangle even on an analytical plane.

Portions of Njoya's later work are more explicitly political as he, along with other Kenyan clergymen, began reacting to the specific events and contexts of daily life. One collection of sermons, delivered from the pulpit at St. Andrew's in Nairobi during 1984–1986, is critical of the Moi government, but not stridently or mindlessly so. In fact, in some of these early sermons he occasionally took pains to mention some good things about the government.[67] For example, in one passage that was, on the whole, critical of certain government policies, Njoya nonetheless drew a comparison that surely must have pleased President Moi: "If the church cannot plead for the poor, oppressed, hungry and marginalised, if it cannot plead for those ostracised from politics like Oginga Odinga and Charles Njonjo and others, it has no reason to exist. Moses pleaded with God to forgive those who had worshipped a golden calf, and in response God declared a general amnesty the way that our President forgives and declares amnesty for a certain category of prisoners on *Jamhuri* [Independence] days. This can, through our prayers, be extended to all prisoners with politically-related offenses."[68] In the same sermon he stated that the government and the churches were not really fighting each other, because, in fact, there were aims held in common. Both "are fighting the attitude, negligence and indifference of those who take advantage of the poor and exploit them saying, 'I am not my brother's keeper,' 'Don't speak the truth because it will antagonise big people,' or 'Leave politics to politicians.' . . ."[69]

One critique castigated government leaders for corrupting "tribes." According to Njoya, the problem in Kenya was not tribes, which God had created and which were therefore "clean," but rather the "leaders, the elites, the ruling class . . . who must stop using the word 'tribalism' for their internal disagreements. If they disagree on what amount of national *ugali* [porridge] and *sukumawiki* [vegetable greens] each leader should enjoy, let them not bring tribe and race into their discord. . . ."[70] His use of food metaphors to criticize leaders for painting their disagreements over "eating" and power as "tribalism" is quite striking. In a different sermon, and in relation to a slightly different question, Njoya used the imagery of food and obesity to refer critically to another group of power holders—those lodged in the church. These passages are worth citing at some length:

> Looking at the problem of Judas in the church, we can compare it to the problem of members who have grown impervious to the Gospel and continue in the church like excessive fat in the body. The church herself can grow big in size without growing spiritually, this again being like ceasing to grow up in order to grow fat. The church may therefore suffer heart attacks, strokes and hernias due to the disease of obesity, characterised by bureaucratic formalism, dogmatism, the struggle for positions, and the stealing of church offerings by church committees and treasurers. Obesity is as big a problem in a developing church as it is among the rich who have more to eat than their bodies need. Churches which grow overweight with worldly power and wealth cannot discharge their prophetic responsibilities. . . .
>
> A healthy church is one whose members and leaders are spiritually healthy because they are filled by the Holy Spirit and are in right relationship to God. When we have a healthy church, without obesity, this leads to having a healthy nation. With a healthy member of the church, you have a healthy family. For if the church can become fat with toxic substances like selfishness, nepotism, heresy, apostasy and idolatry, how much more can a country or family suffer? If the church exercises, eats less and slims, she will become more effective in her ministry in the world. Instead of concentrating on her own bodily survival, she will reach others.[71]

In a sense, therefore, Njoya finds fault with both sets of power holders—those in the state and those in the church. That he would use the same sets of metaphors and imagery, those pertaining to food, eating, and obesity, to describe difficulties in both state and church is surely significant, for his parishioners understand implicitly that power has to do with consumption. They also certainly understand that power is not restricted to either the state or the church and that the political kingdom includes a significant spiritual dimension.[72]

The third Kenyan cleric is Anglican bishop David M. Gitari. In one of his essays Gitari essentially sketches a fourfold typology of church-state relations. The categories are as follows: In the first, churches identify themselves with the goals, intentions, and powers of the state, actively adapting themselves to the state's positions. In the second, churches passively retreat into what he calls the "sphere of the purely religious" and refrain from making any statements on the power of the state. The third category is what he calls critical and constructive collaboration with the power of the state. Lastly, there is resistance or opposition to the state. Gitari's thoughts on these matters do not seem entirely consistent.[73] On the on hand, his phrase "sphere of the purely religious" coupled with the fact that he would even go to the trouble of constructing such a typology makes it reasonable to infer that Gitari thinks that it is possible to separate the state and the political from the purely spiritual. On the other hand, however, the thrust of a later passage appears to contradict this:

> Involvement in the affairs of the State means that the Christian Church will exercise the prophetic ministry of Judgment. Judgment means that the Church will constantly remind people of the standard of righteousness and justice which alone exalts a nation. The Church will also take a lead in giving moral and practical support to the State when it upholds that standard, and will responsibly criticise the State or those in authority when they depart from it. When society accepts as normal racism, tribalism, corruption or the exploitation of fellow men, Christians cannot be silent. They, like the prophets of old, must speak out and pronounce the will and judgment of God. The Christian community must be an ever-present reminder to the State that it exists only as the servant of God and man.[74]

The driving force and emphatic direction of the prophetic ministry of Judgment, in other words, seems to indicate that it would be most difficult, if not impossible, for those clerics who believe in such a ministry to withdraw from an active involvement in politics.

In a later sermon with which representatives of the government took issue, and amid much controversy, Gitari argued:

> We are living in a time when church leaders have to be very patient, especially when it appears that the truth we are proclaiming is either misunderstood, deliberately distorted or completely ignored. In this country there seems to be a clear misunderstanding on whether the church leaders are at liberty to be involved in politics or not. Bishops and clergy are often told to keep off politics. But at the same time the same people who tell us to keep off politics[,] also ask us to encourage Christians as voters. Apparently to tell people to enrol as party members or voters is not politics; but to challenge injustice in voters' registration is politics. Bishops who speak their minds are told to keep off politics, but there is a Bishop in Parliament who has not yet been warned to keep off politics.
>
> The churches have constantly and patiently to make clear that the gospel of Jesus Christ is concerned about every aspect of human life—intellectual, physical, spiritual and social. It is in the faithful proclamation of the gospel and in the teaching of the scriptures that the Spirit will lead us to apply the message of the gospel to the contemporary world.[75]

Some years later the line between politics and religion seemed further blurred in Gitari's thought. On the eve of the opening of Parliament in March 1993, Gitari preached a sermon on the theme of "The Good Shepherd" in which he explicitly merged parents, pastors, and politicians. In his words once again:

> Jesus said, "I am the good shepherd. . . ." At the eve of the opening of the seventh parliament, I wish to invite you to reflect with me the biblical metaphor of lead-

ers as shepherds. Anyone who has ever looked after his parents [sic] cows, goats or sheep will agree with me that the word "shepherd" suggests leadership and caring. Every person appointed or elected to be a leader, be he an assistant chief, a locational chief, a district commissioner, a headmaster, a principal, a councillor, a member of parliament, a parish priest, a bishop or moderator, a president or even a mother or father, must see himself or herself as a shepherd called to the great task of caring for God's flock. . . .[76]

Is it any wonder, therefore, that there have been clashes in Kenya between secular and religious institutions? To be sure, prior to the introduction and grudging acceptance of multipartyism in the early 1990s, Moi's KANU regime did wish to gain control of the ideological and moral space that the churches occupied. And, from the other side, the clerics resisted, with at least some arguing that politicians should be guided by their theological and moral visions. Just before the political liberalization, Njoya argued that the primary doctrine of Christianity was that God is plural and not mono. He continued, "A country is equally reflected in the pluralistic nature of God and that does not necessarily create disunity. . . . A monolithic institution like Kanu [sic], which shuts all doors and windows to pluralism so that no light or fresh air can come in, undermines God's all inclusive nature."[77] The institutional conflict was clear, but often obscured was the underlying assumption that for most politicians *and* clergymen it was all but impossible to distinguish between a discrete realm of spirituality and a separate kingdom of politics. For both sides in these disputes, politics and religion were but two sides of the same coin.

Senegalese Islam

The elision of spirituality and politics transcends formal religious affiliation. It appears in both Christian and Islamic theology and practice throughout middle Africa. The difficulty in drawing a hard-and-fast line between these nominally different power domains is also apparent in the relations between the Senegalese variant of Sufi Islam and the Senegalese state. Moreover, and in contradistinction to the Kenyan case, here there are no serious conflicts between the state and the heads of the major brotherhoods. Since the early days of independence, the Khalifes have been content to support the governments of Senghor and then Diouf, while Senegalese politicians have returned the favor.

At the heart of Senegalese politics lies a series of patronage networks organized around the larger of the Sufi brotherhoods. For many years the classic works on Senegalese politics argued that the government had to reach and nurture political arrangements with the Khalifes. Put briefly and directly, the kernel of the exchange was that the government would see that the Khalifes received support, deference, respect, and—quite importantly—a say in certain policy matters that directly affected their economic and political interests. In exchange, the Parti Socialiste (PS) governments of Senghor and Diouf would receive the electoral support of the Khalifes and their religious followers at election time.[78] The electoral exchange was based on the understanding that the power of the Khalifes enabled them to "deliver" the votes of their disciples because they were entirely dependent on their patrons for material support, general protection, and the Khalife's intercession on their behalf so that they might be admitted to paradise after death. In consequence, the disciples would literally "follow" the political instructions of their marabouts to whom they were beholden. This was the core of the "Mouride model."

In recent years, however, the political evolution of events on the ground coupled with the persuasive analyses of a new generation of scholars has begun to change our understanding of the dynamics of Senegalese politics. Villalón's study of Fatick argued convincingly that the disciples were not completely without political resources: they could, and did, possess some leverage because they were able to get the marabouts to compete for their allegiance and loyalty.[79] In addition, Linda Beck has argued that the relative stability of Senegalese politics plus its unusual absence of extensive ethnic mobilization can be explained through attention to a series of shifting accommodations to patronage systems. She traces variants of these patronage systems among the powerful Mourides and the Toucouleur, and arrestingly explains secessionist tendencies among the Diola of the Casamance as a consequence of their failure to obtain entrance to the patronage systems. Beck also argues that there has been a greater separation of politics and religion under what she calls "modern Mouridism" than there has been in the past.[80] And while I certainly agree that these matters have surely become less blatant than they once were, some of the evidence I have already presented indicates that there nevertheless remains a sense in which the "boundaries" between the political and religious realms are quite artificial.

In the period before the 1983 elections, and more specifically at the conclusion of the Grand Magal of Touba at the end of 1982, the Khalife-General of the Mourides issued a *ndigueul,* effectively a binding instruction on the members of the order. The Khalife praised President Diouf for his great availability to the Mouride brotherhood and then went on to note the large number of development projects accomplished at Touba during the past two years. He then said, "The Mourides have only Serigne Touba [the order's founder, Ahmadou Bamba], and anyone who is effectively engaged in working for the consolidation of his [Bamba's] path is entitled to their gratitude. President Abdou Diouf has worked for the promotion of Touba and the Mourides, in consequence and in return I ask that all *talibés* [disciples] give him more than he has given to Touba." Then, in a veiled reference to the upcoming election, the Khalife added that the Mourides knew what sort of support he expected from them. In his reply, Diouf's representative at the ceremony, Prime Minister Habib Thiam, praised the moral and religious probity of Sheikh Ahmadou Bamba, while renewing and restating the government's availability to listen to the advice and recommendations of the Khalife-General.[81] As far as the precise meaning of the *ndigueul* was concerned, one of the lesser Mouride Sheikhs put it this way: "The Khalife-general of the Mourides has asked us to vote for Abdou Diouf. A good Mouride must fear and love his khalife, following his *ndigueul.*"[82]

Others followed suit. The Khalife-General of the Tidiane order, Abdoul Aziz Sy, reminded his disciples that when President Diouf visits him at Tivaouane, "he is welcomed there first as a son, a full member of the large family and a disciple of the brotherhood." Like his Mouride colleague, the head of the Tidianes was explicit, leaving nothing to chance or misinterpretation. He asked everyone to support the president, and then, speaking specifically to his *talibés,* he again indicated to them the principles that should guide the good disciple who must submit himself to the recommendations of his sheikh in whom he has placed all of his hopes both for this world and for the next. And, as the press reported, he then concluded with this: "'I invite you to support the chief of State with the same determination as your guide [Sheikh],' the Khalife said in substance."[83] All of these endorsements carried some weight with the *talibés,* for Diouf was elected with almost 84 percent of the popular vote. His nearest competitor, Abdoulaye Wade of the Parti Démocratique Socialiste (PDS), received roughly 15 percent.[84]

In the run up to the 1988 elections the Mouride Khalife-General again issued a *ndigueul.* Once again, unsurprisingly, he instructed members of the order to support Abdou Diouf and the PS. The state-controlled Senegalese daily, *Le Soleil,* reported his words as follows:

> Touba is everything for us and Abdou Diouf ceaselessly supports us in the development of this common patrimony. In all domains he contributes to the pursuit of the work of Serigne Touba [Ahmadou Bamba]. If we were endowed with the power to elect, we would do it and he would be maintained for life. Now, this power to decide who will or will not guide a people belongs only to Allah. We humans can only bring our votes to he who merits our choice. In the present context and in light of his constant solicitude in favor of our community, Abdou Diouf is the man who merits our votes. Not to vote for him, would be for the Mourides who we are a pure and simple betrayal of Serigne Touba.[85]

The 1988 election again pitted Diouf against Wade, but this time the results were a bit closer. After the official count was announced, many of Wade's urban-based PDS supporters—especially those at Cheik Anta Diop University in Dakar—rioted. They could not believe that their candidate had actually lost, and they took to the streets. The government declared a state of emergency and imposed a curfew; Wade was arrested for an attack on the security of the state.[86]

There are indications that although many followed the behest of their spiritual leaders as they did in 1983, in the 1988 election not all welcomed the *ndigueul* and, in consequence, felt caught between their individual electoral wishes and the desires of the marabouts. Even some of those who did vote for Diouf and the PS felt that perhaps this time the Khalife's instruction was increasingly out of place.[87] It is also worth noting that in 1993 there was no formal *ndigueul.* Although I raise the question again in Chapter 6 during a more sustained discussion of *alternance,* or the electoral rotation of power, here it suffices to say that while the Khalife's endorsement recognized that the ultimate power to decide who would govern rests with Allah, he nonetheless stated that were it in his power, he would maintain Diouf in power for life. Although by 1988 increasing numbers of urban activists were opposed to the regime on other grounds, the Khalife's suggestion certainly violated one of the premises of the moral matrix of legitimate governance and may well have contributed, at least partially, to the unease with which many people received the 1988 *ndigueul*.

Preachers and Politicians

Another important area where the elision between theology and policy is often visible is in the domain of economic policy advice and attention to corruption. I deal with the economic bases of political legitimacy in Chapter 5, but some preliminary attention is now warranted, for it is in these issues areas, and especially where corruption is at issue and morality is in question, that one sees how both politicians and preachers find it relatively easy to shift between the ostensibly political and religious worlds. Although it is difficult to generalize across so many diverse countries and contexts, it nevertheless seems clear that some clergymen are rarely reluctant to offer the state advice on how best to orient the nation's economic policy. In part, and as should already be clear from the Kenyan case, when the clerics see that the poor and dispossessed are being further hurt, then the more courageous among them speak out. Nor, it should be said, are policymakers and political leaders shy in suggesting "policy" activities for various church establishments. There is thus a two-way flow of advice, agenda setting, and preaching. Once again, since preachers and politicians implicitly assume that there are no real boundaries between the spiritual world and the political one, both seem quite happy to recommend policy orientations for the other. All this quite naturally contributes to the further elision of these two realms, as several illustrations demonstrate.

In 1981, for example, the Catholic bishop of Kumasi, the Right Reverend Dr. Akwaasi Sarpong, called on the Limann government to end the subsidy for feeding secondary school boarders throughout the country. The money, he argued, could be better spent to provide education for the children of the truly needy. He felt that it would be an injustice for the children of some taxpayers to lack privileges that the children of the Ghanaian rich were enjoying. The bishop also deplored the fact that "greed, immorality, stealing and vanity had become the order of the day."[88] Similarly, somewhat later that year, the Christian Council and the National Catholic Secretariat appealed to the government to reconsider its economic priorities so that the provision of basic needs would take priority over luxury items.[89]

Throughout the Limann administration certain Ghanaian clerics continued voicing their qualms about fundamental injustice. Speaking to the twentieth annual general conference of the International Movement of Catholic Students (Pax Romana) Ghana Federation, the Catholic bishop of Accra, the Right Reverend Dominic Andoh, stressed the need for the state to ensure that labor agreements observed the norms of justice and equity so as to respect human dignity. He argued that since the purpose of the state was to bring about the common good, it could not disregard the economic activities of its citizens but should promote them in a suitable manner at all times. The bishop further regretted that when a few people had accumulated excessive wealth, most working men labored daily in acute need of the necessities of life. The bishop stated his belief that pay should not be determined in terms of goods, but rather in terms of the laws of justice and equity.[90]

The flow of advice and implicit criticism from segments of the clergy did not stop after Rawlings took over in early 1982. Furthermore, Rawlings and his PNDC government were not reticent about asking the churches to subscribe to their vision of policy. More specifically, at times the government was quite candid about asking the churches to dabble in the realm of economic policy and development. Speaking at the fifty-fifth anniversary of the Ghana Believers Church, the central regional secretary, Lt. Col. Baidoo, told his listeners that the churches could not only devote their attention to the spiritual development of their parishioners; they also had to educate them to be useful citizens so that they could thus contribute to the task of national reconstruction. In addition, Baidoo wanted the churches to educate the population on the dangers of bush fires and on the importance of a primary health care program while, at the same time, starting self-help projects to improve their environments.[91] Certainly in this case, the government wished to have the support of the churches for its economic policies.

Calls for a similar involvement in economic development policy also went out from sections of the clergy. One, the Right Reverend Daniel Okpoti Okerchiri, apostle-general of the Cherubim and Seraphim Church, made the plea right after his consecration as the first supreme head of the Church's Council in Ghana. That Okerchiri would use that particular solemn occasion to call upon churches to assist the government in its Economic Recovery Program just underscores the importance of this matter. More concretely, he said that the churches should use their spiritual influence to awaken in their congregations the desire to assist the government in all economic development projects. "'If the church isolates itself from development programmes of the day, it would be failing in its duty. The function of the church and the government should therefore be complementary to each other,' the Apostle-General stressed."[92]

Islamic clerics in various countries also pronounced their views on the state's economic policies. One account of the religious ceremonies marking the end of Eid-el-Fitri under the Babangida military regime in Nigeria is instructive on several levels. First, the specific ceremony reported occurred at Dodan Barracks in the presence of the head of state. The imam of the barracks, Alhaji Sanni Ibrahim, urged the government to continue demonstrating justice and fair play to all Moslems and Nigerians, because that would be in accordance with the dictates of the Koran. He further asked trade union leaders, scholars and teachers, and students to avoid negative reactions to national political issues. He reassured them that the government's policies were designed to make life—in the words of the press account—"more meaningful." The ignorant, he continued, had to be educated so that they might better understand the government's policies. This was clearly an example of a sanitized, pro-government sermon coming from Babangida's military chaplain. In this regard it fit nicely with some of the patterns evoked earlier in this chapter.

The chief imam of Lagos, Alhaji Liadi Ibrahim, delivered a second sermon an hour later. The alhaji was also largely pro-government, but in this case he chose to address specific economic issues. He blamed the market women for the rising price of food items in the markets. He wanted to know why they were selling *garri*, a staple, at ₦40 a tin. And he asked, "Is it President Babangida who sells garri at ₦40 a tin?" He then warned the women that they should fear God.[93] General Babangida was doubtlessly delighted with both sermons. Each, however, points to an elision of policy and theology in which the clerics commented freely on policy issues while, from time to time as in the Ghanaian case, representatives of the state did not hesitate to suggest to the clergy what they thought the church's mission actually was, or should be.

This elision is particularly apparent in matters pertaining to morality and corruption. To be sure, when there are persistent tensions between politicians and preachers, it is usually easy for one party in the dispute to cast aspersions on the morality of the other, a pattern that has been evident in Kenya. In 1995, for example, the Roman Catholic bishops issued a stringent pastoral letter that indicted the government on a variety of issues. It concluded that the government had lost "the moral credibility to govern" the country.[94] Such biting pastoral letters also appeared regularly during Mobutu's tenure in Zaïre. In 1990, for example, and in the context of a generally scathing indictment of the regime, the bishops wrote, "All legal arrangements should be made in order to avoid that a minority or group of citizens could confiscate power and impose it on the people for its own profit."[95]

In Ghana, on occasion, there have also been charges and counter-charges of weak or questionable morality hurled between the state and the pulpit. In November 1982 there was an attempted coup against the Rawlings regime. Coups are always high-tension affairs, but in this case anxiety was even higher. It seems that shortly after the abortive coup was announced, a pastoral letter from the Christian Council of Ghana was read in some churches. In addition, also in November 1982, the Catholic bishops released a letter of roughly similar contents. Both epistles called on the PNDC government to hand over the reins of power to a duly constituted national government because its seizure of the state from the Limann administration had in no way been justified. One editorial noted: "It may not matter whether or not the structure of the Catholic hierarchy has been democratised, that is to say whether the Bishops were speaking for the broad masses who form the congregation; but it is becoming increasingly evident that the Church has aligned itself with the forces of oppression and exploitation in the country."[96] The controversy continued, with the government doing all it could to discredit the relevant clergy. One government official, speaking from the pulpit of the Apostles Revelation Church at Tadzewu in the Volta Region, stated that the government was certainly aware that men with questionable characters had successfully infiltrated several congregations and were doing all they could to set the church against the people, thereby reversing the ongoing revolutionary process of the Rawlings regime. According to Colonel A. N. Tehn-Addy, commander of the Border Guard, these were people "who have cheated and fed fat on the sweat and blood of others [who]

would want to reintroduce and maintain the system of oppression that existed before the December 31 revolution." The colonel then emphasized that the People's
Defence Councils (PDCs) were based on the principles of "truth, honesty, love,
peace and happiness which the life of Christ teaches" all Christians. He also urged
the churches to continue to preach against black-marketing, smuggling, and
profiteering.[97]

Some weeks later another official urged church leaders to relate their religion
to the PNDC's revolutionary struggle, instead of asking the government to relinquish power. Under no circumstances, the official claimed, would Ghanaians go
to the polls to transfer power to a selected few individuals. As the journalist covering the event put it, "The Acting Deputy Secretary said Jesus Christ himself was
a revolutionary because he did not countenance people who indulged in mal-
practices in the church and stressed that both the teaching of the Bible and the
current revolutionary process were almost the same. . . ."[98] This message, Jesus as
revolutionary whose teachings were similar to the PNDC's current practices, was
emphasized in one form or another. Some time later, for example, General Arnold
Quainoo, the Army commander, told his troops that the PNDC possessed a "strong
spiritual foundation" and would not be deterred by "parasitic tax dodgers and people
masquerading in cassocks."[99]

There is a widespread understanding among various clergy that they have the
right, responsibility, and duty to help steer ordinary people and officials of the state
toward a moral and righteous path. The onetime patriarch of the Methodist Church
of Nigeria, Dr. Bolaji Idowu, stated directly that if it were necessary to steer politics and politicians toward righteousness, then the church had a right to participate in politics, and that the church could not afford to be neutral in any aspect of
national life.[100] When heads of state and other politicians are not on the receiving
end of these moral lessons, they often agree with the thrust of them and do not reject such obvious and open pastoral involvement in the political kingdom. In Nigeria, to cite one case, both General Buhari and the clerics were, at least on the level
of public rhetoric, quite keen on rooting out corruption. Buhari declared a "War
Against Indiscipline," and some pastors were happy to enlist. The Anglican bishop
of Kwara diocese, the Right Reverend Herbert Haruna, urged the government to
recover stolen wealth from former politicians so that it might benefit the poor.
Haruna likened the end of the Shagari administration and Buhari's military takeover
to a "redemption" from the hands of the unjust politicians who were bleeding the
nation economically, noting that "we should all be morally, economically and politically emancipated and see that discipline crowns all our actions since discipline
is the first order in heaven."[101]

Since virtually everyone is, by definition, against corruption, there would appear to be widespread recognition that if—on this question—pastors may play at
politics, then politicians may return the complement and play at preaching.[102] General Buhari used an Eid-el-Fitri celebration to urge Nigerians to adopt self-sacrifice,
self-restraint, purity, and total submission to God's will. According to the general,

only these things could help to rid the nation of corruption and indolence. Buhari also urged Nigerians to shun greed, materialism, and indiscipline. In this case, Buhari, speaking on a religious holiday, used the occasion to transmit a message that was both political and religious.[103]

The more than occasional overlap between the roles of politician and prelate further erodes the boundary between politics and religion, church and state. Sometimes their spouses recognize and understand this elision with crystal clarity. Mary Lar, the wife of a prominent Nigerian politician, Solomon Lar, is a case in point. In response to a question posed during the Shagari regime about whether she had occasion to encourage or discourage her husband in his plunge into politics, she replied: "You see, I had never wanted to marry a politician but a church minister so that we can devote our time to the service of God. Spiritually my husband is serving God and politically he is devoting his total service to humanity which is one of the doctrines of Christianity. So I always encourage him to succeed in his duties because people wanted him to serve them."[104]

J. J. Rawlings rarely constrained his impulse to mount the pulpit. For example, shortly after seizing power he granted an interview to *Jeune Afrique* that later appeared in translation in the Ghanaian press. He noted: "A long time ago I began to see the moral fiber of my country being destroyed. Corruption, lack of integrity in the Judiciary, the police and the so-called dominant group, the misuse of Christianity. I thought I could find a way out by joining the forces but I realised the Armed Forces institution was no better. So there was a time I had wanted to be a priest." And then, when the interviewer asked him why he was talking about waging a holy war and what it really meant, he replied: "All that is filth, all that is unclean, all that is corrupt has to be done away with and thrown into the waste paper basket. We will have to curb the greed of the dominant group. That is why I keep talking about the national character of my country, because it is a strong, powerful and pure character."[105]

That early ambition to become a priest and to purge the world of the unclean and the corrupt often came through in Rawlings' speeches and talks. Without regard for classic distinctions between church and state, he would happily address spiritual themes on secular occasions and secular themes on spiritual occasions. It made no difference. The two realms were one; it was virtually impossible to distinguish between them. In a speech at a nondenominational thanksgiving service in aid of new laws on marriage and inheritance, Chairman Rawlings stated that "God's glory . . . resides in us and we must allow it to shine among men." Moreover, since man was created in God's image, he could—as he grows more intelligent and develops individually—eventually project a more accurate and sharper reflection of the creator. Rawlings also argued that truth had been crucified well before Christ, and it was still being crucified long after Jesus had come among us. He continued, saying that "for our deeds to reflect the true image of God," we would have to discover and come to terms with our failings while trying to eliminate them.[106]

At times Rawlings would even go so far as to admit that he was preaching a ser-mon. For example, in 1986 his Easter address to the nation began this way:

> Fellow countrymen and women, we are coming to the end of the Easter ac-tivities. During this time, some of us have heard a lot of sermons, and I am sure that one more sermon will not break the back of anyone. But even if I preach a sermon tonight, it will be a sermon removed from the realms of [? sermons] where the body prepares a place for the soul. We want to deal with down-to-earth prac-ticalities. My brothers and sisters, it is considered correct and proper for human beings to reject, and when necessary, to destroy evil, vice, or anything that is un-clean. But man or human beings in their ignorance also tend to destroy, in fact have the tendency of crucifying the truth, virtue, or that which is Godly and good. And most often this is done as a result of ignorance. The most famous example I can give you was one time when I was invited to preach to some brothers and sis-ters. I said: Look up on the hill, the Calvary Hill I believe it must have been. And what do you see? They said Jesus Christ and two robbers. So I said: You see? There is Jesus Christ representing good, virtue, and truth and the two robbers repre-senting vice or that which is considered evil. And yet both have been crucified. As I have said, vice and virtue crucifies at the same time as a result of ignorance. . . .
>
> The centrality of Christ's message is justice. In fact, I have to admit that you and I have not done justice to the opportunities that have come our way. What is the meaning of the 31 December revolution? Was it a mere outburst against anti-social practices? No. The Revolution is a call to liberty, the liberty to be, to produce, to develop and enrich our Ghanaian African non-aligned posture. Was it not Christ who identified the criminal conspiracy of the money lenders, money changers, and money doublers? Why, in point of fact, am I speaking of the tremen-dous and formidable obstacles which stood in the path of Christ? . . .
>
> The PNDC is committed to achieving moral, economic, and spiritual excellence. . . .[107]

Regardless of the accuracy of his Biblical references or interpretations, it is nonethe-less striking that Rawlings felt comfortable enough as a preacher to explicitly adopt that role and to commit the PNDC government to "spiritual excellence."

Nor was the PNDC chairman shy about telling pastors how to go about their business. When addressing the closing session of the First National Pastors' Con-ference at Achimota School near Accra in 1987, Rawlings called on the clergy to try to contain the unscrupulously wealthy who would try to purchase elections for the District Assemblies. Rawlings further noted that "pastoral duties are those which reach beyond the church building, into the community with concern for both the spiritual and material well-being of the people in their day-to-day lives." Finally, he concluded by drawing a parallel between a pastor trying to develop the poten-tial of his flock and the PNDC. To his way of thinking, the PNDC was trying to create the basic conditions for Ghanaians to be their own shepherds.[108]

Finally, to return to a continuing theme of this work, one may discern a certain elision between pulpit and politics in certain aspects of the broader paternal dis-course in middle Africa. Perhaps because he was concerned about the amount of negative publicity his basilica had received, at the end of Ramadan in 1987

Houphouet-Boigny decided to present a mosque to the Islamic population of Cocody-Riviera in Abidjan.[109] Obviously, and very much in keeping with the preferred paternal metaphor and linguistic imagery that the regime favored, the account in the Ivoirian press noted that this "gift" from the head of state would of course inspire in the Muslim population feelings of gratitude toward Houphouet. El Hadj Tidiane Ba, who responded to the presentation of the keys to the mosque, noted that a mosque was first of all a place to gather and pray. In his words, it was also a "school where one taught the values incarnated by President Houphouet-Boigny, namely love of one's neighbor and tolerance." Here, then, we have both the paternal "gift" of a mosque and the notion that in this particular mosque the values that will be conveyed are those incarnated by President Houphouet-Boigny.[110] And, to be sure, there is a real sense in which middle Africa's more paternal rulers like to see that both their publicity apparatus and men of the cloth present them as gifts from God to a grateful nation and its children. In the words of Pastor Monsia of the Evangelical Church of the Awakening, "Houphouet-Boigny is a precious gift of God to yesterday's Côte d'Ivoire. And the Côte d'Ivoire of today is a precious gift of Houphouet-Boigny to Ivoirians." Then, further developing his theme, Pastor Monsia noted that "the word of God teaches us to obey the authorities. There is no authority that fails to come from God. And the authorities that exist were instituted by God. That is why those who oppose authority resist the order that God has established, and from this fact bring condemnation on themselves." These words, as well as the obvious confusion between the political and spiritual spheres that they reflect, could only have been music to Houphouet's ears.[111]

The Elision of State and Civil Society

An examination of the parameters of the political as they pertain to formal religion easily leads one to consider a different binary opposition, that which scholars have established between state and civil society. In the past fifteen years political scientists have "migrated" from a heavily focused concern with the state to study other topics they deem to lie beyond the state's analytical frontiers. Conventionally defined as the public space that exists between the state on the one hand and the family on the other, civil society—especially as it is seen to relate favorably to the process of democratization—has become a new intellectual shelter for many political analysts. Perhaps because of the relative ease of gaining access to certain organizations, many of these studies focus on urban-based associational life. Ecological movements, women's organizations, various professional associations, certain religious bodies, and non-governmental organizations are all topics that have attracted analytical attention. Many of these are important phenomena, while others are simply urban-based shells created to tap into funds from an international donor community that has embraced both democratization and civil society as concepts worth funding.[112] My intent is not to review thoroughly this voluminous body of literature.[113] Suffice it to say that although extremely useful empirical studies have emerged from this perspective, there remains the question of where one draws the line, theoretically and empirically, between the state and civil society. Where, in other words, are the parameters of the political?

Formal religion is in some ways an illustrative case in point. While formal religion presumably falls within the realm of civil society (at least in parts of the West), the middle African understanding and experience of its relationship to politics and power is quite different, as we have already seen. In 1984, for example, the Senegalese government midwifed the birth of an association of imams, the Association Nationale des Imams du Senegal (ANIS). The state's imprimatur was apparent throughout the association's initial meeting. The minister of culture, Abdul Kader Fall, presided over both the opening and closing ceremonies, and the closing ceremonies were attended by the usual collection of ministers, the diplomatic corps, and representatives of all the Islamic brotherhoods. Cardinal Thiandoum had also shown his respect by attending the opening ceremonies. In his remarks, Minister Fall underscored the significant congruence between this congress marking Senegalese Islamic unity and the national consensus that Abdou Diouf had articulated. For Fall, as for so many others, there was no opposition between church and state. This was a false problem because he saw no essential opposition between government and faith, and because God would always be involved in the affairs of individuals. The minister further stated that imams were both spiritual intermediaries and important factors in the maintenance of national unity. He also maintained that this new organization was not a copy of the structures of the state, but was simply a means of permitting the imams to contribute the weight of their religious authority more effectively. The minister did not see this as a conflict of interest because both religion and the government were interested in bettering peoples' lives. ANIS, furthermore, would enhance the already good relations existing between religious leaders and the head of state. Fall also expected the new association to help the state combat social scourges such as prostitution, alcoholism, and drugs.[114]

In 1984 the Ghanaian press reported a peaceful demonstration in Accra against the Ghana Muslim Representative Council (GMRC). It would appear that the major issue motivating the protest was financial accountability. Those demonstrating wanted the government's auditor general to conduct an inquiry into how the GMRC had spent its internal and external revenues since 1973. More specifically, one major item at issue was how the GMRC had spent its money on the annual pilgrimage to Mecca. The protesters prepared a petition for Chairman Rawlings which they presented to the regional administrative officer. That the demonstration was directed toward the government, and not toward the religious organization itself, indicates that analytical lines drawn between civil society and the state lack clarity and precision. It is quite clear that dissident Muslims seemed intent on bringing the state back into the affairs of the religious organization, and the very political actions of the protesters—a march, a demonstration with placards, a petition to the government—indicated that perhaps the actors themselves did not perceive a dividing line between the two realms. A clear elision of the purported boundary lines between church and state, and between state and civil society, exists in this and in many similar cases.[115] Such crude binary oppositions serve as guides neither to empirical research nor to theoretical understanding.

Labor and Business

Labor and business are two domains that most American and U.S.-based scholars tend to view as part of civil society. But in middle Africa, where the parameters of the political kingdom do not precisely coincide with the theoretical imaginings of Western social science, both of these areas are understood as falling well within the political sphere. Part of the reason for this is that the society's generalized paternal model of legitimate governance has thoroughly penetrated both areas. In Cameroon, as in other parts of the region, labor participates in the ritual acts of presence that are a necessary part of the local power game. When, on the occasion of the New Year, "the trade union [*syndical*] family of Mfoundi" presented its best wishes for the holiday to the prefect and head of the local section of the RDPC, its president used the ceremony to "thank the prefect for surrounding the trade union family of the Mfoundi with such solicitude since his recent assumption of office."[116]

The same pattern has obtained in Zaïre/Congo where, more often than not, the paternal pattern was quite explicit and affected most aspects of labor-management relations. A letter from a worker at Gécamines in Musoni to the president director-general (PDG) of the firm in Lubumbashi underscores the pattern: "We have come to launch a moving call to your paternal availability which you expressed personally during your visits of initial contacts with the workers . . . who greeted you warmly. . . . Mr. PDG, we no longer manage to eat more than 15 days out of 30 and when we eat, what accompanies our foufou? . . . [Salt and hibiscus from their compounds.] . . . We beg you because we can no longer support this rhythm of alimentation, despite our good will to serve the company, we cannot serve it without eating. . . . Forgive us, but we are counting on your paternal availability."[117]

Ordinarily in the private and parastatal sectors, labor and management are both part of the larger political family, and, as the examples immediately above demonstrate, there is no ambiguity as to who are the "parents," who are the "children," and who gets to "eat." Both labor and management have their assigned roles to play within this broad political family, and that helps to define the parameters of the political. In most such organizations, both public and private, there is an annual ceremony at which the management awards its loyal workers with medals marking five, ten, fifteen (and so forth) years of good and loyal service to the firm or the parastatal. Such events, like the periodic ordinations or other religious ceremonies, the annual presentation of wishes for the New Year noted above, and the administrative transfer of power from one representative of the state administration to another, are highly choreographed and ritualized with much consistency across both time and space. It is worth emphasizing that the decorations awarded at these ceremonies are state awards, and there is usually a representative of the relevant government agency or ministry present to do the honors and to present the awards to the meritorious workers. Refreshments are generally served, and in certain cases the event turns into a party for management, labor, and their families. In 1988 the awards ceremony at the Bank of Zaïre took place concurrently with the annual gathering to celebrate the New Year and to present the greetings and best wishes of the workers to the management and vice versa. The event occurred in the shadow of a difficult economic year during which there was some tension between management and labor. As is customary, the union shop steward (who at this time was still representing the state-controlled union structure that was part of the MPR) responded to both the festive atmosphere and the specific short speech of the bank's governor. He concluded his remarks as follows:

> Citizen Governor [of the Bank of Zaïre], during the year that has just finished, certain of your children would not have behaved themselves, perhaps, as good sons of this family and through their errors have wounded your paternal heart. We sincerely regret these faux pas and we apologize for them. Receive, Citizen Governor, this round of applause as a sign of thanks, as a request for forgiveness and, finally, as an earnest request for all you are able to do for us this year. Happy New Year Citizen Governor. Happy New Year Citizen Vice-Governor. Happy New Year Mr. Principal Director and Happy New Year to the entire family of the Bank of Zaïre.[118]

Many companies actively seek to advertise these ceremonies, paying for space in the local media. Sometimes these are labeled clearly as advertising, at other times they are presented as "publicity-reporting." What does not vary, however, is the general ceremony, the presence of the state, and the paternalistic overtones of the various speeches. The notion of the "family festival" is often invoked explicitly, and there is often a "family photograph" accompanying the story. One such Senegalese ceremony featured a representative of the Ministry of Labor to award the medals to the meritorious workers, as well as a noteworthy response from a representative of the workers. This employee of Sechoy and Company phrased his thanks in the following way:

> It pleases me to underline this burst of generosity because the management [la direction] that leads the destinies of this company has spared no effort so that a team spirit and agreement reign in our bosom, which favors and continues to favor this climate of social peace in which we bathe. This is why I seize this occasion to thank and to congratulate all those who contribute to this just cause. Our thanks are addressed most particularly to the senior father of our dear company M. Franchi for his devotion to the workers' cause, for his very elevated sense of responsibility, his constant solicitude and availability. If the company has arrived at this stage it is thanks to your personal determination. . . . I would not know how to terminate without thanking your dear spouse, Mme. Antoinette Franchi, who with her unquestionable clairvoyance has placed herself at your side with love and abnegation for the good operation [marche] of the enterprise.[119]

Comparable ceremonies elsewhere do not vary much at all.[120]

The strong structural resemblance between these business ceremonies honoring good workers, state ceremonies of installation or retirement, and the priestly ordinations that we examined earlier in this chapter are striking. All usually feature representatives and/or guests from other sectors; there is a "family" spirit displayed and explicitly evoked; and throughout there is an emphasis—sometimes directly stated as immediately above, sometimes simply implicit—on the notion of the good "father of the family" and his happy, loyal, grateful, and loving children. In addition, all three sectors (business, state, religious) sooner or later get around to underlining the importance of the main "players" as actors on the playing field of power, although the precise form of power may well vary. The continuities in these regards across time, space, and specific sectors (i.e., business and labor, the state, formal religion) are arresting.

Sports

Sports is another case in point. An important topic that occupies much popular attention in middle Africa, sports has thus far eluded the sustained critical scrutiny of political scientists concerned with this part of the world. It has escaped attention because, in the West, sports is seen as part of civil society. In this part of the world, however, ministries of sports abound, and the sector is thoroughly permeated with politicians and political issues, as the earlier treatment of the Zaïrian Leopards demonstrated. This subject itself warrants extended attention; here I confine myself to a few remarks to illustrate the larger point concerning the elision of the boundary between state and civil society.

In general, the state is in charge of the organization of sports in middle Africa. The relevant ministry is responsible for organizing domestic leagues for club play, setting the rules and regulations that govern both the matches and the organization of the various athletic clubs, and seeing that the country is well represented in important international competitions. The reach of the state in this domain is extensive, and virtually all states in the region have regulations on the books that ban from the playing fields ostensibly undesirable practices such as sorcery, although it is practiced quite widely. The relationship between, for example, soccer and politics is well understood, and many a wealthy but aspiring politician has used sports as a springboard into political life because of the visibility and celebrity that control of a major team can bring.[121]

The favorable publicity and other symbolic benefits that a successful national team can bring to a head of state are equally important. Delirious crowds, photo opportunities with the young athletic heroes, an infusion of national pride and national unity, and the declaration of unexpected national holidays can all become political advantages. In March 1984, for example, the Cameroonian national soccer team, the Unconquerable Lions, won the fourteenth Africa Cup of Nations in Abidjan. Never one to miss a good political bet, President Paul Biya declared a national holiday. Congratulating the players and their coaches, Biya called them all "worthy ambassadors of the Renewal," noting that this victory was the "work of the entire Cameroonian nation" and that the sporting triumph consecrated "the victory of the politics of National Renewal and moralization that we have been pur-

suing since 6 November 1982."[122] As Cameroon was in the midst of a difficult political transition, Biya shrewdly took the opportunity to present the ever-popular
Lions as the "ambassadors" of both the nation and his own political program.

The political advantages of a successful sports program, and especially of a winning national soccer team, are such that when things are going badly, the state will
try actively to improve the situation. In 1988 President Mwinyi spoke publicly on
Tanzania's poor performances in international competitions. Describing the national
team as a "madman's head on which everyone could learn how to shave," Mwinyi
suggested that Tanzanians were tired of merely being participants and wanted to
win. Since "sports is politics," he continued, the country's athletes were its ambassadors. That, after all, was why the government gave them a national flag whenever they traveled abroad to international matches. The president also suggested
that it was time for all of the concerned governmental and sporting bodies to follow up on the team's preparation. He then expressed the hope that the Ministry of
Community Development, Culture, Youth, and Sports could promote the standards
of sports in the country. More specifically, and in the words of the press account,
"Expressing confidence in Minister Fatma Said Ali and Principal Secretary Zahra
Nuru, President Mwinyi said women were good in up-bringing children and since
sports needed promotion the two ladies were able to face the challenge."[123]

From this account it is quite clear that Mwinyi assumes, and even goes so far as
to state, that "sports is politics." Two consequences flow from this. The first is that
Mwinyi does not seem to draw the boundary line between politics and sports, and
between state and civil society, where it is customarily placed in social science theory. The second consequence is that since, under this world view, sports is politics, the government needs no special rationale or set of circumstances to intervene
in the realm of sports since, by definition, it is part and parcel of the political kingdom and thus well within the parameters of the political. It is also apparent that
Mwinyi has implicitly understood and adopted the culturally valid paternal model
of the family in relating sports to a question of governance. We might speculate
that the implicit internal logic could be represented as follows: If sports is either
unthinkingly assumed or explicitly recognized to be part of the political kingdom,
then government has a legitimate writ to act upon it. But how shall it act? With
which model in mind? In this case it is clear that the family model is there and
plays a role. Because the relevant minister and principal secretary are women, and
thus by intuitive and unarticulated definition skilled at raising or "up-bringing"
children, they are therefore well qualified to raise and to "up-bring" Tanzanian soccer, thus elevating it from its sorry state of decline. The minister and her principal
secretary, therefore, since they are women, presumably have a writ to treat the prin-
cipals and participants in Tanzanian soccer as though they were children.

The prevalence and ubiquity of the paternal and familial model of governance
makes it extremely difficult to draw a neat line between politics on the one hand,
and labor and sports on the other hand. The assumptions—implicit and explicit—
of this political orientation suffuse such diverse domains as politics, state administration, foreign relations, education, labor-management relations, sports, and for-

mal religion. Where, in other words, do we draw the analytical line between church and state? Where, then, is the boundary line between state and civil society? Where are the parameters of the political in middle Africa? At this point, all I can offer by way of tentative and provisional response are the following concluding thoughts.

Conclusion

First, and most obviously, while there is much overlap between the parameters of the political in the West and those of middle Africa (i.e., the state and the formal political sector), there are significant areas of difference. Certainly, because of the nature of power in this part of the world, those who command formal religious powers occupy an important place on the region's political terrain that they might not enjoy everywhere else. The imams, priests, and pastors are political players, and most recognize them as such. They participate in the rituals of power along with other, more "secular," holders of power. In some cases—the Kenyan clerics, for example—their very theology impels them to become involved actively in overt political life. It thus becomes all but impossible to distinguish certain portions of theological doctrine from political thought because the overlap is considerable. And, as we have seen, politicians such as Rawlings and priests such as Monsengwo and Okullu do not hesitate to discuss deities from State House or to speak policy from the pulpit. Middle Africans understand that nominally religious power has important political consequences and so are wary of it while honoring it just the same. The "separation" of church and state becomes a rallying cry only when particular politicians, such as President Moi, do not particularly like what the clergy's political message is or when politicians fear that competition for resources based on confessional loyalties could become a factor in inducing violence and instability, as has occurred periodically in Nigeria. Except under these circumstances, "rendering unto Caesar" makes little sense either analytically or politically, and most of the time, therefore, it does not happen. The parameters of the political encompass a significant religious terrain that is an integral part of politics.

Second, when variants of the familial and paternal model of governance are applied, either implicitly or explicitly, to most areas of daily life it becomes exceedingly difficult to draw even an analytic line between state and civil society. Somewhat earlier I referred fleetingly to the intellectual "migration" of political scientists from a concern with the state to an increased focus on civil society. At the same time, there has been a second "migration," a conceptual one, that saw theoretical perspectives indigenous to Europe and North America travel to Africa. This conceptual migration has been far less visible and has not attracted sufficient attention. As scholars studied various aspects of politics in middle Africa, they brought with them a conceptual apparatus that was almost always based on implicit Western assumptions and models of life and on explicit Western definitions of key concepts and analytical categories. (And because of Western educational dominance throughout middle Africa, this has tended to be true of local academicians as well.)

In other words, although there are important exceptions such as Frederic Schaffer's work on the local meaning of democracy in Senegal, most scholars have assumed that their basic concepts had the same definitions in middle Africa as they did in the West.[124] They assumed both that binary oppositions such as church-state and state-civil society would also be relevant and that conceptual categories such as "civil society" would be ready templates with which one could examine and illuminate politics and political life. But as we have seen, the assumptions do not always work, the categories are not always relevant, and the conceptual definitions are occasionally out of focus because they were generated in a different context, in a different culture, and with a different set of assumptions in mind. Important theoretical and epistemological observations flow from this.

The first is that the putative universality of concepts initially generated, specified, and defined in the West should be examined carefully before we employ them to study politics in areas that have different cultural traditions and understandings. In Chapter 2 we saw that while various aspects of power as we commonly understand them in the West are certainly applicable and valid in middle Africa, others are not. The result is that the definition of power had to be adjusted to account for contextual specificities such as the political centrality of "eating," as well as for the presence, influence, and importance of the spirit world in the realm of politics. Covered in detail earlier, this point need no longer detain us.

The second observation is that Western political scientists have assumed, incorrectly and largely without reflection, that the very parameters of politics that they implicitly understood constituted a conceptual template that they could apply elsewhere without qualification. Stated differently, they assumed that the parameters of the political would be identical in different societies. Let me suggest both that this is not the case and that it does have consequences for what we study and how we come to understand certain political phenomena. Perhaps this will become clearer with some additional discussion.

U.S. citizens, like people elsewhere, grow up with—and are socialized into—a certain understanding of what is and is not political. As is true of most effective socialization, this lesson arrives in multiple ways, through a variety of disparate yet mutually reinforcing sources. More specifically, one reason many U.S. and other Western social and political scientists do not feel entirely comfortable with the subject of religion and politics is that we tend to operate on an implicit, unarticulated understanding that there is both a boundary line between the political and the religious and that we know where that line should be drawn. The United States is, by constitutional definition, a secular society in which there is a formal separation of church and state. So we assume—perhaps because our own lives tend to be secular, or perhaps because we, in the United States at least, live in a society where there is a formal separation of church and state—that there are in fact two distinct spheres of thought and activity: a secular, political sphere that is largely centered in the state and a religious or spiritual sphere that is largely centered in the church. The Biblical injunction to "Render unto Caesar" is then used as an unstated template for our work. In other words, it would then seem "natural" for people raised in this tradition to assume not necessarily that others would share it, but instead that there would be two separate spheres—politics and religion—and that while one could, and should, study how one sphere impinged on the other, one would not ordinarily be led to inquire whether in other societies the parameters of the political could include a substantial and important spiritual terrain. And, of course, we do study the influence of religious forces on politics, and the impact of politics on religion.[125] In each of these cases, however, there is an assumption that we are looking at two different kingdoms, each with its own set of intellectual keys. Although they can and do influence each other, we still treat them as distinct and autonomous spheres of activity.

This chapter has demonstrated that if one wishes to understand certain political and religious phenomena in middle Africa, then this perspective needs revision. Why, after all, should we make the a priori and unempirical assumption that most middle Africans share our views on the relative autonomy of the political and religious spheres of activity? Why should they even share our assumption that there are, in fact, two spheres of activity that are empirically and analytically distinct? Although there are likely to be substantial areas of overlap, the realm of politics, the contours of the political kingdom, may well vary in both time and place. The parameters of the political in middle Africa contain a spiritual terrain that is largely lacking in North America where, contrary to the Western European experience and the success of Christian Democracy, no seriously competitive political party bears a religious affiliation.

This point may become clearer with an example drawn from a different sphere. For example, are labor-management relations part of the "political" realm or do they fall under civil society? With the rare exception of national strikes, in the United States we assume that labor and labor-management relations are beyond the parameters of the political as we implicitly understand them, and this is reflected in several contemporary institutions. First and foremost, there is no serious labor party in the United States. In addition, and second, the absence of labor from our conception of the political realm is reflected in the organization of universities and the division of labor between academic departments and scholarly disciplines. A survey of ten universities, each containing one of the top ten departments of political science, indicated quite clearly that a student wishing to study the politics of labor, or the politics of labor-management relations, would be best advised to seek courses outside of the various political science departments. In fact, of the total number of relevant courses at these ten universities between 1992 and 1998, departments of economics, schools of business/management, history departments, and law schools all ranked above political science, which accounted for only slightly less than 9 percent of the total number of courses.[126]

The exclusion of labor from our understanding of the realm of the political may also be discerned, albeit far more impressionistically, in the organization of non-elite daily newspapers throughout the United States.[127] Typically, there is a news section (often divided into domestic and foreign), a business section, a sports section, and a "culture" section that will include things like the comics, the horoscopes, recipes, stories on women, religion, movies, television, and the other arts. Unless there is a major crisis of some sort (e.g., the disappearance of Jimmy Hoffa, the air traffic controller strike of the early 1980s), for the most part, stories that deal with the "political" are found in the "news" section while articles concerning labor-management relations are generally consigned to the "business" section. Editors simply do not see them as being "political" and thus do not place them in the "news" section.[128] In Western Europe and the United Kingdom, of course, labor parties do exist, and labor-management relations and related issues tend to be understood as being more "political" than they are in the United States.[129] In other words, the parameters of the political realm are not constant across time and space.

Finally, the third critical epistemological and theoretical observation pertains to the question Alasdair MacIntyre raised a generation ago: "Is a Science of Comparative Politics Possible?"[130] MacIntyre, of course, said no. At the time he was writing, MacIntyre adhered to a model of the political and social sciences drawn largely from the physical sciences, and so was looking for the formulation of cross-cultural, law-like generalizations that were capable of being explained by theory. If we subscribe to this definition of the sciences, and of theory, I suspect that the social and political sciences will never make the grade. Behavior is difficult enough to control in a political sense; for many of our most interesting and important questions, it is all but impossible to control in a scientific sense. In a manner of speaking, therefore, MacIntyre's response to the question he asked was enlightening but predetermined. But since I am a minimalist in matters theoretical, I prefer to follow Abraham Kaplan, who sees a concatenated theory "as one whose component laws enter into a network of relations so as to constitute an identifiable configuration or pattern."[131] The search for identifiable patterns and configurations across disparate cultures is possible, but a close attention to institutions is surely not the only procedure worth following.

MacIntyre also had grave doubts about what the pertinent units of comparison should be, arguing that a political party in one cultural setting was unlikely to be the same as a political party in a different setting. He then wondered skeptically whether this precluded valid comparisons and generalizations.[132] There are obvious and extraordinary differences between Mobutu's MPR and Tony Blair's Labour Party in Britain. This said, if we make careful allowances for the very different cultural, material, and historical contexts in which these two political parties find themselves embedded, then enlightening comparisons in the search for identifiable patterns and configurations are possible and may occur. But MacIntyre's concern over the unit of comparison remains apposite. While we may compare institutions such as political parties, state bureaucracies, and the like, we also need to expand the scope of our endeavors to include comparisons of our most basic concepts, such as power; cross-cultural comparisons of our conceptions and understandings of the parameters of the political; and, as we see in the next chapter, probing comparisons of our culturally different ideas concerning the fundamental forces of political causality.

4. | **Alternative Causalities**

Ordinary individuals, as well as sophisticated and powerful politicians, employ complex and contextually sensitive mixtures of different modes of political causality.[1] They display, in other words, several alternative understandings of the causal forces shaping political life. As we shall see, in this regard middle Africans are no different than anyone else, and three modes of political causality seem particularly relevant in this part of the world. First, there is the contemporary, modern, and scientific understanding of causality. During the Zaïrian political liberalization of the early 1990s, for example, Bishop Monsengwo addressed the reopening of the Sovereign National Conference in these terms: "On the contrary, we ourselves have not even yet begun, as a Sovereign National Conference, the serene self-criticism of our past, the reading of our history to discover the objective causes of the bankruptcy of our society so as to avoid them in the construction of our new political system."[2] Here we find implicit assumptions that there are "objective causes," that we may discover and then study them, and that such newly acquired knowledge can be used to construct solutions for the problems that have troubled society in the past. The rational relation of means to ends, the belief in the possibility of progress, and a notion of the validity of scientific or objective thought as a way to achieve this progress all undergird the bishop's remarks. Similarly, although it pertains to a far more mundane matter, one finds the same tacit perception of causality in the following remarks by Bell Luc René, secretary-general of Cameroon's Central Province, at the opening session of the 1985 annual congress of the provincial football committee. "Trainers and coaches," Bell underlined,

> must be educated to be able to teach the science of football. They must assert themselves and imprint a discipline and rational methods of work. As for the directors of the clubs, they must respect the distribution of labor within the club. Such respect, without doubt, will lead to the avoidance of numerous conflicts that tear

our teams to pieces. It is therefore not a question of directors setting themselves up as coaches. As for the players, they must impose a discipline on themselves and always bear in mind that they defend a cause, that of their club, their province, or that of their country.[3]

Football, like any human endeavor, may be approached scientifically by insisting on a rational division of labor within each club, the avoidance of conflict, hard work, and dedication. In this way the members of the club will realize their larger aim, presumably a championship.

A second understanding of political causality is spiritual and religious. In some cases, believers express this in a manner so that political or economic actions and their consequences flow naturally from either sin or virtuous behavior. In January 1992 the Assembly of Kinshasa (Catholic) Abbés conveyed a message from the pulpit of the Cathedral of Notre-Dame. Part of it reads as follows:

> How sad it is to have to ascertain that the political options taken by our society have been for a society without God. From whence [comes] the suppression of courses of religion, a bad conception of secularity, inversion of values, return to magical [*fétichistes*] practices, paganism and the cult of personality. All that has thrust us into a material and mental underdevelopment such that the country has truly become a Zaïre victimized by disaster. Underdevelopment is always the expression of sin, because it always goes in opposition to the growth of man's virtualities. The project of the Creator by definition tends toward an improved condition, a superior condition.[4]

Obviously, in this vision the causal explanation of underdevelopment has less to do with either comparative advantage or good governance than it does with the violation of God's laws.

At other moments when people use a spiritual and religious understanding of causality to analyze events, they often invoke a version of either the deity or its arch-antagonist to explain a political phenomenon. So, for example, in the immediate wake of the coup d'état that brought General Buhari to power in Nigeria on the eve of 1984, Habibu Shagari, a nephew of the deposed president, described the coup as "as act of God no one could have changed." Shagari's son, attorney Mukhtar Shagari, added, "It was God who gave Shehu power and it was he who took it from him."[5] In an attempt to crack down on what he termed "subversive activities" in Kenya, in 1982 President Moi told one crowd, in the words of the report, that "some people were misleading others not knowing that they will not escape from the ensuing chaos. He said subversive elements were people who were being led by the Devil, adding that everyone knows the Devil hates peace and was using his disciples to cause chaos in Kenya."[6] Do the Shagaris truly think the Buhari coup was an act of God? Does Moi really believe in the Devil? I do not know, but for present purposes it is not necessary to judge the sincerity of these beliefs. It is readily apparent, however, that they have resorted to an alternative form of political explanation and causality. Even if Kenya's president is completely cynical in manipulating the satanic imagery, we may still assume that as a shrewd politician addressing his constituents he has a certain purpose in mind. That purpose, more-over, is more than likely to communicate his political message to people in a causal mode they will have confidence in and understand. In making this argument and in subscribing to the notion of the satanic leadership of certain "subversive" ele-ments, Moi understands that many of his compatriots find this sort of religiously tinged political causality intellectually and perhaps spiritually congenial. Of course, it is also possible that Moi, a born-again Christian, also believes in the devil and the devil's influence on politics. Moreover, we also know that some devout Chris-tians in the United States explain acquired immune deficiency syndrome (AIDS) as a divine retribution meted out to sinners.

Sorcery, the darker side of power, is the third and final mode of causality and occupies the lion's share of our attention in this chapter. Many middle Africans un-derstand sorcery as a mode of causality because they are persuaded that the forces of the night exert an influence on daily events and national politics. People in all spheres of activity are sure that sorcerers and spirits play an important role in every-day life, influencing larger political outcomes and affecting individual life chances and one's various possibilities. A few initial examples will suffice. In the mid-1980s an article in the sports section of the Kinshasa daily *Elima* noted that things in Kisan-gani were getting out of hand. The article related:

> Decidedly, it will not be soon that we shall see our football divorced from magi-cal practices. In Afkis [the Kisangani football association], the open practice of [using] gris-gris [charms] has gone beyond the tolerable. [And] [t]hat in the view and in the knowledge of the referees and the directors of this association. . . . A recent case: Armed with great nerve, a director of a team began pouring more than a liter and a half of blood contained in a white plastic receptacle on the floor of the corridor of the locker rooms. Everyone who was to take his place on the plat-form of honor at Lumumba Stadium had to walk over it. . . . Evidently, the play-ers of the opposing team had to walk over it, for the area is an obligatory passage to reach the field. . . ."[7]

The intent, and the logic, appears to have been that if the opposing players trod through the blood, then the spell or magical properties of the blood would throw them off their game. The match ended in a one-one tie, and the journalist noted that it was the team that had resorted to the dark arts that did not play particularly well. As we shall see, although such beliefs and practices permeate virtually all ac-tivities, the sports pages—and especially the coverage of football—are important because sports is one of the few sociopolitical sites where one finds a relatively open and lively discussion of the occult.[8]

A second case comes from the Côte d'Ivoire in the early 1980s and pertains to a widespread belief that there are marabouts who are able, through their magical prowess, to multiply bank notes. (It should be noted that in this context a "marabout" refers not to a religious holy man, but to a master of the occult who may or may not be Muslim.) Moussa Koumbaré, a powerful marabout, enjoyed a reputation as someone who could bring about the multiplication of bank notes through magical means. When the wife of Sar Harouna, a gardener, fell ill, he sought out this marabout, who was also reputed to be a fine healer. He brought with him his savings, the sum of 1,225,000 CFA francs, in the hopes that Koumbaré's magical powers would be able to double the amount. After administering the requisite treatment to the bank notes, the marabout gave the gardener a package and told him not to open it for one week. At the end of that time, his money, newly multiplied, would be there. When Sar Harouna opened the package he discovered no bank notes. Subsequent inquiries turned up the fact that others had had more or less the same experience with the marabout, who had left town to hide in Upper Volta.[9] Of interest here is not so much the swindle itself, but the fact that its success was predicated on people's beliefs in an alternative form of causality and in a different form of power. The gardener acted on his belief in an alternative causality and, in this case, paid a steep price for it. It would be possible, of course, to dismiss this case merely as an example of extreme gullibility or simple ignorance. But this incident seems to me to be less about simple "ignorance" than it is about a clever charlatan recognizing that people who subscribe to an alternative mode of causality would probably find his larcenous propositions perfectly reasonable and logical.

To render the notion of these three alternative modes of causality more vivid, let us consider an election. The scientific, rational, and modern understanding of political causality might proclaim, "It's the economy, stupid," on the grounds that certain actions and conditions have predictable consequences that voters can rationally relate to each other. In the United States, for example, if the economy is flourishing, it becomes even more difficult to unseat an incumbent president. The religious mode of political causality might view the returns of any particular election as the result of God's will or intervention. And the third mode of understanding political causality might well see, and explain, the results of an election as being due to the fact that the victorious candidate was able to enlist to his cause enough of the most powerful sorcerers to have been decisive.

Middle Africans apply these three alternative modes of understanding causality to explain life's daily events as well as more dramatic instances of high politics. Furthermore, these alternative modes of explanation are by no stretch of the imagination mutually exclusive. People simultaneously hold complex, inconsistent, and often contradictory views on the nature of causality, which they weave together in a manner that emphasizes different causal understandings depending on the specific contexts in which they find themselves. In some circumstances they will see a political event as the result of a rational and predictable concatenation of events; in others they will explain a political event as a consequence of divine intervention; in yet another they will have no trouble accepting that the incantation of a powerful sorcerer caused a particular event. So it should not surprise us, to return briefly to one of the examples cited above, that Bishop Monsengwo could feel quite comfortable adopting a scientific understanding of political causality.

In a way, middle Africans select from a range of alternative modes of political causality much the way they choose among alternative Western and indigenous medical systems. In a fine study of medical anthropology in the Lower Zaïre region of that country, John Janzen found that although most people widely recognize the efficacy and utility of Western medicine and medical treatment at hospitals, indigenous doctors, prophets, and local cures do not necessarily disappear. In its proper context, indigenous Kongo medicine is every bit as commonsensical as the type of medicine purveyed at the local hospitals. For some illnesses, it is perfectly rational to seek the advice either of a herbalist gifted in pharmacological cures that make use of local plant life, or of someone with certain magical knowledge (*nganga nkisi*) who may be adept at treating diseases with emotional roots. Similarly, people recognize that an illness that does not respond to medicinal treatment is probably caused by conflict, tension, or hostility in human social interactions and may thus need a different sort of cure. People thus try, first, to discover the context of the illness and then to determine which form of health care (Western or indigenous) will produce the most efficacious treatment. In addition, people use the two systems concurrently by seeking relief from the symptoms of a disease at the hospital and then seeking the cure from the local healer who is better able to cope with the "causes" of the disease which may ultimately be rooted in the interaction of human emotions such as greed, envy, or jealousy. There is thus a system of complementary medical pluralism in which the two health systems exist side by side. In other words, there is no evidence that people who have been exposed to, and make use of, Western medicine believe that it will ever replace indigenous medicine or render it obsolete.[10] A comparable complementarity exists in Cameroon.[11]

In addition, at various times and in certain contexts, people have no hesitancy about mixing and matching both medical and religious cures. Emmanuel Milingo, the former archbishop of Lusaka, discovered in 1973 that he had a gift for healing. Through prayer and physical contact, Milingo was able to cure a Zambian mental and physical disease called *mashawe* that Western medicine often dismissed as psychosomatic or hysterical. The throngs who sought solace from Milingo's ministry both in Lusaka and more recently in his Vatican exile, probably had little difficulty in accepting, at least in the healing context, Milingo's belief in the occasional need to exorcise the devil.[12]

To avoid misunderstandings, let me state directly the argument of this chapter: Middle Africans choose from among these three modes of understanding and of interpreting political causality. Their choice of a precise mode is, more often than not, a consequence of the political or economic context in which they find themselves. At certain times, therefore, politicians will act on the basis of a scientific mode of causality as, for example, when they are interacting with representatives of the World Bank. At other junctures they may act, and reason, on the basis of a religious mode of causality. It is God's will that the poor suffer or that Senegalese *talibés* in rural areas vote for Abdou Diouf and the PS. At still other moments they may resort to hiring sorcerers to enhance their hold on power. These three modes of political causality coexist and are certainly not mutually exclusive. The epistemological implications of this for Western social science theory, and especially for political science, are serious. Starkly put, social scientists need to pay more attention than they have done to ascertaining whether there is a proper fit between their own theoretical assumptions about causation on the one hand, and the various alternative causal modes that the people they study actually employ on the other. In a probabilistic world, the closer the fit, the more likely a theory will explain and perhaps even predict various behaviors successfully. Various contemporary strands of social science theory thus need to accommodate, better than they have done thus far, the different alternative causalities that many individuals employ regularly.

Two caveats need attention. First, middle Africans are in no way unique in this regard and are certainly not the only people in the world who resort to alternative causalities. If one looks closely enough, various alternative causalities may be found to coexist in virtually all societies. And second, although I have chosen to present these three alternative modes of causal understanding because of their political relevance for middle Africa, one should not assume that these are the only three that exist either in this part of Africa or, for that matter, elsewhere. One example should suffice.

In the waning days of the Reagan administration (1981–1989), Donald Regan—President Ronald Reagan's former treasury secretary and White House chief of staff—was forced out of office. By his own admission somewhat bitter about his experiences in government service, this former chairman of the board and chief executive officer of the financial conglomerate Merrill Lynch published a scathing memoir of his frustrations in the White House. In his own words:

> Virtually every major move and decision the Reagans made during my time as White House Chief of Staff was cleared in advance with a woman in San Francisco who drew up horoscopes to make certain that the planets were in favorable alignment for the enterprise. . . . Although I never met this seer—Mrs. Reagan passed along her prognostications to me after conferring with her on the telephone—she had become such a factor in my work, and in the highest affairs of the nation, that at one point I kept a color-coded calendar on my desk (numerals highlighted in green ink for "good" days, red for "bad" days, yellow for "iffy" days) as an aid to remembering when it was propitious to move the President of the United States from one place to another, or schedule him to speak in public, or commence negotiations with a foreign power.[13]

Regan then suggested that this delegation of control over the president's calendar was critical because "the President's schedule is the single most potent tool in the White House, because it determines what the most powerful man in the world is going to do and when he is going to do it."[14]

The seer, Joan Quigley, agreed and was not shy about claiming responsibility for the timing of presidential press conferences, speeches, and travel arrangements. She also took credit for recreating Nancy Reagan's unfavorable public image and defusing the Bitburg crisis when Reagan was criticized for speaking at a cemetery in Germany that contained the remains of some of Hitler's SS troops. Quigley also claimed that her advice to both Ronald and Nancy Reagan on their images was the Teflon in the "Teflon Presidency." Furthermore, Quigley revealed that she was "heavily involved in what happened in the relations between the superpowers, changing Ronald Reagan's 'Evil Empire' attitude, so that he went to Geneva prepared to meet a different kind of Russian leader and one he could convince of doing things our way. Improved relations, *glastnost* and *perestroika* may, in some small measure, have come out of this."[15] In this context, astrology is an alternative understanding of political causality based on the positions of the heavenly bodies.[16]

The remainder of this chapter focuses on sorcery as an alternative mode of understanding political causality in middle Africa. After briefly defining the phenomenon, the following section traces the ubiquitous and important role of sorcery in various scenes of daily existence. The courts, family, and the treatment of women are all aspects of life that sorcery touches. I then devote attention to football, in which one can see clearly the impact of sorcery as a mode of explanation and causality. In addition, as suggested earlier, the sports pages of the daily newspapers are one of the few places where one can actually find a relatively open and honest discussion of sorcery and its effects. The discourse on sorcery contained in the sports pages is thus worth noting and makes certain aspects of this phenomenon appear in sharp relief. Finally, the last section presents a self-reflective and retrospective case study demonstrating how my own previous studies of Congolese/Zaïrian politics have offered explanations which, although worthwhile at times, nevertheless failed to provide a complete picture of certain significant aspects of political life. In doing this we temporarily abandon the ordinary realm of quotidian politics to focus on a type of high politics that occurs throughout middle Africa.

One final word of explanation. Because many Africans find discussions of sorcery and other related matters demeaning and distasteful, it has always been extremely difficult for political scientists and other social scientists concerned with national and international politics to discuss the effects of sorcery on politics and political understanding. Many African intellectuals think that these practices are "primitive" and are concerned that others will stigmatize them and their culture as "backward," "irrational," and "unscientific." Others, perhaps taking their cue from a legacy of Western missionaries, find sorcery to be contrary to Christianity. North American and European students of politics took their initial set of cues on this subject from their African colleagues, from African politicians who were consciously trying to build their nations and did not view such imagery at all favorably, and—especially in the United States—from the zeitgeist that accompanied the Civil Rights movement. None wished to propagate a negative image of Africa or her peoples, and, at least in Africanist political science, the scholarly agenda initially followed the political orientation of the first generation of nationalist political leaders. Today the scholarly community (African, European, North American) is more self-reflective and self-critical. Although anthropologists have long provided enlightenment about the importance of sorcery in village life and politics, in recent years they and other social scientists have extended their studies of sorcery and the spirit world by linking them to both the national state and other contemporary political phenomena. David Lan has enlightened us about the role of spirit mediums in the

Zimbabwean war for independence, and Peter Geschiere has shown us how sorcery is a thoroughly modern and contemporary phenomenon, as well as how it interacts with the post-colonial state in Cameroon.[17] Moreover, Achille Mbembe's stimulating integration of the "universe of the night" into his history of the Southern Cameroonian maquis and Comi Toulabor's work on how magic and symbolism contributed to Eyadéma's political power in Togo have also taught us much.[18] Because of the sensitively engaging work of these scholars, as well as the indisputable fact that alternative causalities are well distributed in time and space, a forthright discussion of such matters now seems possible.

The Banality of Sorcery

Sorcery is a notoriously difficult term to define precisely, and I do not spend much time doing it here.[19] Writing of witchcraft—and I use the terms *witchcraft* and *sorcery* interchangeably—one Kenyan legal scholar defined the concept and those who practice it as a "supernatural power" and "people who are possessed of, and practise such power," respectively.[20] In the view of a Cameroonian magistrate intent on bringing sorcerers to justice, sorcery is "being in touch with occult powers to do evil things, the art of producing, through certain practices, effects contrary to natural laws, the art of foretelling the unknown."[21] A Zaïrian columnist put it this way: "Sorcery is a universal phenomenon. Certain people possess, in effect, supernatural gifts, mysterious powers that they can put in the service of good or evil. Sorcery is spoken of when these powers are placed in the service of evil with the unique goal of hurting the entourage. That is why the population takes vengeance against the evil-doer when he is unmasked."[22] And a Cameroonian clergyman noted further, "The belief in sorcery is explained by the fact that the African being . . . wants absolutely to know the *why* of things. . . . [And] we can say that sorcery is due to *the fear of the future and the ardent need to know.* . . . Sorcerers are generally considered as the principal causes of sickness and death."[23] Sorcery, therefore, is about spiritual and supernatural aspects of pain and explanation—causing pain to others and explaining things to oneself. It is also, in some contexts, a means not only of causing pain but also of protecting oneself and loved ones from the pain and spiritual aggression of others. Finally, it is a means of effecting certain outcomes in the material world by actively precipitating the intervention of the spirit world. Under certain circumstances, therefore, sorcery might well be instrumental in obtaining a promotion or even winning the lottery.[24]

Sorcery in Daily Life

That organic intellectuals such as a legal scholar, a magistrate, a columnist, and a preacher would all have something to say about sorcery underlines its importance as a quotidian phenomenon.[25] Sorcery is an integral part of daily life for many middle Africans in both rural and urban areas, something the press reflects regularly. The illegality of sorcery dates from colonial times, and today various governments prosecute purveyors of the occult with differing degrees of eagerness. As in most societies, however, it is rarely the powerful or the wealthy who come in for legal scrutiny. Instead, to the extent that judicial authorities pursue such crimes, they tend to target the occult activities of ordinary urbanites and villagers. Press coverage of the courts thus provides a window on some of the daily dynamics of sorcery at the local level, as a few examples should illustrate.

In a case heard before a Ghanaian court, a man had lost two of his wives in a tragic traffic accident. Since sorcery is most often seen as the cause of such events, the widower suspected foul play and thus sought the services of an "herbalist" who, after consulting his oracle, came to suspect a woman residing in the widower's village. They then confronted the suspect, but she denied any involvement. They nevertheless forced her to endure a trial by ordeal to prove her innocence. As part of the ordeal, the accusers shaved her hair and smeared her body with charcoal powder. A rope was then placed around her neck; after some incantations, the rope tightened. At this point her accusers interpreted this tightening of the rope as a sign of guilt, and the herbalist and the widower declared her to be guilty of having caused the traffic accident through sorcery. The woman was later set free, and she then reported the matter to the police who arrested the herbalist, charging him with unlawful trial by ordeal. The court sentenced the herbalist to a C600 fine or twelve months' imprisonment in default. Others who were present at the ordeal received C200 fines or six months' imprisonment.[26]

In a similar vein, a police sergeant caught a Nigerian herbalist secretly reciting incantations at the entrance of a court in the hopes of affecting the court's deliberations in a case in which he was accused of having robbed his younger brother. The sorcerer pleaded guilty to the charge of trying to influence the legal proceedings through sorcery and threw himself on the mercy of the court. The magistrate sentenced him to six months' imprisonment at hard labor, intending this stiff sentence to deter others from trying to predispose the judicial system through sorcery.[27]

In Côte d'Ivoire, too, sorcery is illegal, and the early 1980s saw the passage of severely repressive legislation. In the words of the statute, "Is punished with an imprisonment of one to five years and a fine of 100,000 to 1,000,000 francs whoever gives himself up to practices of charlatanism, sorcery or magic, likely to trouble public order or to injure persons or property." The first trial under this statute concerned five individuals accused of killing the principal of a primary school. The accused were all related to the deceased and included a younger brother, an uncle, the widow of the victim's father, a cousin, and one other person whose relationship to the principal was not clear.[28]

Several different themes emerge from the reporting of these cases, as well as from many others like them. The first is the importance of family. It is not accidental that those accused of sorcery are often related to the victims of these occult practices. An account of a Senegalese case in the mid-1980s described the circumstances of Thianor Ngom's death. The somewhat circuitous story is that young Mbaye

Ngom, son of Malick Ngom, had been ill and bedridden for a long time. Mbaye's relatives accused his father of having bewitched the youngster so that he could steal his vital force. Two of Mbaye's cousins then decided to take matters into their own hands. They beat Malick Ngom brutally; under the pressure of this physical torture, he "admitted" that he had, in fact, stolen his son's vital force and had given it to Thianor Ngom. To salvage the honor of their family, two of Thianor Ngom's nephews then beat him to death.[29] In this tale, as in so many others, family members play a prominent role largely because sorcery enables a socially "acceptable" translation of some of the violent tensions and rivalries that oppose husbands and wives, fathers and sons, and uncles and nephews. Sorcery is, according to Bogumil Jewsiewicki, a principal means of social action that masks an insidious violence that is often directed against those to whom one is closest.[30]

The second theme that emerges from an examination of the usual presentations of sorcery appearing in the local press concerns the victimization of women. Women often find themselves on the receiving end of accusations of sorcery. Moreover, sometimes these accusations turn tragically violent. Northern Tanzania, for example, has repeatedly witnessed outbreaks of fatal violence against elderly women accused of practicing witchcraft. Villagers frightened of their alleged powers either hack them to death with machetes or turn their homes into funeral pyres.[31]

The third and final theme that emerges from these cases is the very banality of the phenomenon. Sorcery is portrayed as an everyday affair that touches the lives of villagers and urbanites in numerous ways. When the law is invoked and the courts are involved, as they occasionally are, judgments come down against those segments of society that have the least power, the least wealth, and thus the least ability to insulate themselves from the power of the state. There is a double standard is at work here that involves social class and political standing. There is ample evidence that many powerful politicians believe in sorcery and at times may even practice it, but they are not the ones who are brought before the courts and accused of charlatanism or disturbing public order. Several examples illustrate the point.

President Moi may decry publicly the practice of sorcery and the lynching of those accused of it, but there is evidence that some Kenyan parliamentarians have been known to practice, or place their faith in, the darker arts. The Kenyan state, however, does not appear to waste much time pursuing such police inquiries in the halls of Parliament. Furthermore, and in a related vein, throughout the 1980s and 1990s there have often been indications that the KANU state itself has promoted ethnic violence when it has suited its own purposes of either remaining in power or appropriating more wealth. When Mombasa was wracked with ethnic violence in 1997, resulting in scores of deaths and thousands of displaced people, the police finally called a press conference to announce that they had arrested a seventy-three-year-old sorcerer whom they had charged with casting a spell on nine of the suspects involved in the violence. Two of the nine were KANU activists, but the real architects of the violence went unpunished. Parenthetically, I need scarcely add that a police investigation that trumpets at a press conference the arrest of an elderly sorcerer who had cast spells causing others to engage in violence demonstrates quite clearly the belief in an alternative understanding of political causality.[32]

Similarly, although Ghanaian courts may fine herbalists, while briefly out of power in the early 1980s J. J. Rawlings objected to a commission of inquiry being formed to investigate him and declared his willingness to go to any fetish shrine in the country with his accusers so as to establish the truth. Rawlings stated that if his request to do this were granted, he would invite all of Ghana's political leaders since 1966 and "those criminals to go along with him and we shall see who will die."[33]

Nigerian politicians and legislators may also draft laws outlawing sorcery of various kinds, but that says nothing about their own beliefs or the place that sorcery might hold in them. For example, in the waning days of the Shagari administration in 1983, federal legislators in Lagos were stunned to discover that one of their number had discovered certain "charms" in their official residence on Victoria Island. The cleaning help of one of the legislators had discovered a large gourd with a black object in a plastic container. After touching the object, the janitor developed a sprained arm and was taken to the hospital for treatment. Several of the lawmakers protested, claiming that they would not move into their flats until they had been thoroughly disinfected.[34] The pervasive fear and caution concerning "magical" objects and fetishes also speaks to an implicitly held alternative understanding of causality. What "caused" the cleaning help's sprained arm was not awkward or strained movement, but rather having touched the magical object. What, then, would be the effect of this understanding of causality when it is applied to the political realm? How does sorcery affect legislation? Are Nigerian politicians and legislators—at least some of them—operating on the basis of an understanding of political causality that in no way resembles the implicit understandings of political causality that undergird Western theories of legislative behavior? And what are the implications of this for Western political theory?[35]

Sorcery and Soccer

On 14 June 1984 Bobutaka, the celebrated striker and high scorer of Zaïre's Vita Club, died in the middle of a match against Matonge when he was tackled by the goalkeeper just as he was about to register a goal. One of the subsequent commentaries in the press began with the headline query, "Who Killed Bobo?" To be sure, the press coverage explored why there was no ambulance on the field, why other medical facilities were lacking, why team authorities permitted Bobo to play even though he had been suffering from headaches for several days, and why the terrain was so uneven. It also mentioned the "mentality" of the players and the team officials, a veiled reference to occult forces. Despite the attention to these diverse factors, it is nonetheless significant that the headline query was not "Why Did Bobo Die?"; not "How Did Bobo Die?"; not "What Caused Bobo's Death?"; but "Who Killed Bobo?" That the press would pose the question in this manner speaks to the salience of sorcery in the world of Zaïrian soccer.[36] In searching for the causes of Bobo's death, the headline may be read to indicate either a primary belief in malevolent agency rather than in a scientific understanding of disease, or a religious understanding of divine predestination and providence. Under the assumptions of either mode of causality, there is room for neither coincidence nor chance. In consequence, explanations emphasizing conspiracy also abound.

The influence of the occult on soccer has long been a subject of lively debate and concern throughout middle Africa. On one level, all governments subscribe to the international rules and standards that categorically prohibit such practices. On another level, however, especially when there are international championships at stake, high-ranking government officials either look the other way or cooperate actively in facilitating the presence of sorcerers in the game. In all cases, this has occasioned much debate throughout the area.

The Rules

In virtually every African state, sorcery is strictly forbidden in the realm of sports. Various international governing bodies prohibit it; no state wishes to see its teams disqualified from international competitions because of it. Most states usually delegate the enforcement of these rules either to the Ministry of Sports or to the local football federation that organizes competition between clubs in the first division and is ultimately responsible for the selection of a national team to represent the country in important international competitions. For example, the Zaïrian Ministry of Sports published the official rules of its football championships in 1980. They were unambiguous on the question of sorcery, and the banner headline read "Fetishistic Practices Are Prohibited!" Article 12 was formal on the subject: "Any club surprised in flagrante delicto of fetishistic practice as much on the field as in the sporting installations will lose the match by forfeit. Whoever observes a case of fetishistic practice on the field, in the sporting installations (halls, toilets, locker rooms, locales, etc.) or in the immediate vicinity of these must instantly inform the commissioner of the match who will proceed to the verification of the facts and will make note of them in his report."[37]

The Zaïrian ban was well in line with the international prohibitions of the day. The African Football Confederation (AFC) sent a circular to all member states in late 1979 indicating that it would no longer tolerate certain practices. More specifically, the AFC declared that it would penalize any "superstitious" teams participating in its competitions. The circular was signed by AFC secretary-general Mourad Fahmy and stated that "superstition and other (*juju*) practices not only create useless confrontation between teams and officials but also harm the formation of the youth and the affirmation of their personality." In consequence, and in an attempt to put paid to "these harmful practices," the confederation's Organizing Committee decided that henceforth all prematch formalities had to be conducted in the locker rooms. And to give the measure some teeth, the AFC further declared that any team that refused to go into the locker rooms would not be permitted to play and would forfeit the match. The reason for this new regulation was that visiting teams often believed that the premises had been bewitched and that if they set foot in the visiting locker room at the opponent's stadium, they would expose themselves to the harmful influences of the other team's sorcerers and magic charms. These fears were so widespread, and teams were so wary of exposing themselves to the malevolent influence of sorcerers before a match, that visiting teams often refused to consume the food and drink that their hosts provided for them for fear that they would be ingesting magical potions that would detract from their performance.

A report generally approving of these rules in the Tanzanian press noted that one Kenyan club had published a balance sheet showing that it had spent several thousands of shillings on witchcraft. And, until it had been stopped, the Tanzanian national team had traveled with a *jujuman* officially dubbed "Discipline Officer."[38] The Senegalese Football Federation also found these measures commendable. Its then president, Amadou Abdoulaye Ba, noted that "the passion, indiscipline and a mystical inclination have exceeded permissible limits."[39] Or, as Ydnekatchev Tesema, Ethiopian minister of sports and then president of the AFC put it, "If there is a scourge that we must combat with energy in Africa, it is sorcery [*fétichisme*] in sports. It is not admissible that in the middle of the twentieth century one can see manifestations of gris-gris [charms], of amulets, that perturb the regular unfolding of competitions." He continued, noting that youth "had to have confidence in themselves and not in sorcerers or other dark forces to claim to obtain results."[40]

In the early 1980s it was widely known that many African club teams, as well as the national sides, openly resorted to sorcery and magic. In 1980 Just Fontaine, coach of the Moroccan national team, was interviewed in the Senegalese press. When asked if he was afraid of gris-gris, talismans, or other magical charms, he responded categorically: "Not at all." When asked if such items could influence the result of a match he was equally abrupt: "If that had an influence, Africans would have been champions of the world for a long time."[41] But this facile reply masks a host of beliefs, practices, and social tensions that social scientists cannot dismiss lightly. If the rules prohibiting sorcery are clear, and they are, it is equally clear that they have usually been honored only in the breach. When the AFC met in Cairo in 1988 in an attempt—in the words of a Tanzanian editorial—to "restore the game's bright image," "superstitious beliefs in the game" were still a major problem.[42] And in 1998, after the fall of the Mobutu regime, the sports ministry of the Democratic Republic of the Congo urged its national soccer team to avoid magic charms and sorcerers in their competitions for the Africa Nations Cup. The cabinet director at the ministry, Emmanuel Mukaz, urged the team to respect the Ten Commandments, to perform honest work, and not to touch any fetish. He added, "There is plenty of proof that fetishes cannot help us win. For example, during the World Cup in 1974 a whole plane was sent filled with witch doctors and it created a lot of trouble."[43] Of course, such a statement would not have been necessary had the ministry official been confident that his team was uninvolved in such practices.

The Practice

Throughout middle Africa it is simply assumed that football clubs and national teams will resort to the darker powers to enhance their athletic performances on the field. An article in the Senegalese press, for example, relayed an account of a Ghanaian victory in a semifinal match in the 1982 Africa Cup of Club Champions tournament between Asante Kotoko of Ghana and the Senegalese Diaraf club that occurred at Kumasi, on Kotoko's home field. Adopting a restrained and mournful tone, the account lamented that it took the Senegalese team five hours to clear customs and that the Senegalese directors were involved in a physical set-to with Ghanaian soldiers at the airport. Furthermore, "the entrance formalities were very simply pitiable for the players were all deprived of their things [objets] including their amulets."[44] Noteworthy is that only passing and tangential mention is made of the "amulets" of the Senegalese players and the fact that the Ghanaians confiscated them. So common are amulets and other such magical paraphernalia that it was just simply assumed that the players possessed them and that these would be something for the opposing side to target in an attempt to affect the psychological climate and thus the eventual outcome of the match.

One Zaïrian critical commentary from the early 1980s noted that belief in magical charms and fetishes was widespread because there were "naive people" who put their faith in their "mysterious efficacity." The article lamented that among the believers in such matters were political cadres and even intellectuals, and that most clubs in Kinshasa had formed "research committees" to find individuals who, for a serious sum, could harness the occult to facilitate happy results for the club. Once the right person was found, the mysteries of the spirit world resided in the pockets of the players, in magic handkerchiefs, and in pots that were jealously guarded in the locker rooms. These things, the author lamented, rather than training and hard work, now dominated the Kinshasa football league.[45]

Teams elsewhere also seek to exploit the power of the occult, and the press in Côte d'Ivoire has documented that clubs in Abidjan can spend large sums on sorcery. For example, in the early 1980s the annual published budgets of many clubs candidly listed the salaries of the teams' sorcerers as an ordinary budgetary expense. In general, this expense tends to rank behind stadium upkeep, players' salaries, equipment and health, and the coaches' salaries. But the sorcerers do rank ahead of transportation and "diverse," and the phenomenon of sorcerers involved in the sporting life is so well accepted and understood that there is little or no effort to hide such things. In addition, the director of one Abidjan football club noted that he could spend 200,000 francs CFA on sorcerers before a local match and that this figure could be multiplied by five before an African international competition.[46] There are, in other words, serious financial interests involved, for the sorcerers themselves seem primarily motivated neither by the love of the sport nor, in the case of international competitions, by feelings of national pride. Echoing the situation in Côte d'Ivoire, a 1982 inquiry in Zaïre noted that "the most reputed sorcerers [*féticheurs*] now form a bourgeois class. . . . On the eve of [a big match] a 'marabout' can easily bring in Z10,000 without counting the [other] material advantages if his prognostications come about. And as the appetite develops while eating, they become versatile, blackmailing the leaders of the teams."[47] Sorcerers do not ply their craft for free.

That material interests play a role in these matters was also apparent in the stance taken by the Ivoirian Association of Sports Medicine in 1982. After meeting for a seminar of reflection, the association noted with great regret that there were still many clubs in the Ivoirian Football Federation that did not employ a medical team. They also denounced the fact that sorcerers received better treatment at airports and hotels than did the members of the association, and that even when a team physician was present, he usually had less influence over the players than the sorcerer did. The association particularly objected to sorcerers who used concoctions of unknown origins to induce vomiting several minutes before a match.[48] The association's protest, in other words, seemed to be about money, status, and science. Money, insofar as the doctors were unhappy because there were still teams that did not employ their services in sports medicine; status, because even when they were employed, they were not often listened to and, at times, were stranded at airports or in hotel lobbies while everyone else made a beeline to consult the sorcerer; and science, because they sought to maximize the potential benefits of a scientific medical approach to the medicine of football and thus found the presence of sorcerers throughout the various Ivoirian teams somewhat "backward," although they did not use that term.

Knowledge and tolerance of sorcery in soccer often reaches the highest levels of the state. In the aftermath of "Côte d'Ivoire 84," an international tournament at which the home team, the "Elephants" of Côte d'Ivoire, exited from the competition before people had expected them to, Minister of Youth and Sports Laurent Dona Fologo granted an interview to the local press. Even though the Elephants had not been successful, the minister was still pleased with the results of the tournament because he was able to make President Houphouet much more aware of the importance of football than he had been previously. "With regards to football," Fologo stated, "the President today is a new man. He knows that in Africa it is a powerful instrument of social, moral, civic, and political education. It is a phenomenon which gathers peoples together, something a man of politics cannot be indifferent to." He then added that another positive consequence of having hosted the championship was that all Ivoirian leaders had realized that sorcery had run its course and had to come to an end in Côte d'Ivoire. The minister as much as admitted that during this tournament the "pursuit" of sorcerers to influence favorably the outcome of the matches had been "excessive, expensive, and destructive." No more. "I consider that there is only one 'fetish' that is worth the effort to worship: that is work," he said. "The player must be in physical condition . . . [and] must be technically and physically capable. . . . There is no more place for sorcerers, most of whom are in reality intelligent swindlers who know how to exploit a situation of naivety and disarray of which we are often the victims."[49]

Fologo's stance against these practices in Ivoirian football did not result in their disappearance, as he himself recognized in an interview several years later: "But after a small lull, I see that believers in sorcery have returned even stronger. I can affirm that the last two matches of Africa [an Ivoirian club] in Côte d'Ivoire were not spared from these practices. If fetishes could make a team win, Africa would be the world's champion. But we are last!"[50] The pressures—political, moral, economic—in favor of sorcery are considerable. In 1989 the then president of Stella Club of Abidjan spoke to the press about some of these matters. "Finally I realized," he said,

> that at Stella, there are people who are fundamentally nasty, adept at occult practices and always ready to work against the interests of the club. A [club] president who leaves never leaves a clean place. He wants whoever succeeds him to fail, so that he can be rehabilitated. . . . Today, you see, I have been pushed toward unsportsmanlike practices. I have been forced to do fetishes. Finally, each director has his [own] sorcerer and his [own] player. All the sorcerers neutralize each other to the point that when they predict a score in our favor, it is registered against us. What do you want me to say? Many people who pretend to be with us, in fact work against us.[51]

Many club presidents feel pressure to succeed and thus feel obligated to seek every possible means to improve the performance of their teams. Even if they themselves do not believe in the efficacy of sorcery, it is almost certain that some of their board directors, financial backers, trainers, coaches, and players do.[52] Or even if they do not, they are at least agnostics on the subject who nevertheless wish to hedge their bets in case all of the physical conditioning, tactical training, and shrewd player personnel maneuvers do not bear fruit. Even players may well feel pressure to conform to these practices when they, themselves, may not actually believe in sorcery. Joseph Antoine Bell, a Cameroonian goalkeeper who played in Côte d'Ivoire during the 1980s, noted: "I detest the fetish as I detest the lie. Sorcerers are my enemies. I am able to put up with them sometimes, perhaps to please the [club] directors. . . . And it is difficult for me to believe that a man who does not even know what it is [a football] can help me to play better."[53] In football, as in politics, people resort to alternative understandings of causality depending on the particular context of the moment. Moreover, there is no reason to assume that people are in any way adverse to entertaining—or at least tolerating—several different alternative understandings of causality at the same time, just as they seem to have no difficulty in believing that different sorts of health care systems can coexist without problem. The nuanced views of Gbonké Martin, Bell's coach, illustrate this: "The 'fetish' is psychological. But the players have understood that work pays more. You see Lébry: he has returned to his best level through incessant work! The psychological support of the 'fetish' is real, but it can in no way come before serious work which is the unique path to success."[54]

The Discourse

Middle African discourse surrounding the role of sorcery in soccer is extensive, appearing regularly in the sports pages and, from time to time, in popular literature as well. Although there are some variations, many of the discussions describe in scathing terms the activities of the sorcerers while deploring the substantial influence they wield. In general, they are ashamed of the image this presents to the outside world, and they argue for a more "scientific" or "rational" approach to the game. Although this discourse is invariably written from the perspective of those who would like to abolish sorcery and is thus not a genuine debate, it nevertheless both frames and distinguishes clearly two distinct alternative understandings of causality. The following extract from one of Nigerian columnist Achike Okafo's essays is indicative:

> There is an attitude which a good many Nigerian sports men and women seem to have now which often proves to be their bane in competitive sports. Only very few of them seem to believe that their success or failure in a given competition is in large part dependent on, and determined by their proficiency, requisite skills and adequate preparation or lack of these. Often times, you hear in sports circles discussions bordering on fetishism and ridiculous superstitions. There are now in our forward lines players who before a football match begins demoralise themselves with negative thoughts. They believe, for instance, that they can't score a goal except they kick the ball from a particular point. . . . That's all because some haggard-looking fellows with no ideas of the dimensions of a football pitch nor the rules of the game have made some wild claims. . . .
>
> There have been instances where contestants refuse to subscribe to the familiar courtesy of handshakes with their opponents, in some sports because of their pathological fears and illusions that are totally inexplicable in the light of reason and common sense. . . .
>
> Even at the National Stadium, we witness some bizarre ceremonies that border on occult practices being carried out to the embarrassment and shame of spectators. What has football to do with pigeons and rabbits that these are introduced into fields of play in the event of a contest? What are those dishevelled men with long chewing-sticks doing in our field of play? It has now reached such ridiculous limits that certain sports men and women would not want to participate in events that are fixed on certain days of the week or months of the year. . . .
>
> However, to make any significant mark in sports we need a reorientation in our attitudes to competition, to cultivate greater confidence in the abilities and endowments of man to perform, and rely on a more rational basis for analysis in event of victory or defeat, not a blind faith in the talismanic efficacy of relics. . . .
>
> Away with those phoney beliefs, I say.[55]

These passages clearly indicate this contest pits "skills," "preparation," and "proficiency" on the one hand, against "ridiculous superstitions" and "negative thoughts" on the other. One side is full of self-evident "common sense" and "the light of reason," the other is prey to "pathological fears and illusions." The rational and the phony are locked in struggle. While Okafo offers no physical description of the forces of light, one may reasonably infer that they look better than the "haggard-looking" and "disheveled" champions of darkness.

The same one-sided discourse deploring the influence of sorcery and the spirit world on the world of soccer is also present in many accounts of Zaïrian/Congolese football, and popular literature often echoes the press. One of Zamenga Batuke-zanga's novels, *Sept frères et une soeur* [Seven brothers and a sister], describes a football match in the following way:

> The suspense was total with ten minutes left: the two teams were still tied. Who is going to win? In the two blocs thus formed, one noticed with surprise beings dressed strangely in raphia. They could be seen spitting mouthfuls of palm wine mixed with chewed kola nuts; at certain times, one could see a type of mud leaving their mouths that they spit in the direction of the players. It was whispered that these bizarre beings were the representatives of some very celebrated *nganga nkisi,* or sorcerers. Thanks to their magic, the *nganga nkisi* made the legs of the players that they supported lighter, more supple, and also quicker than those of the others which got heavier, becoming incapable of scoring a goal.[56]

An account in the press blamed officials of the Kinshasa Football League (LIFKIN) for such sorry spectacles as the one Zamenga describes above: "Since instead of using its authority to block the road to the grave-diggers of our football who camouflage themselves behind chimerical practices, LIFKIN seems to act in connivance with them. We have for proof football matches played at the 20th of May Stadium during which the locker rooms are taken by the assault of armies of sorcerers."[57] After reiterating that success in sports rests with serious training rather than with "charlatans," one commentary castigated a "dishonoring" display that occurred during the halftime of a major match between two of the dominant teams in the league (Vita and Imana). "The lawn momentarily liberated by the players was, in effect, invaded by imposters who paraded with an infernal rhythm, going out and then returning in turn, one with a goblet, one with a packet of fetishes that they ostentatiously dumped in the goals. Even the poor nets would have given in under the snout thrusts that these 'nganga' inflicted on them."[58]

One Zaïrian football coach with a degree in physical education argued that fetishes and magical charms just were not going to do the trick when the country was confronting "technically evolved football." And, according to this particular observer, the deep belief in the influence of sorcery was a cause for concern among those who possessed "a scientific vision" of the future of football.[59] A Zaïrian social scientist, however, notes that those involved in the various facets of football may not actually perceive a dichotomous opposition between a belief in sorcery and a more scientific approach to the game: "Major sports teams see there [in sorcery] the key to their victory to the point that before an important sporting event, they will retire from the course of habitual life accompanied by a sorcerer who completes, through mystical and spiritual training, the tactical and technical training which has already been accomplished."[60]

As we have seen, sorcery—as well as the alternative understanding of causality it incarnates—is an everyday occurrence in middle Africa. Its impact is easy to spot in the local courts, as well as in football and other sporting events.[61] In this regard, therefore, it is a completely banal phenomenon affecting people in both rural and urban areas. In some ways the influence of sorcery on high-level national politics throughout the region is equally banal yet has been much less obvious even to serious political analysts. In the following section I reflect on certain aspects of politics in Congo/Zaïre to explore why this has been so.

The Perils of Explanation in Congo/Zaïre

Political life in the Democratic Republic of the Congo (DRC, formerly Zaïre) has always created difficulties for even the sturdiest theoretical frameworks of the political and social sciences. The Congo's size, diversity, complexity, and rough-and-tumble politics have usually defied parsimonious explanation. To be sure, deft students of Congolese politics have produced some noteworthy theoretical analyses—both intelligently elegant and "thickly" descriptive—and their substantial contributions have certainly added to a progressive cumulation of knowledge.[62] Nonetheless, theoretical shortcomings remain. In addition to the empirical complexity of Congolese politics, there is another reason why our theories have come up short. Put simply, most of the theoretical frameworks that Western social scientists have generated make certain implicit culturally based assumptions about causality and explanation, about the parameters of the political, and about the nature of power itself. And while these assumptions might make perfect sense in the cultural contexts in which they were originally derived, when confronted with Congolese realities they have often seemed either seriously incomplete or slightly out of focus.

This section explores alternative notions of causality, explanation, and power, arguing that political scientists need to think systematically about the occult and the role of supernatural forces in politics—topics that our political theories either dismiss or, more usually, simply fail to consider because they lie beyond our culturally specific understandings of where the parameters of the political are actually located. I also argue that our predominantly Western social scientific theories are often based on an implicit understanding of causality that may, at times, be quite incongruent with the causal assumptions of Congolese political actors and that if we are to understand political behavior more fully, we need to pay greater attention to these usually tacit understandings of the contours of the political universe and of the causal forces which shape it.

The Disclosures of Mobutu's "Liberalization," 1990–1997

When President Mobutu announced the end of the Second Republic in April 1990, the political landscape changed virtually overnight. New political parties, new newspapers, and other outlets for the free expression of political ideas appeared almost immediately. In addition, at least for the relatively brief moment of its existence during 1991–1992, the work of the Sovereign National Conference also encouraged a public sharing of information and ideas that Mobutu's single party, the MPR, had never permitted. It seemed as though the newspapers were filled with astonishing revelations almost daily. Congolese from all walks of life embarked on a still incomplete process of trying to discover, understand, and explain what had happened to their country during the years since independence.

The political ramifications of these disclosures concerning the actual operational methods of the Mobutu regime were substantial and certainly contributed to a politically poisonous atmosphere. Even the most fervent Mobutists soon concluded that the regime had lost any semblance of political legitimacy. While the eventual emergence of Laurent Kabila as the Congo's new political leader after seven months of armed insurrection certainly surprised most observers, by late 1996 and early 1997 there was no longer any doubt that the Mobutu regime was living on borrowed time.[63]

The continuous stream of new disclosures during the 1990–1997 "transition"— in effect, new data—have forced me to rethink and to confront certain theoretical and epistemological shortcomings in Western social science in general, and in some of my own small contributions to the study of Congolese politics in particular.[64] As an illustrative case in point, I begin this examination of alternative causalities with a brief biography of a major political figure of the Mobutu regime, Dominique Sakombi Inongo. I focus on Sakombi, a onetime pillar of the Mobutist political order, for two reasons; first, because he was a powerful politician who was at Mobutu's side during much of the Second Republic; and second, because his public confession prompted me to reevaluate some of my previous analyses of Congolese politics.

Sakombi Inongo

Although Sakombi was born in Kinshasa in 1940, his maternal language was Lingombe and his family had roots in Equateur Province among the Ngombe people living along the Mongala and Congo Rivers. His father was a fisherman, and he had a Catholic upbringing. He attended secondary school in Kinshasa with the Scheutist Fathers and later continued his studies at Louvain and then, from 1961 to 1965, at the Free University of Brussels (ULB). He returned to the Congo and in 1966 began his professional career as an instructor in the faculty of medicine at Lovanium University in Kinshasa.[65] His entry into the political world occurred while he was at the university, and for a while he held both his position at Lovanium and that of principal secretary (Chef de Cabinet) of the minister of information. Sakombi's political star rose with Mobutu's, and, as an *originaire* of Equateur who was well connected by birth and education, he soon came to occupy several important positions in the Second Republic. He became Mobutu's minister of information in 1970 and was thus the spokesman for the government. Two years later, in 1972, he also became the national secretary of the MPR for propaganda, information, and the press. Moving easily between the various interrelated arms of party and state, Sakombi held the position of minister of national orientation from 1973 to 1975.

Sakombi then served a stint as a member of the national legislature from 1975 to 1977. A nonelective office, the position required neither that legislators campaign for reelection, nor that they attend to the needs of their constituents; nor were they to advise or criticize the Mobutu government. Even drafting legislation was not a high priority in a regime where the president's spoken words literally, and immediately, became the law of the land. Sakombi was thus able to take on the position of regional commissioner (governor) of the city of Kinshasa from 1976 to 1978. In addition, he also served for a time as secretary general of the party youth wing, the JMPR, and Mobutu twice named him as a member of the MPR Political Bureau (1974–1976, 1981), which, after Mobutu himself, was the state-party's preeminent decision-making forum. Sakombi returned to the government as information and propaganda minister from 1983 to 1985, and Mobutu later named him Congo's ambassador to France and the United Nations Educational, Scientific, and Cultural Organization (UNESCO) in Paris. His next posting was as Congo's ambassador in Dakar. He then returned to Kinshasa, and the Cabinet, in 1988 as minister of information for the third time. Although he left the government in January 1990, he was still named to the MPR's Central Committee.

At other points in his political trajectory, Sakombi served as the president-general of the Association of Former Students of the Scheutist Fathers, an influential grouping of many of the regime's important political figures who hailed from Equateur Province, and along the way Mobutu named him as a grand officer of the National Order of the Leopard—another significant political honor and status marker during the Second Republic. He was, by any reckoning, certainly among the "best and brightest" of the Mobutist political order; an influential and powerful politician; in the words of the Kinshasa street, a *grosse légume* [bigwig]; and a well-recognized "Baron" of the regime.[66]

As minister of information and propaganda, Sakombi had the job of singing the praises of the Guide and Helmsman of the Authentic Zaïrian Revolution, the Father of the Nation, Mobutu Sese Seko—something he did loudly and often. He was a modern-day griot of the single party, a praise-singer in the employ of, and politically dependent on, his political master. For example, in describing Mobutu's frequent trips around the country in the 1980s, Sakombi wrote that "the Guide knows what pleases the militants of the MPR, he knows thoroughly their most secret aspirations." These trips, he continued, have "an immense value. And, especially, they permit this prodigious man to know his country and its inhabitants to perfection. Thus, better than all of us, the Father of the Nation knows what is most suitable for his people."[67]

After Nguza Karl i Bond, a former foreign minister and member of the MPR Political Bureau, broke with Mobutu and went into exile in the early 1980s, he wrote an accusatory memoir entitled *Mobutu: ou l'incarnation du mal zaïrois* [Mobutu: or the incarnation of the Zaïrian sickness]. This work presented a critical and seamy picture of life in the upper reaches of the regime. The prominence of corruption, as well as the influence of sorcery, poisonings, and other unsavory doings—especially among an informal grouping composed of Mama Mobutu and the wives of other high-ranking officials known as The Syndicate—were all detailed.[68]

Sakombi, then momentarily out of power, wrote a short book in direct response to Nguza's attack, *Lettre ouverte à Nguza Karl i Bond* [An open letter to Nguza Karl i Bond], in which he criticized Nguza for projecting "an image of Zaïre close to the clichés of the ethnologists of a short time ago. That of an African multitude, cut off from all intellectual heights, barbarous and possessing no awareness of its destiny." Sakombi obviously seized on Nguza's recitation of the sorcery, magic, and political machinations of Mobutu's mandarins and their spouses but rejected them as an unseemly and misleading subject for discussion—implicitly likening these tales to those once told by colonial ethnologists intent on presenting Congolese as "backward" and "primitive." He also reminded Nguza of the passionate discussions and debates—presumably quite modern, intellectual, and rational—in the MPR Political Bureau.[69] For his efforts in this matter, Mobutu welcomed Sakombi back into the upper echelons of the regime.

At the time I wrote a review essay, jointly examining Nguza's memoir and a social scientific study by three Belgian economists.[70] I argued that "despite obvious dissimilarities, there [was] a fundamental sense in which the explanatory tasks [were] identical." As far as Nguza's work was concerned, the review noted only that his account of The Syndicate was "fascinating and all-too-brief." Nowhere, however, did my review mention the use of sorcery to maintain influence. Furthermore, at least for me, the work ultimately "[fell] short in its analytic task" because it focused "almost exclusively on the symptoms of the Zaïrian sickness [in other words, Mobutu] without setting us in search of the cure."[71] On the other hand, I lauded Bezy and his collaborators in these terms:

> In stark contrast to Nguza's single-factor analysis and diagnosis of the Zairian sickness, . . . Bezy . . . although addressing the same problem, stresses entirely different explanatory variables, follows a very different—and deeper—line of inquiry, and is ultimately a vastly more satisfying analysis. The authors' research perspective tries to avoid a simple conjunctural analysis by exploring "the coherence, change and movement of a given socio-economic system, the specific articulation of its subsystems, and the contradictions, mutations and structural continuities of this system since the colonial period" [Bezy's words]. And herein lies the great strength of this book; political events since independence are analyzed and evaluated in light of Zaire's social, economic, and political evolution since the early colonial period. We are thus better able to see, and perhaps understand, how a Mobutu could have been produced.[72]

In retrospect, it seems clear that my own unstated assumptions concerning the nature of political causality blinded me to the possibility of alternative causalities. It is not that the economists were wrong and that Nguza was right; nor is it that sorcery and the power that comes with it explain everything. But it does, in certain contexts, explain some things. Equally important, and as Nguza's memoir illustrates, under certain circumstances political actors make decisions, determine policy, wield power, and implement political action on the basis of an implicit understanding of political causality in which the spirit world plays a critical role. More specifically, this is most likely to occur either when they try to influence or understand immediate events, especially when these are uncertain. Sorcery finds its political niche in helping people cope with contingencies and in helping politicians pursue and defend power.

Sakombi related that sometime in 1990 God visited him and that, in consequence, he converted. He broke with Mobutu shortly thereafter, and in 1991 he founded a church called The Voice of God. During the next five to six years he traveled across Zaïre and Europe, attending prayer gatherings and religious conferences where he confessed the magical practices that he had embraced to curry favor with Mobutu.[73]

Thus, in April 1992, two years after the political opening, a newly penitent Sakombi came forward. At a "national day of repentance" organized by prayer groups and independent ministries of the city of Kinshasa, the former Mobutist baron and erstwhile defender of the old order bore witness to his involvement in the *ancien régime*, naming names and providing details on many of the regime's abuses and excesses. Such public confessions are not unique to Congo, and we have recently witnessed similar phenomena in South Africa and a number of post-authoritarian societies. At an open-air gathering of roughly ten thousand people, Sakombi spoke of the political importance of magic and sorcery in the highest reaches of the Mobutu regime.

A contrite Sakombi maintained that beginning around 1971 Mobutu had cast a series of satanic spells on the people of Zaïre, which kept them politically quiescent, their loyalty to his regime unquestioned and assured. He testified that the regime had dumped tons of "mystical products" into the River Congo at its source in Katanga to achieve this political effect. Furthermore, according to the former minister, this scheme was why the regime banned the importation of all foreign beers during 1976–1978. In this manner, even the wealthy, those who could afford to buy imported beer, would be obliged to drink the local products and would thus be politically bound to Mobutu and incapable of posing a threat to his continued rule.[74]

Political scientists rarely consider these sorts of data and generally assume a political world governed by a different set of causal forces. As a case in point, my own earlier fascination with the political economy of beer in the town of Lisala certainly operated in light of a different understanding of political causality. While I did note that "political legitimacy and stable beer prices would thus seem to go hand in hand," the explanatory connection emphasized the fact that—in the words of a bureaucratic memorandum—the "stability of these [beer] prices ensures the confidence of the population in the Father of the Nation" and that political unrest might ensue if people did not have an assured supply of beer because important aspects of local social life such as weddings (bridewealth), funerals, and just plain socializing depended on it. If the beer did not flow, then people might well become unhappy and choose to blame the government. The causal link, in other words, was a political-economic one between an ample supply of cheaply priced beer and political quiescence.[75]

Both my logic as well as my unstated and unexamined assumptions about causality were the same as far as the international dimension of the question was concerned. Although I can unearth nothing I wrote directly about the ban on the importation of foreign beers, the following comment is illustrative of my thoughts at that time: "From a national perspective, beer-belly dependency poses a dilemma for the regime in power. Zaire cannot afford to spend $15 million per year on its beer industry [for imports of hops and malt] at a time of financial crisis. Such expenditures do nothing to end the crisis and contribute to a further evaporation of the state's precious supply of hard currency."[76]

My analyses were not wrong, but they were incomplete, missing as they did a significant dimension of the politics of beer. Moreover, I would now also maintain that the reason they were incomplete was because the theoretical orientations I was immersed in (political economy, social-class dynamics, bureaucratic politics, cultural pluralism) all shared a dual shortcoming. First, they simply did not consider the possibility that sorcery was important to understanding politics at the national level. Sorcery, after all, was beyond the parameters of the political as they were implicitly understood in most Western social science. And second, they failed to recognize, even as a hypothetical possibility, that Congolese political actors operated, at least part of the time, in a world with a substantially different understanding of causality and causal forces than most Western social and political scientists possess.[77] Once in the field, immersed in Lisala's bars, I gradually learned the important effects of sorcery and spirits on local life.[78] The prevailing scholarly paradigms, however, assumed a different universe of political causality—one that neither conceived of the possibility nor encouraged the application of this localized knowledge of sorcery to the realm of social scientific explanation.[79] Had I been more attuned to the importance of sorcery as an alternative mode of causality, I might well have sought to explain—at least in part—the politics of the 1973 Zaïrianization of the economy in those terms. The local acquirers might have made use of the dark arts to insure that they would be among those chosen to take over the European-owned commercial houses. They might also have explained their success, or failure, in those terms. But that hypothesis simply did not occur to me.[80] So "natural," so powerful, so hegemonic are the unstated assumptions of causality in the prevailing paradigms that it never dawned on me that this was something worth questioning. Nor did it occur to me that there could be one or more alternative causalities.

At the same open-air prayer meeting, Sakombi also spoke of how Mobutu's new national anthem, La Zaïroise, came to be adopted as part of the regime's political campaign for cultural authenticity. Sakombi testified that this song was adopted under satanic conditions. He was told to go to the OAU Village in Kinshasa to pick up the musical scores from an important "marabout" (or sorcerer), and then to take a plane to collect the members of the MPR Political Bureau and bring them to Mbuji-Mayi. He further relates:

> I had taken the bewitched scores, had put them in my briefcase, then I went to look for the members of the Political Bureau: Madrandele, Ileo, Nzondomio, Kithima and others, without them knowing anything about this. . . . Before leaving, I had recited the prayers that I had been told to say over these scores. Finally, I distributed them in the room. The members of the Political Bureau were astonished, asking what this was all about. But in touching the paper, they were bewitched. Thus all these old men began singing like children. This was recorded and that tape was bewitched again. Thus when it was played on the radio, all the people began to sing. . . ."[81]

My own analysis of a small portion of the Mobutist state's campaign for cultural authenticity agreed with neo-Marxist analyses in their emphasis on the regime's desire to protect the interests of the dominant politico-commercial bourgeoisie and also noted that the imprecision in many of the key concepts (*révolution, radicalization*) probably contributed to the continuing "'mystification'" of the Congolese people. "None the less," I wrote,

> neither of these analysts adequately addresses the fact that the notion of *authenticité* has been grasped not only by the political leadership . . . but by many ordinary folk as well. The idea of an authentic way of doings things, of a recourse to ancestral customs, as well as the concomitant pride in these traditions is one of the striking achievements of the Mobutu régime and should not be minimised. Zaïrians are now proud of their heritage, and this is no little change from the currents of thought relevant both in the First Republic and in many other parts of the continent.[82]

In other words, and at the risk of belaboring the point, while seeing the authenticity campaign as a cynical mechanism of political control and domination in the hands of a ruling bourgeoisie intent on maintaining its privileged position, I also understood it as a manifestation of cultural nationalism, or of nation-building. The new national anthem was part of that. But sorcery and magic did not enter into the explanatory equation. Nor did my analysis pause to consider that such a "cause" would be worth exploring were the relevant data ever to become available.

Sakombi's public testimony is also remarkable for the alternative notions of causality it displayed. Present and intermingled were assumptions that both the dark forces of the occult and the power of divine intervention could and did result in certain political outcomes. Sakombi's belief in divine intervention was also present in an interview he granted in late 1997. His political touch still deft, after the fall of the Mobutu regime Sakombi reemerged as one of Laurent Kabila's confidants, for a time even managing communications and public relations in the president's office. When asked to explain how an architect of "Mobutism" such as himself happened to arrive at Kabila's side, Sakombi replied that his political orientation under Mobutu was "satanic." After his conversion, however, he saw Kabila's liberation of the country as "an instrument of God." "God told me," he said, "that I should bring my spiritual and political contribution to President Kabila and the AFDL" (Alliance des Forces Démocratiques pour la Libération du Congo). In describing one of his early meetings with Kabila, Sakombi transmitted to Kabila the message "that I had received from God concerning him. That is what I did, in revealing to him notably that the prophetic destiny of the DRC and his mission at the head of our country as the chosen instrument of God for the realization of the marvelous plan that God had for the DRC."[83]

Other Evidence

Sakombi's confession is only an illustration. Other former officials also came forth and testified publicly.[84] Not all, however, freely admitted their failings. Some made use of the recently unshackled newspapers to castigate Mobutu. In these cases the format was often a bitter and accusatory "open letter" to the president. Nendaka Bika Victor, a former minister and once head of the political police, wrote such a letter to Mobutu. Resentful at the way he had lost his position in the government, Nendaka publicly resigned from the MPR, rebuking Mobutu for the humiliating way the regime had recalled him from his last post as ambassador to West Germany. Initially placed under house arrest, he was subsequently exiled internally to Equateur Region. "During my detention," he wrote, "I lived a situation which was at least unusual, namely that they took my blood, my fingernails, my hair and God alone knows what they did with them. It goes without saying that this may be placed [se situe] in a direct line from the false legend stating that Nendaka would have to, if only for twenty-four hours, exercise the functions of the head of state."[85] The unstated but nevertheless clear implication is that sorcerers used his blood, nails, and hair to create either a potion or a spell that would preclude his ever superseding Mobutu.

The reports of the Conférence Nationale Souveraine (CNS) detailed similar machinations and comparable accusations at some length. Many of these were cast in the idiom of witchcraft. In May 1992, for example, Jacqueline M'Polo Ekonda, the widow of Maurice M'Polo, who had been assassinated in 1961 with Patrice Lumumba, testified before a committee of the CNS in these terms: "It must be said: our politicians, as veritable vampire-humans, live only from blood. At night they do not sleep. At night our politicians organize assassinations and seek whom to kill. That is why they have chronic insomnia and even hallucinations. They spare no one: young and old, civilians and soldiers, pagans and Christians . . . all pass over. Whose turn will be next? Who will be their next victim?"[86] Given the belief in sorcery as an alternative form of political causality in this part of the world, we may reasonably assume that many who heard her testimony interpreted it quite literally.

Published accounts of the nexus of sorcery and politics, often without the religious overlay, also began appearing during the early 1990s. Emmanuel Dungia, a former agent of the regime's security services, published two books which detail at some length the influence of sorcerers and other occult powers in the politics of the Mobutist state.[87] He maintains, for example, that Mobutu's marabouts habitually accounted for 3 percent of the government's budgetary expenditures—which was more than the Health Ministry received. Additionally, he notes that marabouts helped to prepare Mobutu for his meetings with foreign heads of state. When Mobutu met French president François Mitterand in 1981, this preparation was not a briefing in a conventional sense but rather consisted of the marabouts' active intervention to make sure that Mitterand would be prevented from acting to destabilize Mobutu's political power. These magical preparations included Mobutu gently walking on a picture of the French president that was sitting on a leopard skin; Mobutu peering at a photograph, concentrating with all his force on the eyes of his diplomatic adversary while pronouncing a certain formula; Mobutu placing his cane on Mitterand's picture before going to bed in the evening; and Mobutu avoiding sex for three days before arriving in Paris for the summit meeting. The meeting was a spectacular success for the Congolese president. At a time when Mobutu feared that Mitterand, a newly elected Socialist, might review France's policy of support for his regime, he and the French president met in an atmosphere that was reasonably cordial. This diplomatic success, however, came at a price. The marabouts received more than $4 million and some gold bullion for their efforts.[88]

In addition, the marabouts were also pressed into national service after the second invasion of Shaba/Katanga (Shaba II) in May 1978. In this case their powers were enlisted to help seal the borders, rendering them invulnerable against further rebel incursions. They accomplished this by slitting the throats of sheep and uttering the appropriate ritual incantations over the spilled blood at designated border positions. This, too, depleted the state's coffers. But it is at least conceivable, since there was no Shaba III, that Mobutu and his minions believed that magical blessings and blood of the lamb were sufficient to safeguard the national territory against further invasions.[89] It can almost go without saying that maraboutic briefings and preparations before a summit meeting are scarcely consistent with contemporary theories of international diplomacy, bargaining, and negotiation as political scientists in the West have elaborated them. Preserving the territorial integrity of the state through incantations said over bleeding sheep is similarly beyond the scope of the theoretical explanations that international relations theory provides.

Finally, Congolese have long appreciated that there is a link between money and political power. In the Congo, however, a popular understanding of this connection is not necessarily consistent with the perception of the political role of money most commonly found in treatments of interest-group or electoral politics in the West. For example, many reports have noted that at least some of Mobutu's political power derived from the magical effect that certain symbols on the national currency had on the population, thus further reinforcing the president's hold on high office. One commentator and occasional correspondent affiliated with the Catholic Faculty in Kinshasa argued that the five million zaïre banknotes that Mobutu had introduced into general circulation possessed a "diabolic spirit" and that people should reject the currency for that reason. "In effect," he wrote, "take one of these bills and observe: placed there are two curious signs of the cross generally utilized during black masses by high-ranking Indian hypnotists and by the priests of the 'Prima Curia.' This satanic spirit is conveyed by these cursed bills through the horrible and lugubrious effigy of the man from Gbado-Lite with the insolent look. . . . There is in these bills an evil spell-casting spirit."[90]

Moreover, many Congolese (and other middle Africans) are certainly aware that the president's portrait on the currency has an importance transcending its role either as symbol of the nation or as a manifestation of a cult of personality. It also speaks to a certain type of power and political surveillance. One newspaper column expressed it this way:

> Hasn't it always been said that everything Mobutu's enemies say, he knows it for he is always with them? It is true that one must be insane to believe that in the fact of carrying Zaïrian money on one's person, the Field Marshal-President is watching you. But during the reign of President Mobutu many acts were accomplished under the effects of the devil. It is why the marabouts hold a preponderant place in the life of the Field Marshal-President. But all leads us to believe that this is the reason why President Mobutu had the 20 makuta banknote with the picture of Prime Minister Lumumba on it disappear.[91]

In this light we should be able to see that Sakombi's seemingly simple hagiographic statement cited previously—"the Guide knows what pleases the militants of the MPR, he knows thoroughly their most secret aspirations"—can also be understood as a thinly veiled and rather chilling allusion to Mobutu's powers of political surveillance. Mobutu was, after all, always with his compatriots in the form of his portrait on the national currency. This presence gave him the ability to hear political opponents plotting against him because they always carried "His" money on their persons. It seems apparent that the theoretical principles of mainstream, Western neoclassical economics do not readily permit an appreciation of the role of currency in political surveillance. Nor does orthodox economic theory lead us to consider the possible economic or political effects of a bewitched banknote bearing magical symbols connoting black masses and satanic influence.[92]

This alternative understanding of the use of the currency is also at odds with political scientists' visions of the state, their perceptions of state's role in intelligence gathering and political surveillance, and their views of how the state coerces its citizens. In an earlier study of the Zaïrian state I examined the Mobutu regime's political police. The relevant chapter analyzed the tasks of this secret organization: coercion and control, information gathering, and symbolic reassurance to the regime's politically insecure ruling class.[93] What I did not appreciate then, and am frankly only just beginning to see now, is how sorcery and the world of the spirits were enlisted into, and became part of, the state's surveillance mechanisms, as well as parts of its coercive and repressive arms. The empirical evidence was there, but the prevailing theoretical orientations toward the state common in the West did not enable me to focus on it with any clarity.

For example, although I noted that the Kitawalists, a religious group that had withdrawn from all contact with the state, refused to accept any national currency, it did not occur to me why the one exception they allowed—the old twenty makuta note that bore the likeness of Patrice Lumumba—was significant.[94] At the time I was writing, it seemed that refusing the rest of the currency because it had Mobutu's portrait on it was merely a symbolic way of demonstrating their disaffection and disdain both for the state and for the specific person of the ruler. It was that, of course, but it was also a great deal more. We might now also hypothesize that the Kitawalists' refusal to accept currency with Mobutu's portrait indicated a fear of exposing themselves to the magical powers of surveillance that the currency imparted to Mobutu. Clearly based on an alternative understanding of causality, this hypothesis remains, at least for the moment, untested. For my purposes here, however, it is sufficient simply to note that it is not a hypothesis that Western political and social scientific paradigms of politics and the state could have produced because their unstated assumptions and understandings of the relevant causal forces in politics are rather different.

Other Visions

Sakombi's testimony, and indeed the entire thrust of this chapter emphasizing the banality of sorcery in middle Africa, raises several possible objections. Let me address them directly. First, critics might object that this analysis is far too anecdotal. There are three lines of response to this criticism. The first is simply to restate the old adage that according to a certain experiential scholarly wisdom, the plural of anecdote is data. This reply need not detain us. Charles Jones, however, advances a second, more compelling response in a review essay dealing with some of the memoirs that emerged from the Reagan administration in the United States. Writing in the context of American politics, Jones argues that when they are well done, memoirs (such as Donald Regan's discussed briefly earlier) can provide additional and previously unknown details on important political events; they can illustrate the strategic thinking of an administration; they can show the interactions among high-ranking policymakers; and they can offer perspectives on the high and mighty that differ from those in the media. Although Jones deplores the specific problem of the "inside tidbit" such as the revelation of astrology in the White House, he still argues that memoirs should not be dismissed out of hand.[95] His position is ultimately one of skeptical mistrust that requires verification, a stance whose scholarly caution I appreciate.

A third possible response to the charge of "anecdotalism" is simply to ask, "What are data?" Data, of course, do not exist independently of the theories that generate them and order them into meaningful theoretical and explanatory patterns. Our tendency, therefore, would be to dismiss Sakombi's testimony, as well as Dungia's revelatory memoirs, as mere anecdotes when they provide information that our usual theories of political behavior cannot account for or accommodate comfortably. But if our theoretical orientation recognizes the existence of alternative understandings of causality that people do act upon, then Donald Regan's revelations about astrology in the Reagan White House become data. The same may be said of Sakombi's testimony. The better our theories, in other words, the more likely it is that scholars will come to see that certain "insider tidbits" and "revelations" are data when seen through a conceptual lens that is able to infuse them with analytical meaning.

Two further examples from Uganda should demonstrate the point. In 1991 the Kenyan press reported that Uganda's President Yoweri Museveni had argued publicly before a London audience that sorcery was the reason that demand for cotton (one of Uganda's major crops) was so high. Sorcerers had brought this about by ensuring that whoever wore clothing made from synthetic materials would develop a skin disease. Museveni was further reported to have stated: "As a result, our witchcraft has forced Europeans to abandon synthetic materials and to return to cotton." The article that relayed this information took a rather dim view of these statements, editorializing that this is something "modern-day" Africans do not wish to be associated with and that "Museveni's remarks will not do much to erase any image Africa may have as a backward and superstitious continent."[96] Similarly, in 1998 the international media reported that the Ugandan government had arrested a witchdoctor because he *failed* to warn security officials that the rebels of the Lord's Resistance Army (LRA) would attack the town of Rackoko in northern Uganda. A member of the security forces stated, "We arrested him because he predicted that the LRA would attack Rackoko but instead of informing us, he kept quiet." During this particular attack, one civilian and one soldier were killed, and thirty people were reported abducted.[97]

These two incidents are anecdotes only if one does not have a theoretical orientation capable of recognizing them for what they, in fact, are: demonstrations of the political potency of an alternative understanding of political causality. Museveni would appear to understand the success of Uganda's cotton crop on the world market and in international trade not so much as a function of a competitive price, or of better quality, or of a comparative advantage, but rather as being due to the work of a team of Ugandan sorcerers. The president of Uganda, in other words, advanced a different explanation that presupposed an alternative understanding of causality. The second incident speaks to the same point. The witchdoctor was arrested not because he used his dark arts to predict an LRA attack, but rather because after predicting the attack he refrained from sharing his foreknowledge with the state's security apparatus. If one's scholarly inquiry is guided by the tenets of our usual and accepted theories of the state, or of rebellion and revolt, or of neorealist international relations, this is a "colorful" anecdote that has no meaning within current intellectual parameters and is thus dismissed. If, on the other hand, one can admit the possibility of alternative causalities, then the reasons why security officials took the sorcerer into custody become explicable. Their job is to protect the security of the state, and in keeping his prediction quiet, the sorcerer—in their view—had committed a grave infraction. It is unimportant whether scholars believe in the accuracy of such predictions. Personally, I do not. What matters in explaining political behavior—in this case, the decision of the security forces to arrest this individual—is that *they* believe in these predictions and act on them accordingly. Analysts who fail to consider the causal assumptions and understandings of the people whose political actions they are trying to explain run the risk of completely misunderstanding the wellspring of political behavior.

A second possible objection to the line of analysis in this chapter concerns the veracity of the sources cited. For example, are Sakombi's accounts true, and how can we know this? Let us break this question down further. Did the Mobutu regime really dump tons of "mystical products" in the Congo River? And if so, what specifically were they, and did they have any demonstrable effect—chemical, political, or otherwise? Did Mobutu and others around him actually believe that this action would create ties of political loyalty between ruler and ruled as people consumed beer brewed with the treated water? Even if the products were not placed in the river, was Sakombi persuaded that this had nevertheless happened, and was he, therefore, telling the truth to the best of his knowledge? Regardless of whether this or other comparable events actually occurred, is there a significant portion of the population who believe that such events are possible and occur frequently, and who undertake their own political action in light of that knowledge?

Regrettably, I cannot answer all of these questions. I do not know whether the authorities truly filled the river with "mystical products." If they did, I do not know what these were, or whether they had a demonstrable effect on people who were exposed to them. Nor, unfortunately, can I say with any certainty whether Mobutu and his mandarins actually believed that brewing beer with "treated" water would forge bonds of political loyalty between the father-chief and his people. Here, however, it strikes me as a most reasonable suspicion that more than a few high-ranking officials might well have entertained these—or similar—sorts of beliefs. But, to be candid, although it is a strong suspicion, I cannot be absolutely certain. Was Sakombi telling the truth about this, as well as about the other incidents to which he bore witness, at least in the sense that he was speaking openly and to the best of his knowledge? I think so. What, after all, would have been his motivation to lie? He claims to have undergone a religious conversion, and there is no reason to doubt his sincerity. To be sure, in a most cynical way, in the early 1990s he might have simply wished to distance himself from the obviously failing Mobutu regime. And while such an explanation is possible, other former political barons did this in more conventional ways by simply pointing to the regime's corruption and the pervasive economic regression that had occurred under Mobutu. Had this been Sakombi's desire, he could have easily done the same without the magical mystery tour. While there is obviously ample room for disagreement in this matter, I do believe that Sakombi's testimony had the ring of sincerity. But in a fundamental way the answer to the last question posed above, in many ways the easiest of the questions, renders moot all such speculation. Regardless of the whether the incidents actually occurred; regardless of whether Mobutu actually believed in sorcery; regardless of whether Sakombi's testimony was sincere; it is absolutely certain that there are large numbers of Congolese and other middle Africans who believe in sorcery and thus would have been prepared to accept explanations for familiar political phenomena (such as the new national anthem) that were rooted in the alternative causalities that they lived with every day and that were thus accepted unthinkingly and without further examination. Furthermore, at least in the Congolese case, Mobutu and his regime used these beliefs, and the fear they inspired, to promote political quiescence in the face of increasing repression and declining economic well-being.

The epistemological implications of this seem rather large. Depending on the context, theoretical explanations need, at the least, to take into consideration a political world in which there are alternative and quite operative notions of causality at play. Moreover, and in consequence, all causal theories will need to be examined for how well they cope with these alternative causalities. Critics might object that one of the problems with the alternative causalities I have elaborated is that they require that the political analyst actually get into the heads of the population under study to determine both if and how they perceive cause and effect. Fair enough. But is this requirement not true of all other explanatory frameworks? Is not one of the great attractions of the rational-choice perspective that there are times and contexts in which many different peoples will behave like the proverbial *homo economicus* and do understand causality as a function of the maximization of gains and the minimization of losses? Ordinary individuals tell us that this is so, and we believe them. We believe them, moreover, because they are consistent in expressing this and, importantly, because we are easily able to observe their behavior—some of which might reasonably be adduced to be consistent with this particular understanding of causality. In addition, our explanatory frameworks need to flow not only from the specific subject matter at hand, but also from the particular, complex, and contextual understandings of causation that the people whose behavior is under scrutiny actually use. Unfortunately for the scholar, notions of political causality are not always articulated, often remaining subjacent. Theorists of whatever contemporary stripe might well find it enlightening, and perhaps more than occasionally troubling, to probe the relationship between their paradigm and the alternative causalities employed by the people whose behavior they are trying to explain.

Let me again be as clear as I can be about the thrust of my argument. We need not discard political and social scientific theories derived from the West. I do not recommend this, for within their limits, they are useful analytical tools. There are many areas of middle African political life where they capably provide us with valid, even compelling, explanations of contemporary political phenomena. Although I have been critical of my own previously published analyses, I am still prepared to defend them as competent, if at times uninspired, treatments of Congolese politics. They are incomplete; their patterns of explanation are culturally specific; and they are perceptually limited. They are not, however, invalid, because there are many areas of overlap between the political realm of the West and the political realm as it is understood in the Congo and much of the rest of middle Africa. Furthermore, there are indeed times when Congolese will act politically on the basis of an understanding of causality that is quite consistent with the assumptions of certain political theories of Western origin.

When such congruence exists, there is no reason why a Western theoretical perspective cannot enlighten us concerning those aspects of middle African politics. But the congruence between Western and middle African visions of the frontiers of the political kingdom is not perfect. Similarly, there are often different, alternative understandings of causality that can, and do, come into play in any given society. When this occurs, theories generated with one set of causal assumptions in mind are unlikely to provide us with entirely satisfactory explanations of political phenomena and may actually impose the scholar's perceptions on other people. In such cases, however, we need theories and explanations that are flexible and subtle enough to incorporate other perceptions of political reality and alternative visions of causality and explanation. Political scientists, and all who would pretend to work on theory and explanation, need to pay much greater attention to other ways of knowing, both popular and endogenous. How might this be done?

While I have no definitive answers to this question, several suggestions follow. First, I think it essential that we listen carefully to what people are saying and not be too quick to dismiss stories, tales, and points of view that may—at first blush—seem nonrational. If someone tells us that a certain political outcome is God's will, or the result of the intervention of the spirit world, or a consequence of some other form of alternative causality, we need to take them seriously whether or not we share their perceptions or beliefs. They may not necessarily be suffering from a form of false consciousness or a mystification by the hegemonic ideological order. Instead, they may simply be operating politically under an alternative understanding of causality, or a different perception of the parameters of the political, or a culturally specific and contextually immediate understanding of certain key political concepts.

Second, I also think it important that political scientists expand the range of primary source materials that they invariably consult. The parameters of the political, as well as stunning examples of alternative causalities, may be found in the world of sports, theology and formal religion, and popular literature. Similarly, proverbs, jokes, rumors, group discussions in various locales, and popular music have much to tell us. Newspapers in middle Africa also need to be consulted, not so much because they inform us about what is actually going on in the arenas of high politics and policy decision making (a rare occurrence at best when they are under state control), but because if read carefully they may provide us with indications of how people understand basic concepts such as power, the contours of a society's political parameters, and hints of some of the various alternative causalities that may be at work.

Third, scholars may need to be more understanding and accepting of slightly different "rules" of evidence. For example, one of the Congolese autobiographies that Jewsiewicki collected relates the story of an individual whose wife gave birth and then began having difficulties with his father's wives. In his words,

Neither my wife nor child had a health of iron. One evening I called my father and told him that I was going to leave him to go live elsewhere, because his wives had a grudge against me. My father was opposed to this because I didn't have any proof. But how could I have proof in a domain as mystical as sorcery? 'The proof,' I answered him, 'is that, during the night, I see only your wives torturing me in a dream and, during the day, either it is I who suffer or it is my wife and my daughter who do not feel well. And that owl comes to hoot on my roof, what is it looking for? And these will-o'-the-wisps?'[98]

Are dreams evidence of sorcery? Of intent to do harm? I cannot say for certain, but since individuals in middle Africa often act politically on the basis of such evidence, and proof, students of politics may need to rethink slightly, and enlarge, the categories of information deemed acceptable as evidence in support of their various theoretical explanations.

Referring to Sakombi's public confessions and revelations concerning the role of sorcery and magic in the Mobutist state, one commentator wrote the following: "To credit this hypothesis appears irrational. But we are Africans and Zaïrians. Furthermore, numerous compatriots among the collaborators of the ex-guide, have already stigmatized the *'maraboutage'* and the cult of fetishes so honored in the presidential entourage."[99] I am neither African, nor Congolese, nor irrational. At least I like to think I am not irrational. Simply put, and at the risk of some repetition, we need to include other perceptions of power, other understandings of causality, and other visions of the contours of the political realm in our theories of political behavior. I advance these suggestions not as a competing approach but perhaps as a complementary, or parallel, theoretical and epistemological imagination which would enhance our understanding of the motivations behind certain manifestations of power and other political phenomena. In short, we all need to understand better how Congolese and other middle Africans comprehend and interpret their political world. In doing this, is it too farfetched to hope that we might also come, someday, to perceive with sharper clarity the contours of our own political world?

5. Matrix I—The Father-Chief
Rights and Responsibilities

In January 1989 Kenya's weekly newsmagazine, *Weekly Review,* published a two-page year-end review essay entitled "The Presidency '88: Consolidation of Power."[1] It recapped the political events surrounding the presidency in 1988 from the regime's perspective. A banal and predictable treatment of the year's political changes, the text of the article itself is of little or no interest and need not occupy our attention. But the photographs and their captions are another matter entirely. In them, President Daniel arap Moi appears in a series of "characteristic" poses, almost as though they were pictures at an exhibition. First, at the top of the initial page of the article, the editors show the president holding a book, presumably a Bible, while taking the oath of office which a bewigged magistrate is administering. The caption is "An onerous task. . . . President Moi being sworn in as Kenya's leader at Uhuru Park in March." Then on the same page we see him as a "Teacher" in full academic regalia, dignified and solemn, at the University of Nairobi's graduation ceremony. On the following page he appears as "Commander-in-Chief" while inspecting a military honor guard at ceremonies on Kenyatta Day. In this image his facial expression seems serious, concerned, capable, and perhaps a bit distant, as though these were the qualities necessary to ensure national defense. A different photograph shows Moi as "Provider" while inaugurating new buses to be added to Nairobi's fleet of commuter transportation. Here there appears to be a small smile on his face as he inspects the interior of one of the new buses. The fourth image shows him as a "Fatherly figure," being greeted by smiling children at the airport on returning home from a trip abroad. In this photograph he appears to have plunged into the euphoric crowd of youngsters and seems to be wearing a wide grin. Finally, the last photograph shows him as a "Supporter," sitting and smiling while rooting for the Gor Mahia football team. Accompanied by a another important politician, a clapping and happy Paul Ngei, in this image Moi is doffing a Stet-

An onerous task..... President Moi being sworn in as Kenya's leader at Uhuru Park in March

Consolidation of Power

The year 1988 was one of further consolidation of the power and prestige of the presidency in Kenya. Right from the start, President Daniel arap Moi set the tone for the year by declaring an early general election. When it came on March 21, the general election (preceded by the Kanu queue-voting nominations on February 22) helped remove some of the leaders who had either been critics of government and party policy or had otherwise fallen foul of the government. Then in one deft stroke, soon after the election, President Moi showed who is boss in the country by removing the experienced, increasingly powerful and much respected Mr. Mwai Kibaki from the national vice-presidency and replacing him with a relative newcomer in politics, Dr. Josephat Karanja. In his cabinet and other appointments, President Moi sent signals for continuity as well as change by retaining the majority of ministers in his previous cabinet on the one hand, and creating a number of new minis-

tries and appointing new faces to the cabinet, on the other. As the activity related to the general election and the ensuing appointment of cabinet and senior government officials ebbed towards mid-year; the president turned his attention to other matters of state,

Teacher..... at last year's University of Nairobi graduation ceremony

especially to the then looming educational crisis when the majority of the candidates who had qualified for entry into the four public universities failed to gain selection in the initial intake. President Moi intervened and directed that the universities admit the majority of candidates. Eventually, more than 7,000 students would gain admission.

In a year that was characterised by general and party elections and celebrations of the first Nyayo decade and the nation's 25th Independence anniversary, the president maintained a high public profile and a heavy schedule of both public and private engagements. After being returned unopposed and sworn in for his fourth term as head-of-state at the general elections early in the year, President Moi was again returned unopposed as president of Kanu during the national party elections which he called in September. Even at the party elections, President Moi's hand was evident when a new team of his choice was elected to party national offices, including Karanja as vice-

Figure 5.1. Paternal Authority and Political Legitimacy. Source: *Weekly Review,* 6 January 1989.

Kenya

president of the party to replace Kibaki, thus ending an anomaly that had existed since the general election in March whereby the vice-presidency of the party and that of the country were held by two men.

During the later half of the year, the president turned his attention to persistent rumours to the effect that a post of prime minister was in the offing. At a rally at Nyeri in June, he effectively quashed the speculation by declaring categorically that there would be no post of prime minister in Kenya. As the year wore on, however, matters of state security, including a government crackdown on political dissidents and a sudden and unprecedented increase in incidents of poaching and general acts of banditry took centre stage and the president spent much of his time and considerable energies rallying the nation to greater unity and spearheading the fight against poaching and banditry.. Preparations as well as the actual celebrations of the two important national anniversaries were the dominant political events during much of the last quarter of the year, however, and a public transport crisis and the sudden resignation of a senior cabinet minister, Mr. Kenneth Matiba, made waves but in no way rocked the ship of state.

Even in the midst of far-flung domestic activity, President Moi did not neglect foreign policy. Apart from inviting and meeting with a large number of foreign leaders and other dignitaries in Kenya, including most heads of state

Commander-in-Chief..... inspecting a guard of honour on Kenyatta Day

and heads of government of neighbouring countries, the president made a number of state visits abroad, among which the most important were to the People's Republic of China, Egypt and Iran. Among African countries, the president visited Tanzania and Zambia during 1988. One of the most significant foreign policy developments came towards the end of the year, with the re-opening of diplomatic relations with Israel and President Moi's vigorous defence of the decision in the face of vehement criticism from the Arab world.

Fatherly figure..... with children who had gone to the airport to welcome him home from a trip abroad

Provider..... inaugurating new additions to the fleet of Nyayo commuter buses

Supporter.....with Mr. Paul Ngei at a Cup Winners' cup quarter-final match involving Gor Mahia

son, presumably while approving something that occurred on the field. Since Moi, a Tugen (Nandi), and Ngei, a Kamba, are socializing while supporting Gor Mahia— a team Kenyans usually understand to be an important Luo symbol—the image also conveys a message about ethnicity and national unity.

Several observations seem worth making here. The first is that the text is almost irrelevant. The five photographs occupy thirty-four of fifty-seven column inches, or roughly 60 percent of the total. Second, comparatively speaking, there is a striking similarity in these Kenyan photographs and their respective captions to the qualities Zaïrians normally ascribe to their vision of an ideal administrative superior. A previous investigation of this imagery demonstrated that Zaïrians would like their political superiors to be patient teachers, sociable friends, competent and decisive decisionmakers, and, above all, generous and caring fatherly providers.[2] Finally, and most importantly, in both Kenya and the larger middle African context, these photographs and captions speak directly to an implicit vision of the cultural logic of political legitimacy. It is therefore significant that the smaller photographs depicting Moi's paternal virtues fall below the larger one showing him taking the oath of office. Paternal authority and political legitimacy are thus linked inescapably; the combination is quite thinkable.

As we have seen, this implicit model of the family, and especially the idealized paternal role that usually accompanies it, permeates daily discourse throughout middle Africa. By no stretch of the imagination is it confined to the upper reaches of the polity or to the political class that typically dominates the state. A letter to the editor entitled "The Role of the Man in Cameroonian Society" captures well the prevailing point of view:

> Cameroon is composed of men and women. In addition, we all know that "a single hand does not solidly tie a parcel." Moreover, the "woman" at the man's sides always needs him in such and such a circumstance, although this need is reciprocal. Thus the role of the Cameroonian woman is only complementary to that of the man.
>
> What is, therefore, the role of Cameroonian man in society?
>
> In the family (the more limited society) the man is father and chief.
>
> His role as father consists of nourishing his family from the sweat of his brow, in bringing up his children, in educating them, dressing them and caring for them. In brief, he must insure the material and moral guidance [*encadrement*] of the entire family.
>
> As head of the family, man directs his own. He draws up the household budget in agreement with his wife. He guides his children after a conversation with his companion [wife]. He supervises his children and his wife. He counsels them and punishes them if that proves necessary.
>
> The above roles must emanate from the love that a father and a chief has for his own.
>
> We ascertain with regret that very few men play their roles, especially in the bosom of the family. Several limit these roles to nourishing and paying the school costs [*écolage*]; they buy medicines when the situation becomes worrisome.

The juvenile delinquence that Cameroonian society currently knows is caused principally by the absence of the fathers of the family from their homes. . . .[3]

I discuss the advisory and "complementary" role that the discourse assigns to women in the next chapter. For the moment, however, let me simply note that both the photographs of President Moi and this rather idealized letter touch on most of the responsibilities of political fatherhood.

Consolidating the enumerated characteristics, as well as adding a few that we have discussed fleetingly in earlier chapters and document at greater length in this one, a more comprehensive list of paternal and legitimating responsibilities would include the following. First, as the initial premise of the moral matrix indicates, the political father-chief must be a provider; he must nurture and care for his political children. He must see to it that his family has enough to eat and that they have decent clothing, shelter, and health care. In addition, the political father is also a teacher; he must raise his children, making sure that he educates them by ensuring that they have the resources to attend school, but also by furnishing them with a larger sense of morality and an ethical compass. The father must also love his children and demonstrate that love by showering them with the things that they need and by caring for them in myriad ways. In times of unexpected crisis, he must be there for his children with aid and succor, generously given. Safeguarding the unity of the political family is a critical responsibility—one that a devoted father will not neglect. Lastly, the father-chief must know how to maintain parental discipline and order within the household for the good of the children and the entire family. There are always wayward children, and the father must not hesitate to punish them. He must also, however, be able to reintegrate them back into the family's bosom once they have recognized the error of their ways by humbly and penitently asking forgiveness of their generous and caring father. So great is his paternal love that he cannot refuse their requests for pardon and absolution. We also see in Chapter 6, when discussing premises three and four of the moral matrix, that political fathers may not eternalize themselves in power. They must permit their children to grow up and to succeed them eventually. At that point, too, we consider that political father-chiefs also have to consult and listen to the voices of the wives and their adult children.

Political father-chiefs also have certain rights within the family. Contained within the implicit model of the family, fathers have the right to receive love, respect, and gratitude, provided they discharge their paternal obligations to the best of their abilities. In addition, the chief (and the two roles are usually so intermeshed that it becomes all but impossible to distinguish them) also has the right to respect, deference, and, occasionally, certain types of tribute, perhaps in the form of a repayment of the enormous "debt" his children owe him. Importantly, and again assuming that they have fulfilled their responsibilities, both father and chief have the right to eat, and even eat well. Peter Seitel's study of Tanzanian folktales speaks to the point. The Haya system of land ownership was a male domain in which the chief distributed land to men he considered prominent and worthy. The symbolic and social ramifications of these arrangements were expressed symbolically in the Haya aphorism *"Akulisa niwe akutwala* [the one who feeds you is the one who rules you]." According to Seitel,

> The verb "feed" in this context refers to providing land for growing food. The proverb means that the person who provides one with the land that sustains him is the same person to whom one owes allegiance and, moreover, the person who has the socially sanctioned right to control many aspects of one's behavior.
>
> In this system, the chief is the ultimate landowner and also the ultimate ruler. He "feeds" his people and rules them. The same principle applies to each point of land distribution down the line: at each level, the distributor "feeds" the distributee and, therefore, rules him. The lowest level of distribution is from father to son. A father apportions a plot of land from his own holdings when his son marries. At that point, and before it as well, the father provides land that feeds the son; this is said to be a basis on which a Haya father "rules." A son owes his allegiance to his father, and through him to his clan, and through the clan to the chief.[4]

In other words, if the father nourishes and nurtures, he has the right to rule and, I would submit, a right to "eat" as long as his political children are well nurtured. But when there is hunger, it would be unthinkable for the chief to eat, and this is the basis of the second premise of the matrix: namely, that there are limitations on just how much the father-chief may consume in conditions of scarcity while his children suffer from hunger. This set of imprecise calculations is never entirely transparent, or perhaps even conscious, but we may discern their broad outline in the discourse surrounding questions of corruption and the unequal distribution of wealth among social classes. There is thus a very real economic basis, and limit, to the legitimacy of any political father-chief in middle Africa.

This chapter addresses certain dimensions of these economic factors. It is not a treatise on economics, but instead demonstrates how tacit economic calculations are presented, understood, internalized in the daily discourse, and then incorporated into the moral matrix of legitimate governance. It also touches on the role of the father-chief as provider, his ability to "pardon" children who have strayed from the family path, and how the popular discourse represents excessive corruption, or "eating." As will become apparent, these factors all play into the unarticulated logic of legitimacy.

Nurture and Nourishment

Editorials in the Kinshasa press captured nicely the imagery that a father-chief such as Mobutu Sese Seko wished people to internalize: "For the Father of the Nation, his constant worry has always been to assure each daughter and each son of this country the means to nourish themselves, clothe themselves, maintain their health and educate their children." Or, with a slightly different emphasis, "Restarting the economy has remained for several years the principal preoccupation of Zaïrian authorities. This work, as is known, has always been at the center of the worries of the Father of the Nation who has not ceased consecrating to it most of his energy and time."[5] Then there were also Mobutu's own words, usually emblazoned across page one. More than occasionally, the "Thought of the Day"—which was almost always a quotation from President Mobutu—evoked similar themes. For example, "Today all our attention, all our efforts, all our means, we consecrate them to the search for paths capable of leading us out of the preoccupying economic situation that we are passing through. For us, the people must eat and eat well; they must be cared for and be well cared for; they must be housed and housed decently."[6] Naturally, Mobutu regularly used the royal "we."

The Zaïrian president was never alone in presenting the country's economic situation as his constant and most preoccupying concern. Most other middle African leaders and mass media put forth the same rhetoric. Moi, for example, would occasionally remind his listeners that, in the words of one radio report, "it was the responsibility of the government to take care of all Kenyans regardless of the[ir] material or social status." Similarly, a comment made almost in passing in the context of trying to justify a parliamentary pay raise also indicates how deeply rooted is the notion of politician as provider. The article began, "It might sound like a lot of money, *but in a country where leaders tend to be regarded as providers,* the proposals contained in the national assembly remuneration (amendment bill) seeking to increase the earnings of elected representatives in parliament are nothing to write home about."[7]

The prevalent paternal discourse emphasizes that although the political father has the responsibility of providing the population with food, clothing, shelter, health care, and other basic necessities, people should not view these as rights or entitlements. Instead, they are "gifts" from their generous and loving "father." So, for example, when in 1987 the Bulungu General Hospital received a shipment of pharmaceuticals and diagnostic equipment, the press presented these materials as "a gift of the President-Founder" of the MPR to Bulungu's party militants.[8] Naturally, when receiving a "gift" from one's father, there is an expectation of a fulsome expression of "thanks" in return. To be sure, however, there is variation in the extent to which middle African political fathers adhere to the script. Mobutu, Moi, Ahidjo, and Biya have reveled in the role, while Diouf and the Tanzanian leadership have at times seemed slightly less enamored of some of the more blatant paternal trappings of power. Rawlings has occasionally tried to reject it entirely. For example, in 1984 the Ghanaian press featured an article indicating that Chairman Rawlings had donated a Land Rover to a Catholic mission hospital along with a variety of medicinal drugs. Rawlings was not at the small ceremony, but the materials were presented on his behalf by the regional medical officer. The very next day a correction appeared in the paper noting that these "were not personal gifts from the PNDC Chairman." The items in question were a donation to the government, and Rawlings had simply directed that they be routed to this particular hospital.[9] Rawlings thus falls at the extreme end of the continuum in this regard. Most of the other middle African heads of state would have immediately claimed that the transfer of the car and the drugs was, in fact, a gift from the loving and solicitous political "father."

The features of the normal paternal exchange appear clearly when the "father" deals with university students. A letter to the editor, for example, thanked President Moi for "his generosity and wisdom" while making a brief stopover in Bombay. When Moi met with Kenyan students there, "his fatherly advice about studying hard and thwarting tribalism was relayed to all Kenyan students. . . . Above all," the letter continued, "we would like to thank the president for the US$8,500 . . . that he gave us. This was a blessing to some students who were financially handicapped and waiting for money from home."[10] In a comparable vein, the opening of a new student restaurant at the University of Yaoundé elicited the customary paternal language from the press: "Profoundly touched by this solicitude of the government, through the chancellor, the students addressed a motion of thanks and support to the Head of State, H. E. Paul Biya." In his brief impromptu remarks, the university chancellor made it clear that this new dining facility had come about "thanks to the personal solicitude of the president of the Republic who unblocked the funds necessary for its construction."[11] Quite literally in this case, the father feeds and nourishes.

In other instances, the father houses. In 1985 thirty-five Zaïrian student families were threatened with eviction because the national housing office wished to reclaim their apartments and rent them out to those who could afford to pay more for them. When a delegation of student spouses visited Mama Bobi Ladawa, the First Lady, she conveyed to them the presidential decision favoring the students and canceling the eviction order. The students greeted this decision with "an explosion of joy." An editorial reported that "as a father of the family worried about the living conditions of all his children, and more particularly about tomorrow's cadres . . . the presidential attitude brings into relief the permanent solicitude for the happiness of the daughters and sons of Zaïre over whom he watches day and night."[12] Finally, student turbulence may call forth both the father's caring and solicitous side, as well as his stern visage as a disciplinarian. Cameroon provides a case in point. In 1980 complaints and disturbances on the Yaoundé campus resulted in a student boycott of classes. President Ahidjo augmented the scholarship funds available, thus reminding students of his "solicitude," but at the same time he "invited" them in no uncertain terms to return to their classrooms.[13] Some years later a columnist noted that when Ahidjo speaks to Cameroonian youth, they often hear a dual voice: "that of the Father, affable but untiring who does not cease to remind his children of what is just and good and of what is not, and that of the Chief who tells one and another what he expects of them."[14]

Paternal gifts and largesse are also apparent in the world of sports. The political father's backing for the national soccer team is symbolically important because of a commitment to nationalism and national identity, but the actual manner in which that support expresses itself generally reinforces the prevailing paternal model. Although not inclined to be a sports fan, Houphouet-Boigny knew how to cash in on a soccer success. When the Elephants, Côte d'Ivoire's national side, qualified for "Egypt 86" (the African Cup of Nations soccer tournament), Houphouet ceremoniously received the Elephants and rewarded them all. In addressing the players as "my very dear children," he made it clear that because the Elephants represented the entire Côte d'Ivoire: "I will take the Elephants of Côte d'Ivoire personally in charge. . . . Everywhere the honor of Côte d'Ivoire in this game will be engaged. I will not say more to you. You will not lack for anything with me. Even your brothers who have gone outside Côte d'Ivoire, notably in France, will be part of the Elephants [and] will benefit from the same solicitude as you."[15] And in 1997 President Moi personally donated the healthy sum of three million shillings toward the preparations and training of Kenya's national team, the Harambee Stars. Parenthetically, when the president's official salary was raised in 1994 the press recorded the new figure as 1.2 million shillings per year.[16]

The image of paternal generosity also extends to the state's more conventional economic policies. Raising producer prices, increasing salaries, and other such measures are generally presented as the work of the head of state. Obviously, politicians everywhere like their constituents to see them delivering material benefits, and middle Africa is no exception. In this part of the world, however, the presentation of such policies in the local press usually emphasizes, in one way or another, aspects of the preferred paternal and familial imagery. To cite only one particular instance, when Cameroon's Ahidjo raised the price per kilogram paid to cocoa farmers in 1982, the press noted, "This decision must, therefore, be considered as an encouragement and as an appeal of the head of state to Cameroonian peasants to redouble their efforts. . . ." Fathers generally encourage their children to work harder. And when Paul Biya took over the presidency after Ahidjo stepped down in November 1982, one of the very first things he did was to raise salaries.[17] In addition, to commemorate the first anniversary of his accession to the presidency, Biya also saw to it that salaries were "revalued." Such measures taken in the hopes of increasing one's political popularity are universal. In middle Africa, however, where the familial imagery and paternal metaphor reflect a deeply rooted moral matrix, many ordinary citizens almost certainly understood the measure as both a paternal gesture and a gift to the people. At the same time, they might also have seen the new salary level as either a cynical device to boost political popularity or as a commonplace aspect of the state's larger economic policy. In this cultural context, these are not mutually exclusive explanations.

In Chapter 4 we saw that political father-chiefs can command, or at least prefer to be understood as having the ability to command, certain occult forces. In this context a description of one of Biya's visits to the town of Bertoua is of interest. When he traveled there in May 1983, the area had remained bone-dry for two weeks. On the appointed day, the morning was bright and sunny. But as the time for Biya's arrival approached, the sky became more somber. The president deplaned, but just as his motorcade started to move, the skies opened and it poured. All of the ceremonies took place in the rain. According to the journalist covering the event, "A group of [party] militants of a respectable age chased away people who came to ask them why they had not stopped the rain. Their response was clear: 'Paul Biya has brought us the benediction of the heavens, we should be very proud of it.'" He then noted that the rain brought with it a promise of great fertility after a period of extended dryness.[18] Biya, in other words, has the power to bring with him the "gift" of rain and fertility. To be sure, rain is often associated with renewed life, prosperity, and good times. The chief who brings rain thus enjoys a certain legitimacy, in that it would be unthinkable to remove him while times were good.[19]

In a slightly more mundane context, Mobutu also liked to see himself presented as the bringer of light and the bringer of water. When he arrived in Boende for a brief visit in 1980, people were astounded that the electricity worked and that the water flowed from the faucets for the first time in quite a while. The population's "joy" because of this, and of course because of Mobutu's visit, was heightened because Mobutu had also brought a substantial monetary "gift" for the age grade into which he had been ceremoniously inducted in 1977.[20] Zaïrians surely understood that local authorities had turned on the water and the electricity so as not to incur Mobutu's wrath. Yet without excluding this cynical interpretation, on a symbolic level Mobutu was still bringing the gifts of water and light, and his appearance was also intimately connected with a generous financial gesture to the local members of his honorary age grade. On this level, the paternal "generosity" was apparent for all to see.

On occasion the paternal metaphor and imagery yields pride of place to a more maternal motif. One Swahili praise poem, for example, called President Nyerere the first person to respond to the needs of the people, comparing the nation to an infant wishing to be breastfed. Throughout the poem the author calls Nyerere's work extremely difficult, and he compares the president to a hardworking mother who supplies food and mother's milk for her child's needs.[21] Although the motif of nurture is apparent here, as is the notion of comparing the population, or the nation, to a child looking for the mother's breast, since the vast majority of heads of state in this part of the world are men, the metaphors and imagery usually take on a paternal and masculine cast. This is not to suggest, however, that maternal imagery and metaphors are in any way excluded. In fact, when Ruth Perry—a former banker and onetime senator—became the head of Liberia's transition council in 1996, thus effectively becoming for a brief time the head of state, she described her meeting with the three main faction leaders who had chosen her (Charles Taylor, Alhaji Kromah, and George Boley) in these terms: "Believe you me, I signed the cross immediately and said a little word of prayer. . . . Each one of them expressed their feelings, their willingness to work with me, and they said they would give me their fullest cooperation, that I will have no problem with them; that I should relax, because I am their mother. And because they used the word 'mother', it filled my heart. I almost burst out in tears." And when she was asked to send a message to the hundreds of thousands of Liberian refugees that the civil war had created, she replied: "I am asking all Liberians, wherever they are, if you have a brother that you know is holding arms, talk to that brother. Let them give this woman a chance. She is your mother; she is your friend; she is your aunt; she is your sister. Give her the support so that we can try to bring peace to this our country where there is little hope."[22]

At times, too, the presidential spouse is associated actively with paternal gestures demonstrating great compassion. First Ladies often participate in social actions demonstrating that the father actually cares about his children, and thus—in some small ways—they help in "softening" the father's occasionally stern visage. One example should suffice. In 1985 Mobutu and Mama Bobi returned to Kinshasa after a trip to Senegal and Togo. Upon arrival, the press report mentioned that they had learned with great sadness of the small airplane crash that had occurred in their absence that had claimed approximately twenty lives. Scarcely had they descended from the plane when both Mobutu and Mama Bobi visited the site of the accident to console the families of the survivors. The columnist noted that this action of "paternal comfort" was "one of the marks of the permanent solicitude of the Guide [Mobutu] towards his people. . . . Once more the Father of the Nation has shown us that his marriage with the entire Zaïrian people reaffirms itself in everyday acts, and that it is in misfortune that veritable love is proven."[23]

Regardless of whether we speak of paternal generosity and solicitude, maternal care and nurture, or the ability of the head of state to use his occult gifts to shower his children with rain and thus the very conditions of life, these "gifts" and "generosity" require repayment. Part of the usually unspoken understanding of this exchange is that in return for such parental gifts and generosity, the political "children" must be grateful. They must show deference and accord respect. They have to accept the wisdom of their political father and honor his political wishes for, at least according to the usually implicit model, they know that he has their best interests at heart. Debts incurred must be repaid.

On some occasions, however, the amount of expected "repayment" can be staggering. In 1983 the Executive Committee of the PDCI decided to move Côte d'Ivoire's capital from Abidjan to Yamoussoukro, Houphouet's home village. The formal announcement from the Executive Committee noted that "the work of the President receives the approbation of a large number [of people], for this transfer would not only respond to economic and sociological imperatives, but would constitute an expression of the gratitude of the country to the Father of the Nation."[24] Needless to say, in many countries it would be politically unthinkable to suggest moving the nation's capital to repay a moral debt to a sitting head of state. But in middle Africa the structure of the moral matrix and the paternal and familial metaphors associated with it make such an outcome eminently thinkable. To cite another case, in 1985 Mobutu accused Libya's Muamar Kadhafi of having sent terrorists into Zaïre from Burundi. Speaking directly to the Zaïrian people, the editorialist reminded them that

> Mobutu has granted you his affection and has sacrificed his health and the best years of his life for you. Today you have the sublime duty to demonstrate again once more your indefectible attachment to his person and to his clairvoyant policy for the invulnerability and dignity of greater Zaïre and for [his] safeguarding of the gains of the revolution.

> Certainly, the anger and the indignation that you manifested last week through the grandiose marches that saw you unfurl massively on the arteries of the country to denounce the diabolical aims of Kadhafi . . . and express your total support for Guide Mobutu Sese Seko, testifies to your political maturity and your loyalty toward the Head of the Party.[25]

Of course, anyone witnessing such a march would not mistake the coerced participation that actually occurred with the massive, spontaneous outpouring of support that the discourse imagined. Nonetheless, it is noteworthy that the editorialist would choose to express himself in these terms. The "sublime duty to demonstrate" is clearly a repayment for Mobutu's paternal affection, for the sacrifice of his health, and for his "gift" of the best years of his life to the Zaïrian people. Parental guilt trips would appear to be universal.

At other times, the repayment is more harmlessly symbolic. In 1984 Ivoirian Gabriel Tiacoh unexpectedly won a silver medal in track at the Los Angeles Olympic Games. On returning home, Tiacoh—the only Ivoirian to win a medal that year—received a hero's welcome, including a reception at the presidential palace. At that event the medalist addressed the following words to the president: "Permit me, Mr. President, to thank you personally. I thank you wholeheartedly, in my name, in the name of my mother and also in the name of my entire family. This Olympic medal belongs to you, also, it returns to you by right." At that point the athlete placed the medal around Houphouet's neck, while—according to the report—the president wiped away a tear. Then Houphouet returned the medal to Tiacoh, wishing for an even greater harvest of medals at the 1988 Seoul Olympics. Finally, the reporter noted that this particular "family festival" concluded with a cocktail at which point the president raised his glass in a benediction that Ivoirian youth would often gather such honors.[26] In this "family" celebration there are perhaps echoes of pre-colonial custom in the ritual offering of the medal (or perhaps the fruit of the hunt) to the chief, and also perhaps in Houphouet's speedy return of this offering to the young athlete.

Such pre-colonial echoes occur commonly, because father-chiefs usually wish to conflate the two roles. Being seen as a chief, receiving gifts of tribute in one's capacity as chief, can enhance one's political legitimacy. There are several reasons for this. In the first place, being named as chief, or as a member of an age grade, or as an honorary member of a clan, lineage, or ethnic group can create fictive ties of familial solidarity with a portion of the national population, thus contributing further to the idea of the large national family. Second, and equally important, receiving customary gifts and tribute from the representatives of a group's elders is, for the father-chiefs, a way of being perceived as a customary as well as a national authority. In this way it is possible to join the two spheres of contemporary life, and their respective powers, in the person of one individual. Put differently, and to reemphasize an analytical theme raised in Chapter 2, this is a way of maintaining the unity and indivisibility of power in a single individual. Furthermore, since the forces of the occult tend to have certain of their roots in rural areas, such ceremonies subtly remind people that the father-chief has access to the world of sorcery. In 1980, for example, Mobutu received at one of his homes members of a Mongo age set that had traveled to the capital to congratulate the president on his fiftieth birthday and on the marriage of one of his daughters. The members of the delegation offered Mobutu birthday gifts including two spears, traditional pieces of currency, a sculpted tusk of ivory, a checkers game carved in malachite, and the sum of Z5,000 in currency.[27] And once Tanzania's Ali Hassan Mwinyi, a head of state far less given over to paternal flourishes than either Mobutu or Houphouet, tried to honor the party "elders." In 1987 he thanked the elders for their support, and they replied with customary gifts: a traditional stool, a machete, an axe, a hoe, a drum, a flask, a piece of cloth for his wife, and material for a suit for himself. The stool is a common symbol of authority, and the hoe has an equally common association with food and fertility. The elders also informed the president that the machete was for slashing economic saboteurs, the axe was for chopping off all elements of favoritism, and the hoe was to dig out the roots of irresponsibility at places of work.[28]

In both Ghana and Nigeria the prevalent discourse accords customary chiefs places of great respect and legitimacy for certain things.[29] One Ghanaian columnist put it this way:

> Ghanaians are a people who hold their chiefs or traditional rulers in reverence. . . .
> Our chiefs are political leaders, traditionally, and occupy positions of *primus in-
> ter pares* in our society. We make them feel we love and respect them. Therefore,
> we do not misbehave in their presence. Whatever they say is final and their au-
> thority is so immense that we do not challenge or oppose openly or publicly what-
> ever judgement they give in their court. Thus we acquiesce, without question, in
> our dealings with our chiefs. . . . Because of unquestioning acquiescence on our
> part, a chief can say, "I have put my feet on it" when it comes to adjudicating on
> a case between two warring groups.[30]

Although in the 1980s J. J. Rawlings was certainly not given to the facile acceptance of any form of "traditional" authority, on his return from a trip to Latin America and Cuba the press caught him in a photograph with other members of the PNDC government on the airport tarmac. The image showed Rawlings and the others looking on most attentively as "Nii Adokwei, Klolo Wulomo of Labadi is seen pouring libation to welcome Chairman Rawlings."[31]

There is a real sense in which chiefs, and sometimes elders, both touch and represent certain forms of spiritual legitimacy and power with which even skeptical father-chiefs like to associate themselves. One glowing account by another chief of Oni Sijuwade Olubuse II, a Yoruba monarch, put it this way: "To the Yoruba-speaking people all over the world, ODUDUWA is the ancestral father. And as Oba Sijuwade reminded me recently in his palace, a reigning Oni is Oduduwa, and Oduduwa is Oni. . . . I had no doubt in my mind that this god-king had certainly made a rendezvous with his royal destiny. Certainly, there is a divinity that hedges the brows of kings. Oba Sijuwade does not need to engage in tortured sophistry to establish his claims to a divine right to rule his people. He personifies that divine right."[32] Paternity, ancestry, and a tinge of divinity are all legitimating factors in middle Africa; they are attributes that most of the region's father-chiefs wish to display.

At times the dominant discourse in Nigeria displays an interesting variation on the theme of political paternity. As we saw in Chapter 1, Nigerians have adopted the paternal and familial metaphors, but there have often been disputes as to just who was to be the national father. One response to these conflicts has been to shift the locus of political paternity from the president and head of state back to Nigeria's customary rulers. An editorial written toward the end of the Shagari administration noted that

> The writers of our constitution wanted to avoid any misunderstanding between the "fathers" of the nation and the politicians, that was why they decided to isolate traditional rulers from partisan politics. Although philosophers recognise that every man is a political animal, a traditional ruler, regarded as the father of all the people in his domain, should restrain himself from any action which will make a section of his subjects see him as partisan. Since all his subjects are not likely to belong to one political party, there is no way that he can play politics without estranging his relationship with some of his people.[33]

Also of interest is that the definition of politics is implicitly restricted to the sphere of party politics and that "politics" should not in any way sully the role and neutral position of the "father." The Owelle of Nimo in Anambra State expressed this view of the chiefly father being above the fray of electoral politics during the 1983 elections. As the dispatch put it, "The Owelle said that as the father of Nimo community, he welcomed all the six registered political parties to the town and assured them of equal protection."[34] In any electoral setting politicians like to collect endorsements, and in Nigeria they know that a blessing from one of the royal fathers can carry some weight. In 1992 Major-General Shehu Yar'adua, a presidential candidate, illustrated the point first by recognizing the Oba Badagry as father and then by asking if he could become his "favoured child." At the Oba's palace, the candidate openly sought the Oba's electoral blessings in these terms: "I know that as a traditional ruler you are not supposed to play politics. Though all of us (aspirants) are your children, I am sure that you as a father have your favourite child. I wish to be that, your favoured child. I therefore present my humble self to you as one who is working hard to build a bridge between the past and present as well as to correct the mistakes of past leaders."[35]

Chiefly fathers also watch out for the well being of their children. In 1989 prominent customary rulers went to then president Ibrahim Babangida to plead for the reopening of the nation's universities. After meeting with the general, Oba Sijuwade said, "The majority of us abhor indiscipline and we will, from now, take it upon ourselves, seriously, by talking to our sons and daughters to see that they are well-behaved."[36] As we shall see presently, both national father-chiefs and the more localized and ethnically circumscribed chiefly fathers care deeply about discipline.

Nigeria's chiefly fathers are also valued as advisers in the political discourse, if not in reality. When Babangida finally stepped down after the nullified June 1993

presidential elections, his farewell address to the Nigeria public stated: "My gratitude is without bounds to our most respected royal fathers who have served as
sources of inspiration to me and my Administration, and as volunteer 'fire fighters'
in many communal and national crises. I hope they will continue to place their
wise counsel at the disposal of successive administrations. . . ."[37] Parenthetically,
that the Nigerian state and media would—at least in their public discourse—present
the "royal fathers" as valued advisers constitutes an interesting historical reversal
of one of the dictates of the Lugardian theory of indirect rule which saw the state,
in the person of the district officer, as an "adviser" to the chiefs.[38]

One last observation on variations in the discourse is worth making. Although
it is not a usual occurrence, in some middle African contexts it is quite possible for
a woman to take on the role of chief and thus don the parental mantle that goes
with it. In Cameroon, for example, one village had gone without a chief for two
years after the death of the last incumbent. During that time the village had remained an "orphan." Eventually one of the deceased chief's daughters was elected
to replace her father. In that role, like her father before her, she would have to "look
after the life of all the people through political, economic, social and cultural guidance [encadrement] and that in peace and [with] respect for public order."[39] In other
words, although the sub-prefect presiding over the installation ceremony did not
say so directly, she would have to be a parent to her people.

One unfortunate consequence of a discourse that emphasizes this imagery and
these metaphors is that political fathers often portray, and perhaps even come to
think of, their fellow citizens as children dependent on their father, or mother, for
gifts, advice, wisdom, and a sense of political direction. Mature, thinking, reflective adults who have their own political preferences, orientations, and ideas are
thus transformed into immature children unable to make decisions without substantial paternal "guidance." So when Houphouet would travel to a region of Côte
d'Ivoire where, on occasion, people had expressed displeasure, they were likened
to "sons and daughters, turbulent but always faithful" to their "Father-President
[whose] wisdom and mansuetude [are] known."[40] Similarly, when conforming to
the unstated understandings of political and electoral "gratitude" toward the father-
chief, the discourse patronizingly deems the population to be "mature." When Paul
Biya received 99.98 percent of the vote in the January 1984 presidential elections,
a journalist recorded and evaluated the event in these terms: "The Cameroonian
people voted en masse, the Cameroonian people voted in order and discipline, the
Cameroonian people voted with enthusiasm, if I am to believe the . . . echoes that
have reached me. This signifies that once more, this Cameroonian people has
confirmed its great political maturity and its civic sense."[41]

This infantilization of the population has aroused the anger of more than one
middle African intellectual. Celestin Monga, a Cameroonian scholar writing in an
Ivoirian magazine in 1991, sent an open letter to President Biya: "The empty and
simplistic slogans that adorn the front page of the Cameroon Tribune every day must
cease and people who have interesting things to say must be permitted to do so—
and I can assure you that there are many of them in this country. The time of the

'fathers of the nation' is largely over. Cameroonians are not children that you may judge to be 'mature for democracy'. . . ."[42] Of course, it would be quite thinkable for a political "father" simply to dismiss an "intemperate" opinion such as this as the point of view of a wayward, misguided, and politically "immature" "child" who has regrettably strayed from the family. But if these "difficult" and "troubled" children show proper remorse, the father can reintegrate his wayward sons and daughters into the bosom of the large national "family" through an act of presidential and paternal magnanimity and forgiveness.

Punishment and Pardon

Father-chiefs often have a dark, nasty side. The prevalent discourse presents this as a consequence of the need to maintain unity within the family, the need to make sure that "children" receive proper "discipline" so that they will grow and "mature," and the need to see that "children" who have erred receive the requisite punishment. There is a sense in which middle African discourse authorizes and accepts harsh discipline and punishment as long as it is balanced by the father-chief's kind, loving, and paternal persona. This pattern is replicated in different countries, in different spheres of life, and at different levels of the sociopolitical hierarchy. One may discern it, for example, in an account of a Ghanaian eastern regional minister lecturing his administrative subordinates that henceforth they would have to account for all money and every liter of gasoline they received. The report continued, "Mr Amoah further told the [department] heads that while they must be strict in checking laziness, lateness to work and absenteeism, negligence of duty, corrupt practices or any tendencies that tended to put their entire public service into disrepute, they should also be sensitive to genuine problems of their subordinates."[43] An administrative father-chief, like a political "father," must be firm and rigorous, yet at the same time understanding and compassionate.[44]

There is also a place for firm, authoritative behavior in the sphere of education. In 1983 Amady Fall, professor of modern letters, delivered a speech to mark the occasion of the annual distribution of prizes at the Commercial Lycée of Kaolack, Senegal. Professor Fall noted that the first form of authority a child encounters is parental authority, which is determinant in the child's evolution. More than that, however, the child is constantly bumping into all forms of authority in everyday life. He noted that in pre-colonial Africa children had to obey almost everybody— even those adults they did not know but who nonetheless felt obliged to correct and discipline them for an infraction of recognized norms, customs, or standards of behavior. Where schools were concerned, Professor Fall argued that "an efficacious and sure teacher conserves an authority which becomes his principal arm." In his own words, "The word of an authoritarian schoolmaster has more force, it is more convincing."[45] There is, in other words, a place for autocratic behavior when dealing with children.

Similarly, the discourse recognizes that fathers, men, have certain rights over women, even if a specific mention of them comes in a highly critical context. A 1989 newspaper article relayed the sad, first person testimony of Soppi M., a then recently divorced Cameroonian woman. Married for ten years, but having filed for divorce, Mme Soppi discovered that her five children, including her raped daughter, "belonged" to her former husband; that she had no real rights in the marriage; that she did not have enough money to wage a lengthy legal struggle; and that she found herself standing alone before the justice of men. The author then relates how she was able, with the aid of an attorney, to get an exit visa for herself and her children. At the airport while going through the bureaucratic formalities necessary before leaving, she discovered that even though she was in the middle of divorce proceedings she could not legally leave the country without the consent of her husband. When she broke down and cried, a policeman told her, "Really Madam, do not insist. You must understand that he [her husband] is the head of the family. It is he who decides, you have only to come to an arrangement with him to have his authorization."[46] In a certain sense, therefore, the father of the family legally "owns" the children and, to a great extent, can use the law to control his wife. Far from the highly idealized vision of the *bon père de famille* who wants only what is best for all members of his family, this incident touches on the dark side of paternal authority that, regrettably, is also extrapolated into the political arena.

At least on the level of the rhetoric contained in the discourse, political father-chiefs often seem torn between the two roles. Some of them have delivered public speeches, at times almost soliloquies, reminding their "children" that they are both the father who loves and forgives, as well as the chief who is perfectly capable of applying severe punishment. Zaïre's Mobutu illustrates this nicely. Addressing legislators in 1981: "I am the father of the great Zaïrian family. Even though I know how to love, I also know how to punish."[47] Three years later, announcing the orientation of his new seven-year mandate, Mobutu put it this way: "I speak of our Zaïrian society, a society founded on an authentic conception of values, this same authenticity that makes of the Chief also a veritable father of the family, the father of the Nation. The Chief can chastise, but the Chief must also know how to pardon. After the pardon comes reeducation, so that the sick part becomes healthy again. And in a family, a difficult child remains despite everything a child of the family."[48] And then once again, in 1988 at the closing session of the Fourth Ordinary Congress of the MPR, Mobutu shared with his highest-ranking cadres his thinking on his own role in the polity:

> My own examination of my conscience pushes me to believe that these last years . . . I have acted more as Father of the family, as Father of the great family of the . . . [MPR]. I recognize it and I do not regret it.
>
> But some have concluded from this that this attitude of the Chief signifies that in the Republic of Zaïre [there] reigns the law of laissez-faire and the law of carelessness without consequence, that, for example, one may embezzle freely, because in their eyes, there is neither control nor punishment.
>
> Since I have not been understood, I must henceforth act more as Chief than as Father of the family, to restore order in the house of Zaïre. . . .

> Of course, I shall not cease to be the Father of the nation and as God Himself . . . who created man who is good and merciful, I shall strike forcefully the bad and continue to recompense the good . . . in separating the wheat from the chaff.[49]

Although Mobutu's comparison of himself to the deity stretches credibility beyond the breaking point, it is still worth noting that over the years Mobutu's speeches and actions often displayed a real tension between the gentle hand and the firm hand. Both the image of the loving father and the image of the forceful, punishing chief are lodged well within the premises of the moral matrix, and both, therefore, are quite thinkable and thus legitimate.

Other father-chiefs share the same concerns and also strive for a balance between the two roles. In 1984, for example, Abdou Diouf visited the incessantly secessionist southern region of Casamance to inaugurate a hydroelectric complex. On the one hand, the president was obviously (and literally) there to bring water to the peasants of Casamance in his role as a father who nourishes and provides. On the other hand, however, in a thinly veiled warning, Diouf stated: "It will never be said that I hold the tiller of this country with a weak hand."[50] Two years later Diouf decided to amnesty certain of his "brothers" from Casamance who had been condemned for separatist activities. In sharing his reasoning with the entire Senegalese population on the eve of their national independence day, he maintained, "This care for conciliation should be interpreted neither as a sign of weakness nor as an underestimation of the acts having led to the condemnations. Let it be understood that in my capacity as President of the Republic, guardian of the Constitution, I shall always and everywhere defend the integrity and unity of the national territory against all action, all inclination towards destabilization or disaggregation of the Senegalese nation, from wherever they come."[51]

At times Houphouet also consciously tried to balance the roles of father and chief. In 1983 a labor dispute ensued when the state withdrew the free housing that secondary school teachers had previously enjoyed, leading to an unauthorized strike. Addressing the nation, Houphouet spoke not only as president of the PDCI-RDA "but also as an Ivoirian and as a father. It is evident that whatever my will to pay the liveliest attention to all that touches them, I shall in no case tolerate, as long as the country has confidence in me, that a social body, however important it might be, erects itself as a state within the State, in refusing all collective discipline, and in wanting to serve only fractional and personal interests. Democracies die from their weakness. My love for dialog and for tolerance, my love for Man, cannot be interpreted as a weakness."[52] Parenthetically, the strike ended some weeks later after Houphouet threatened to fire all those teachers who were on strike and to hire unemployed intellectuals in their place. And finally, in 1996 a journalist asked Ruth Perry about the fact that Liberia's faction leaders returned repeatedly to the battlefield to solve their differences. Her reply is consistent with the ambivalence of other heads of state as they attempt to balance the roles of father and chief. "They told me they respect me like a mother, and I hold them at their word, I will treat them like a mother and, if necessary, that means discipline," Perry said.[53]

The power of executive clemency is a widespread constitutional provision throughout the world. In middle Africa, however, a simple judicial power usually attributed to the head of state takes on a rather different meaning because of the prevalence of the paternal and familial metaphors and their role in shaping understandings of politics. We have seen that one of the responsibilities of political father-chiefs is discipline, or punishment, and at times political fathers discipline their wayward children quite harshly. Another responsibility is to grant clemency, to forgive, and to reintegrate the wrongdoer into the bosom of the national family. Although tales of presidential mercy and forgiveness vary according to context, in broad outline the prevailing discourse usually emphasizes something resembling the following general scenario. If a wrongdoer approaches the father-chief on bended knee, publicly recognizes his political paternity, asks humbly and penitently for forgiveness while acknowledging a desire for reintegration into the large national family, then the father-chief is usually so moved that he exercises mercy and magnanimity, and demonstrates his paternal love by granting both political and paternal absolution, thus welcoming the erring child back into the fold.[54] An Ivoirian case is an initial illustration.

In 1973 Captain Sio Koulaou Ernest, along with some other young officers of the Ivoirian army, tried to overthrow the government with a coup d'état. Believing in the power of sorcery and fetishes, Captain Sio apprehended five fishermen who were fishing illegally on Lake Koussou and immolated them on his fetish (which was not specified in the report). In theory, this human sacrifice was supposed to have assured the success of his plot against the government. Sio was condemned, but President Houphouet liberated him after about ten years in jail. Sio then wrote a letter to Houphouet to thank him and to ask him for a personal audience. The text of the letter follows and is worth extensive citation:

> Mr. President and very dear father,
>
> I have the honor to come very respectfully to your excellency to express the feelings of gratitude that animate me. As an infinitely indulgent father, you have deigned to forget the errors of the lost sheep that I was by granting me your pardon for all the evil that I must have done you.
>
> Venerable Father of the Nation, be convinced that your formerly unworthy son has considered carefully and offers a sincere "Mea culpa." I recognize and regret my errors and I beg you to believe that my entire reason for being is to work to merit your pardon made of love and infinite goodness. . . .
>
> Mr. President of the Republic, please accept that I prostrate myself at your feet. . . .
>
> Dear Father, I do not at all have the pretension to ask you to anticipate the projected interview. However, I would like to underline that this meeting is vital for me. Not only would it permit me to signify to you all my regrets, but it would reconcile me with my parents for whom I still remain the ungrateful and pretentious child. For as long as I will not have met you, I will feel overwhelmed by the

weight of my faults and will be able neither to live as a free man nor to go to my village. In effect, my parents, although happy at the announcement of my liberation, require that before receiving me in the family, that I make amends to you. . . .
  Your son, Sio[55]

Houphouet, of course, reveled in the role of the magnanimous and loving father who would never fail to exercise his paternal responsibility. In 1985, for example, 276 parastatal workers went on strike to protest some of the government's economic measures. The government fired them. With the minister of the Civil Service present, they then asked for—and received—an audience with Houphouet. Figuratively descending to one knee, the leader of the delegation noted:

> Our mistake was to have cut off the dialog with the authorities and to have chosen the general call for strike to express our grievances. We humbly acknowledge our mistake. . . . Mr. President, we sincerely regret our attitude which led the government to take some measures which, even though justified, resulted in the dismissal of some of our comrades. These measures put them though a period of hardship. We know of your generosity and your kind heart. Mr. President, therefore we are asking for your clemency which will enable our comrades to return to work.

Houphouet responded in kind: "I am receiving you as a head of family. I recalled in the presence of the holy father, the very holy father, John Paul II, that there is mercy for everything. What you did is an error of youth. If there are people who love you, who want your good as well as the good of the country, they must be your elders with, at their head, your humble servant. . . . You have requested to rejoin the civil servants' family. I agree to it."[56]

Another who at one point sought forgiveness from the president was his long-time political opponent, Laurent Gbagbo. As described in the local press, after six years in exile Gbagbo returned to Côte d'Ivoire in 1988 and apologized personally to Houphouet because certain of his critical political tracts had wounded the president. "I have come; I place myself at your disposition," Gbagbo is reported to have said. Houphouet then replied, "That which he was able to write, he is the only one to judge it. It is not for us to do it. He is a professor; he is going to profess; perhaps he will explain to his pupils that which he has written. As far as I am concerned, he is a brother whom I have rediscovered; there are no problems; he is in the house, at home so that we may build Côte d'Ivoire."[57] Unlike the previously cited speeches and letters, there is at least a possibility that this particular incident of a presidential pardon might not have gone precisely according to the script. The presentation of Gbagbo's reply to the head of state, even as reported in the state-controlled press, obviously did not attain the usual level of the flowery familial dialog between Houphouet and the usual run-of-the-mill penitents. Still, it is of interest that the regime tried to fit even a hardened political opponent such as Gbagbo into the prevailing implicit conception of the paternal pardon.[58]

The paternal pardon is certainly not restricted to Côte d'Ivoire. In 1992 the Kenyan press reported that the Kenya National Democratic Party (KNDP) was to dissolve and rejoin President Moi's KANU. At the time, the KNDP's interim leader, John Chesanga, tried to apply the notion of the paternal pardon to a clear case of parliamentary carpet crossing. Commenting that there were probably people in other opposition parties who were not any more sure of the future than when they were in KANU, Chesanga said, "I urge them not to die in their guilt but come back and repent because KANU is Kenya's mother and will always forgive."[59] Similarly, in trying to bring peace to her troubled land, Liberia's Ruth Perry appealed to the mothers of all guerrilla fighters to lay down their arms. "I extend the olive branch and I forgive our children," she said.[60]

Mobutu Sese Seko also made frequent use of the imagery associated with the paternal pardon. In 1986, for example, Mobutu pardoned approximately one hundred "lost sons" who had spent the previous twenty years in the maquis and who were, according to the regime, responsible for the brief seizure of Moba town in the mid-1980s. They had resolved to reenter the large MPR family, "like the prodigal son of the holy Scriptures." In a particularly Zaïrian twist, the newly reintegrated sons were asked to perform a session of "*animation*," or political cheerleading, and to sing "revolutionary" (i.e., pro-Mobutu) songs at an officers mess. So they sang the Lingala chant "*Sese mokonzi ekolo, Sese tata na bana, mobongisiya Zaïre* [Sese is the chief of the nation, Sese is the father of the family, the builder of Zaïre]."[61] Moreover, like his fellow middle African heads of state, Mobutu often used university students and their "normal" turbulence to highlight his paternal solicitude and to emphasize his willingness to employ the paternal pardon. An editorial in *Elima* noted that the regime had closed the University of Kinshasa in February 1989 because there was disorder on campus. Nonetheless, as the editorialist had it, because the youth carry with them the hopes of the nation and the guarantee of its future, and because the place reserved for student youth in the life of the MPR is of the first importance, "as a good father of the family, the President-Founder has just granted his pardon to the troublesome students and has decided to reopen the closed institutes. This measure of clemency shows once again an illustration of Father of the Nation's grandeur of the soul and also constitutes an act of magnanimity by the Chief of the Party." The editorial concluded laconically that several of the students had already demonstrated their gratitude to the Guide for this merciful measure.[62]

Abdou Diouf would also employ the paternal pardon, although not nearly as often as Houphouet or Mobutu. Furthermore, Diouf's presentation of the pardon was in some ways more thoughtful and subtle, and less predictable. For example, in the wake of the contested elections in 1988, supporters of Abdoulaye Wade's PDS rioted in the streets for several days, and Diouf immediately declared a state of emergency for the region of Dakar. Several months later, on the eve of the Muslim holy day, Aïd el Fitr (Korité), the president conveyed his holiday greetings to the nation on national television and radio. He began by symbolically embracing God and the Koran, for, in the view of some, all power and legitimacy ultimately derive from God. "I wish that God, the Merciful, . . . surrounds us with his generous Grace which, in fact, constitutes the light that illumines our hearts, purifies our souls and guides us on the road of rectitude," he intoned. He then declared that he would end the state of emergency. In setting forth his reasons for making this decision, Diouf stated that he had also introduced an amnesty bill to the National Assembly, which, once adopted, would have the effect of pardoning certain Senegalese who had been convicted of crimes. "President of all Senegalese," he continued, "elected for a new five-year mandate, it is my duty to say to these sons and daughters—since women are also concerned in this amnesty—that the nation does not intend to reject them indefinitely. They were able to follow a bad road. They must not be penalized all their life. I want to give them a new chance, so that they can rediscover their family, their friends, their villages or their neighborhoods, and again harness themselves to the construction of Senegal." Diouf also relayed his decision to meet with Wade, leader of the parliamentary opposition, to discuss the nation's problems. In concluding, he noted, "I am thus making an optimistic bet on the maturity, the patriotism and the wisdom of each of the actors in the political game of our country."[63] Diouf's confidence in the political "maturity" of the Senegalese involved in the political game is particularly telling. The unstated assumption was that if they did not follow his lead in these matters, then they were "immature." In other words, even in Senegal there exists something of the "classic" pattern of paternal pardons. But there are two important differences. The first is that Islam played a critical role in structuring the timing of the pardon, as well as in providing Diouf an occasion to demonstrate to Senegalese that he was, after all, a devout believer in a theological context that also views charity and forgiveness as virtuous behavior. The second is that even if Diouf was totally cynical and that meeting with Wade was simply a political maneuver or for show, he still attributed a role to the opposition in publicly admitting that his regime should confer with them and at least listen to them.

Other heads of state would also periodically resort to the paternal pardon, or a variant of it. Both Ahidjo and Biya, for example, were adept at this, often saving the announcement of these pardons for key anniversaries or holidays so as to maximize the symbolic value already associated with a national occasion.[64] But even where many of the more blatant paternal trappings were missing, regimes still emphasized the act of pardon itself even without the rhetorical baggage. In Nigeria, for example, Shehu Shagari's account of his first one hundred days in office concluded with both a plea for national political consultations among the various political parties and a reminder that he had ordered the immediate release of certain people convicted under the Foreign Exchange Anti Sabotage Act because it was "repugnant to natural justice." Then, in 1981 he pardoned the former head of state, Yakubu Gowon, because he wanted a "spirit of magnanimity and restraint" injected into Nigerian politics and therefore granted the clemency as part of the celebration of Nigeria's twenty-first anniversary of independence.[65] One contemporary commentary on Shagari's administration saw his pardon of both Gowon and the former Biafran secessionist leader Emeka Ojukwu as an example of his attachment to high ethical norms, and especially his belief in acting the role of his "brother's keeper." The author described the pardons this way: "As brothers of his, born by our mother-Nigeria, Shehu's sense of brotherhood overwhelmed all apparently justified fears and grievances expressed by well meaning citizens."[66]

If we envisage the presidential pardon in middle Africa along a continuum ranging from the fully elaborated paternal pardon (à la Houphouet and Mobutu) at one end, to a Weberian bureaucratic orientation at the other end, both Nyerere and Mwinyi of Tanzania, as well as the Rawlings regime in Ghana, would fall closest to the Weberian bureaucratic side. In Tanzania, for example, news articles simply report the facts of the matter. "Mwalimu Nyerere yesterday pardoned a total of 1,919 prisoners to mark his swearing-in as President of the United Republic of Tanzania for five more years." Or, "President Nyerere has pardoned 2,494 prisoners and 65 people accused of economic sabotage and racketeering in a gesture to mark the 22nd Independence Anniversary yesterday." And, "President Mwinyi has pardoned 835 prisoners on the occasion of the 26th Anniversary of the Independence of [the] Tanzania Mainland."[67] Although these articles simply relate the facts of the pardon—in other words, the numbers of inmates and the categories of offenses involved—it is significant that they almost always appear prominently on page one of the newspaper. The pardon, even without its fully explicit paternal regalia, remains important in conveying to people a certain logic of legitimacy and in reinforcing—albeit subtly—a generally unstated familial responsibility of even the less paternally inclined of middle Africa's political leaders.[68]

In some decisions to grant a judicial pardon, especially where the death penalty is involved, it is fair to say that some middle African leaders—whatever other calculations of political advantage might be involved—probably also think deeply about the moral and ethical ramifications of their actions. After his retirement, Léopold Senghor noted that during his years in power the most difficult decision for him was to have refused to commute the death sentence of a man convicted of having attempted to assassinate him. "On reflection," he said, "the death penalty is a decisive weapon, especially in a developing country. You see, there have not been more than four executions in Senegal since independence."[69] In a similarly reflective vein, in 1980 Hilla Limann justified granting certain general amnesties to mark the first anniversary of the Third Ghanaian Republic. In a radio and television broadcast the preceding evening, President Limann explained that he made the gesture "because of our strong belief in the innate goodness of the Ghanaian as human being and in his high sense of the values of peace, freedom and justice."[70] Even Paul Biya, on most occasions perhaps not one of the more philosophical heads of state, thoughtfully noted the following in a radio address to the nation as he commuted the death sentence of Ahmadou Ahidjo and his fellow conspirators in 1984:

> Everybody is equal before the law and no one has the right, whatever services he might have previously rendered to the nation, to place in peril the collective security through ambition or personal interests.
>
> But beyond justice, there is the higher interest of the State and the moral values of respect for life, of humanity and magnanimity which constitute the grandeur of man.

In the name of this interest and these values, and in my soul and conscience, I have decided by virtue of the powers the constitution confers on me, to commute to detention the death sentence pronounced by the military tribunal of Yaoundé. . . .

From this painful episode in the political life of our country, history will remember that the President of the Republic, although he had all of the legal means at his disposal to implement the just sentence of the tribunal, preferred clemency in the higher interest of the Nation and fidelity to higher moral values. . . ."[71]

Unfortunately, "higher moral values" have not always been the lodestar guiding middle Africa's father-chiefs.

Corruption and Its Limits

It is a staple of various analyses of politics in middle Africa both to highlight and to deplore the pernicious economic and political effects of corruption. Economically, corruption has the effect of levying a hidden tax on growth and development; it discourages the confidence of investors and international financial institutions and constitutes an often substantial drain on the state's resources. Politically, corruption saps the confidence of ordinary citizens. They know that their taxes may well line someone else's pockets, while economic and electoral competitions will be skewed. Justice, education, and health care increasingly come to be primarily for those fortunate enough to be able to afford them, while the gap separating rich and poor widens, and the foundations of the entire polity are brought into disrepute. Confidence erodes and, of course, legitimacy declines as removing the present regime by whatever means necessary becomes an increasingly thinkable option.[72]

While there is much that is meritorious in these analytical treatments of corrupt practices, many middle Africans frequently place a slightly different emphasis on these things. As we saw in Chapter 2, power in this part of the world is often seen as the ability to control and consume both people and resources—the ability to "eat" in both literal and figurative senses of that term. There is also a sense in which, because they are powerful, people expect their father-chiefs to "eat" and even eat well. This is one of their rights, and if they observe certain limitations, it will be quite thinkable that they continue to do this. Is this a culturally determined carte blanche for corrupt practices? No. It is simply a recognition that power is not always manifested in the same ways in different cultural contexts. Furthermore, the second premise of the moral matrix of legitimate governance sets limits, however imprecise and unamenable to equational precision they may be, on just how much father-chiefs and other officials may consume. Put briefly, the father-chief may eat, and eat well, but not while his political children go hungry. Or phrased in a slightly different idiom, in 1990 Zaïre's Catholic bishops criticized the regime for, among other abuses, its inattention to "the philosophy of the traditional system, notably the economic solidarity of the prince with all his people."[73]

A retrospective essay reflecting on the origins of the coup that ended the Acheampong regime and brought J. J. Rawlings briefly to power in 1979 makes the point nicely: "The nation was in crisis. There was general despondency. The economy had run down and as Flt.-Lt. Rawlings put it at the trial, 'people were dying of starvation in the teeth of few well fed, who even had the chance of growing fatter when the economy of this country was dominated by foreigners, especially Arabs and Lebanese[,] when successive governments had failed to question about their nefarious activities.'"[74] The same point was also apparent in the 1983 Christmas sermon of the Reverend Festus Segun, the Anglican bishop of Lagos. The bishop spoke of the fear of hunger in Nigeria because food production was lagging, and prices had skyrocketed. People, moreover, were afraid of poverty because of unemployment and the retrenchment of workers. The situation was "grim," and Bishop Segun lamented the increasing financial insecurity of Nigeria's masses "while the greedy selfish few, swim in the ill-gotten wealth, and display sheer indifference to the needs of the others."[75] The references to the "greedy selfish few," the "ill-gotten wealth," and the display of "sheer indifference" to others speak to a perceived relationship between corruption, conspicuous consumption, and rising social class tensions in a period of sustained economic deterioration. Corruption and economic decline continued unabated under various military rulers. Despite the usual protestations to the contrary and the succession of "wars" against "indiscipline" and other forms of corrupt behavior, extralegal appropriations flourished with the soldiers in charge. Speaking specifically of the Abacha regime in the middle and late 1990s, one civil rights attorney noted that "when the soldiers have eaten enough, he retires them."[76]

Although it had virtually no influence in such matters and certainly could not say what all knew—namely, that the major example of corrupt behavior, of excessive "eating," was Mobutu himself—the state-controlled Zaïrian press nevertheless frequently railed against corruption. For example, a 1981 editorial castigated "gluttonous" cadres who had become middlemen in the agricultural sector but who were no longer interested in developing the valuable land the state had given to them.[77] Another columnist criticized a cadre for embezzling public funds and then taking severe actions against those who had denounced his activities. Commenting on the cadre's unpersuasive defense of his actions, the journalist noted that "all reasons are thus evoked by this type of hierarchical chief to defend [his] cake."[78] For another columnist writing in 1983, the pillage of national resources, as well as the widening gulf between the vast majority of the population and the very privileged minority resulting from it, had created a situation of such alarming proportions that it had become, in his view, "worse than colonization."[79]

Some of the same conditions are evoked elsewhere as well. One letter commenting on events in The Gambia in the aftermath of the Jammeh coup against Dauda Jawara noted that "while the Gambian people were living in abject penury, Jawara and his colleagues continued paying themselves fat salaries."[80] Similarly, a critical letter published in Kenya noted that constant reports and editorial correspondence on the subject of corrupt officials were not presenting outsiders with an especially favorable image of the country. In his words, "Legislators who have tended to prosper materially in recent years have been those who have avoided raising the dust for the sake of the electorate. The catchphrase seems to have been *Kula matunda ya Uhuru pole pole bila kelele* [Take what you can quietly without making waves]."[81] A more literal translation of the Swahili phrase would be "Eat the fruits of independence slowly, without noise."

Not all middle African states were as corrupt as Nigeria under military rule or Zaïre under Mobutu. Although corruption existed in Tanzania under both Nyerere and Mwinyi and certainly got progressively worse throughout the 1980s, it was still on a far smaller scale than elsewhere in middle Africa.[82] People perceived Nyerere, especially, to be honest—as someone who did not "eat" and thus as being physically "thin." A poem published in the *Daily News* in 1980 described Nyerere as someone whom Tanzania still needed: "NYERERE, father of the nation, / You have done much for us. / Your unprecedented contribution, / To build our nation. / You get a meager return, / Yet you don't complain. / Whom shall I compare you with? / You are very audacious, / Too benevolent and a benefactor. / . . ."[83] Similarly, a 1971 Swahili praise poem noted that Nyerere was "number one" in Africa and Tanzania among leaders who care about their people's welfare because he is unlike others who are interested only in lining their own stomachs ("*wasotunisha tumbo zao*").[84] And Nyerere himself was often in the forefront in the various campaigns against corruption, racketeering, and economic sabotage. In 1981, for example, while addressing the nation's youth and speaking to over 6,800 new party members, he noted that a "party of eaters [*Chama cha Walaji*]" could not pass for a revolutionary party, and asked the new members to reject the idea that CCM was the basis for their personal enrichment.[85]

Oftentimes abuse of the state's automobile fleet, or some other question pertaining to cars, would exacerbate sentiments against corruption in public life. A 1986 Ghanaian editorial inveighed against what it called "Pajero politics," taking note of the many Pajeros, Land Cruisers, and other sport-utility vehicles that roamed the streets of Accra and other major population centers. The vehicles themselves, whether rightly or wrongly, had become associated in the popular mind with government officials (who, on their salaries, certainly could not afford to drive them). The editorialist noted dryly that "when members of the public see such vehicles lined up outside a nightclub or hotel, a question mark arises in their minds. . . ."[86] Moreover, a 1982 *Elima* editorial evoked a similar theme. Noting that although public officials ought to serve as good examples for the population, the reality was rather different. The essay observed that certain public officials declared their state vehicles "obsolete" after minor damage; once the cars were put back into proper shape they were then resold to the same officials who had them declared outmoded in the first place.[87] A decade later, during Mobutu's partial liberalization, the CNS set up a Committee on Stolen Property. The committee's final report noted that although Zaïre was one of the poorest states in sub-Saharan Africa, it was also one of the continent's largest importers of luxury automobiles. In addition, the report also noted that in 1989 the budgetary rubric "purchase of vehicles" represented 10 percent of the total national budget and that the sums expended on the health and education sectors did not even receive 3 percent of the total.[88] Even in Tanzania this was a concern that had bred cynicism by the end of the 1980s, although the theft and abuse occurred on a much smaller scale than elsewhere in middle Africa. When asked how she differentiated between corrupt leaders and other citizens, a typist replied: "A look at the luxurious saloon cars they are driving, their mansions and life styles which do not correspond to their incomes, will tell you all."[89]

In general, and throughout the region, regardless of the degree of complicity of the father-chief or the political class, clergy more than occasionally deplored both endemic corruption as well as the decline in morals that accompanied it. In 1980 the then Roman Catholic archbishop of Lagos, Dr. Olubunmi Okogie, used his annual New Year's message to call on Nigerian leaders to resist greed and to live a life of sacrifice and moral courage.[90] Some years later one of his colleagues, the Catholic bishop of Jos, Dr. Gabriel Ganaka, told a television audience that any act of political corruption, but especially election rigging, is an "abominable offence against humanity."[91] And, in Senegal, during his 1982 Tabaski sermon the imam of the Great Mosque of Saint-Louis, El Hadj Oumar Diallo, said that those who appropriate public goods must be punished without shame, regardless of who they might be.[92] On this question as well, therefore, there is again a blurring of the boundary between the political and religious spheres.

Certainly, clergy are not the only people concerned about declining public morals. During the 1980s and into the 1990s editorialists throughout middle Africa beat the drum steadily with essays and opinions castigating corruption and deploring declining moral standards. The Nigerian *Daily Times,* for example, took note of the work of the National Ethical Re-orientation Committee in 1983 and commented, "Really, the rate of corruption, bribery, indiscipline, immorality, cheating, idleness, drug addiction, armed robbery, smuggling and other vices has currently assumed an alarming proportion in this country."[93] Another editorial presented roughly the same laundry list of illegal, yet common, practices and remarked, "To eliminate corruption and enthrone a just and morally sound society, Nigerian leaders should lead the country by good examples. A demonstration from above of an iron-will to eradicate corruption amounts to more than half the battle against it. . . ."[94] And a 1983 Ghanaian editorial, reflecting on the preceding Limann administration, noted that a "war" against corruption was necessary to restore dignity to Ghanaian society. "For years," the editorialist wrote, "corruption has eaten like a festering sore into the body politic of the Ghanaian society. It was taken for granted that corruption was a legitimate means of doing business and conducting affairs of the state."[95] In Ghana, as in so many other parts of middle Africa, corruption in the normal conduct of state affairs had become thinkable and thus legitimate. Even more to the point, the familial and ethnic pressures often brought to bear on those within the state and thus able to "eat" were such that it gradually became unthinkable and illegitimate *not* to engage in such activities.[96]

Although they themselves might well have been involved in corrupt practices, father-chiefs, too, often contributed to the invective against corruption. Beginning with his 1977 speech on what he termed the "Zaïrian sickness [*le mal zaïrois*]," Mobutu would regularly take officials to task for their corrupt activities. In that particular speech he observed, correctly, that "everything is sold, everything is bought in our country. And in this traffic, the possession of an ordinary parcel of public power constitutes a veritable currency of exchange against the illicit acquisition of money or of a material or moral value, or moreover, the evasion of all sorts of obligations." The most basic and legitimate rights of the population were thus exposed to an "invisible tax" that officeholders would then openly and brazenly cash.[97] Of course, Mobutu criticizing corruption was roughly equivalent to the Pope criticizing Catholicism, and fifteen years later the CNS's Committee on Stolen Property concluded its report noting, "In truth, there was no place in this country for virtue, particularly in the matter of public management." The committee deemed that "the responsibility of the political authorities of the Second Republic is, in this regard, total."[98] Virtue and honesty had, over time, become unthinkable in state officials.

In 1982 Abdou Diouf, a far less venal politician than Mobutu, denied accusations of corruption leveled against him, stating, "I am faithful to the oath that I took before the Nation on the occasion of my accession to the supreme magistrature. We want to have a clean [*propre*] government to construct a clean, transparent State [*cité*]. A house of glass. . . ."[99] And, some months later in an address to the nation, Diouf spoke at some length of the need to cleanse Senegal's political and economic morals. "It is not tolerable," he said, "that some people use the powers conferred to them by their positions of responsibility to enrich themselves, in an illicit manner, to the detriment of the collectivity."[100]

Time and the close observation of behavior have made many middle Africans cynical about the motives of their politicians. They are thus unlikely to accept such statements at face value. On one level, father-chiefs and other public figures are well aware of this, and they know that while they may "eat," conspicuous consumption—especially during a period of general economic hardship—would be perceived as excessive and wrong. When in 1982 Diouf, for example, decided to forgo two months of his salary in solidarity with Senegalese peasants who were then suffering, one local journalist evaluated his action, remarking that the president's gesture was, first of all, a human one and that this was important because power brings additional responsibilities and power holders need to show a human face rather than hiding behind the disembodied, anonymous visage of the state.[101]

In other words, austerity has to be shared or legitimacy will diminish markedly—a point made explicitly in a Ghanaian editorial during Limann's administration: "It has become very embarrassing to preach the tightening of belts to the Ghanaian public because in the midst of the austerity imposed on the people, the leaders always flouted their affluence. We are sure, however that Dr Limann can safely preach sweat, blood and toil for as long as he can ensure that the austerity will be uniformly spread around."[102] The succeeding PNDC government also recognized and, presumably, accepted the point. In 1983, for example, a ranking member of the PNDC tried to explain the rationale behind the current budget. In the words of the newspaper account covering the speech, "The PNDC, unlike past governments, is not asking Ghanaians to tighten their belts while its members loosen theirs, Mr. John Ndebugre, the Upper East Regional Secretary has said. He said the leadership of the PNDC is honest and its members are equally facing the same economic hardships all other Ghanaians are experiencing at present."[103]

Father-chiefs, therefore, must nourish and nurture. They may discipline and punish but must also forgive and pardon. And while they may eat within reason, they may not overindulge their appetites while the population, their political "children," are suffering from hunger. These are, in brief, some of the rights, responsibilities, and limitations on the father-chief contained in the first two premises of the moral matrix of legitimate governance. In Chapter 6 we examine the rights, responsibilities, and limitations set forth in the third and fourth premises of the matrix that pertain to women and the alternation of power.

6. Matrix II—Gender and Generation
Women, the Paternal Order, and the Alternation of Power

The third premise of the moral matrix of legitimate governance concerns the position of women and how the prevailing political discourse positions them in the polity.[1] Put briefly, the discourse often implicitly defines the parameters of the political so as to exclude women from the realm of politics while consigning them to the arena of small, localized development projects. This cognitive and definitional exclusion results in both a "structured invisibility" and a "structured silence"; in consequence, their voices are rarely heard in the political arena except in the carefully controlled, state-dominated, and state-organized venues that formal "women's organizations" usually provide.[2] Women, however, do have a voice. Even where the paternal order is most pronounced in middle Africa, the prevalent discourse provides them space to act as counselors to the political "fathers" and further requires father-chiefs to listen to their counsel, heed their advice, and treat them (and by extension other politically disadvantaged segments of the population such as workers, farmers, and students) with dignity and respect. Moreover, although politicians and others spoke increasingly of democracy throughout the late 1980s and 1990s, they have been much less likely to advance claims of equality— especially where women are concerned. The complementary and advisory roles which the implicit paternal language and familial metaphors assign to women are changing quickly, however, and women throughout the region are increasingly aware of international legal changes, the various United Nations conferences and publicity on women, and other initiatives designed to alleviate the plight of women throughout the world.[3] The swift diffusion and critical importance of these external influences and ideas means that this premise of the matrix is shifting rapidly, making it most difficult to speak with certainty of the idealized roles that the dominant political discourse assigns to women. What remains certain, however, is that as in Latin America, Japan, the United States, and elsewhere, considerations associated with gender in middle Africa are complex and contextually sensitive, emerging as they do from complicated processes of social and political construction.[4]

Senegalese author and literary figure Mariama Bâ framed some of these issues, especially the economic ones, in a 1979 speech pertaining to the national day of the Senegalese woman. In her own words:

> I wish, before this assembly, that my voice, unauthorized though it may be, also remains the expression of the most numerous women, the most deprived, the most deserving perhaps, relegated to a silence despite themselves. I want my voice to be confused with those of city workers, living in the peripheral neighborhoods, . . . mothers unbalanced by a thousand hungers in their bellies. I want to be the interpreter of the woman farmer that malnourishment, [and] the search for water . . . fade prematurely. . . . I would like to reverberate, without anger, but in ringing echoes, all the strangled voices, the voice of oppressed sisters . . . who have heads buzzing from uncontrolled maternities, heads buzzing from all the fatigues which are their daily lot. . . .
>
> If equalizations, not negligible in their content and orientation, tend to level Senegalese man to the level of his companion in many social, cultural, judicial domains, segregations persist, still too vexing that we should forget them; insufficiencies are situated, visible and depressing, requiring the woman, in her accession to positions of political and administrative responsibility, an exhausting investment of all her resources, [that is] unknown to men.
>
> Decisive changes will be born from the reconversion of mentalities. From a well coordinated complementarity must surge forth a mutual support [coude à coude] fruitful for all.
>
> Man, without rancor and without hate, is invited to descend from his pedestal of inherited and unjustified privileges. In our times let him forget, without nostalgia, the Lord that he was, to become a worker, along side a female worker, for the harmonious edification of the State [cité]. To engender new attitudes let his instinct of domination cede place to comprehension and to humility. . . .[5]

But Bâ's voice was "unauthorized." Much closer to the thinkable mainstream in these matters was a 1985 Nigerian editorial. "The Nigerian woman," the editorialist opined, "like members of her sex in almost every culture, has long been recognised as the weaker sex. She was perceived to be on the average, more virtuous than her male counterpart. But far from being exploited, repressed or treated with levity as many a feminist would have us believe, the Nigerian society has always recognised and respected the God-ordained and cultural roles of our women." The essay then recounts that a small percentage of Nigerian women have debased womanhood through their illegal pursuit of material gain: "In what appears their determination to secure equality with men—a determination we consider misguided on account of the fact that our society places no obstacle on their path to self-actualisation, one reason we find some of them in many respectable positions and noticed their presence in many professions—our women have been engaged in armed robbery operations, smuggling, hard drug trafficking, brothelkeeping and other such ignoble pursuits and negative tendencies which were once thought to be the exclusive preserves of men."[6] In contradistinction to Bâ's vision, although the present inequality between men and women is also simply assumed, here the quest for equality is seen as "misguided." Furthermore, there is also an assumption that such inequality is divinely inspired. This editorial is one of the clearer statements of the usually implicit notion that a woman's equality has no real place in the pantheon of contemporary cultural values in this part of the world—at least no place according to the men who have the discursive power to write editorials such as this one.

Mariama Bâ's vision, however accurate it may be, is almost certainly profoundly upsetting to the prevailing powers and is therefore not widely diffused. If (as the Nigerian editorial would have it) the role of women is "God-ordained" and "cultural," we must still elaborate the component characteristics of the idealized vision of women in middle Africa that power holders in the paternal order find acceptable and worthy of diffusion. As always, although the eight major countries under examination display variations in the prevalent imagery, there is nonetheless substantial congruence of some of the more central ideal characteristics. In this vein, an account appearing in the Zaïrian press in 1982 lauding Mama Bobi Ladawa on her thirty-seventh birthday merits attention, for it touches on many of these desired traits.

The author, Essolomwa Nkoy ea Linganga, was for many years an authorized and favorite public spokesman of the Mobutu regime. Since the themes he sounded in this particular essay were all hardy perennials, commonly advanced and widely diffused, it thus seems certain that the political powers heartily approved of the thrust of his analysis.[7] In his words, as the nation's First Lady, Mama Bobi was naturally the "first [female] citizen of Zaïre." To celebrate her birthday, Mama Bobi spread her joy to people in difficulty, as well as to the ill in Kinshasa's hospitals. "To the latter, the Citizen Presidente made a generous gift of hundreds of sides of beef, thousands of chickens, and dozens of thousands of eggs." These gifts again demonstrated Mama Bobi's "maternal solicitude" toward the sick and others in need. In engaging in these and other comparable actions, she was the "mother of 25 million Zaïrian women and men." She had, in other words, become a symbol of the "grandeur of the soul" intent on easing the suffering and pain of the needy. In consequence, everybody appreciated her good upbringing, her high moral values, and her excellent qualities as a mother of a family. Moreover, the article continued, the First Lady "applies herself to the task of following the subtle conceptions of her illustrious husband . . . of whom she is a much listened to counselor."

Concluding his journalistic birthday card, Essolomwa noted, "That is to say that Mama Bobi Ladawa plays a preponderant role in the political and social life of the country. For, if on several occasions, she is seen tirelessly accompanying the Head of State on his long journeys . . . if she is regularly seen entertaining the wives of diplomats and other political personalities, equally she does not miss, devotedly and with abnegation, taking part in the country's social activities."[8]

The motifs evoked are striking. The First Lady is, of course, an ideal woman. She is a repository of high moral values and has become a national symbol of the assumed and preferred virtues of motherhood. She is a valued counselor to her husband. She is the mother of the large national family who shows her devotion to her national "children" through acts of maternal solicitude such as donations of food to the sick and needy. Curiously, although she "feeds" and "nourishes" just as her spouse does, these actions are seen as charity rather than as being political. She has a political role, but it is limited to accompanying the president on his trips and supporting him by entertaining diplomats and political dignitaries.[9]

This chapter examines political language, metaphors, and imagery as they pertain to this rather idealized vision of women as mothers, counselors, and providers of succor. We shall see that the treatment of women, and gender relations more broadly, has to do with basic questions of inclusion and exclusion. Who shall be included in the polity? Who shall be excluded? Who will enjoy full rights and responsibilities? Who will play a "complementary" role? Is the preferred role of women, at least according to the dominant imagery, only that of counselor, hostess, and, as we saw in Mama Bobi's case, provider of food and aid to the needy and sick? Who will have power? Who will "eat"? Or, in Bâ's words, who will be "unbalanced by a thousand hungers in their bellies"? All these questions touch on fundamental aspects of political life under the middle African paternal order.

Basic questions of political succession also concern the political fathers. One of the responsibilities and limitations contained in the fourth premise of the moral matrix is that power may not be wielded permanently and that, in consequence, there must be an alternation of power. In other words, since good fathers must permit their children to grow up, eventually succeeding them, political fathers cannot monopolize power indefinitely without having their legitimacy diminish markedly. Failure to allow their political "children" to "grow up" and to succeed them would be unthinkable and illegitimate. Issues of political succession are thus critical. Alternation of power also concerns inclusion and exclusion. In this matter, however, the critical factor is not gender, but generation. As we shall see, in adopting an implicit notion of generational rotation as a method of achieving political alternation, the reliance on an idealized historical model of transfer of power between two groups of elders, or between fathers and sons, tends to exclude both women and youths. The ascension of these groups would be quite "naturally" unthinkable and thus illegitimate. Generational succession and the passage of power between different political generations that accompanies it is a key to understanding the logic of legitimacy in middle Africa.

This chapter explores the third and fourth premises of the moral matrix. It begins with the presentation of women in the dominant discourse, focusing on their definitional exclusion from the political realm, their "approved" role as counselors and advisers, and their more general position within the paternal order. The second portion of this chapter examines the usually unstated assumptions pertaining to the illegitimacy of eternal power and the consequent importance of generational rotation. I pay particular attention to successions in Senegal, Tanzania, and Cameroon, for these cases illustrate well how the paternal order presents and understands political succession.

Women and the Paternal Order

Mama Bobi's birthday card nicely indicates one way in which the prevailing language and imagery restricts the "political" role of women. In having her "political" role restricted to counseling her husband and entertaining dignitaries, Mama Bobi—and by extension other women—is confined within a "political" universe whose parameters are both narrow and gendered. In ways both subtle and obvious, the political language of middle Africa either reduces the political space women may enjoy or, in some cases, excludes them entirely from the realm of effective politics by suggesting that their true tasks lie elsewhere. In a 1982 speech before the National Council of the Parti Socialiste, for example, Abdou Diouf called on the party's organizations for youth and women to play an active role in its social project. "Already our valiant sisters who do not want to remain at rest in the combat for the diffusion of our party and for national construction," the president intoned, "have been mobilized to support concretely the government's economic projects, thus honoring the PS."[10] Similarly, in 1988 Ghana's First Lady, Nana Konadu Agyeman-Rawlings, called on women to do away with their negative attitude of dependence on men. She maintained that women should have the courage to involve themselves actively in public affairs so as to help reshape the country's future. On one level, Mrs. Rawlings had issued a ringing cry for the end of dependency and an involvement in public affairs. At the same time, however, this call was tempered by her assertion that, in the words of the press account, "the country needs women who can effectively contribute to the development of their communities and also maintain some degree of personal economic independence by engaging in productive work."[11] Public affairs, or a key portion of the political realm, is thus equated with community development, financial independence in the household, and productive work.

Other examples of this conceptual exclusion abound. In 1982 an interviewer asked the president of a provincial branch of the Organisation des Femmes de l'UNC (OFUNC), the women's wing of the Cameroonian single party, whether Cameroonian women liked politics. She replied: "The Cameroonian woman wants to be interested in the affairs of her country. To this end, she has an interest in having weight within the Union National Camerounaise. This interest shows itself through massive participation in party meetings, and in public demonstrations such as official holidays, welcoming officials or the high personalities of the Republic." But when asked about the participation of women in the cultural, social, and economic development of the nation, she noted that for the women it was a question of cultivating the "taste of work, whether it concerns work on the land, in the household, at the office or even in commerce."[12] Party meetings provided little room for independent, unscripted political activity. Nor, for that matter, did participation in choreographed demonstrations or in welcoming visiting dignitaries. In a similar manner, Mme Yaw Aïssatou, in 1989 the minister of social affairs and of the feminine condition, noted that Cameroonian women benefited "from the government's constant solicitude, as attest the multiplicity of national mechanisms for the integration of women and the importance of projects and programs implemented to improve this situation."[13] Again, we see that women are shunted conceptually from the political realm to an arena ostensibly full of "projects and programs."

Kate Kamba, a Tanzanian MP and head of the Tanzanian Women's Organization (Umoja wa Wanawake wa Tanzania, UWT) in 1983, replied to a question concerning the definition of women's liberation. She noted: "We should not talk of men collecting firewood or washing dishes as liberating women. Rather, we should talk of taking services closer to the rural women so as to lessen the burden of her having to walk miles and miles to get water, medical care or even the firewood with a baby on her back." She then argued that if women had access to child care centers and medical facilities nearby, their burden would be diminished, and, therefore, they could participate in other developmental activities. The MP further maintained that she did not really see "how you can separate politics from the rest of life."[14] And while this is undoubtedly true, it would nonetheless appear that she has effectively excised much of the easily recognizable core of the political realm from her conception of politics as it pertains to Tanzanian women.

A structured political invisibility of middle African women results from this conceptual exclusion. Nigeria provides one glaring instance of this phenomenon. In 1986 the then president, Ibrahim Babangida, noted, "We have deliberately adopted the policy of involving all sections of our community in the decision-making process and it is our belief that our people are sufficiently mature to be allowed to express their views on any issue, to be consulted and to be encouraged to come forth with a consensus. Because we know that we must unite to solve our problems by ourselves, we have involved the workers, the business community, the traditional rulers, religious leaders, the Press and others, not the least, members of the intellectual community, in the search for solution to the myriads of problems we face."[15] Although we may certainly question just how sincere and widespread Babangida's "consultations" actually were, the omission of women as a distinct category of individuals involved in the general's idealized process of political decision making was, to say the least, striking.

Certain images and metaphors often used in reference to women also tend to present them as inhabiting a social, cultural, and economic world that exists outside the parameters of the political. In 1982 Senegal celebrated its eighth annual national literacy week. An article in *Le Soleil* called attention to this fact, emphasizing that most illiterates in the country were women. A female official asked to comment on this noted that any type of development excluding women was an impossibility and that women simply did not think about participating in development without first assuming a certain responsibility for it. Such accountability would not be possible if women were illiterate. The article then reminded its readers that women were the "pillars of the family and thus of the nation" and that, therefore, the Senegalese government's action plan accented the role of women in the management of family affairs, as well as in the organization of local cooperatives and small businesses.[16] Put slightly differently, the article saw literacy as a tool women could use to improve their performance in economic development, rather than as a means of fostering their political participation or accession to genuine political power.

Given the close relationship between food, eating, and power in middle Africa's cultural context, images of food are particularly telling. Although women are often pictured as being instrumental in the production and preparation of food, they are rarely portrayed as "eating" in the sense of displaying power. Nor, for that matter, does the discourse often show them feeding others—something they most assuredly do. The result is to deepen their structured political invisibility, thus further removing them from reciprocal relations of power. Because they have been symbolically excluded from the realm of power, and because so many of their productive activities are defined explicitly and understood implicitly as cultural or economic, their resulting structured invisibility in the political realm helps us to understand why this paradox exists. President Diouf could thus publicly recognize and laud their "courage, imagination, and spirit of initiative" in changing alimentary habits and mind-sets about food so as to enable Senegal to become self-sufficient in food production.[17] Furthermore, the press often mentions women and food in the same breath. In 1986, for example, Senegalese authorities decided that the theme of the fifth Woman's Fortnight (a period devoted to women's issues and concerns) would be the role of the woman in Senegal's quest for self-sufficiency in food. As "pillars of the family," women were educators, mothers, and providers of nourishment. They, after all, were in charge of food production for family consumption. Even more, they were in charge of food preparation: "In effect, culinary art and the presentation of a dish counts for much in the adoption of that dish. And in this domain, no man disputes them the *chieftaincy of the kitchen.*"[18] It can almost go without saying that this particular position and title bring them no effective power.

The early days of the ostensibly radical Rawlings' regime saw the Ghanaian media present seemingly contradictory images of women. On the one hand, the press would often associate women with a set of strikingly benign and powerless images. So the *Daily Graphic* would cover, with a photograph, Ghana's "Ideal Womanhood" show. And what was the purpose of this one-month training course organized by the National Mobilisation Committee and the Fellowship of the Ghana Christian Women? During the sessions women were taught "dressmaking, bakery and cookery."[19] Even under the Rawlings revolution, ideal women cook and bake. They do not make trouble; they do not agitate politically; they do not go outside the regime-approved and -controlled organizational structure to "participate" in politics or to develop bases of effective power. Ironically, during roughly the same period some women were doing precisely that. Mrs. Rawlings as well as others were highly critical of Accra's market women, whom they thought were engaging in a "selfish" black market trade known as *kalabule.* The First Lady of the Revolution did not like this and argued that the participation of women in the national economy could never be assured until this trade was ended and the women in question changed their attitudes. According to Mrs. Rawlings, the "real" Ghanaian woman was "a loving and caring mother or sister."[20] Apparently, in other words, Accra's market women—some of whom were quite wealthy and powerful—could not be "real" women unless they renounced the source of their wealth, power, and independence.[21]

Certain countries—Nigeria, Senegal, and Côte d'Ivoire among them—hold annual beauty pageants to select and crown a young woman to serve as the national "Miss" for a year. Such events usually receive widespread press coverage and can usually be counted on to put forth a particular image of womanhood. One press report described the 1980 edition of the annual "Miss Nigeria" contest as follows:

> And as always, the focus has been on the true ideals of perfection in womanhood as part of the search for perfection in our social and cultural life. Especially, the emphasis has been on what the woman, as the source of new life, should symbolise in our ideas of beauty in looks, behaviours and activities.
>
> Perhaps, this explains why in the tradition of every ethnic group in Nigeria, and indeed all over Africa, the celebration of womanhood is an important event in the socio-cultural calendar.
>
> The rite of passage from girlhood to womanhood is marked with the parade of beauties who are adorned with the very best in dresses, makeup and ornaments. Such a parade usually marks the end of their formal training preparatory for adult life. This includes learning both the art and craft of motherhood and being a wife in etiquette, appearance and dressing.
>
> These cultural values in our perception of womanhood therefore prescribe standards of social conduct and expectations for whoever is so lucky to emerge as the queen in any given year.[22]

Here the discourse presents women as wifely beauties, as the "source of new life," and as practitioners of "the art and craft of motherhood." Critics might object that many societies, including that of the United States, have such annual beauty pageants and that perhaps the Nigerians, Ivoirians, and Senegalese learned such activities from watching how Westerners treat their own women. While this probably is the case, it is nevertheless striking that the themes permeating the discourse are quite consistent.

Emphasis on the preparation of food, on the role of motherhood, on the social and cultural importance of women is present even among many of the best educated and most accomplished segments of the female population throughout middle Africa. As an illustrative case in point, in 1980 the *Daily Times* ran a story about Winifred Odeinde, the chief librarian of the Central Library in Lagos. Mrs. Odeinde noted that "women as mothers of the nation have a very delicate role to play. Whereas the education of a man is said to be the education of an individual, educating a woman means educating a nation." Continuing, she stressed the importance of education, adding:

> Education is a continuous process. . . . There are assorted books on how to look after one's home, children and husband. There are educative books on cookery, home management, business, marketing etc. Such books are meant to be borrowed and read by our women as these would give them knowledge which would make them enlightened, broad in views, vast in current affairs and consequently be-

come respectable, intelligent women, because at this stage of our nation building we cannot afford to accommodate lazy and unintelligent women.[23]

Or, there is also the example of Cameroon's First Lady, Jeanne Irène Biya, who entertains elite women and the spouses of important political dignitaries each year shortly after New Year's Day. Powerful elite women, ministers and legislators among them, can always be counted on to offer Mme Biya a bouquet of flowers because, in the words of the article relating the event, women "know well the language of flowers."[24]

In other words, the very language and imagery that these reports employ and evoke subtly remove women from the political kingdom by placing them either in a world of small-scale economic development and small commerce, or in a world of motherhood and child rearing, or in a world of cooking and food preparation. As far as politics is concerned, the occasional exception notwithstanding, they are present but invisible. And although a treatment of "women's" organizations in middle Africa is well beyond the scope of this book, the existence of state- or party-controlled women's organizations, government ministries and departments devoted to women's issues, and other ad hoc attempts to organize and control women from above all also contribute to this structured political invisibility. Moreover, these organizational initiatives are certainly consistent with the state's frequent attempts to control the symbolism and imagery pertaining to women.[25]

Women as Counselors

Women have a voice in middle African discourse, but its range is limited. It is ancillary, rarely heard in public, and generally confined to a restricted array of subjects. Ultimately based on an idealized and perhaps increasingly unrealistic conception of the women's role within the family, the implicit model suggests broadly that women "complement" and support their spouses. In general, when middle Africans—especially men—speak of the "complementary" role of their wives and other women in these discussions, it should be understood that the term usually connotes a distinctly secondary, often subordinate role and a most unequal status. In turn, one of the husband's responsibilities, especially on questions that pertain directly to the children and the household, is to seek his wife's advice and input into any major decisions.

When Fatoumata Ka was elected president of the women's wing of the Senegalese PS in 1982, she gratefully accepted the position while praising the qualities of President Abdou Diouf "who incarnates the most precious virtues that the education of the Senegalese woman can bring to man: humility and firmness, generosity and a sense of justice." Addressing her organization, Mme Ka affirmed that "for us it will be about accepting, at the sides of our brothers, the numerous challenges that menace us."[26] In a related vein, a Nigerian commentator reflected that the society's customary, authoritative institutions "fostered ambivalence in the way the average Nigerian man sees his woman." Continuing, the author also noted some of the tensions and contradictions involved:

> He wants her to be a partner in progress when it comes to campaigning and voting for him to win a political position but not when it comes to her being elected or being voted into such positions in her own rights. While recognising her potentialities in being used as a ladder to climb up to positions, her man continues to see the Nigerian woman . . . as an appendix to himself and any benefits she gets out of those high positions have to be channeled through him, to her. . . .[27]

Similarly, in 1987 Mrs. Rawlings urged Ghanaian women to start asserting themselves in the country's social and political development. Elaborating, she noted that throughout Ghana rural women have traditionally had the role of being consulted before the decisionmakers (presumably their husbands) arrive at final decisions. The First Lady noted that this phenomenon indicated the importance of women in decision making, arguing that this common country practice should be used in building the nation.[28] Indeed, this right of consultation is pervasive, especially in rural areas. Some Ugandan women, for example, make no bones about the fact that should a husband fail to consult on matters directly relevant to his wife and her children, he would no longer be the effective head of the household. One woman put it this way:

> If a man insists on not respecting his wife and not including her in decisions, he would have failed to be the head of the household. If women are the ones who are more concerned with the family and take the time to sustain the family, then she is fit to be the head of the household, not the man. Though we think that a man should be the head, many women think that a woman should be the head of the family because of the work she does and the great care that she takes of the family.[29]

Even in urban areas among the educated elites, however, there remains at least a residue of this notion of consultation. Mary Lar, the wife of Solomon Lar, who was governor of Plateau State under the Shagari regime, spoke of this in an interview in 1980. Herself an educated individual and the principal of a government secondary school, Mrs. Lar replied as follows when asked about her advice to her spouse in discharging his duties:

> It appears that I'm now using the Press to communicate with my husband: Well, he is on stage now and my advice to him is that he should act well and to the best of his ability and conscience, so that when the time comes and he steps down, he will be able to look back with pride and say "Thank God." I also advise him to always have the people in mind whatever he does, and to keep up his veritable qualities. In an effort to keep those qualities, he should proceed prayerfully and endeavour to strike a balance between state affairs and those of the family.[30]

Although, under the circumstances of a public interview, her "advice" was quite banal and predictable, the very question, as well as the response, underscores the legitimacy of this notion of consultation between spouses, and the fact that it is both a correct and accepted role—a thinkable role—for the wife to advise her husband. Despite her own considerable accomplishments, the question encouraged Mrs. Lar her to think of herself as a counselor to her politically powerful husband. It should also be noted that the interviewer did not ask Mrs. Lar what advice her husband, the governor, habitually gives to her in her role as a secondary school principal. He, after all, is not seen primarily as a counselor.[31]

Being accepted as counselors and advisers, however, does not mean that the mainstream of contemporary middle African thought accepts women as the equals of men. Mariama Bâ understood this. Some men often use religion as a justification for their political, social, and economic dominance. Even Kenya's contentious clerics do not advocate equality in these matters. One of the Reverend Timothy Njoya's 1984 sermons illustrates the point.

Speaking at a service at the University of Nairobi, Njoya directly addressed what he termed "God's Policy on Marriage." The pastor began with the notion that men and women are equal both before each other and in the eyes of God. But, Njoya quickly added,

> This does not contradict the fact that man is the head of the wife (Eph. 5:23), because head does not mean better, higher, superior or master, but head in the order and structure of marriage. Head is head in terms of leadership like a chief in a location is head of that location. In a certain location you may find doctors, lawyers, judges, commissioners and very wealthy people being subject to the power of the chief and obeying the laws under the chief's act. The chief himself may have a small national position and may not be very literate, but in terms of government, he is the head of the location and all those residing in it. So, being head does not mean being more intelligent, more powerful, wiser, superior or better, but a leader in one's family.
>
> My wife, who has a degree in Business Accounting and another in Political Science, is more intelligent than me in administration. Yet, I am the head of the family. In my wisdom as head of the family, I have left almost all matters of administration to her. If anything goes wrong, an appeal may be made to me, but this does not usually happen. Marriage consists of mutual delegation of authority. . . .
>
> Therefore, Christian husbands should follow the example of Christ who loved the church and gave Himself for her. They should accept their role as leaders without feeling threatened by their wives when their wives are more educated, have higher salaries or bigger positions. Christian wives, as Christians, should likewise subject themselves to their husbands and uphold them in their headship in the family.[32]

Men and women may well be equal before God, but not in the household where, according to Njoya, it is quite clear which of the parties gets to delegate most of the authority and which has the right to hear appeals. Women may be more educated than their mates, have higher salaries than their mates, but are advised to submit themselves to their husbands because the male is, after all, still the head of the family.

One may not ultimately agree with Njoya's position in this matter, but he is thoughtful and intelligent. Others are less so. In Lisala, Zaïre, in 1975, one of my informants, an official in the local branch of the Ministry of Justice, argued strongly that the administrative principle of "unity of command" should also be applied in the household. This doctrine required that there be an ultimate, unquestioned authority with final decision-making power. In his household, of course, he was the authority. When, for the sake of argument, I accepted the principle but asked why the woman of the house could not command, he became upset and angry. "Because," he fumed, "when we make love I am on top," adding that when he went out to philander there was no danger that he would return carrying someone else's child.[33]

In a more public forum in 1989, a prominent Kenyan politician and then an assistant minister, John Keen, argued that African society had no place for women in high office and that they should only have strictly subordinate roles.[34] Keen, in other words, was making the argument that the very thought of a woman in high office was untenable. Whether it comes from the thoughtful or the closed-minded, this systematic devaluation of women in both public discourse and private conversation has consequences that can be unpleasant. When, even under the best of circumstances, the treatment and popular understanding of the political role of women sees them as being nothing more than "advisers" and thus usually in a position subordinate to that of men, who are heads of the household, problems will develop. One thing this means is that—over the long term—as inequality becomes rooted in patterns of thought and implicit understanding, certain terrible things become quite thinkable.

One ghastly and tragic example occurred in Meru, Kenya, at the St. Kizito Mixed Secondary School in 1991. Briefly, on 13 July 306 male students attacked an overcrowded girls' dormitory containing 271 young women. During this grisly incident nineteen girls died from suffocation in the ensuing panic or were crushed to death while trying to escape. In addition, the marauding students raped or gangraped more than seventy of their classmates. Many other injuries requiring hospitalization were reported. Help did not arrive until three hours after the attack, and many of the young victims lay bleeding, suffering from shock before receiving help. The punishments meted out to the guilty parties were, to say the least, mild. Four boys were found guilty of manslaughter and received sentences of four years each; three others were given probation. One careful observer, editorialist Hilary Ng'weno, noted "the lot of our women and girls is lamentable. We treat them as second-class beings, good only for sexual gratification or burdensome chores. We bring up our boys to have little or no respect for girls. It is revealing, for instance, that those so adept at fulminating against the ills of society are generally silent about gender issues in this country."[35] Similarly, and tragically, in the immediate aftermath of the attack, the school's headmaster was reputed to have said that the St. Kizito boys "meant no harm; they only wanted to rape."[36] If an educator, even one intent on shielding himself from the bureaucratic consequences of this terrible episode, can maintain that rape "meant no harm," then rape and other atrocities become all too thinkable.

Equality is elusive in both popular and political culture. For example, Fela, the well-known Nigerian singer and recording artist, insisted that "they're not on the same level with men. . . . Equality between males and females? No! Never! Impossible! Can never be! It seems the man must dominate." He further inveighed, "Men are the masters, not women" and "A woman has to respect her husband. . . . They need you to show authority, man." For Fela, a man whose music reached millions, the role of women in society was "to keep the home smooth, the children happy, the husband happy. To make the husband happy, that's a woman's job. Women got no other work than making the man happy."[37] In Nigeria's more clearly political domain, in 1987 Kehinde Olurin, the wife of the Oyo State governor, publicly called on women to be more concerned about the educational measures necessary to develop their potential instead of asserting their equality with men.[38]

As we have seen, for some the thought of women in high office, let alone the presidential palace, stretches belief beyond the breaking point. By the end of the 1980s, however, people were beginning to discuss the idea. One column, the Nigerian author's tongue firmly planted in his cheek, put it this way: "The Nigerian woman is best suited to rule the country. . . . What is very clear is that since independence only men have had all the flesh of the political grub. And how they stuffed themselves to bursting point, teetering on the edge of explosion, while the women stood at the fringes and suffered deprivation of sorts."[39] Some months later, however, the *Daily Times* began publishing several more serious essays on the question of a woman president. One op-ed piece argued that it was time for a woman to be president of Nigeria. In the author's words:

> In our cultural background, a woman is regarded as the property of the husband, and treated just like one of the accessories in the home. She must dance to the tune of the husband. Using the Bible and the Quoran to justify their myopic views, these male chauvinists argue that a woman's role is to be found in total submission. . . .
>
> In Nigeria today, many a woman is occupying important positions. The time is ripe therefore for a woman president. . . . They are sometimes far more stronger at heart and bolder than men. . . .
>
> A woman President will reduce the high level of corruption in the country. There would be no "back door" obligations to be fulfilled. As we know, the making of a good nation starts right from the family, the women are good managers of their home, it is their right to lead this nation, taking up the leadership mantle. Our women are not [sic] longer totally dependent on the men like it was in the past. . . . If politics is a dirty game: violent and corrupt, then it is the fault of the men. . . .[40]

Although this essay argues in favor of a woman as president, it does so largely in terms of the familial language and metaphors we have been examining. This essay thus makes an explicit linkage between the home and family (women manage these very well) on the one hand and the affairs of the state (which they should be given a chance to manage because the men have proven to be violent and corrupt and have thus made a total hash of it) on the other. In this case, therefore, the writer gives serious expression to a rapidly evolving point of view but does so in a manner quite consistent with the language, metaphors, and premises of the moral matrix.[41]

For some, however, no argument would ever convince them that a woman should be president of Nigeria. One hard-liner put it this way:

> My own opinion is that a woman should never be the President of Nigeria unless all men are extinct and only one man is alive. Even in that case the man should take over as President. . . . The Presidency of Nigeria is not a woman's job. . . . Whatever a woman is, in Africa, she is not qualified to be President because she is a woman.
>
> God created women to serve other purposes and not to lord it over men. . . .
>
> Our fathers never gave women a chance to interfere in the affairs of men. They were no fools. They knew what they were up to. Today we have given women a chance. As a result they have polluted all our sacred enclaves and shrines. That is why today, they are aiming at the Presidency. Their secret plan is to mount a coup against men and take over all offices of state. They will not succeed in our life-time. Let them take it from me. They will fail woefully.[42]

Similarly, a 1990 letter to the editor in Kenya noted: "Given that mothers are excellent in caring for their children, much better than the fathers, we feel that our country's leadership, which has been in the hands of two African men for over a quarter of a century, should be surrendered to women."[43] Although the intellectual level of this discussion is not particularly high on either side, such discussions are occurring not only in Nigeria, but elsewhere in middle Africa as well. This debate is but one sign that a thought once unthinkable (a woman as president) is in the process of gaining a certain legitimacy.

Evolving Norms

The image the Zaïrian press habitually presented of both the first Mama Mobutu and Mama Bobi Ladawa, Mobutu's second wife, is quite common throughout middle Africa. In Cameroon, for example, although Ahidjo's four official wives never received all that much press coverage, Biya's wife is regularly the focus of articles on certain ceremonial occasions when the writers laud her maternal qualities, her generosity toward the needy, her grace and elegance, and her ability to create a family atmosphere.[44] Mme Houphouet never received the attention in the media that either Mama Bobi or Mme Biya did, but when she did appear in the pages of *Fraternité Matin* it was almost always in conjunction with occasions that permitted reporters to emphasize her loving, generous, and maternal qualities. She was, in the words of the national president of the Association of Ivoirian Women, "the spiritual mother of all Ivoirian women." In addition, Houphouet's elder sister, Mamie Faitai, was also known as "the mother of mothers."[45]

In Senegal, however, Senghor's wife—perhaps because she was French—never received much coverage. That situation changed, albeit quite gradually, after Abdou Diouf came to power. In the early years of his rule, Elisabeth Diouf initially maintained a low-key presence in the national media. On the appropriate ceremonial occasions the press would note her presence touring the country, opening hospitals and rural dispensaries and generally distributing gifts to women and to the needy.[46] But by the end of the 1980s and the beginning of the 1990s, Mme Diouf was receiving press coverage that was more consistently emphasizing her maternal qualities, as well as her social and religious conscience. One photograph, for example, showed her smilingly and lovingly holding a baby. The caption read: "A moment of tenderness: Mme Diouf could not resist the temptation of holding this baby in her arms."[47] Another article noted her presence at a meeting dealing with the economic advancement of rural women, remarking that nothing could be more "natural." After all, her attendance was simply an extension of her "faultless engagement which she does not cease to demonstrate" of her aid to the disinherited, of her assistance to the "voiceless who in all circumstances know how to count on 'The First Lady of the Country' who spares neither effort nor initiative to alleviate those in disarray . . . who are in need without any distinction." The piece further maintained that all of her initiatives were

> marked with the seal of humanity, discretion, a serenity capable of meeting all challenges, but with a rare efficacity the secret of which is only that determination to attenuate the sufferings of her fellow citizens. . . .
>
> In permanent contact with the real country and the deep country, Mme Elisabeth Diouf is decidedly, on all fronts of humanitarian action, admirably seconding the Head of State in his quotidian quest for remedies to the ills which the most impoverished [démunis] suffer from. . . .
>
> This legendary availability is manifested at all levels. All the social categories of our country have been entitled to the solicitude of Mme Elisabeth Diouf, affectionately called "Tata Elisa." It would be superfluous to enumerate all her social actions so many and diverse are they. . . .[48]

That the preferred and dominant image of various middle African First Ladies heavily emphasizes an idealized vision and understanding of maternal qualities and characteristics should not surprise us. After all, until recently the image of the First Lady was not all that different in the United States, parts of Western Europe, or even in Japan, where the Emperor's wife played a comparable role. As worldwide feminist currents of thought have taken hold, the highly idealized "maternal" role of the First Lady has declined. But for most of the period under examination, the image, as well as the metaphor of the "national mother" that usually accompanied it, was pervasive in middle Africa. So, too, was the notion that a woman should complement her husband, seconding him and supporting him in all that he did while, of course, taking care to see that the children were raised properly and the home ran smoothly. She should, in other words, stand behind him. A publication highlighting President Ibrahim Babangida's "nuggets" of "wisdom" underscores these points. It contains, for example, a photograph of the general and his wife attending a sporting event. They are both silent, watching the event. Mrs. Babangida, however, is seated on a slightly lower chair than her husband is. The caption reads:

"Behind Every Successful Man." The symbolism seems apparent. The same volume reprints extracts of some of Babangida's speeches on a variety of subjects. Speaking to the Nigerian Army Officers Wives Association, the president noted: "Perhaps more than in any other profession, we in the army believe that, an officer who cannot maintain discipline in his home, cannot successfully maintain discipline in his unit." And, "Afterall [sic] it is said that behind every successful man, there is a woman. The reverse is equally true—that behind every unsuccessful man there is also a woman." He continued, "While it is true that the up-bringing of the children is the duty of both parents, it is also a fact that the mother has the greater influence on the child straight from birth. The father's role here is supportive and complementary."[49]

This imagery also exists at other levels of the social and political hierarchy. One Nigerian chief commissioned a book about himself and devoted several pages to his spouse. Some of this commentary is worth reproducing.

> The old cliche that behind every successful man there is a woman could not be more true than in the case of Lolo Grace Chizoman Egwunwoke and HRH Eze Onu Egwunwoke the Eze Oha I of Ihitaoha Uratta. . . . Chizoman has a graceful elegant carriage and disposition. She welcomes guests warmly to their home with radiant smiles. . . . She plans with and supports the Eze always. Lolo, in addition, helps in the execution of some of the plans. . . . Lolo Egwunwoke cannot help being "a twenty-four hour a day house wife." . . . According to Lolo, although she also employs some kitchen staff for the palace, she cooks all Eze's meals personally. This is so because she enjoys providing those personal touches Eze's eating habits demand. . . . She has seven children, six males and one female.[50]

Contemporary and constructed, these images of "traditional" life and family values should not be confused with anything resembling a historical baseline. They do constitute, however, something of a cultural baseline against which one can evaluate and, to the limited extent possible, gauge some of the enormous changes that are occurring.

Certain aspects of these transformations could be seen even in the state-controlled media during the 1980s and 1990s. The Tanzanian *Daily News* could report that a magistrate had maintained that husbands "have no right to beat their wives because women are entitled to the same dignity as men." Moreover, an editorial could argue: "This revolution must combat the erroneous assumptions about women's abilities, life patterns, skills and desires. Women must not be regarded as mere appendages of their men, but as responsible people deserving all rights in society."[51] Changes of this sort, however, even in the realm of public discourse and political discussion, are always uneven and are never unidirectional. At roughly the same time, for example, Aboud Jumbe, then vice-chairman of the CCM, could tell a gathering of the UWT at the Kivukoni Ideological College that, in his words, "I think the main problem is that you women have so far been too soft in exercising your rights. You need to be better organised and have a strong leadership if you really want to bring change."[52] In a similar vein, eight years later, President Mwinyi participated in a seminar on Women and Development. Although lauding the contributions of many women to national development and criticizing men for putting the burden of caring for the family on women's shoulders, the president nevertheless maintained that the women's approach to tradition often harmed their progress. He wondered aloud, for example, why a mother-in-law had to interfere with a son's marriage, especially if the wife was unable to bear children. The press report also noted that "the President's views were shared by other participants who said more often than not women were to blame for setbacks in the general thrust for women's emancipation and social advancement."[53]

However slowly, some important norms pertaining to gender relations are changing. A tale conveyed in the Cameroonian press during 1982 illustrates this. The article recounts an incident that occurred at Tala in Lekie in the Centre-Sud province. For several years a young bureaucrat had lived with a young woman whom he loved and wanted to marry. They had already had children together, and they wished to make their union official and legally recognized. On their wedding day, their friends and families gathered to attend the ceremony at the civil clerk's office. While asking the couple all the usual questions necessary to drive home to them the heavy responsibilities of marriage, they had to stop at the one concerning the choice of matrimonial option. (Cameroonian law permits selection of either a polygamous or a monogamous option.) The groom wanted the polygamous option because he thought it would be unworthy of a "notable" such as himself to have only one wife. In addition, he also wanted to take some precautions in light of possible troubles in the household that might eventually arise. The journalist noted that the bride, however, simply would not for any reason accept sharing her household with another wife. He speculated both that this reluctance might have been because of her egotism or because she had been raised as a Catholic. Regardless, the couple could not reach a compromise, and they canceled both the wedding and the planned reception.[54] Unfortunately, no follow-up to this story was published; the article itself simply stated the facts of the case without too much editorial comment. To be sure, the author speculated on the bride's motives for getting cold feet rather than the groom's, but there was nonetheless a tacit acceptance of the fact that the couple did have to agree on the matrimonial option.

Other signs of change are apparent as well. In Ghana, for example, a female columnist could argue in favor of equal opportunities for men and women in the sphere of education. "Trends in the world are changing," she wrote. "Women are challenging old notions about their status. Let it not be said therefore that while this process was going on all over the world, Ghanaians turned the clock backwards by reemphasising the false notion that men realise themselves through hard work while women do so only through the material gain from the institution of marriage. . . . What is good for men is equally good for women and vice versa: education is as good for both men and women as marriage is for both."[55] And Mrs. Babangida, who in other contexts was quite willing to "complement" her spouse, argued in 1987 that women should be partners in the decision-making process and should not be relegated to the background in development programs.[56] At the same time, however, many of these regimes continued to attribute whatever progress had been made in easing the situation of women, not to mention their "emancipation," to the benevolent "clairvoyance" and progressive inclinations of the national "political father" and continued to insist that the woman's first role was that of "mother of the family."[57]

Of course, none of this should in any way imply that women lack agency or are incapable of taking direct action. As we saw in Chapter 1, when women believe that their interests are threatened seriously, when they believe that their societies are in crisis, when they feel that the father-chief is no longer consulting them or listening to their concerns, they do not hesitate to act. Health care, school fees, the salaries of their husbands, and the general well-being of their children are often key issues for them. In Nigeria, for example, in 1980 an industrial action by nurses and midwives created a shortage of labor in the health sector, resulting in the refusal of many state-owned hospitals and clinics to admit new patients. In consequence, about one hundred pregnant women from various parts of Lagos besieged the premises of the National Assembly, demanding prenatal care and begging both legislators and passers by for help in saving them from an "untimely death."[58]

Similarly, in 1987 five thousand market women marched through the streets of Benin City protesting against the increase in secondary school fees from ₦50 to ₦60 per term. When the women tried to enter a state hall, the police opened fire with tear gas. Then the chief superintendent of police appealed to the women and asked them to send up some of their number to present their grievances to him. This calmed the demonstrators momentarily, but they again began agitating when the police official told them that he would see to it that their grievances were sent on to the "appropriate quarters."[59] It is perhaps significant that the women decided to renew their agitation when the police superintendent informed them that their concerns would be sent to the "appropriate quarters." Perhaps they knew, or could guess, how the "appropriate quarters" would treat their grievances. Both of these incidents speak to the question of women's voice and the need for serious rather than pro forma consultation, or what we might call a consultative voice.

In 1991, the wives of state officials and teachers in Mbanza-Ngungu, Zaïre, met at a local market to protest their treatment at the hands of the state. As Zaïre's economy and protracted political crisis had become progressively worse, their sense of powerlessness and general discontent had risen to a point of near desperation. Because of this they proposed to go on strike against their husbands. The statement they issued reflected their frustration:

> If we, the wives of all the categories of bureaucrats, well known for our legendary maternal patience, and our acute sense of patriotic duty, have come to this point, we are fed up with the state [le pouvoir] which has not been able to direct this country.
>
> Our husbands . . . have often been on strike because the state has rebuffed them and pretends that it understands nothing. We agree with them. Because the state must ameliorate the salaries of our husbands, we their wives will have to go on strike against our husbands who are also our employers if the latter do not review living conditions of everyone in their respective homes.[60]

Finally, in 1992 the mothers of some of Kenya's political prisoners staged a hunger strike and a series of demonstrations in Uhuru Park in Nairobi to protest the incarceration of their sons. The police rioted and beat the protesting women severely. In an attempt, perhaps, to shame them, some of the women stripped and began taunting the police, defying them to continue the beating. While the regime's friends denounced the action of the women as shameful, others applauded their courage in confronting the state and in "voicing" their protest.[61] Because the women were on the street and protesting, each of these instances may be taken as an indication that the states were violating the third premise (and perhaps several others as well) of the moral matrix and that women were calling into question the regime's legitimacy.

Generational Rotation

The fourth premise of the moral matrix holds that permanent power is illegitimate and that political fathers, therefore, have to let their children grow up, mature, take on ever-increasing responsibilities in the conduct of their own affairs, and eventually succeed them in power. In other words, there needs to be political alternation. Support for the notion of rotation of power among elites appears to be widespread. A letter to the editor of *West Africa* put it this way: "The problem in Africa is that men without vision and hardly any education, lacking experience in management or dealing at the international level, stay in power decade after decade. A new day must come to save Africa!"[62] Another correspondent, this time writing in reaction to some of Captain Jammeh's less-than-democratic actions after seizing power in The Gambia, complained that "Gambians would like to know why their overwhelming demand for term-limitation for the presidency was thrown overboard, considering that the main justification for the coup against the democratically elected government of Jawara was that they had stayed too long in power. . . . Are these not clear signs of an impending dictatorship?"[63] And, in a similar vein, an essay written not too long after Léopold Senghor's announcement that he would relinquish power, but just before it had actually happened, appeared in the Nigerian press. Using Milton Obote's return to power in Uganda as a springboard to present his thoughts on the question of tenure in office, Ebenezer Williams wrote the following:

> The one truth which stares everyone in the face of this Ugandan drama, however, is this unwillingness of the average African leader to surrender power. Invariably, once in power the African leader is always in power; and in his attempt to keep his post and retain his title, he would do anything, however heinous. He would enthrone thugs. He would opt for the one-party system. He would promote himself from Prime Minister to President, from President to president-for-life, and from president-for-life to emperor. . . .
>
> Name it, in almost every African state those who have ruled for the last 10, 20 years, still consider themselves the legitimate and ordained rulers of the people.

> Which is saying that the only way to change a government on this continent is through the barrel of a gun. The only way to remove the African from office is to cut his throat. Which is sad, very sad.

The essay then noted that Africans would need to be reeducated "to know that no position is permanent."[64]

While many observers and commentators believe that such desired political rotation should come about through multiparty elections, other methods are also possible and thinkable. The implicit and usually unstated model of the idealized family recognizes as legitimate a demographically regular rotation and passage of power between different political generations. Moreover, such a generationally sensitive transition might well come about as the result of a generational shift within an electorally dominant or even a single political party. The rhetoric surrounding the transfer of power between Léopold Senghor and Abdou Diouf in Senegal in 1981 is most instructive in this regard.

Senegal

Léopold Senghor, Senegal's first president, resigned from office on 31 December 1980 after having served in that capacity for two decades. News of the impending resignation first appeared in both the French and Senegalese press about a month before the actual event. One front-page editorial put it this way:

> In a world prey to delirium, where the exercise of power is too often, alas, perceived as lasting eternally, to renounce it of one's own accord, apart from any physical or juridical infirmity, proceeds from the peculiar. . . .
>
> Here, one assassinates to remain in a position of command; there, one fixes elections; elsewhere, one organizes coups d'état in blood and tears, and here is what he [Senghor] says to us, that one must know how to leave the table, and without turning around. . . .[65]

Several days later another commentator wrote that "habitually, we know that around us, systems and institutions created by men who make them their [own] thing, who install themselves in an immutable manner, in thinking of the Providential and the eternal. Senghor, by renouncing such practices, will make of this act, on our continent and for an entire generation, an incomparable pedagogic element." The author then noted that over the past several centuries people held that any system conceived was to be "eternal" and that in Africa, "all these men are installed royally, without believing and thinking for an instant that there are limits." Then, referring to Senghor and Diouf but resorting to the well-worn familial metaphor, the author noted:

> The child of the house who succeeds him, enjoys his aid and will benefit, necessarily, from the solidarity and the assistance of members of the family to preserve the indispensable unity and cohesion that the father had known how to maintain. Let us wager that today, as a grandfather, he will keep vigil. An experiment, a lesson in democracy. . . . It is time for the children of the house of the great family,

let us say the people, to find each other, think, and to join together to remain in the line of continuity.[66]

Senghor, in other words, was demonstrating through his actions that power was not eternal and that in stepping down he was becoming, in effect, a "grandfather" who would continue to watch over the actions of his children, who were now going to be in charge of the family's fortunes. Of course, as a grandfather, the former president was well on his way to becoming an ancestor.

Senghor's address to the nation on the day of his resignation explicitly underlined his conception of the generational aspects of the political change and is worth citing at some length:

> In truth, my will not to be a "President-for-Life" was an open secret for, as is known, I refused, among others, a proposition for a bill that tended to make me a President for life. Better yet, in an interview with the Dakar weekly *Afrique nouvelle,* in May 1976, I said: "During the several years of life I have remaining, I would like to confide my dreams to other hands. From my election in 1960 my principal problem has been to put together a team to replace me on the political plane." It was clear.

The outgoing president also noted that there were two reasons for his resignation; one was based on principle, the other on fact:

> Firstly, a reason of principle. I have always been against a life presidency, I have always been in favor of an alternation in power, whether it is a question of an alternation of parties expressed in free elections, or an alternation within the confines of the same party through the rise of young people. . . .
>
> Concerning the reason of fact, it is that I have just become seventy-four years old. And while, for my age, I do not feel too badly, I can no longer work, the month of vacation excepted, on the average of ten hours a day including Saturdays and Sundays. The position has to be left and the flame passed to the following generation.[67]

Senegal was caught in a serious social and economic crisis at the time of Senghor's resignation, and this may have had something to do with his decision to resign because he did not wish to have anything to do with the potentially painful measures that a structural adjustment package would have imposed. This, however, in no way dilutes the generational logic of his publicly stated reasoning. It merely, and quite expectedly, indicates the possibility that the first premise of the moral matrix concerning the notion of parental nurture also had its role to play in the trajectory of these particular political events.[68]

It was readily apparent that the "father" was leaving and that in his departure there was a lesson to be learned about alternation of power. The president of the Supreme Court noted that Senghor's political comrades felt "orphaned." He also remarked that although he was not a seer, he could nonetheless predict that grandmothers of the twenty-first century would teach their offspring that in Senghor there was, "once upon a time, a Head of State who had understood that only the power of God is unattackable and absolute."[69] Others, of course, also picked up on the theme of generational change. A Senegalese student in Paris wrote to *Le Soleil* that from the instant Senghor had chosen to elevate Abdou Diouf to the post of prime minister in 1970, he had "promoted an entire generation of men and women. It is the first trait of a democratic opening." He also noted that Diouf represented a generation that would be both "technocratically competent" as well as "political."[70]

Unlike the transitions in Cameroon and Tanzania that occurred several years later, the Senegalese succession was quick and complete, for, in addition to resigning the presidency, Senghor also promptly relinquished his position as president of the PS. Diouf thus assumed the leadership of both party and state, eliminating the possibility of a rupture in the unity and indivisibility of power.[71] Moreover, Diouf was always quick to credit Senghor for the transition and to pledge his loyalty. In a 1982 interview he affirmed that "I am loyal to Senghor whom I consider my father on the plane of affection." And he continued, "I refuse all personal opposition between President Senghor and President Diouf. I have for President Senghor respect, admiration, veneration." But he also noted that he and Senghor had received different educations and had enjoyed different life experiences and that, therefore, it would be quite normal for them to govern differently.[72]

Diouf publicly stated that both he and the PS were in favor of political alternation but insisted that it emanate from the people, rather than as the result of a negotiation between politicians.[73] But by the end of the 1980s opposition politicians were increasingly calling for a change in power. Unsurprisingly, in doing so they increasingly came to evoke the theme that Diouf had been there long enough and that a change was thus needed. In making this argument, I would speculate that they were, in effect, tapping into the fourth premise of the moral matrix by reminding the voters that it was time for another generational change. One opposition politician, Abdoulaye Bathily, phrased his argument this way in 1987:

> Abdou Diouf has been in power ever since independence, from the president's cabinet to ministerial posts. He has been prime minister for 10 years, and president since 1980. Up until now, the situation has not been improved, especially over the last few years since Abdou Diouf came to power. People were expecting an improvement of their living [and working] conditions. . . . And what we have seen is the result of the implementation of the IMF and World Bank conditionalities; the situation of the country has worsened. So our support for Abdoulaye Wade's candidacy stems from the fact that we think that the time is ripe for a . . . qualitative political change in the country.[74]

In other words, whether consciously or not, whether cynically or not, Bathily evoked here premises one and four of the moral matrix. Fathers must nourish, and they must not eternalize themselves in power. Diouf failed to nourish and failed to relinquish power in a timely manner. His twenty-year run as president ended in 2000, when the Senegalese electorate voted him out of power in favor of Abdoulaye Wade.

Cameroon and Tanzania

Since we examined the major events of the Cameroonian succession in Chapter 2, here I simply note that although the rhetoric of this transition between Ahidjo and Biya resembled the comparable Senegalese case in some ways, there were also areas of difference. To be sure, in the Cameroonian transition Ahmadou Ahidjo and his minions in the media certainly emphasized that the departing president had resigned, in part, because he had no desire to eternalize himself in power. Two days after his unexpected speech of resignation, one commentator reminded his readers that Ahidjo had several times previously indicated that he would not remain in office forever. "'I shall not eternalize myself in power' . . . President Ahmadou Ahidjo declared last May to journalists of the national and international press. . . . At the Congress of Maturity at Douala in February 1975, while presenting the balance sheet of his seventeen years in power, Ahmadou Ahidjo recognized that an 'immense work has been accomplished with the aid and support of the Cameroonian people' and thought that the conditions were fulfilled [*réunies*] to 'think of rest.'" Ahidjo, the claim went, had actually been thinking of retiring at several junctures but had always acceded to the demand of the Cameroonian population that he retain his office.[75] Similarly, in an interview some months after his resignation, Ahidjo stated:

> The deep reasons for my resignation do not comprise any mystery. I said, a long time ago, at the moment when some proposed a lifetime presidency to me, that I did not have the intention to eternalize myself in power. For me, power is a means of serving the people and the nation. My intimate conviction is that a reasonable period of time is sufficient to do this and to permit a head of state to give his full measure. Too long a duration exposes [one] to wear and tear and fatigue. For the exercise of supreme power is an absorbing task which requires a physical and moral tension at every moment.[76]

Based on the violent events that followed over the next several years that were detailed in Chapter 2, cynics might reasonably argue that these initial protestations of Ahidjo's wish not to occupy power forever were simply so much rhetorical window dressing and that either he realized that he had stepped down prematurely or he really was intent on maintaining control over the polity from his position as head of the party. While these interpretations have much merit, it is still of interest that the government's publicity machine chose to present Ahidjo's resignation in terms of his desire to avoid eternalizing himself in power.

In some respects, however, the discourse surrounding the Cameroonian transition differed from the Senegalese case. As we have seen, Senegalese media and politicians tended to emphasize the continuity in change that a rotation of political generations brings. In Cameroon, on the other hand, a slightly different set of motifs were underlined in the wake of the succession. The media in Yaoundé saw the great event as a tribute to Ahidjo's careful and minute preparation (even though his resignation seemed to have come as a near-complete surprise) and as a sign of the political "maturity" of both the Cameroonian people and the nation's political institutions. One of the regime's preferred editorialists noted: "It is still to him [Ahidjo] that we owe the maturity that the circumstance requires"; and "He also prepared men among whom, with perseverence, he cultivated the elevated conscience of national responsibility."[77]

In contrast to the experiences of Senegal and Cameroon, where the initial announcements caught people by surprise and the actual transitions were accomplished quickly, Tanzanian President Nyerere clearly and convincingly stated his desire to withdraw from the presidency and gave people enough time to absorb the news before it actually happened. Indeed, the announcement in 1984 that Nyerere was going to step down initiated a lively series of letters to the editor.[78] Several letters opposed the resignation. One of the more interesting of these wondered whether Nyerere's "long reign has created within us a psychological dependence on him. We now ask: If Mwalimu for any reason is out of leadership shall we be like lost sheep? Shall we be like a boat without a helmsman? People ask these questions because they think (rightly) that Mwalimu is growing old. But Mwalimu is only 61 years and in good health. How old is Reagan or Andropov? In fact if anything Mwalimu may do a good ten years of leadership if the people and himself do wish."[79]

Nonetheless, most correspondents thought that people should honor and respect Nyerere's desire to step down. One put it this way:

> It is good for all of us to realize that no one leader is indispensable all the time. It is also dangerous to make people, leaders and the led, believe that only one person is capable of leading others. My view is that there will always be good and capable leaders so long as the criteria, principles and procedures for their selection are sound and acceptable to the majority of the society. . . .
>
> It is also my view that a good leader should be able to prepare for his smooth succession. This is more so in a society like ours where we do not have a multiplicity of political parties with different leaders. Smooth succession will ensure a stable society in future for which posterity will thank the preceding generations.[80]

Another correspondent argued that nobody lives forever and that Nyerere should step down now because that would give the nation a qualified adviser. Moreover, he argued, there would always be a qualified successor even if that person could not yet be identified.[81]

Yet another expressed things this way, and his letter to the editor is worth citing at some length:

> In true democracy wherein the sovereignty of the nation resides in the people, really and practically, the question of who is leader is not vital, because, if he is good, fair enough; if he is useless, he is sure to be removed rapidly, safely, and in accordance with the constitution.
>
> A good father does not wish to live for ever so that he looks after his children and guides them throughout their lives. A good father, painful though it be, wants

to see his children established and leading independent lives, running their own affairs, in their own homes, far from their father's house.

For this he trains them from childhood to make small decisions for themselves and run (or perform) small housekeeping chores for the good of everybody in the home. In this way, the father makes sure that when he is gone and not there to supervise things, his children will continue to guide their own lives without pain.

Mwalimu, being a good father, has told us in advance that he does not wish to stand for the Presidency in 1985 because he wants someone else to take charge while he (Mwalimu) is still physically able to guide this new man through and across pitfalls and hurdles.[82]

Unlike Ahidjo, Nyerere appears to have genuinely believed that it was time to step down from the presidency. Like Senghor, part of the reason he might have felt this way was because of economic crisis and widespread popular frustration with his economic policies. But when the BBC asked him why, he replied, "I am retiring because basically I think it is time I retired. I have been leading my country for 23 years. Well, it is time I step down and let someone else."[83] And, some months later, he also noted that "when one person becomes president of a nation for a very long period, people begin to fear changes in leadership. They ask: When Mwalimu leaves, what will happen to the country? But I wish to say again, whether we like it or not, changes in leadership are inevitable. There is no man who will live forever. And there are many shortcomings in waiting until such time when death compels changes in a nation."[84] But like Senghor, Nyerere also sounded a theme of generational change and passage. One report of a speech in June 1985 noted that Nyerere had said that he "had decided to retire in order to help the nation move from the post independence leadership to that of the next generation. . . . Amid applause Mwalimu said he and his colleagues had taken over leadership after independence without any experience of running the government but at present there were many young people who had acquired vast experience of leading the country."[85]

Although Nyerere did hand over the reins of the state to Mwinyi, he remained as chairman of CCM until 1990. At that time he again sounded what was by then a familiar theme: It was inevitable that he retire. Addressing elders and party leaders in Dar es Salaam, Nyerere was categoric: "'There is no mincing words about it. I cannot retain this position for life,' he said, adding that even if death was determinant 'one should not pester God to take his life.'"[86] Nyerere's sentiments against eternalization in power were quite strong. When, also in 1990, Idris Abdul Wakil, president of Zanzibar, retired, Nyerere praised him in these terms: "Ndugu Wakil is not a species of leaders who cling onto leadership and think that they would continue forever."[87] Both Tanzania and Senegal, then, were probably exceptional in middle Africa in that their leaders were willing to contemplate their own succession and to act on it. In both countries, a sense that eternal power was unthinkable and illegitimate, coupled with an implicit understanding that, in the polity as in the family, new generations must be permitted to rise and to ascend to positions of power and influence, facilitated two smooth and peaceful political transitions. Elsewhere in the region the tendency of political leaders to overstay their welcome thus contributed to making political agitation against a "bad" father thinkable and thus increasingly legitimate.

In an unexpected way, even the course of events in Côte d'Ivoire where Houphouet-Boigny did, in effect, hold a lifetime presidency, underscores the importance and relevance of the notion of generational rotation. Although Houphouet remained in office until his death in 1993, throughout his lengthy tenure the nation's mass media would occasionally present election results, especially within the ruling PDCI, as reflecting a normal rotation of generations. For example, in the aftermath of single-party elections in 1980, Philippe Yacé, then president of the National Assembly and secretary general of the PDCI, opened the first legislative session of 1980 with an important address. After heaping the usual and customary praise on the "clairvoyant" President Houphouet, Yacé stated:

> The composition of our Assembly has permitted an efficacious work of highly technical quality thanks to the sum of the experiences and the knowledge that you have put in the service of our institution. It is significant enough to specify that the average age of the legislative corps is 47 years old, the oldest among us being born in 1898 and the youngest being only 31. This range of generations represented here has given us the advantage of allying the profound knowledge of the country of the most aged with the enthusiasm of the youngest, the wisdom of the former balancing the ardor of the latter. And since the solution of wisdom and reason often remains in the synthesis of the tendencies that are present, our discussions have generally led to temperate decisions, easy to apply, and of a real scope. To this symbiosis of age we have added one of competencies.[88]

Implicit here is the idea that slowly, progressively, youth and the rising generation should increasingly be included in the legislature's work and that, therefore, a gradual rotation of generations within the party is desirable.

That idea was made explicit several years later when the PDCI Political Bureau met and declared after its gathering that "after calling on the militants to come together now in order to build the country in love and brotherhood, the Political Bureau rejoiced that the quarrels between generations, which are deplored elsewhere, do not exist in Ivory Coast. In fact, the elders have agreed to progressively withdraw from public affairs to make room for the youth, thus ensuring a smooth takeover and continuity. . . ."[89]

Underneath these contemporary concerns with the rotation of political generations lies an older, usually implicit model of generational rotation within certain ethnic groups. In 1989, for example, *Fraternité Matin* sent a reporter to Orbaff, a village of 6,000 people located approximately twelve kilometers from Dabou. The reason was that the Adjoukrou people were having a major ceremony to mark the passage of power within their ethnic group from one generation to another. The mayor of Abidjan presided over the ceremony, and many other national personalities were in attendance. The article then noted that the Adjoukrou had known several sacred regimes during their existence. One was an automatically transmitted, individualized, gerontocratic authority that was primarily religious. In this case, the eldest male receives this power upon the death of the present incumbent. "The other, however, is dictated by a care for the democratization of power: political and religious power belongs to an age class and its transmission is done through a ritual inherited from the ancestors." Once accomplished, the rising age class would be responsible for the exercise of political and religious power; they would invoke the Gods and the ancestors in ceremonies that would guarantee fertility, prosperity, peace, and independence. Moreover, they would henceforth be responsible for organizing festivals, sanctioning other age classes whenever they might be remiss in their duties, and convoking and presiding over village assemblies.[90]

In other words, many Ivoirians and other middle Africans might find it perfectly thinkable to view the transmission of power along generational lines as something quite familiar and natural. Tellingly, however, the article made no mention of the female members of this group who might as well have been politically invisible during the ceremony. The structured invisibility of women and the notion of rotational generation feed into relevant but usually unarticulated notions of both democracy and legitimacy in a variety of complex and occasionally contradictory ways, as do previously examined conceptions of the father-chief's rights and responsibilities. Chapter 7 explores how the four premises of the moral matrix, as well as local understandings of power, the parameters of the political kingdom, and appreciations of alternative causalities, help to shape both implicit conceptions of democracy and a logic of political legitimacy in middle Africa.

7. | Democracy and the Logic of Legitimacy

The moral matrix of legitimate governance, endogenous definitions of key political concepts such as power, an understanding of the parameters of the political, and an appreciation of alternative comprehensions of causality all contribute to the continuous elaboration of a largely unarticulated mapping of the politically subjacent terrain. This politically subjacent arena is home to our pretheoretical notions and unspoken assumptions about what is politically thinkable and what is not. It is the locus of our sense of what is, or is not, politically legitimate behavior. In other words, an understanding of subjacent politics can tell us much about the cognitive and intellectual terrain on which politics occurs. In this regard, a knowledge of the politically subjacent is, or should be, a necessary first step and a foundation for all political and social scientific explanations.

This chapter recapitulates portions of the argument made throughout. It also revisits the moral matrix of legitimate governance, demonstrating once more how it structures notions of political thinkability and legitimacy in middle Africa. In so doing, I reflect on what the politically subjacent arena might mean for the eventual success or failure of ongoing democratic experiments in this part of the world. The relationship between legitimacy, democracy, and "democratization" will also attract our interest. Before approaching these tasks, however, some of the epistemological issues and questions that this work has raised along the way need to be addressed. More specifically, three questions command attention. First, has the moral matrix changed over time? Second, is there anything essentially middle African about the logic of legitimacy this book has presented? Third, and obviously related to the second question, are various concepts such as power and the parameters of the political, as well as certain fashionable analytical distinctions such as state–civil society and church–state, universal? These are difficult and contentious matters; definitive answers are elusive. Rudimentary reflections are the best I can offer at this point.

Epistemological Issues

Historical Change?

Middle Africa's moral matrix is not timeless and unchanging. Nor does it sit in splendid isolation. It is the historical product of severe ruptures and gradual evolution, generated both endogenously and exogenously. To mention only one of the many indigenous societies in middle Africa, Wyatt MacGaffey reminds us that although there is a recognizable regional tradition that has evolved over 2,500 years, BaKongo "are one product among many of the continual changes and adaptations this evolution entailed." In later years, he notes, "the BaKongo have been in contact, sometimes intense contact, not only with the rest of the region but with Europeans since the end of the fifteenth century; their language is full of buried Portuguese, French, and English terms, recording that history."[1] Historians and other historically inclined social scientists could make virtually the same statement about any of the societies comprising the eight contemporary states of middle Africa (Senegal, Côte d'Ivoire, Ghana, Nigeria, Cameroon, Congo/Zaïre, Tanzania, and Kenya). All have evolved considerably; all are the products of both internal and external forces. J. D. Y. Peel, for example, provides an excellent study of this in Western Nigeria. He pitches his historical sociology of the Ijesha Yorubas at the micro level to account for roughly eighty years of incorporation into wider social and political units, demonstrating convincingly that change results from a complex interplay of endogenous and exogenous factors. He also pays special attention to how the Ijeshas "discovered" the Nigerian state and then made use of it in their own political calculations.[2] From a wider, regional perspective encompassing Equatorial Africa, a region more or less coterminous with the limits of the expansion of Western Bantu languages that today covers parts of Congo/Zaïre, Cameroon, Gabon, and Congo-Brazzaville, Jan Vansina reminds us that amidst the enormous changes the entire area developed an enduring tradition and a certain cultural and historical unity that resulted from it. "Traditions," wrote Vansina, "are self-regulating processes. They consist of a changing, inherited, collective body of cognitive and physical representations shared by their members. The cognitive representations are the core. They inform the understanding of the physical world and develop innovations to give meaning to changing circumstances in the physical realm, and do so in terms of the guiding principles of the tradition. Such innovations in turn alter the substance of the cognitive world itself." Such traditions need autonomy to endure across time and tend to die out when they lose, for whatever reason, their ability to innovate.[3]

The moral matrix of legitimate governance has evolved and continues to evolve. Using an examination of political discourse as a point of entry, I have argued that the imagery of father, family, and food is culturally relevant and politically important, and it strikes a responsive chord throughout middle Africa. Political legitimacy in much of this region is based on the tacit normative idea that government stands in the same relationship to its citizens that a father does to his children. There is a substratum of belief which views paternal authority as thinkable, and thus legitimate, as long as the implicit understanding of rights and responsibilities contained in the moral matrix is not violated. In other words, when political leaders behave as responsible fathers; when they care for, nurture, and nourish; when they do not seek eternal power and respect the normal rotation of generations; when they do not "eat" too much, especially in times of hunger; when they respect and listen to their mothers, wives, and daughters, and other marginalized groups, it becomes increasingly unthinkable to challenge them. Their political legitimacy and thus the broader stability of the polity are thereby maintained. But when they violate the implied cultural norms and unarticulated expectations of political "fatherhood," their legitimacy erodes; tensions mount; and instability, repression, or both ensue. Under those circumstances, it becomes all too thinkable to contemplate the removal of a political figure who has violated the trust and expectations implicit in the moral matrix of legitimate governance. In middle Africa these removals have been effected through military coups, political insurrection, and the ballot box.

The matrix that structures implicit and usually unarticulated notions of thinkability (and thus of legitimacy) is itself the product of a multifaceted historical evolution that I am unable to present in any great detail, for to do so would require a much different book. Elsewhere, however, I have sketched—at least in the Zaïrian/Congolese case—the origins of this imagery and of the matrix.[4] In brief, and at the risk of broad-brush generalization, parts of the origins of the moral matrix may be found in the various traditions of the pre-colonial polities that make up the eight states of middle Africa. The importance of an ideology of kinship, the occasionally close congruence between the familial and the political, and the important role of the father (even in matrilineal societies) all played a role. Also significant at times was, in some places, a close association between the role of chief and the overarching family structure. In any number of societies, people came to think of the chief as their "father," and his authority thus had a paternal patina at times. Pre-colonial chiefs, like their self-styled contemporary counterparts in the presidential palaces, had two faces. One was benign, paternal, and smiling; the other was snarling, harsh, and repressive. One pardoned, the other punished. The father-chief could, and did, traffic with the forces of the occult and was able to bring these to bear, using fear as an implement of rule when necessary. Sometimes the father-chief acted as a "Big Man," receiving tribute and "eating" his fill but redistributing food and other resources as necessary to alleviate hunger, as a reward for political support or to consolidate certain social and political ties. In addition, there was in many of these societies an ongoing generational rotation that saw power pass from one group of male elders to the succeeding generational age grade in orderly fashion. Women (and youths) were excluded from effective power in this way and thus in many cases found themselves consigned to the role of silent counselor to their husbands, brothers, nephews, or sons. These pre-colonial traditions varied widely in middle Africa, however, and it mattered enormously whether one lived in a village micro polity or in a larger kingdom or state. Middle Africa's diversity of pre-colonial political forms defies easy generalization.

It is also difficult to generalize about which of these orientations survived the colonial period, and to what degree. Colonialism profoundly transformed most of them; the social, economic, and political changes were devastating. Nonetheless, the colonial powers often patterned their relations with middle Africans after an idealized vision of the authority relationship that existed at home between parent and child. There was, even among the most liberal and sincerely motivated colonizers, a deep-seated paternalism that had an impact on these societies. Both colonial administrators and European missionaries tended to treat Africans as children. Colonial schools, for example, often diffused a role model for their teachers that was heavily laden with explicitly paternal imagery, and teacher training manuals reflected this. The colonial state, the missions, the educational establishment, and—where applicable—large European firms in the private sector all reinforced the message that Africans were children and that the European authority figure was like a "father."

The thinkability of the basic notions of father and family that many middle African rulers exploited when they took power in the early 1960s took root in this fertile terrain that both pre-colonial and colonial influences had irrigated. Once independence arrived, parts of middle Africa witnessed the growth of a personality cult surrounding the "father" of the large national "family." Given the historical trajectory, such an eventuality—especially if the father-chief respected his rights and responsibilities—became all too "natural," all too thinkable, and all too hegemonic. The considerable changes resulting from the area's multiple inclusions into a world of states in the midst of a cold war, a world of markets, and a world dominated economically by an increasingly global capitalist nexus and a technology of coercion that considerably enhanced executive power, meant that whatever pre-colonial political safeguards had once existed to contain and correct political abuses receded into the mists of memory.

The colonial period represented a massive exogenous influence even though, as Jean-François Bayart reminds us, Africans often exerted their "revenge" on the state and other external influences by adapting to them, shaping them in creative ways, and eventually making them at least somewhat congenial to local society and culture.[5] Given the enormous influence of the colonial period, the post-colonial thickening of worldwide communications networks and the diffusion of mass media and education, it is today virtually impossible to discern what influences are primarily endogenous and which are mostly exogenous. Ideas are engines of change, regardless of their provenance. As we saw in Chapter 6, this is quite apparent in the awareness that many African women have of various international conferences and events marking the trajectory of the women's movement and in the anger they feel when their governments abuse them. And, as we shall see presently, other ideas such as democracy have also had an effect throughout middle Africa and are resulting in ongoing changes in the moral matrix.

Essentialism?

Although my focus has been on the eight states comprising middle Africa during roughly 1980–1995, none of the political metaphors, imagery, or discourse I have described and analyzed is unique. A diligent search can surely uncover examples of these same words and expressions in other times and places as well. For example, in Chapter 2 we noted that one of the localized faces of power in middle Africa had to do with eating and that the metaphors of food and consumption prevalent in the discourse provided an avenue for understanding an important local dimension of power that standard, canonical definitions of power within the discipline of political science tend to miss. In Muscovy, the historical core of Russia, provincial administration under Ivan III (the Great, 1462–1505) had to get by with limited resources. One of the ways the central government maintained its administrative agents in the field was through an extractive arrangement known in Russian as *kormlenie,* or feeding. In effect, the central state gave the newly appointed governors a "feeding," and they lived off the food, goods, and services that the local peoples provided. Some of the governors were quite rapacious, "feeding" themselves enthusiastically and excessively.[6] Moreover, but in a rather different context, the American lexicon of distributive politics has long included expressions such as "pork barrel" and a "piece of the pie." In addition, Anne Norton reminds us:

> Consumption, in the material sense, remains a compelling and popular metaphor in American political culture. We continue to expand through eating. Indices of national consumption are used as measures of economic health, along with the Gross National Product. Self-consciousness of America as a culture of production and consumption has not resulted in a diminution of eating metaphors but in their proliferation and refinement. They are less obtrusive. Economic language is so well established that the corporeal referents of *corporate, incorporation,* and *product* are rarely recognized.[7]

Nevertheless, however similar the references to food and eating may be, what differs is the intuitive understandings people ascribe to them and the degree to which, if any, they become part of the politically subjacent realm.

Similarly, although Chapter 4 presented an extended examination of sorcery as an alternative mode of causality, we noted that it often appeared in complex contextual mixtures when people wished to explain, understand, and influence the events of daily life as well as certain aspects of politics. But we also saw that the resort to the occult often occurred in tandem with other modes of causal understanding such as the modern scientific mode, as well as the religious or spiritual mode. Middle Africans, like most of us, have a propensity to mix and match alternative modes of causality depending upon the circumstances of the moment. Furthermore, such intellectual procedures in the daily quest for explanation and understanding of the political world are certainly not limited to these eight states. Reliance on alternative understandings of causality may be quite universal—a point that is often obscured largely because of the contemporary intellectual and political prestige of science. Many Americans might feel slightly uncomfortable juxtaposing examples of middle African sorcery and the reliance of the Reagan White House on astrology, yet both represent attempts to deal with the unknown, control uncertainty in a world of political flux, understand political phenomena, and influence political events. Both are alternative modes of causality, and we need to understand and appreciate them as such, rather than simply dismissing them as isolated instances of "bizarre," "idiosyncratic," or "exotic" political behavior. Other peoples at other times have always employed, and continue to employ, alternative modes of causal understanding. Science, sorcery, and spiritual modes of causality are all distributed widely in time and space. Astrology, to provide another example, has long played a prominent role in Indian politics.[8] In other words, the political importance of sorcery in middle Africa is merely a local manifestation of a universal phenomenon. There is nothing "essentially" or uniquely middle African about it.

Universal Concepts?

Throughout this work, but especially in Chapter 3, I have argued that the parameters of the political, which political and social science takes for granted, are not necessarily a universal given. Let me clarify. Politics is a universal activity. To the best of my knowledge, all societies distinguish certain types of activities they deem to be political. But as we saw, activities that people see and understand as political in one society may not be conceived as political in another. Although variability in the parameters of the political does not challenge the omnipresence of politics, it does call into question the universality of certain binary analytical distinctions such as state–civil society and church–state that political scientists and other students of politics employ habitually in constructing their theoretical edifices. Such dichotomous distinctions generated and applied in a society with an implicit understanding of one set of contextual factors at work may, or may not, be suitable for application in a different society in which the cognitive understanding of the parameters of the political varies markedly. The application of such theoretical distinctions in societies with different sets of assumptions concerning the nature and boundaries of the political terrain may obscure more political phenomena than they illuminate. Or, even if they are suitable, scholars will have to exercise caution in their use and will need to control for these contextual variations in how each society maps the contours of its political arena.

Most directly in Chapter 2, when we examined representations of power, but more generally throughout this book, I have questioned the facile assumption often made in the social sciences that basic concepts, usually generated and elaborated within the confines of a specific society, are necessarily universal. Once again, let me be clear. I do not propose to discard orthodox definitions of basic concepts such as power. These can, and do, enlighten us in a wide range of political contexts. In middle Africa, far from the locales where they were initially generated, these definitions shed light on many political phenomena. The theoretical notions of Dahl, Lukes, Weber, and others do provide analytical clarity concerning the use of power when a rampaging warlord and his band descend on a village brandishing AK-47s demanding both the money and the wives of unarmed farmers. Such manifestations of power are universal. Others are not. The difficulty is that because most standard social scientific concepts, as well as their most common operational definitions, were generated in different societies with different unstated assumptions concerning the parameters of the political and the nature of political causality, they will therefore tend to miss (and misunderstand) certain politically significant phenomena. They will not necessarily be wrong, but they might well be incomplete or slightly out of focus. The retrospective examination of my own analyses of Congolese politics in Chapter 4 demonstrated this point. Political discourse can, in these situations, provide us with certain clues as to where we might look to unearth understandings of power that may have local significance and applicability. As we saw earlier, while canonical definitions of power are attuned to AK-47s, they are not sensitive to notions of food, eating, consumption, and ample physical girth as indicators of political power. Nor do they easily accommodate the spirit world, the role of the ancestors, or the use of sorcery and the occult arts as implements of power. Yet these local comprehensions of power are absolutely critical if we are to understand and explain how middle Africans perceive and construct their political world and why their political behavior takes certain of the forms that it does. The close examination of various forms of middle African political discourse in this book thus also responds to the challenge of Sills and Merton, noted in Chapter 1, that the social sciences need to incorporate "the basic ideas of African, Asian, and other non-Western thought into the Western paradigm."[9]

My argument, in other words, is neither as radical nor as fundamental as the one Oyeronke Oyewumi advances in her study of Yoruba women. Adopting both an insider's perspective as a Yoruba and an outsider's perspective as a professional sociologist, Oyewumi focuses on the concept of gender. Her startling thesis, summarized simply, is that Western concepts of gender were introduced from abroad into Yoruba culture. She maintains, therefore, that gender is neither universal nor timeless. Her sociological examination of Yoruba society demonstrates that gender is simply not a fundamental organizing principle of Yoruba society. "Women," she argues, is not a basic or universal category, and the subordination of women is not universal. This is a case where a Western concept, gender, has been incorrectly assumed to apply to an African society.[10] My synopsis obviously cannot do justice to her wonderfully rich argument and the wealth of evidence she brings to bear. Nor does my limited knowledge of the literatures on Yoruba society and on theories of gender permit me either to applaud or to deplore her effort. Suffice it to say, however, that even if we momentarily suspend judgment on its validity, her work nonetheless raises a stimulating hypothesis that cannot be ignored and ought to be considered in the wider context of explaining political phenomena.

Democracy is another contentious concept whose universal applicability should not be assumed a priori. Once again, our customary definitions occasionally either miss the mark or, as is perhaps more usually the case, are not quite congruent with local experiences and understandings. When local perceptions do not align conveniently with notions assumed to be universal, it becomes all too easy for social scientists and other analysts of politics simply to dismiss certain endogenous ideas as manipulative and politically cynical ploys calculated to preserve the less than benign, antidemocratic rule of an incumbent leader. On one level such analyses are often accurate, and I do not dispute them. It is, for example, quite difficult to take the following statement of Kenya's President Moi with anything other than a grain of salt. Speaking in 1990 before the introduction of multiparty elections, Moi maintained: "As Kenyans, even before the changes in Eastern Europe, we had our own democracy. We cannot turn around and say we had no democracy and that from now on we should proceed toward democracy. We have always had a genuine democracy, and it is a perfect democracy—one which is beneficial to us and one which the citizens themselves see as useful."[11]

On a different level, however, caution is warranted. Several statements of Ghana's J. J. Rawlings shortly after his second coup merit attention in this regard. In his speech to the nation on 5 January 1982, Rawlings stated that his seizure of power was not a conventional military coup, but something else:

> It is rather to create by this action an opening for real democracy. Government of the people, by the people and for the people. . . .
>
> This should also create the necessary atmosphere in the rural areas to enable the Food Distribution Corporation and the allied agencies as well as private distribution networks to ensure the movement of food supplies and commodities throughout the length and breadth of our country.
>
> This in the light of our stated acknowledgement that democracy is not realised merely by having a machinery for registering voters and getting them to vote every four years, but also by there being a machinery for identifying the needs of those voters in between the election periods, and monitoring the realization of those needs. . . .
>
> Let the world know that Ghanaians want a government with an agenda, not just a talking shop and that this is a democratic revolution to assure for our people the basic conditions of their survival: their right to eat and feed their families, to be clothed, to attend to their health needs through the provision of basic medical facilities, the right to education for their children, so that what they themselves have not been able to attain, their children can work towards.[12]

Of note is that Rawlings advanced two reasonably distinct definitions of democracy. Initially, he echoed Lincoln's often-quoted line from the Gettysburg Address and called for a "government of the people, by the people, and for the people." But then he suggested a different vision of democracy that explicitly included food, the distribution of food, the avoidance of hunger, and an almost moral economic vision of the right not to go hungry. Democracy in this view was not limited to the ballot box.

Rawlings' disdain for elections remained constant for some time. Several years later Radio France asked him whether he believed in democracy. In reply, he noted:

> What do you mean by democracy? A procedure whereby the mass of the people are manipulated, cajoled or misled by promises into voting for a few preselected candidates, who, after they are elected, will have no further interest in the electorate until another election is approaching? If this is what you mean—the outward procedure of Western-style democracy, the trappings of the ballot-box—then no, I do not believe in it.
>
> But I believe very deeply in democracy which enables the people to participate at all levels and all the time, not just once every few years, in building a better society. This is what we are working towards. . . .[13]

According to Rawlings, there was clearly more to democracy than simple elections. Yet in evaluating whether Ghana was becoming democratic or even consolidating democracy, it would seem quite "natural" for most political analysts to focus on elections, or their absence, or on the number of political parties, or on whether the elections resulted in an alternation of power.[14]

To cite but one prominent example, Michael Bratton and Nicolas van de Walle are explicit about this in their excellent work on regime transitions. "The most basic requirement for democracy," they write, "is that citizens be empowered to choose and remove leaders. Thus, democracy is defined in this study as a form of political regime in which citizens choose, in competitive elections, the occupants of the top political offices of the state."[15] In other words, the operationalization of Lincoln's conception of democracy, as well as of other common notions that in some ways derive from it, is easily (if only partially) achieved by focusing on elections. To their credit, however, Bratton and van de Walle "recognize that elections alone are not a sufficient condition of democracy." They are, however, "the principal and necessary condition of democracy, the first step without which democracy cannot otherwise be born."[16]

Elections in the formal arena of the state are generally understood to be well within the parameters of the political. But Rawlings' initial emphasis on food and hunger is significant in light of the analysis presented here. If middle Africans implicitly understand that food and eating are related to power, and they conceive democracy at least partially as a form of empowerment, then it should not surprise us that Rawlings would include attention to food, the distribution of food, and the right to avoid hunger as part of one of his definitions of democracy. I suspect, however, that few students of politics would build factors such as food distribution or hunger into their operationalizations of democracy. Yet in middle Africa a political leader who feeds and nourishes, who brings rain, and who does not eat while others go hungry enjoys much legitimacy. As long as the other premises of the moral matrix are respected, it would be quite unthinkable to remove him from office—whether with bullets or ballots. Let me thus disagree with Bratton and van de Walle. Legitimacy is "the first step," not elections. Elections, however free and fair they may be, will not be a way station on the road to democracy unless people understand them to be, in some measure, compatible with the implicit premises of the moral matrix of legitimate governance.[17] They must, in other words, tap into and resonate within the realm of subjacent politics. Should they fail to do this, no matter how cleanly and transparently they were conducted, they would not speak to the prior "first step" of legitimacy, and the democratic experiment would therefore be built on a foundation of sand. Similarly, however democratic a new constitution might be, if it does not in some way achieve a degree of congruence with the underlying moral matrix and the domain of the politically subjacent, it probably will not succeed. In other words, neither democratic elections nor democratic constitutions are always legitimate, as the experience of Weimar Germany should remind us.

Frederic Schaffer's superb study of the various layers and meanings of democracy in Senegal, both imported and homegrown, demonstrates how an analysis might take local concepts seriously. He notes that there are distinct differences in how members of the Senegalese elite use the French term *démocratie* and how relatively uneducated members of the Wolof-speaking majority use the Wolof word *demokaraasi*. There is, in the translation, an important shift in cultural points of reference and thus in understanding. For the group without formal education, *demokaraasi* can at times simply mean the achievement of agreement. This consensus, moreover, often connotes a form of community solidarity that people express using a family idiom. In this view, Senegalese are all members of the same family, they are all relatives, and all families have parents and thus hierarchy. Schaffer further notes that this communal solidarity can also refer to a distributive evenhandedness that people often evoke using the metaphors and imagery of food. But this understanding of impartial distribution is limited and implies no equality between a husband and wives, a mother and her children, or a religious leader and his disciples.[18] Rural and uneducated Senegalese thus appear to ground their understandings of *demokaraasi* in the moral universe of life in the local community. As Schaffer expresses this, "The result is what we might call a folk concept of *demokaraasi* that differs in important ways not only from views of *démocratie* or *demokaraasi* generated by the French-speaking elite but also from the American concept of democracy." *Demokaraasi*, in this context, means sharing with those who are needy and have nothing to offer in return, and an important purpose of *demokaraasi* is to ensure material security, especially where food is concerned, through community solidarity.[19]

Schaffer's discussion of the meaning of elections in Senegal is also noteworthy, for they are imbued with cognitive nuances that would be quite foreign to most theorists of democracy. Those Wolof-speaking voters who are mostly uneducated perceive elected officials as they would Wolof kings: as essentially unaccountable. In their eyes, therefore, elections are not about accountability; they are a way to benefit materially from the candidate's power and wealth. In addition, if communal solidarity is an important conceptual foundation of *demokaraasi,* then electoral factionalism could conceivably divide this moral and communal unity. The act of voting, in consequence, might not always be understood as an unmitigated good, and Schaffer notes that because of this some Senegalese opt not to vote at all. If accountability comes into play at all in these circumstances, it may be more about the distribution of resources through private channels than about enforcing public standards of morality. As Schaffer puts it, "The broader point is that similar institutional arrangements in different cultural contexts are not necessarily imbued with similar meaning. While Senegal shares with the United States the most significant feature of institutional democracy (regular elections), ideals of *demokraasi* among Wolof speakers depart in significant ways from American ideals of democracy."[20] As is true of most key political concepts, democracy has locally relevant and important meanings that the standard definitions political analysts usually employ tend to miss. So, too, does power. So, too, does legitimacy.

Throughout this book I have equated political legitimacy with thinkability. In doing this I have departed from a lengthy and distinguished scholarly tradition that flows from Max Weber's seminal analysis of three forms of legitimate domination, or authority: rational/legal, traditional, and charismatic.[21] In advanced industrial nations today, rational/legal authority is most often associated with the state. For example, Rodney Barker writes that legitimacy "is precisely the belief in the rightfulness of the state, in its authority to issue commands, so that those commands are obeyed not simply out of fear or self-interest, but because they are believed in some sense to have moral authority, because subjects believe that they ought to obey."[22] And, for Richard Merelman, "in the center of rational/legal legitimacy resides the principle of instrumental rationality" that is given institutional life in liberal democratic states through "bureaucracy, courts, parliaments, and science."[23] In other words, the state is central to the concerns of most scholars writing in this tradition; it is a widely accepted paradigmatic template. Failure to accord the state pride of place in reference to legitimacy would be most unusual. In other parts of the world, however, the state evokes different histories, passions, and understandings. In equating legitimacy and thinkability, I create analytical space for other possible matrices combining mental and emotional images of local importance and relevance. As we have seen throughout this intellectual journey, in middle Africa one such template features the imagery of father and family. Political fathers and national families are thinkable and thus legitimate.

When middle Africans, and others who have not participated in the elaboration of these putatively universal concepts, engage in cross-national discussions of them, they may find that there are disjunctures between their implicit models and understandings of the parameters of the political, key concepts, and modes of political causality, on the one hand, and those of their interlocutors, on the other. Rawlings came close to giving voice to this situation of occasionally and partially conflicting of sets of implicit cognitive models in a telephone interview he granted a New York City radio station in 1984. He then stated:

> In talking about Abraham Lincoln it meant that I knew something about your history and you didn't know anything about my history. Some of our children are told at school that Lake Victoria was discovered by David Livingstone, which is

not true. David Livingstone was led to that Lake by African blacks. So when I talk about the human factor I am talking about the way people must have felt prior to the French Revolution. I am talking about the way your ancestors must have felt when they decided that "we are going to revolt against the British overlords" when they attempted to re-impose themselves. I am talking about the world of ignorance, I am talking about the world of the oppressed man, I am talking about a level of reasoning that cannot find any analogy or equation in your society.

And yet when I have to deal with your mentality I have to perceive—or let's put it this way—I have to answer your question through your perspective and not mine. . . .[24]

Rawlings here obliquely touched on the question of different implicit models and some of the dissimilar perspectives and understandings that result from them.

To reiterate, most political analysts probably would not include escape from hunger as part of an operational definition of democracy. From Rawlings' perspective, however, the premises of the moral matrix of legitimate governance might make it seem "natural" for him to do so. The widespread significance of nurture and nourishment as one of the rights and responsibilities of the father-chief and, additionally, the importance of metaphors of food and eating as they relate to implicit understandings of power would make avoidance of hunger seem like a reasonable and compelling factor to include in any definition of democracy. On the other hand, given their fascination with elections, the number of political parties, and electoral alternation as indicators of democracy, some Western analysts and policymakers might be inclined to dismiss concerns about food, eating, or communal solidarity as unimportant or, as is perhaps more likely, never even consider that they might be critical either to local conceptions of democracy or to its eventual consolidation. When such reservations are expressed by heads of state with no commitment whatever to democracy who are intent only on retaining power, analysts are, on one level, correct in dismissing these statements as self-serving. But as I have tried to show throughout this book, there are deeper levels of analysis.

The Matrix Revisited

This study has argued that the four largely unarticulated and implicit premises of the moral matrix of legitimate governance structure middle African notions of what is thinkable and thus politically legitimate. The first and second premises concern the rights and responsibilities of the father-chief as discussed in Chapter 5. As long as he nurtures and nourishes, his legitimacy is maintained. The father-chief may eat, but not while people are hungry. In providing for his political children, he is entitled to gratitude as repayment for the debt incurred. The father-chief must exert discipline when necessary but is obliged to pardon offenders if they make a sincere act of contrition before him. The third premise, examined at length in Chapter 6, concerns the role of women in the polity and the notion that while the matrix does not see them as equal to men, their advice and counsel must be sought and heeded. The fourth premise, also elaborated in Chapter 6, concerns the illegitimacy of eternal power and understanding that there should be a rotation of power between political generations.

The premises of the moral matrix are not laws. Nor are they, standing alone, explanations. They precede explanation, however, in so far as they indicate the parameters of the range of thinkable political choices that are likely to be available in any situation. I would submit that our chances of arriving at vigorous and valid explanations of political phenomena increase as our understanding of the contextual possibilities becomes more firmly rooted in those things people believe to be "natural" and thus not worthy of explicit articulation because they are "obvious." The premises of the moral matrix are, in other words, cultural predispositions that reflect these usually unstated, implicitly obvious understandings of certain political phenomena that people—largely through socialization—"intuitively" come to understand as a "natural" part of the order of things. They are rarely discussed, much less called into question. This is why, in effect, I have had to try to discern them indirectly, through a study of discourse and the politics of the quotidian.

This book has examined the discourse of eight states, and while we have seen that there is a recognizable configuration of metaphors, words, and images among them along each premise of the matrix, there is also a range of important variation. As far as premise one is concerned, we have seen that the notion of political paternity was most fully elaborated in Côte d'Ivoire under Houphouet-Boigny, Zaïre under Mobutu, Cameroon under both Ahidjo and Biya, and Kenya under Moi. In various Nigerian regimes the very soul of the political struggle was over who might become the father of the Nigerian family. In Ghana there was some paternalism under Limann in the early 1980s, but the accession of J. J. Rawlings muted that particular theme because it was inconsistent with Rawlings' brand of populism. Of the eight states, the paternal metaphors were least striking and least prominent in Senegal and Tanzania. In Tanzania, Nyerere's personality and socialist ideology made him uncomfortable with such paternal imagery, although his style of rule often contained paternal aspects. In Senegal, Senghor's intellectualism made explicit references to his role as father of the nation unacceptable until he announced his retirement. Diouf was both slightly less intellectual and slightly more paternal than his predecessor but was still considerably less given to employing the paternal metaphor than many of his brother heads of state. Significantly, however, in all eight states—regardless of the degree of prominence of the paternal metaphor—familial imagery of other sorts was quite common.

The second premise of the matrix concerned the limits on consumption and, by extension, corruption. While railing against the evils of corruption seemed to be national pastimes in most states, there were clearly some differences—not so much in the intensity with which the local presses reported about corruption, for in general they all did, but in the degree of corruption that seemed to be acceptable. Although always a difficult phenomenon to measure empirically, we know that in Zaïre and Nigeria billions were stolen; Kenya, Côte d'Ivoire, and Cameroon were probably not too far behind. In Senegal, Ghana, and Tanzania the degree of corruption might not have been any the less, but the scale certainly was, thus reflecting the more modest economic prospects and circumstances of those three states. In addition, Nyerere, Rawlings, and Diouf remained quite a bit "thinner" than some of the other heads of state did. At various times during their stays in power all three were at least willing to undertake certain sorts of symbolic gestures indicating that they were not "eating" to excess while others suffered from hunger. In Diouf's case, however, my impression is that both his paternalism and his girth tended to increase with his tenure in office.

Premise three of the matrix pertained to women. In general, what has been called "First Ladyism," or the cult of the First Lady emphasizing her role as a loving, maternal, and supportive adviser, seemed to be quite important in Zaïre, Nigeria under Babangida, and Cameroon during Biya's tenure. It progressively took hold in Senegal during Diouf's stay in power. Moi's divorce precluded this discursive option in Kenya, while Houphouet's mother and elder sister only occasionally called forth the same sorts of devoted and loving press coverage that were characteristic of some of the other more paternally inclined regimes. Nyerere's spouse was almost never mentioned. Nana Rawlings, like Elisabeth Diouf, gradually became more prominent as the regime wore on. The great paradox here was that although the First Ladies, and women in general, were seen and expected to nurture and nourish, in their cases this was not associated with eating, feeding, or power. Powerless providers, in most places they suffered from a structured invisibility that effectively removed them from the parameters of the political and confined them to small-scale development activities. They had to be treated with respect, however, and when they were not, as in Kenya in the early 1990s and Zaïre in the late 1980s and early 1990s, it became increasingly thinkable to question the regime and to protest against it.

The fourth premise of the matrix concerned the illegitimacy of eternal power and the importance of generational rotation. This theme—albeit with some variation—came through quite clearly in the study of the successions between Senghor and Diouf in Senegal, Nyerere and Mwinyi in Tanzania, and (to a slightly lesser extent) Ahidjo and Biya in Cameroon. In other states the importance of generational rotation was often present in the discourse, but the head of state was usually seen to be an unstated "exception." Instead, it emerged when discussing subjects such as the replacement of older parliamentarians or ministers with younger ones and the constant prominence given to bureaucratic retirements in the daily press coverage in Senegal, Cameroon, Zaïre, and Côte d'Ivoire.

The fact that there is such significant variation along each premise of the matrix underscores a point raised in Chapter 1. Namely, it is impossible to calculate the analytical weight of each premise of the matrix. In other words, there is no way of knowing whether violations of one premise can be counterbalanced by respect for the others. Nor can we state with assurance that any one premise is necessarily any more important, or central, to a comprehension of legitimacy than any other. "Legitimacy," as David Beetham usefully reminds us, "is not an all-or-nothing affair."[25] The politically subjacent realm does not credibly lend itself to such calculations. Its analytic strength and utility, however, has three main components. First, it provides us with a road map to the politically thinkable and unthinkable. It is thus a guide to "common sense," "natural," and hegemonic understandings of legitimacy. Second, and in consequence, it furnishes us with a mechanism to discern the cognitive range of acceptable political possibilities and alternatives in any given society. To return to an earlier example, Microsoft may be dismantled, but it will not be nationalized. That would be unthinkable. Third, part of the reason that the politically subjacent domain and the moral matrix are so powerful and important is that they engage our emotions. Images of father, family, and food touch emotional reservoirs within us. When the metaphor of father and family is projected onto the political arena, politics can acquire a significant emotional intensity. Politics in middle Africa, like politics everywhere, is fraught with passion.[26]

Moreover, although there is substantial variation along each of the premises of the moral matrix, there is still a recognizable configuration of political and cultural factors that gives the politics and political cultures of these states a certain analytical cohesiveness. They all have in common an implicit understanding of power that is often expressed in metaphors of food and eating. These are, moreover, consistent with the emphasis on nurture and nourishment in the moral matrix of legitimate governance. Furthermore, they all also share an emphasis on the unity and indivisibility of power, as well as a recognition that power has an important spiritual dimension. These common areas of agreement lead to a mapping of the parameters of the political that seems consistent in all eight states. Finally, people and politicians throughout middle Africa understand that sorcery is an alternative mode of political causality. The variation between states along the dimensions of the premises of the moral matrix occurs within these common parameters of the political, with a broad agreement on the comprehension of key political concepts, and with an unstated understanding of the political importance of alternative modes of political causality.

Legitimacy, Democracy, and "Democratization"

Close attention to political language and imagery has led me to explore the realm of the politically subjacent and to probe the moral matrix of legitimate governance. The matrix is really a series of cultural predispositions and implicit understandings that provide some underlying cognitive structure to those political words, concepts, images, institutions, and behaviors that we consider to be thinkable and thus legitimate. Let me emphasize that the moral matrix can aid us in understanding basic questions concerning political legitimacy, for it touches on the thinkability of certain types of relations between rulers and ruled, the duration of political mandates and succession, the expectations concerning the economic benefits necessary to maintain political legitimacy, and the amount of wealth that rulers may legitimately "eat." It points us in the direction of a greater understanding of those political phenomena that middle Africans view as "natural" and accept without deliberate reflection. The moral matrix, and the entire approach to political legitimacy that undergirds it, can also shed at least some light on certain aspects of middle Africa's current political unrest, as well as on the continentwide thrust toward "democratization."

The quotation marks surrounding "democratization" are deliberate. Although "democratization" has been a word heard with much frequency throughout middle Africa, as well as the rest of the continent, it is not the correct term to describe the political trajectory since 1989. It is certain that the entire continent is in the throes of a period of pervasive political change. Also certain is that there has been, in many states, a retreat from the single-party or military authoritarianism—whether of the left or of the right—that dominated Africa's political landscape in the 1970s and 1980s. Much less certain is whether these transformations will result in anything resembling democracy—however we may define that occasionally disputed concept.

In saying this, I fear that both political history and the history of political analysis may be repeating themselves. In 1960, when much of Africa achieved independence, most analysts and observers in the West believed, somewhat optimistically, that the end of formal colonialism would inevitably lead to the institutionalization of democratic rule. There was much optimism in 1960 because virtually all of the new states professed a belief in democracy. After all, was not democracy the very antithesis of colonialism? To be sure, there was much disagreement over the best means of achieving this goal, but the goal was present. Much of the debate focused on the applicability of multiparty politics in an African setting. Even those who argued in favor of single-party regimes (whether they were politicians or analysts) often did so in the context of an overarching democratic mind-set. Democracy, they reasoned, could not be attained without development, and development could best be achieved through a one-party system guaranteeing both economic progress and national unity. Both democracy and development were necessary to build the nation, and the early 1960s was the era of nation building. But things soon went awry; the result was neither democracy nor development.

At that time most believed that the Western constitutions bequeathed by the imperial powers would be respected. Few thought that multiparty, ostensibly democratic, systems would within five or six years give way either to single-party dictatorships or military rule. These developments surprised most of us, although both Frantz Fanon and W. Arthur Lewis sounded prescient and exemplary cautionary notes on the antidemocratic dangers of the single party.[27] The reasons why these early democratic experiments failed were many and varied. First, the constitutions that had been hastily grafted onto the new states in the waning days of colonial rule were often slightly modified copies of the constitutions in place in the metropole. The European democracies, however, had had years, in some cases centuries, to evolve these governmental forms.[28] As the imperial recessional sounded, they were hastily implanted in African soil, where people were untrained in their use, unaccustomed to or unaware of their often unwritten norms, and ill at ease with some of their assumptions. Institutionalized opposition, for example, might well have felt uncomfortable to many who placed a genuine premium on community and consensus. Opposition parliamentarians often willingly crossed the carpet and came over to the majority's side so that they and their constituents could benefit from the advantages of being in the Government. The institutional trappings of parliamentary democracy never really had the time to gain acceptance or become rooted in the subjacent realm of the politically thinkable.

Second, there were often failures of political leadership.[29] Leaders who might well have once been genuine democrats soon developed a taste for the power and perquisites of office. In Ghana, as in many other countries, those in power soon equated legitimate political opposition with treason. An early foretaste of this attitude was seen in Kwame Nkrumah's modestly titled book, *Ghana: The Autobiography of Kwame Nkrumah.*[30] The dilemma, a serious one, was the following: If the nation and the political leader were one and the same, then how could legitimate political opposition be expressed without attacking the nation by committing treason? The usually unstated notions of the unity and indivisibility of power contributed to the tendency that many leaders had to try to monopolize the levers of state command. In this context, without proper preparation, "eating alone," or not sharing power, became all too thinkable as politics often became a struggle— occasionally violent—to see who would get to occupy the sole seat at the national dinner table.

A third reason, closely associated with the second in many places, also became visible. Perhaps because they had so long been denied chances to become wealthy under colonialism, many leaders also began to convert their public offices into opportunities for the accumulation of private wealth. Those in positions of authority and control began to "eat." Over time it ultimately mattered little if they "ate" because of personal venality—although there was much of that—or because they were latter-day "Big Men" under pressure to redistribute the fruits of *Uhuru* to their families, communal networks, and ethnic kin. The effect of this behavior, regardless of its motivation, was to sap further the foundations of the polity so that in extreme cases it became unthinkable *not* to exploit one's parcel of authority in this way. The fourth reason these 1960-vintage experiments in democracy failed was because of massively rigged elections. Once it became clear that one would no longer be able to "eat," much less "eat alone," were an election to be lost, the incentives for illegal electoral manipulation became overwhelming. Early democratic optimism faded into cynicism as voters realized that there was no way in which their leader could have possibly achieved 99.9 percent of the vote. Unworkable constitutions, corrupt politicians, fraudulent elections, and declining economies combined to usher in both the military coup and the era of the single-party regime. Both were profoundly antidemocratic.

A similar wave of democratic optimism accompanied the liberation of Portuguese Africa in the mid-1970s. Here, too, hopes were belied as both Angola and Mozambique opted for variants of Marxism-Leninism and later descended into civil war, fueled in both cases by the intervention of powerful external actors. Moreover, and more recently, in our euphoria over 1989 and all that it has come to signify, we have forgotten 1979—a very tough year for tyrants. Somoza fell in Nicaragua, the Shah in Iran. In Africa a bubble of hope emerged as the regimes of Idi Amin in Uganda, Emperor Jean-Bedel Bokassa in Central African Republic, and Francisco Macias Nguema in Equatorial Guinea came to an end and as the civilian regimes of Shehu Shagari in Nigeria and Hilla Limann in Ghana reclaimed power from the military after national multiparty elections. These were shortly to be followed by a majority-ruled and ostensibly democratic Zimbabwe.

That bubble burst. These positive and hopeful developments were soon dashed on the rocks of increased repression, corruption run amok, poor domestic policy choices, increasing debt, staggering economic decline, and various forms of less-than-benign external intervention—whether in the form of a pernicious cold-war rivalry, the aggression of the South African apartheid state, or the increasingly dominant economic policy position of the officials of the various international financial institutions such as the World Bank and the International Monetary Fund.

In late 1989 Gabon's President Omar Bongo was quoted as saying, "The wind from the East is shaking the coconut trees."[31] He should have added, although he did not, that in consequence some of the coconuts were going to fall. And fall they did. On one side of the conventional, though misleading, left-right political continuum, long-serving autocrats such as Ethiopia's Mengistu Haile Mariam and Somalia's Mohammed Siad Barre departed under violent circumstances. Bénin's Mathieu Kérékou, a onetime Marxist, had his power stripped by a national conference but then returned to power after winning a democratic election. Also at one time a Marxist, Congo-Brazzaville's Dénis Sassou-Nguesso departed from power peacefully, only to return, undemocratically, after a brutal civil war. Zambia's Kenneth Kaunda relinquished office to Frederick Chiluba after a democratic election and has remained in the political wilderness ever since. Ironically, and sadly, Chiluba has used many of the same antidemocratic mechanisms that Kaunda himself once employed to ensure his own political dominance. On the continuum's other side, Liberia's Samuel Doe and Joseph Momoh in Sierra Leone also gave up their political ghost. The violence in those two tragic countries has yet to abate. In 1994 the murder of Rwanda's Juvénal Habyarimana triggered a genocide that plunged Rwanda, and all Central Africa, into a war and political crisis of unprecedented proportions. On a much happier note, the end of the apartheid state in South Africa gave way to democratic elections in 1994 and then to the presidencies of Nelson Mandela and Thabo Mbeki. This multifaceted and exceedingly complex process has now well begun, and the dynamics of political change, as they so often do in Africa, seem to be occurring with near-complete disregard for Africanized versions of Western ideologies, the sensibilities of great power patrons, and the theoretical ruminations of social scientists.

In retrospect, it seems clear that both the independence governments of the 1960s as well as their successors of the 1970s and 1980s progressively squandered whatever popular acceptance they might have once had. In the midst of today's upheavals, all we can safely say is that the majority of single-party states and military regimes long ago proved themselves to be politically bankrupt. We cannot yet say with any certainty what forms of government will emerge, whether these will be legitimate, or if they will be democratic.

As has been true of the rest of the continent, the range of political variation in middle Africa has been extremely wide. As of this writing, no transition has occurred in Kenya since the death of Jomo Kenyatta in 1978. And no transition has occurred in Cameroon since Ahidjo's resignation in 1982. In the 1990s multiparty elections of varying degrees of international acceptability were held in both states. Moi and Biya are still in charge. Côte d'Ivoire, like the other states, instituted multiparty elections, but Houphouet's successor Henri Konan Bédié and the PDCI retained control until a military coup in late 1999 brought General Robert Guei to power. Guei promised elections, but those of October 2000 were a sham because the Ivoirian courts had decided on dubious constitutional grounds that a major opposition leader, Alassane Ouattara, was not legally entitled to stand. Laurent Gbagbo (the one serious candidate who was permitted to run) and his supporters refused to accept Guei's fraudulent claim of victory. Civil disturbances followed, and the general fled the country. The outcome remains uncertain, although for the moment Gbagbo appears to be the new occupant of the presidential palace. Gbagbo, too, has tried to exclude Ouattara from electoral competition. In Congo, the Mobutu regime fell to armed insurrection in 1997. Since then the Congo has been the site of civil war, external military intervention by her neighbors, and a new regime. Laurent Kabila (1997–2001), Mobutu's initial successor, had questionable democratic credentials.[32] He was assassinated in January 2001 and was succeeded by Joseph Kabila, his son, who remains in power at least for the moment. This succession was conducted under the watchful eye of Angolan and Zimbabwean military forces and was realized without the benefit of any democratic procedures.

More optimistically, Nigeria returned to civilian rule in 1999 after democratic elections that saw the end, finally, of what some had called the permanent transition.[33] Nigerians elected Olusegun Obasanjo as their new president. A former general and former president, Obasanjo had peacefully and willingly handed over power to the civilian regime of Shehu Shagari in 1979. Although no transition had occurred in Ghana since Rawlings' second coup in 1982, Rawlings agreed not to stand for reelection in December 2000. These elections were successful, peaceful, and democratic. Opposition candidate John Kufuor defeated Rawlings' incumbent vice-president and was inaugurated in early 2001. In Tanzania, although the CCM remains in power, multiparty elections have occurred regularly. Benjamin Mkapa was elected to succeed Mwinyi in 1995 and won reelection in 2000 despite substantial electoral irregularities on Zanzibar. In Senegal, Abdoulaye Wade and his PDS emerged victorious in the 2000 election, and Abdou Diouf relinquished power.

To lump all of these complex and varied political trajectories under the heading of "democratization" is misleading, arbitrary, and premature. On this point I must continue to disagree with Bratton and van de Walle, for the empirical picture is far more complicated than the rubric of "democratization" actually indicates.[34] To be sure, some of these experiments will become democracies; others will not. Given the political and analytical experiences of the first wave of democratic experiments—the failures of the early 1960s—caution is warranted on this subject. If nothing else, those failed experiments should have at least taught us that a label such as "democratization" confuses a normatively desired end with a still bewildering and most uncertain process whose direction is far from unilinear and whose ultimate destination is far from determined. It is a process whose outcome defies prediction. But it is also a process whose complexity creates room for both optimistic and pessimistic interpretations because the moral matrix of legitimate governance permits a range of politically thinkable outcomes.

Finally, are the four premises of the matrix, as well as middle Africans' implicit understandings of key concepts such as power, the parameters of the political, and appreciations of alternative causalities, compatible with democracy? In other words, do middle African perspectives on legitimacy lend themselves to democratic outcomes? Given the varied political trajectories of the eight states of middle Africa over the past forty years, the answer is yes—and no. Let me elaborate.

First, everything contained in the four premises of the matrix can be reconciled with contemporary, widely accepted notions of democracy. As long as political "fathers" continue to nurture and nourish, creating the economic and political conditions that permit people to "eat"; as long as they themselves do not "eat" too much and refrain from eating while others are hungry; as long as they do not eternalize themselves in power and respect the normal rotation of political generations; and as long as they treat their political "wives" and "children" with dignity and respect, listening to their counsel and hearing their voices, it will be quite thinkable and legitimate that they continue in office. Or, phrased in a different idiom, as long as political leaders develop the economy so as to encourage the growth and distribution of resources that allow people to become better off; as long as they do not engage in ostentatiously corrupt practices—especially during periods of economic decline; as long as they show themselves willing to relinquish power and leave office; as long as they cherish civil liberties and treat their populations with respect, honoring their views and preferences, their political legitimacy will remain robust. Nothing in the matrix precludes this, and the four premises even encourage it. The moral matrix, in other words, can be quite consistent with democratic practice.

The new generation of political "fathers" will, however, have to widen the range of people with whom they consult, listening carefully to the voices of those who were once either disenfranchised or consigned to positions of structured invisibility. An argument could be made, for example, that women cannot effectively fulfill their role as "counselors" unless they are represented in positions of power and influence in far greater numbers than they are currently. The new political "fathers" will also have to expand the categories of people who are able "eat" and thus share in the fruits of *Uhuru*. The existence of too many hungry, "thin" people will sap the foundations of any would-be democratic polity. At the same time, of course, even though many of them have been long-starved for power, they cannot "eat" too much. Men with "big tummies" must not overindulge their appetites.

Similarly, there is nothing inherently antidemocratic in middle African understandings of the parameters of the political realm. That the political kingdom in middle Africa includes a considerable spiritual terrain is not, in and of itself, antidemocratic in any way. Nor is there necessarily anything antidemocratic in the resort to alternative modes of causality. Here, however, we must be careful to distinguish the intellectual operation (sorcery as explanation) from the political operation (sorcery as a means of achieving a political end). To be sure, there is, as we have seen, a dark side to sorcery, and those who employ the occult arts are feared and occasionally hated. Although democracy is not necessarily about liking other people, it is—or should be—about freedom from fear. As we have seen, sorcery can be used, as it was in Congo/Zaïre, to induce political quiescence. When this occurs, largely because of fear of the consequences, it becomes unthinkable to challenge a father-chief steeped in the dark arts. Sorcery as an implement of statecraft, especially when its effects are feared, poses a problem for both the spirit and the practice of democracy.[35]

But perhaps the biggest impediment to democratic practice in middle Africa is the notion of the unity and indivisibility of power. If "power is eaten whole" throughout much of the region, how can it possibly be shared among competing and contending forces in a democracy? If fear of losing the only seat at the national dinner table impels violent preemptive action, what hope is there of developing a less apocalyptic vision of political competition? If political leaders are unwilling to share even the symbolic dimensions of power, what hope is there for an eventual democratic outcome? Heads far wiser than mine will have to answer these questions. Positive answers, favorable to democracy, are not beyond the realm of the possible, for the politically subjacent realm in middle Africa permits, as it has always done, a wide range of creative, thinkable, and thus politically legitimate solutions to emerge from the moral matrix of legitimate governance.

NOTES

I. METAPHOR AND MATRIX

1. David L. Sills and Robert K. Merton, "Social Science Quotations: Who Said What, When, and Where," *Items* 45, no. 1 (March 1991): 3.

2. Michael G. Schatzberg, *Politics and Class in Zaire: Bureaucracy, Business, and Beer in Lisala* (New York: Africana, 1980).

3. Michael G. Schatzberg, *The Dialectics of Oppression in Zaire* (Bloomington: Indiana University Press, 1988), 71–98.

4. See Jean-François Bayart, *L'état au Cameroun* (Paris: Presses de la Fondation Nationale des Sciences Politiques, 1979); Achille Mbembe, *Afriques indociles: Christianisme, pouvoir et état en société postcoloniale* (Paris: Karthala, 1988); and Achille Mbembe, "La palabre de l'indépendance: Les ordres du discours nationalistes au Cameroun (1948–1958)," *Revue française de science politique* 35, no. 3 (June 1985): 459–487.

For an early attempt to extend the analysis to Cameroon, see Michael G. Schatzberg, "The Metaphors of Father and Family," in *The Political Economy of Cameroon*, ed. Michael G. Schatzberg and I. William Zartman (New York: Praeger, 1986), 1–19. A better developed, more comparative analysis may be found in Michael G. Schatzberg, "Power, Legitimacy, and 'Democratisation' in Africa," *Africa* 63, no. 4 (1993): 445–461.

5. See, for example, Samuel Decalo, "Modalities of Civil-Military Stability in Africa," *Journal of Modern African Studies* 27, no. 4 (1989): 547–578.

6. Robert W. July, *The Origins of Modern African Thought: Its Development in West Africa during the Nineteenth and Twentieth Centuries* (London: Faber and Faber, 1968); and Steven Metz, "In Lieu of Orthodoxy: The Socialist Theories of Nkrumah and Nyerere," *Journal of Modern African Studies* 20, no. 3 (1982): 377–392.

7. See, for example, Irving Leonard Markovitz, *Léopold Sédar Senghor and the Politics of Negritude* (New York: Atheneum, 1969).

8. Crawford Young, *Ideology and Development in Africa* (New Haven, Conn.: Yale

University Press, 1982); and David Ottaway and Marina Ottaway, *Afrocommunism* (New York: Holmes and Meier, 1981).

9. Ilunga Kabongo, "Déroutante Afrique ou la syncope d'un discours," *Canadian Journal of African Studies* 18, no. 1 (1984): 13–22.

10. Alfred Schutz, *The Phenomenology of the Social World,* trans. George Walsh and Frederic Lehnert (Evanston, Ill.: Northwestern University Press, 1967); Peter L. Berger and Thomas Luckmann, *The Social Construction of Reality: A Treatise in the Sociology of Knowledge* (Garden City, N.Y.: Doubleday-Anchor, 1966); Nelson Goodman, *Ways of Worldmaking* (Indianapolis: Hackett, 1978); Nelson Goodman, *Of Mind and Other Matters* (Cambridge, Mass.: Harvard University Press, 1984); and Jerome Bruner, *Actual Minds, Possible Worlds* (Cambridge, Mass.: Harvard University Press, 1986).

11. Clifford Geertz, *The Interpretation of Cultures: Selected Essays* (New York: Basic Books, 1973); George Orwell, "Politics and the English Language," in *In Front of Your Nose, 1945–1950, vol. 4: The Collected Essays, Journalism, and Letters of George Orwell,* ed. Sonia Orwell and Ian Angus (1946; reprint, New York: Harcourt Brace Jovanovich, 1968), 127–140; Murray Edelman, *Constructing the Political Spectacle* (Chicago: University of Chicago Press, 1988); Kenneth Burke, *A Grammar of Motives* (New York: Prentice-Hall, 1945); and Jan Vansina, *Oral Tradition as History* (Madison: University of Wisconsin Press, 1985).

12. Ronald Inglehart, "The Renaissance of Political Culture," *American Political Science Review* 82, no. 4 (1988): 1203–1230, esp. 1203; also see his *Culture Shift in Advanced Industrial Society* (Princeton, N.J.: Princeton University Press, 1990); and *Modernization and Postmodernization: Cultural, Economic, and Political Change in Forty-three Societies* (Princeton, N.J.: Princeton University Press, 1997).

13. Geertz, *The Interpretation of Cultures,* 312.

14. See the various works of Michel Foucault, especially *The Archaeology of Knowledge and the Discourse on Language,* trans. A. M. Sheridan Smith (New York: Pantheon, 1972); *The Order of Things: An Archaeology of the Human Sciences* (New York: Vintage, 1973); *Discipline and Punish: The Birth of the Prison,* trans. Alan Sheridan (New York: Pantheon, 1977); and *Power/Knowledge: Selected Interviews and Other Writings, 1972–1977,* ed. and trans. Colin Gordon (New York: Pantheon, 1984). Also see Michel de Certeau, *L'invention du quotidien, 1: Arts de faire* (Paris: Union Générale d'Editions, 1980).

15. E. S. Atieno-Odhiambo, "Democracy and the Ideology of Order in Kenya," in *The Political Economy of Kenya,* ed. Michael G. Schatzberg (New York: Praeger, 1987), 177–201.

16. I was a Peace Corps teacher in Cameroon from 1969 to 1971 and did fieldwork in Zaïre from 1974 to 1975. Unable to return to Zaïre because my writings were critical of the regime, I was able to interview Zaïrian exiles and do archival work in Brussels during the summers of 1983 and 1993. I accomplished some preliminary fieldwork in Kenya in 1983, but a longer stay was cut short by the regime during 1984–1985. On this particular experience, see Michael G. Schatzberg, "Two Faces of Kenya: The Researcher and the State," *African Studies Review* 29, no. 4 (December 1986): 1–15.

17. World Bank, *World Development Report 1997: The State in a Changing World* (Oxford: Oxford University Press, 1997), 214, Table 1. The gross national product (GNP) per capita in 1995 U.S. dollars was Tanzania, $120; Nigeria, $260; Kenya, $280; Ghana,

$390; Senegal, $600; Cameroon, $650; and Côte d'Ivoire, $660. No figures were provided for Congo/Zaïre, although it is safe to include it within the same low-income economic grouping. All such statistics must be treated cautiously, however.

18. I am most grateful to Andrew Sessions for performing this yeomanlike task.

19. Useful works on unraveling the meaning of visual sources are W. J. T. Mitchell, *Picture Theory: Essays on Verbal and Visual Representation* (Chicago: University of Chicago Press, 1994); Murray Edelman, *From Art to Politics: How Artistic Creations Shape Political Conceptions* (Chicago: University of Chicago Press, 1995); Catherine A. Lutz and Jane A. Collins, *Reading National Geographic* (Chicago: University of Chicago Press, 1993); and Johannes Fabian, *Remembering the Present: Painting and Popular History in Zaire* (Berkeley: University of California Press, 1996).

20. Foucault, *The Archaeology of Knowledge and the Discourse on Language,* 37–38. For enlightening studies of discourse in South Africa, see Adam Ashforth, *The Politics of Official Discourse in Twentieth-Century South Africa* (Oxford: Clarendon Press, 1990); and Aletta J. Norval, *Deconstructing Apartheid Discourse* (London: Verso, 1996).

21. Auguste Miremont, "Président, bon anniversaire," *Fraternité Matin,* 17–18 October 1981, 1. This and all translations are mine unless noted otherwise.

22. "Bonne Fête," *Fraternité Matin,* 18 October 1982, 1.

23. Michel Kouamé, "Le Chef de l'Etat a dansé," *Fraternité Matin,* 9 December 1980, 14. Also see, "Yamoussoukro—Quand les enfants accueillent le père . . . président," *Fraternité Matin,* 18–20 October 1980, 9.

24. "HOUPHOUET ELU A 99,99%" and "Les Ivoiriens ont manifesté dimanche leur fidélité et leur reconnaissance à leur 'Vieux,'" *Fraternité Matin,* 14 October 1980, 1.

25. "Motion spéciale à l'adresse du Chef de l'État," *Fraternité Matin,* 10–12 April 1982, 1.

26. "On ne sert mieux qu'en servant le pays," *Fraternité Matin,* 18 June 1985, 4–5.

27. "Dabakala: Le préfet Coffi Béhibro de nouveau à la tête de la région," *Fraternité Matin,* 14 February 1980, 8.

28. "Propos du quartier: Merci au Père de la Nation," Letter to the Editor, *Fraternité Matin,* 29 February 1980, 6.

29. "Prime Minister Announces Ivoirian President's Death," La Chaine Une, Television Network (in French), 7 December 1993, cited in Foreign Broadcast Information Service (FBIS), *Daily Report: Sub-Saharan Africa,* FBIS-AFR-93-233, 7 December 1993, West Africa, 25–26 (hereafter, FBIS-AFR). FBIS translates materials from other languages into English.

30. "Mzee Jomo Kenyatta, Editorial Tribute," *Kenya Mirror,* 1 June 1968, 2.

31. "President Moi Speaks; Links Parties, Tribalism," Nairobi Domestic Service (in Swahili), 10 May 1990, cited in FBIS-AFR-90-096, 17 May 1990, 4.

32. Christabel Ouko, "'I Thank God for the Years I Shared with Him,'" *Weekly Review,* 2 March 1990, 24.

33. On hidden transcripts, see James C. Scott, *Domination and the Arts of Resistance: Hidden Transcripts* (New Haven, Conn.: Yale University Press, 1990).

34. "Le Message du Dimanche: En faveur des artistes," Editorial, *Elima,* 26–27 July 1981, 1, 9.

35. "Le séjour du maréchal Mobutu à l'Equateur," *Elima,* 27 August 1984, 15.

36. "Succès total," Editorial, *Cameroon Tribune,* 29 February 1980, 1 (emphasis in original).

37. Jean-Mary Neossi, "La joie de Bertoua," *Cameroon Tribune,* 5 February 1981, 3.

38. Henri Bandolo, "Le Président Paul Biya répond à Cameroon-Tribune," *Cameroon Tribune,* 18 January 1983, 2–4.

39. "Présentation des voeux de la Cour Suprême; Allocution de M. le Premier Président de la Cour Suprême," 30 December 1980, typescript, 1 (Dakar, Senegal: Archives Nationales, "Dossier Politique, Senghor 1980").

40. Serigne Ndiaye Gonzalès, director, National Dramatic Troupe, Théâtre Daniel Sorano, "Un triste et cruel cadeau de fin d'année," Letter to the Editor, *Le Soleil,* 27–28 December 1980, 4. For a similar evocation of the father of the nation, see Amadou Dibor Seck, retired bureaucrat, "Le président Senghor s'en va," Letter to the Editor, *Le Soleil,* 30 December 1980.

41. Jacques Moundor Diouf, "Les 'noces d'argent' de Mgr Thiandoum," *Le Soleil,* 20 May 1987, 4.

42. "Le Pr Iba Der Thiam [minister of education]: 'L'absence d'éducation morale menace l'école sénégalaise,'" *Le Soleil,* 4 January 1985, 4–5. Also see Alioune Dramé, "Raisons d'espérer," *Le Soleil,* 5 April 1991, 1, where Diouf is seen to adopt the profile of the "paterfamilias."

43. "Nyerere Hands over CCM Chairmanship to Mwinyi," Dar es Salaam Domestic Service (in Swahili), 17 August 1990, cited in FBIS-AFR-90-162, 21 August 1990, 15.

44. Halima Shariff, "You Are Pillars of the Nation, Elders Told," *Sunday News,* 11 January 1987, 1. Also see the press coverage of Mwinyi's adoption of two children. Mkumbwa Ally, "Mwinyi Adopts Two Children," *Daily News,* 15 February 1990, 1.

45. "President Addresses Nairobi Rally 23 September," Nairobi Domestic Service (in Swahili), 23 September 1982, cited in FBIS-AFR, East Africa, 27 September 1982, V. R1.

46. "President Moi Details 'Intentions' for Peace," Nairobi, Kenya Broadcasting Corporation Network (in Swahili), 20 March 1992, cited in FBIS-AFR-92-056, 23 March 1992, 3.

47. Lucas M. Kilemba, Taita, "Ethnicity in Kenya," Letter to the Editor, *Weekly Review,* 30 May 1997, 2; and Wilson M. Wadia, Mombasa, "Terrorists," Letter to the Editor, *Weekly Review,* 21 April 1995, 2.

48. Trayo A. Ali, "'The Strength of Our People Is My Inspiration,'" interview with Ngugi wa Thiong'o, *West Africa,* 6–12 November 1995, 1735.

49. Léopold Senghor, transcription of radio address to the nation on 3 April 1970, in *Dakar-Matin,* 6 April 1970, 4.

50. Ibrahima Gaye, "Maturité," *Le Soleil,* 9 April 1980, 1.

51. "Comment: Growing Up Is Difficult," Editorial, *People's Daily Graphic,* 8 March 1984, 2.

52. J. J. Rawlings, "The People Are Awake—2," *People's Daily Graphic,* 4 February 1983, 2.

53. See, for example, Achike Okafo, "Lest We Forget: New Year Resolution," Column, *Daily Times,* 6 January 1982, 7; Nellie Onwuchekwa, "An Autopsy of a Nation at 28," *Daily Times,* 30 September 1988, 11; text of Ahidjo's speech to the nation, *Cameroon Tribune,* 1–2 January 1980, 3; text of Ahidjo's speech to the youth of the nation on the fourteenth annual youth holiday, *Cameroon Tribune,* 10–12 February 1980, 6; "Election présidentielle du 14 janvier 1984," *Cameroon Tribune,* 20 January 1984, 3; "Message de voeux de l'an du président Paul Biya—Le président Biya invite les Camer-

ounais à démontrer leur ardeur et leur foi en nos idéaux," *Cameroon Tribune,* 3 January 1986, 5; and Jean-Pierre Ayé, "Le nouveau gouvernement: Un reflet des diversités régionales," *Fraternité Matin,* 4 February 1981, 1.

54. Attilio Tagalile, "Mwinyi Accepts Nomination," *Daily News,* 16 August 1985, 3.

55. Panteleon Ekwunife, Unibadan, Ibadan, "New Name for Nigeria," Letter to the Editor, *Daily Times,* 16 January 1980, 11.

56. The Rt. Hon. Prince Akweke Abyesinia Nwafor Orizu, *Insight into Nigeria: The Shehu Shagari Era* (Ibadan, Nigeria: Evans Brothers, 1983), 272.

57. Wunmi Osinaike, "Governor Lawal—'A Mother to Her Children,'" *Daily Times,* 8 November 1988, 7.

58. "Sierra Leone: 'The Popular Choice,'" interview, *West Africa,* 12 August 1985, 1635.

59. G. R. Jones, Freetown, Sierra Leone, "Return to the Family," Letter to the Editor, *West Africa,* 14 October 1985, 2166–2167.

60. Adiatu Tejan, London, "Another Moses?" Letter to the Editor, *West Africa,* 1–7 June 1992, 908.

61. "Une atmosphère de famille," *Fraternité Matin,* 4 May 1982, 11; and Félix Houphouet-Boigny, "Sachons nous dépasser," *Fraternité Matin,* 10 June 1982, 4, 25.

62. *Fraternité Matin* (in French), 26 September 1984, 7, cited in "Call for Vigilance Made," FBIS-AFR-84-189, West Africa, V., T3. For other examples, see "M. Fologo à la cérémonie de clôture: Le PDCI, c'est la Côte d'Ivoire," *Fraternité Matin,* 13 December 1982, 15, 19; and *Fraternité Matin* (in French), 26 September 1985, 24–25, cited in "Alliali Addresses Meeting Preceding Congress," FBIS-AFR-85-188, 27 September 1985, West Africa, V., T1.

63. "President Bédié Interviewed on State of the Nation," Abidjan Radio, Côte d'Ivoire Chaine Nationale-Une, 3 July 1994 (in French), cited in FBIS-AFR-94-131, 8 July 1994, 22–23.

64. Isaac Preko, London, "Nkrumah's Followers," Letter to the Editor, *West Africa,* 31 August–6 September 1992, 1468.

65. Ajoa Yeboa-Afari, "Asuma Banda and the CPP," *West Africa,* 18–24 March 1996, 424.

66. "Reactions to Abacha's Broadcast," *West Africa,* 25 September–8 October 1995, 1597. For additional examples, also see "No Multi-Party in Zimbabwe—Let Us Differ in One Family, Says Mugabe," *Daily News,* 4 May 1990, 2; and "Nyerere on Party Democracies," *Daily News,* 17 August 1990, 6–7.

67. Paul Biya, text of speech to the class "vigilance" of the Ecole Militaire Interarmes (EMIA), *Cameroon Tribune,* 31 July–1 August 1983, 3–4; and "'Il ne peut y avoir de véritable soldat sans une certaine éthique'—Déclare le président Paul Biya," *Cameroon Tribune,* 13–14 July 1986, 3. The Cameroonian political police were also a "big family." See, for example, Mouelle Bissi, "Sûreté Nationale—Mm. Mbassi, Mveng, Amougou et Djambou promus commissaires divisionnaires," *Cameroon Tribune,* 9 January 1984, 5.

68. Essolomwa Nkoy ea Linganga, "Symbole de la stabilité, de la paix et du progrès," *Elima,* 11 June 1985, 1, 7.

69. See, for example, "Vittel: La grande famille Franco-Africaine," *Fraternité Matin,* 7 October 1983, 1.

70. "Diouf Delivers Senegambia Anniversary Address," Dakar Domestic Service (in French), 31 January 1986, cited in FBIS-AFR-86-022, 3 February 1986, V., T3.

71. "Front Page Comment—A Stab in the Back," Editorial, *Daily Graphic,* 23 March 1981, 1–2.

72. Abdou Diouf, text of speech upon arriving at Yamoussoukro, *Fraternité Matin,* 9–10 May 1981, 9.

73. On Touré's visit, see *Fraternité Matin,* 29 January 1980, 1; on the 1984 homage, see "Le premier ministre guinéen hier à son départ: Le Président Houphouet nous a prodigué de sages conseils," *Fraternité Matin,* 13 April 1984, 28.

74. "Comment: Welcome, Big Brother," Editorial, *People's Daily Graphic,* 13 March 1987, 2.

75. "Apology Due from Washington," Editorial, *The Standard,* 4 March 1991, cited in "U.S. Apology Demanded," FBIS-AFR-91-043, 5 March 1991, 8 (emphasis added).

76. KNS, "Prière des zaïrois: Le 'Notre Père,'" *"Umoja"* (Kinshasa), 30 September 1991, 12.

77. Pape Marcel Sene, "Conférence de presse de l'Archévêque de Paris—'L'église européenne pourrait beaucoup apprendre de l'Afrique,'" *Le Soleil,* 10 December 1981, 6.

78. Ibrahima Fall, "56e Magal de Touba—Unité, confrérique, prix et développment," *Le Soleil,* 17 September 1981, 6.

79. Amadou Gaye, "Le Khalife général aux fidèles: 'Je vous invite à soutenir Abdou Diouf,'" *Le Soleil,* 29 December 1982, 4. Also see Babacar Dieng, "Louga: 33è anniversaire du magal de Darou Marnane," *Le Soleil,* 5–7 October 1984, 9.

80. Jacques M. Diouf, "Abdou Diouf à Ndiassane—Visite de courtoisie du fils à son père," *Le Soleil Urnes,* 26 February 1988, ii.

81. Mukendi Mwadia-Mvita, "L'homme fort vert et blanc—'Le secret de notre réussite c'est la discipline,'" *Elima,* 21 February 1986, 9.

82. Marcellin Abougnan, "Merci Monsieur le Président!" Editorial, *Fraternité Matin,* 3 April 1986, 1.

83. See, for example, "Papa's Family to Brief Baba," *Daily Times,* 16 May 1987, 1.

84. Bode Ayeni, "Open Letter to Awo," *Daily Times,* 9 May 1988, 11.

85. Bola Olowo, "Nigeria in Shock," *West Africa,* 20–26 May 1996, 779.

86. Ola Rotimi, "Of PPA Presidential Choice and the Nation," *Punch,* 30 December 1982, reprinted in Ola Rotimi, *Statements: Towards August '83* . . . (Lagos, Nigeria: Kurunmi Adventures Ltd., 1983), 11.

87. *Weekly Review,* 14 October 1988, 73.

88. "The Challengers," *Weekly Review,* 16 October 1992, 5.

89. See, for example, "Communiqué: Fête de famille chez Maître Moustapha Thiam (Notaire)" (advertisement), *Le Soleil,* 13 April 1983, 11; and "Communiqué: Sechoy et Cie: Fête de famille" (advertisement), *Le Soleil,* 16–17 April 1983, 8. In addition, for Senegal, see the following issues of *Le Soleil:* 21–23 May 1983, 18; 27 May 1983, 5; 15 November 1983, 2–3; 17–18 March 1984, 10; 28–29 July 1984, 21; 1–2 December 1984, 11; 29 April 1985, 5; 6 June 1985, 3; 3 July 1985, 9; 13–14 July 1985, 11; 12 August 1985, 4; 22 January 1986, 4; 30 April–1 May 1986, 9; 13 August 1987, 2; 4 January 1988, 7; 12 January 1988, 5; 13–14 February 1988, 4; 22 April 1988, 8; 21 June 1989, 10; and 26 December 1989, 9.

For Cameroon, see the following issues of *Cameroon Tribune:* 21 January 1986, 7; 22 January 1986, 5; 4 February 1986, 7; 13 February 1986, 7; 29 April 1986, 11; 25–26 May 1986, 17; 29 May 1986, 17; 7 June 1986, 18; 18 December 1986, 18; 13 April 1987, 11; and 30 June 1987, 9.

For Zaïre, see the following issues of *Elima:* 8–9 February 1986, 9; 18 February 1986,

13; 12 March 1986, 14; 2 June 1986, 14; 20–21 September 1986, 12–13; 1 December 1986, 7; 11 February 1987, 12–13; 4–5 April 1987, 10; 7 January 1988, 9–14; 12 February 1988, 2; 13 April 1988, 14–15; 11–12 June 1988, 5; 1 November 1988, 12–13; 15 November 1988, 10–11; 27 December 1988, 12–13; 31 January 1989, 4; and 18–19 January 1990, 13.

90. Moussa Sadio, "Ziguinchor: Fête de famille au Trésor," *Le Soleil*, 3–4 April 1982, 10; Vieux Doro Ndiaye, "O. P. T.: Vin d'honneur pour le départ à la retraite du receveur," *Le Soleil*, 18 November 1983, 11; and "Economie nationale—Mise à la retraite d'un éminent collaborateur," *Elima*, 26 August 1986, 3.

91. "Nioro du Rip—Fête de famille pour le départ du chef de bureau d'ordre," *Le Soleil*, 23 August 1982, 10; "Mutation à la police de Ndorong," *Le Soleil*, 26 January 1984, 9; M. Mbodj, "En l'honneur de M. Madieyna Diouf: Fête de famille à l'Urbanisme," *Le Soleil*, 13–14 July 1985, 11; Pape Boubacar Samb, "Fête de famille à l'ENAM," *Le Soleil*, 4 February 1986, 9; and "Fête de famille à la gouvernance: La cérémonie a été organisée lors du départ de M. Moussa Ndoye ancien gouverneur de la région," *Le Soleil*, 14 February 1985, 12.

92. "Fête de famille au Jardin d'enfants 'Kër Gune Yi,'" *Le Soleil*, 24–25 July 1982, 4; Maye Mbengue, "L'école sénégalaise d'hier et d'aujourd'hui," *Le Soleil*, 13–14 October 1984, 6; Ibrahima Fall, "M. Kader Fall a exalté le rôle de l'enfant dans la nation," *Le Soleil*, 10 January 1980, 3; Ndiogou Diop, "Fête de famille à l'école franco-sénégalaise," *Le Soleil*, 2 July 1985, 7; and "Les 25 ans du collège Notre-Dame d'Afrique—Une 'Fête de Famille' dans une chaude ambiance," *Fraternité Matin*, 6–7 March 1982, 7.

93. "Gala de l'ENA—Une belle fête de famille," *Fraternité Matin*, 23 June 1983, 3; Essolomwa Nkoy ea Linganga, "Consolider davantage la démocratie," *Elima*, 6 October 1987, 1; and "Présentation des voeux à Mme Jeanne Biya: La cérémonie s'est déroulée dans la simplicité et la cordialité," *Cameroon Tribune*, 4 January 1985, 3.

94. Unfortunately, I was approximately halfway though my reading of the newspapers before I realized the relevance of these photos, so my listings are incomplete. Even so, a full listing of those citations that I do have would be both lengthy and tedious. I here include only those references for Cameroon, Côte d'Ivoire and Senegal for 1986—a year chosen quite arbitrarily. All other references are available upon request.

Cameroon: "Présentation des voeux de fin d'année," *Cameroon Tribune*, 1–2 January 1986, 1, caption: "La grande famille de l'Information et de la Culture: déterminée à faire mieux en 1986"; "Installation du premier secrétaire provincial de la chambre d'agriculture de l'Adamaoua," *Cameroon Tribune*, 29 January 1986, 9, caption: "Photo de famille après l'installation provincial de la chambre de l'agriculture pour l'Adamaoua"; "Le nouveau procureur de la République installé à Eséka," *Cameroon Tribune*, 5 June 1986, 7, caption: "Photo de famille à l'issue de la cérémonie"; "Douze jeunes fonctionnaires ont prêté serment à Ngaoundéré," *Cameroon Tribune*, 6 June 1986, 8, caption: "Photo de famille avec trois agents de poursuite du trésor"; "Séminaire pour la promotion de l'élévage avicole à Ambam par l'INADES-Formation," *Cameroon Tribune*, 4 July 1986, 8, caption: "Photo de famille des autorités administratives des responsables politiques et des encadreurs du séminaire d'Ambam"; "Tubercules, racines, légumes—Un séminaire de réflexion se tient à la chambre d'agriculture de Yaoundé," *Cameroon Tribune*, 10 September 1986, 5, caption: "La photo de famille: les participants au séminaire autour du secrétaire d'Etat"; "Conférence annuelle des responsables des transports—Trois rappels à l'ordre de M. Cheuoua," *Cameroon Tribune*, 24 September 1986, 3, caption: "La grande famille des responsables s'est retrouvée autour de M.

Cheuoua"; "Premier Conseil national de l'OSTC [Organisation Syndical des Travailleurs du Cameroun]—Devenir un organisme dynamique," *Cameroon Tribune,* 3 October 1986, 3, caption: "Photo de famille autour du ministre du Travail et de la Prévoyance sociale à l'issue de la cérémonie"; "Congrès de la FECATENNIS—Une source de fierté," *Cameroon Tribune,* 19–20 October 1986, 15, caption: "La grande famille du lawn tennis réunie autour du représentant du ministre"; "Installation de nouveaux responsables du MINFOC [Ministère de l'Information et de la Culture] à Douala—Traduire dans les faits la politique du Renouveau national dans le Littoral," *Cameroon Tribune,* 18 October 1986, 4, caption: "Photo de famille regroupant autour du gouverneur Luc Loé, les délégués sortants du MINFOC au Littoral, ainsi que la famille de l'information à Douala"; "En clôturant la réunion des responsables centraux et extérieurs du MINFOC—Le Pr. Georges Ngango en appelle à un 'sens aigu des responsabilités,'" *Cameroon Tribune,* 2–3 November 1986, 1, caption: "Le ministre Ngango pose avec la grande famille du MINFOC"; "Installation du nouveau chef de zone CENADEC—Veiller au contrôle régulier de la gestion de la coopérative," *Cameroon Tribune,* 7–8 December 1986, 9, caption: "La grande famille de la zone CENADEC du Mbam a posé avec les autorités administratives et politiques"; "Rétrospective UDEAC 86—Après le sommet de Bata: Communiqué final," *Cameroon Tribune,* 23 December 1986, 3, caption: "La photo de famille des chefs d'Etat à l'issue de l'ouverture du sommet de Bata . . ."; "Campagne d'alphabétisation des adultes—Une expérience originale lancée à Eséka," *Cameroon Tribune,* 25–26 December 1986, 3, caption: "Photo de famille à l'issue du stage autour de M. Mayi Matip."

Côte d'Ivoire: "Installation des municipalités—Kouassi-Kouassikro: M. Assoua Ya Jacob élu," *Fraternité Matin,* 5 February 1986, 7, caption: "M. Jacob Assoua . . . et son équipe posent pour une photo de famille"; "Le Ministre Fologo—Le Président Mobutu est la chance du Zaïre," *Fraternité Matin,* 21 February 1986, 16, caption: "De gauche à droite: Mme Abinader, M. Roger Abinader, l'ambassadeur du Zaïre dans notre pays, M. Dona Fologo et ses enfants. Une belle photo de famille"; "Tombola de la mutuelle: Les gangnants ont reçu leur prix," *Fraternité Matin,* 15 May 1986, 8, caption: "La photo de famille devant les locaux de Frat-Mat"; "13ème Conférences des Chefs d'État de France et d'Afrique à Lomé—La France réaffirme son soutien à l'Afrique," *Fraternité Matin,* 15–16 November 1986, 1, caption: "La photo de famille du sommet de la solidarité africaine"; "Séminaire des secrétaires généraux des mairies—Savoir préparer les dossiers," *Fraternité Matin,* 18 November 1986, 6, caption: "Après le séminaire des maires que symbolise cette photo de famille. . . ."

Senegal: "Saint-Louis—Les centres d'accueil: De véritables foyers éducatifs et culturels," *Le Soleil,* 12 February 1986, 12, caption: "Photo de famille avec le gouverneur de la région au centre Téranga"; "Sommet France-Afrique: La cohabitation à Lomé," *Le Soleil,* 12 November 1986, 1, caption: "Photo de famille lors du dernier sommet à Paris"; "Dakar-Washington: Fructifier les échanges," *Le Soleil,* 12 November 1986, 4, caption: "Photo de famille sur le perron de l'Hôtel de Ville. . . ."; "Première action des riverains: L'Avenue Pompidou fait sa toilette," *Le Soleil,* 6–7 December 1986, 4, caption: "l'A.R.A.P. est née: une photo de famille avec le Maire de Dakar . . ."; "Jumelage aller entre La Flèche et Ntchoréré," *Le Soleil,* 20–21 December 1986, 7, caption: "Photo de famille entre les élèves des deux écoles."

95. See David Laitin's superb study of the Yoruba, in which he defines hegemony as "the political forging . . . and institutionalization of a pattern of group activity in a state and the congruent idealization of that schema into a dominant symbolic frame-

work that reigns as common sense." David D. Laitin, *Hegemony and Culture: Politics and Religious Change among the Yoruba* (Chicago and London: University of Chicago Press, 1986), 19. Also see Katherine Verdery, *National Ideology under Socialism: Identity and Cultural Politics in Ceausescu's Romania* (Berkeley and Los Angeles: University of California Press, 1991).

96. Chief Obafemi Awolowo, "I Have Brought Back with Me a Big Cargo of Satisfaction," text of an address delivered by Awolowo to the Lagos State House of Assembly, Ikeja, 22 January 1980, in Chief Obafemi Awolowo, *Voice of Wisdom: Selected Speeches of Chief Obafemi Awolowo,* vol. 3 (Akure, Nigeria: Fagbamigbe Publishers, 1981), 171 (emphasis in original).

97. Victor Turner, *Dramas, Fields, and Metaphors: Symbolic Action in Human Society* (Ithaca, N.Y.: Cornell University Press, 1974), 63–64.

98. Claude Meillassoux, *Maidens, Meal, and Money: Capitalism and the Domestic Community* (Cambridge: Cambridge University Press, 1981), 47, 86; and Claude Meillassoux, "The Social Organization of the Peasantry: The Economic Basis of Kinship," *Journal of Peasant Studies* 1, no. 1 (1973): 81–90.

99. Pirira bint Athumani, "Azimio la Arusha Limetukaa Moyoni," *Uhuru* (Dar es Salaam), 17 November 1970, 4.

100. Jean Mboudou, "Chronique du vendredi: Le pardon est divin," Column, *Cameroon Tribune,* 29 August 1986, 1.

101. "Solidarité nationale: Abdou Diouf renonce à deux mois de salaire," *Le Soleil,* 14 December 1983, 1.

102. "Graphic View—The Presidential Road Show," Editorial, *Daily Graphic,* 28 January 1980, 2.

103. Aili Mari Tripp, *Changing the Rules: The Politics of Liberalization and the Urban Informal Economy in Tanzania* (Berkeley and Los Angeles: University of California Press, 1997), 180.

104. David G. Maillu, *My Dear Bottle* (Nairobi: Comb Books, 1973), 19.

105. Zenobia Ofori-Dankwa, "Women Advised to Help in Development," *People's Daily Graphic,* 21 July 1984, 1.

106. For hints of this exclusion from the political realm in Tanzania, see Kathleen Mulligan-Hansel, "The Political Economy of Contemporary Women's Organizations in Tanzania: Socialism, Liberalization and Gendered Fields of Power" (Ph.D. diss., University of Wisconsin-Madison, 1999).

107. G. S. Esegine, "A Challenge to Women," *Daily Times,* 3 June 1989, 13.

108. Transcription of Mobutu's address of 25 April 1988 provided by Action des Chrétiens pour l'Abolition de la Torture (ACAT), Berne, Switzerland, 8 June 1988. For a slightly different version, see *Het Belang van Limburg* (Brussels), 1 July 1988.

109. Nairobi Domestic Radio Service, 25 August 1990, cited and translated from the Swahili in FBIS-AFR-90-166, 27 August 1990, 9 (emphasis added).

110. David G. Maillu, *The Ayah* (Nairobi: Heinemann, 1986), 34.

111. Koffi Labitey D., "Eyadema Must Go," Letter to the Editor, *West Africa,* 1–7 March 1993, 320.

112. Howard W. French, "In Gambia, a New Coup Follows an Old Pattern," *New York Times,* 28 August 1994, 4.

113. "Who is Lt. Yaya Jammeh?" *West Africa,* 1–7 August 1994, 1347.

114. "We Won't Overstay—IBB," *Daily Times,* 20 March 1986, 1. This is actually an old and consistent theme. See the analysis and primary materials assembled by

A. H. M. Kirk-Greene, *'Stay by Your Radios': Documentation for a Study of Military Government in Tropical Africa,* Africa Social Research Documents, vol. 12 (Leiden and Cambridge: Afrika-Studiecentrum and African Studies Centre, 1981), 16–18 and passim.

115. Peter Dwaah, "The Fate of Limann," *Daily Graphic,* 5 February 1982, 1, 4–5. Also see Breda Atta-Quayson, "PNDC Will Stay for Long—Declares CDS," *Daily Graphic,* 15 January 1982, 1; and "Radio France Talks to Rawlings," *People's Daily Graphic,* 6 May 1985, 3.

116. George Lakoff, *Moral Politics: What Conservatives Know That Liberals Don't* (Chicago: University of Chicago Press, 1996), 4. Also see George Lakoff and Mark Johnson, *Metaphors We Live By* (Chicago: University of Chicago Press, 1980), in which the authors argue that metaphors create social realities for us and may guide our actions. For comparative applications in different societies, see the collection of essays contained in Dorothy Holland and Naomi Quinn, eds., *Cultural Models in Language and Thought* (Cambridge: Cambridge University Press, 1987).

117. Denis-Constant Martin, "A la quête des OPNI: Comment traiter l'invention du politique?" *Revue française des sciences politiques* 39, no. 6 (December 1989): 793–815. Also see Denis-Constant Martin, *Tanzanie: L'invention d'une culture politique* (Paris: Presses de la Fondation Nationale des Sciences Politiques and Karthala, 1988), as well as the essays in his more recent edited volume, Denis-Constant Martin, ed., *Nouveaux langages du politique en Afrique orientale* (Paris and Nairobi: Karthala and IFRA, 1998).

118. See, for example, Gordon J. Schochet, *Patriarchalism in Political Thought: The Authoritarian Family and Political Speculation and Attitudes Especially in Seventeenth-Century England* (Oxford: Basil Blackwell, 1975); Melvin Yazawa, *From Colonies to Commonwealth: Familial Ideology and the Beginnings of the American Republic* (Baltimore: Johns Hopkins University Press, 1985); Lucian W. Pye, *Asian Power and Politics: The Cultural Dimensions of Authority* (Cambridge, Mass.: Belknap Press of Harvard University Press, 1985) on the paternal dimension of Asian political authority; and Dorinne K. Kondo, *Crafting Selves: Power, Gender, and Discourses of Identity in a Japanese Workplace* (Chicago: University of Chicago Press, 1990) has much to say concerning the prevalence of the "company as family" metaphor in a Japanese factory.

119. Barry Schwartz, *George Washington: The Making of an American Symbol* (New York: Free Press, 1987).

120. In these remarks I am especially mindful of, and grateful to, Carola Lentz's intelligent and engaging critique of my earlier work, which took me to task for underplaying the flexibility and historical variability of the moral matrix. It should be noted, however, that there are important differences in the levels of analysis at which we pitch our respective works. See Carola Lentz, "The Chief, the Mine Captain, and the Politician: Legitimating Power in Northern Ghana," *Africa* 68, no. 1 (1998): 46–67.

121. See Robert H. Wiebe, *Self-Rule: A Cultural History of American Democracy* (Chicago: University of Chicago Press, 1995), who identifies individualism as an important strand in democratic practice and thought since the early days of the Republic. Also see Richard J. Ellis, *American Political Cultures* (New York: Oxford University Press, 1993), who sees individualism as one of five types of value systems.

122. "Comments after Speech at the U.N.," *Washington Post,* 10 December 1994, A12. Also see Ruth Marcus, "President Clinton Fires Elders," *Washington Post,* 10 December 1994, A1. I am grateful to one of my research assistants, Lynda Kellam, for putting together the references and a chronology on the Elders affair.

2. REPRESENTATIONS OF POWER

1. On the importance of local knowledge, see James C. Scott, *Seeing Like a State: How Certain Schemes to Improve the Human Condition Have Failed* (New Haven, Conn.: Yale University Press, 1998); and Clifford Geertz, *Local Knowledge: Further Essays in Interpretive Anthropology* (New York: Basic Books, 1983).

2. W. Arens and Ivan Karp, "Introduction," in *Creativity of Power: Cosmology and Action in African Societies*, ed. W. Arens and Ivan Karp (Washington: Smithsonian Institution Press, 1989), xi–xxix. And, for a fascinating treatment of endogenous notions of power in Java, see Benedict R. O'G. Anderson, "The Idea of Power in Javanese Culture," in *Language and Power: Exploring Political Cultures in Indonesia* (Ithaca, N.Y.: Cornell University Press, 1990), 17–78.

3. See, for example, Christopher L. Miller, *Theories of Africans: Francophone Literature and Anthropology in Africa* (Chicago: University of Chicago Press, 1990); Christopher L. Miller, *Blank Darkness: Africanist Discourse in French* (Chicago: University of Chicago Press, 1985); and David Maughan-Brown, *Land, Freedom, and Fiction: History and Ideology in Kenya* (London: Zed Books, 1985). In addition, for a social scientist who takes literature quite seriously, see Josef Gugler, "African Literary Comment on Dictators: Wole Soyinka's Plays and Nuruddin Farah's Novels," *Journal of Modern African Studies* 26, no. 1 (March 1988): 171–177.

4. For an interesting anti-essentialist argument, see Paul Gilroy, *The Black Atlantic: Modernity and Double Consciousness* (Cambridge, Mass.: Harvard University Press, 1993). The fascinating reflections of Kwame Anthony Appiah also emphasize the importance of an ongoing diffusion of ideas and identities. See Kwame Anthony Appiah, *In My Father's House: Africa in the Philosophy of Culture* (Oxford: Oxford University Press, 1992).

5. Max Weber, *Economy and Society*, 2 vols., ed. Guenther Roth and Claus Wittich (Berkeley and Los Angeles: University of California Press, 1978), 1:53.

6. Bertrand Russell, *Power: A New Social Analysis* (London: George Allen and Unwin, 1938), 35.

7. Robert A. Dahl, *Modern Political Analysis* (Englewood Cliffs, N.J.: Prentice-Hall, 1963), 41. Also see Dahl's discussion of the relationship between power and influence on 50–51, where he argues that two forms of influence, negative and positive coercion— the threat of extreme coercion or the prospect of large gains—are included in the term "power."

8. Robert A. Dahl, "Power," in *International Encyclopedia of the Social Sciences*, vol. 12 (New York: Macmillan and Free Press, 1968), 407 (emphasis in original).

9. Peter Bachrach and Morton S. Baratz, *Power and Poverty: Theory and Practice* (New York: Oxford University Press, 1970), 7.

10. Steven Lukes, *Power: A Radical View* (London: Macmillan, 1974), 34.

11. Dennis H. Wrong, *Power: Its Forms, Bases, and Uses* (New York: Harper and Row, 1979), 2 (emphasis in original).

12. Kenneth E. Boulding, *Three Faces of Power* (Newbury Park, Calif.: Sage, 1989), 10.

13. Michel Foucault, "The Subject and Power," in *Art after Modernism: Rethinking Representation*, ed. Brian Wallis (Boston and New York: David R. Godine and New Museum of Contemporary Art, 1984), 417–432, citation, 428, cited in Eric R. Wolf, "Distinguished Lecture: Facing Power—Old Insights, New Questions," *American Anthropologist* 92, no. 3 (September 1990): 586.

14. Foucault, *Discipline and Punish*, 194.

15. Arens and Karp, "Introduction," xx. They do, of course, refer to a wide range of anthropological writings in their interesting essay.

16. James G. March, "The Power of Power," in *Varieties of Political Theory*, ed. David Easton (Englewood Cliffs, N.J.: Prentice-Hall, 1966), 39–70, esp. 43.

17. On this point see Carla Pasquinelli, "Power without the State," *Telos* 68 (1986): 79–92.

18. Richard A. Joseph, *Democracy and Prebendal Politics in Nigeria: The Rise and Fall of the Second Republic* (Cambridge: Cambridge University Press, 1987), 150.

19. Kole Omotoso, *Just Before Dawn* (Ibadan, Nigeria: Spectrum Books, 1988), 283.

20. Atieno-Odhiambo, "Democracy and the Ideology of Order in Kenya," 195.

21. See, for example, Kipngetich arap Simatwa, "Tribalism in Kenya," Letter to the Editor, *Weekly Review,* 17 May 1991, 4.

22. Jean-François Bayart, *L'état en Afrique: La politique du ventre* (Paris: Fayard, 1989), 10.

23. Antoine Ahanda, "'Nation: Le Point'—La sagesse des proverbes," Column, *Cameroon Tribune,* 25 June 1982, 8.

24. Wilson Kaigarula, "Viewpoint: We Cannot Afford Licences to 'Eat,'" Column, *Sunday News,* 12 January 1986, 3.

25. N'Zinga Nsingi, "Fait du jour: Des 'vautours' en circulation à Kinshasa," *Elima,* 1 December 1982, 2.

26. "Kenya: Democracy Could Be the Loser," *Africa Confidential* 33, no. 25 (18 December 1992): 1–2; and "Reassuring Public Defense," *Weekly Review,* 3 September 1993, 8–9.

27. The *naira* is Nigeria's currency.

28. Matchet, "Doe on God and Power," *West Africa,* 10–16 July 1989, 1123. Also see Comi M. Toulabor, *Le Togo sous Eyadéma* (Paris: Karthala, 1986), 263–264.

29. David W. Cohen and E. S. Atieno-Odhiambo, *Siaya: The Historical Anthropology of an African Landscape* (London: James Currey, 1989), 131.

30. For examples of this theme from Tanzania, see Isaac Mruma, "Aim at Self-Sufficiency—Nyerere," *Daily News,* 16 February 1982, 1; "Mwinyi Urges Hard Work," *Daily News,* 22 April 1984, 1; "Increase Food Production—Call," *Daily News,* 27 April 1984, 3; "Food Priority Number One, Says Salim," *Daily News,* 4 May 1984, 1; "Mwalimu Warns of Food Scarcity," *Daily News,* 17 May 1984, 1; "Grow More, Peasants Told," *Daily News,* 9 July 1984, 3; and Mkumbwa Ally, "Double Food Production, Says Mwinyi," *Daily News,* 15 December 1988, 1. For a sample of Nyerere's voluminous writings on the subject of *Ujamaa* socialism and self-reliance, see Julius K. Nyerere, *Ujamaa: Essays on Socialism* (Oxford: Oxford University Press, 1968).

31. Gichuru Njihia, "Prelates Reject Charges," *Daily Nation,* 29 September 1990, 1–2, cited in FBIS, *Daily Report: Sub-Saharan Africa,* FBIS-AFR-90-215, 6 November 1990, 12.

32. "Comment: Valley of Decision," Editorial, *People's Daily Graphic,* 7 March 1984, 2. Also see "Govt Plans to End Hunger," *Daily Graphic,* 1 July 1982, 1; and Samuel Kyei-Boateng, "'Change Attitudes towards Community Development,'" *People's Daily Graphic,* 1 May 1985, 4–5.

33. Kojo Atsu, "Let's Feed Ourselves—Quainoo," *People's Daily Graphic,* 14 June 1985, 1.

34. "Daily Times Opinion: Of Cakes and Philosophy," *Daily Times,* 7 October 1985,

3. Also see Sampson Onwumere, "Public Affairs: Food: An Attribute of National Power," Op-Ed Column, *Daily Times,* 14 March 1983, 3.

35. Ayodeji Aregbesola, "Politics of Soccer," *Daily Times,* 28 November 1986, 9.

36. Grape Vine, "Soccer and the National Cake," *Daily Times,* 7 April 1980, 3.

37. Mkumbwa Ali, "'Ujamaa Here to Stay,'" *Daily News,* 2 May 1981, 1.

38. Nairobi Domestic Service (radio), 8 January 1991, cited and translated from the Swahili in FBIS-AFR-91-006, 9 January 1991, 5.

39. "KANU Politics: A Familiar Song," *Weekly Review,* 30 September 1994, 12.

40. "Sharing the National Cake," *Weekly Review,* 17 December 1993, 9.

41. A. Fall, "Lunch à l'ITA—Manger Sénégalais, et bien," *Le Soleil,* 29–31 December 1984/1 January 1985, 17.

42. On the Rabelaisian aspects of political life, see the stimulating work of Achille Mbembe, "Provisional Notes on the Postcolony," *Africa* 62, no. 1 (1992): 3–37.

43. A.E. Afigo, Commissioner for Education, Imo State, "The Development of Improved Work Ethic among Nigerian Workers," in Imo State, Nigeria, Establishment and Training Department, Cabinet Office, Owerri, "Report of the Public Seminars on the Objective, Policies, and Programmes of the Military Administration, 23–24 August and 24–25 September, 1984" (Owerri, Nigeria: Government Printer, 1984), 28.

44. Elizabeth Ohene, "Thinking Allowed: Pity the Poor Big Man," Column, *Daily Graphic,* 10 November 1981, 3.

45. Elizabeth Ohene, "Thinking Allowed: Of Cakes and Ale," Column, *Daily Graphic,* 2 June 1981, 3 (emphasis in original). On the question of sharing national cake, see also Arthur A. Nwankwo, *Thoughts on Nigeria* (Enugu, Nigeria: Fourth Dimension Publishing Company Ltd., 1986), 92.

46. Ebenezer Williams, "The Love of Power," Op-Ed Column [?], *Daily Times,* 2 January 1981, 3.

47. Niyi Oniororo, *Letters to Nigerian Society* (Ibadan, Nigeria: Ororo Publications, 1990), 118.

48. Remi Adeagbo, Akoka, Lagos, "Programme Serves No Useful Purpose," Letter to the Editor, *Daily Times,* 16 April 1981, 15.

49. Banji Abeeb, Oshodi, Lagos, "OYSG and Budget of God-fatherism," Letter to the Editor, *Daily Times,* 11 February 1981, 15.

50. Fiagbema Finestone, Warri, "The Answer Lies in Baking a Bigger Cake," Letter to the Editor, *Daily Times,* 9 June 1982, 7.

51. M. Adebayo Belo, "Nigeria's Dilemma," Letter to the Editor, *West Africa,* 16–22 October 1995, 1591.

52. Advisor, Musoma, "Big Bellies," Letter to the Editor, *Daily News,* 23 November 1982, 5 (emphasis in original).

53. Halima Shariff, "Obesity: A Health Hazard," *Sunday News,* 16 January 1983, 6.

54. Wekesa-Mwembe, Untitled, Letter to the Editor, *Weekly Review,* 10 May 1991, 3.

55. Sugut Lawrence Isaac and David Kiplagat Rutto (for Nandi Watch, Eldoret), "Warning to Kamotho," Letter to the Editor, *Weekly Review,* 16 February 1996, 2.

56. Essay Magugudi, "Eating the Country: A Short Story," *Sunday News,* 20 April 1986, 6 (emphasis in original).

57. For details on Maillu and his literature, see Bernth Lindfors, *Popular Literatures in Africa* (Trenton: Africa World Press, 1991), 47–60, 87–100.

58. Maillu, *My Dear Bottle,* 18.

59. Maillu, *My Dear Bottle,* 38, 109.

60. David G. Maillu, *the kommon man–part one* (Nairobi: Comb Books, 1975), 12–13, 13.

61. Maillu, *kommon man*, 91, 100, 102–103, 103–104, 104, 105.

62. Maillu, *kommon man*, 174.

63. Lindfors, *Popular Literatures in Africa*, 54; and Mbembe, "Provisional Notes on the Postcolony," 3–37. See also David G. Maillu, *Unfit for Human Consumption* (Nairobi: Comb Books, 1973); David G. Maillu, *No!* (Nairobi: Comb Books, 1976); Jasinta Mote, *The Flesh,* produced by David G. Maillu (Nairobi: Comb Books, 1975); and Maina Allan, *One by One,* with a touch by David G. Maillu (Nairobi: Comb Books, 1975).

64. On Mobutu's name, see Crawford Young and Thomas Turner, *The Rise and Decline of the Zairian State* (Madison: University of Wisconsin Press, 1985), 153, note 31. On Moi, see "Praise to High Heavens," *Weekly Review,* 2 September 1994, 16.

65. Willy A. Umezinwa, "The African Novel, the African Politician, and the Metaphor of Size," *Imprévu* 1 (1990): 25–42. The novels he discusses are Achebe, *A Man of the People, No Longer at Ease*; Farah, *Sweet and Sour Milk*; Kourouma, *Les soleils des indépendances*; Mphahlele, *The Wanderers*; Ngugi, *Petals of Blood*; and Nwankwo, *My Mercedes Is Bigger Than Yours.*

66. Umezinwa, "The African Novel, the African Politician and the Metaphor of Size," 27.

67. Works of literature containing images of food and eating are numerous. See, among others, Wole Soyinka, *AKE: The Years of Childhood* (New York: Random House, 1981), 30, 91; Sam Githinji, *Struggling for Survival* (Nairobi: Kenya Literature Bureau, 1983), 14, 127; F. J. Amon d'Aby, *Proverbes populaires de Côte d'Ivoire* (Abidjan: CEDA, 1984), passim; Bernard B. Dadié, *Les vois dans le vent (tragédie)* (Abidjan: Nouvelles Editions Africaines, 1982), 59, 112 (original edition by Editions Clés, Yaoundé, 1970); Jean-Marie Adiaffi, *La carte d'identité* (Abidjan: CEDA, 1980), 51; Ngugi wa Thiong'o, *Matigari,* trans. Wangui wa Goro (Oxford: Heinemann, 1987), 50, 60, 113; Meja Mwangi, *Striving for the Wind* (London: Heinemann, 1990), 56, 60; Cheik Aliou Ndao, *Excellence, vos épouses!* (Dakar, Senegal: Les Nouvelles Editions Africaines Africaines and SEPIA, 1993), 12, 15, 137; Ahmadou Kourouma, *Les soleils des indépendances* (Paris: Editions du Seuil, 1970), 18, 23; Lye M. Yoka, *Lettre d'un Kinois à l'oncle du village* (Brussels and Paris: Institut Africain–CEDAF and Editions l'Harmattan, 1995), passim; Ben Okri, *The Famished Road* (New York: Anchor Doubleday, 1992), passim; and Nuruddin Farah, *Secrets* (New York: Arcade Publishing, 1998), 35.

68. Televised press conference of Jean Konan Banny, 30 August 1990, cited and translated in FBIS-AFR-90-171, 4 September 1990, 37.

69. Leandre Sahiri, "Prière à Dieu," *Fraternité Matin,* 16 September 1980, 9.

70. For anthropological confirmation of the importance of food and eating in the invisible world, see the essays assembled in Arens and Karp, *Creativity of Power,* as well as Peter Geschiere, *Sorcellerie et politique en Afrique: La viande des autres* (Paris: Karthala, 1995).

71. See Abner Cohen, *Two-Dimensional Man: An Essay on the Anthropology of Power and Symbolism in Complex Society* (Berkeley: University of California Press, 1974); Mary Douglas, *Purity and Danger: An Analysis of Concepts of Pollution and Taboo* (1966, Harmondsworth, England: Penguin, 1970); Christel Lane, *Rites of Rulers: Ritual in Industrial Society—The Soviet Case* (Cambridge: Cambridge University Press, 1981); and, for a fine analysis of the symbolism of the Kenyan *baraza,* see Angelique Haugerud, *The Culture of Politics in Modern Kenya* (Cambridge: Cambridge University Press, 1995).

72. "The Outspoken Clergyman," *Weekly Review*, 7 January 1994, 5–6.

73. Konde Vila-ki-Kanda, "La fête de la résurrection," *Elima*, 25 November 1987, 1, 7, 8.

74. Mobutu Sese Seko, opening speech at the Fourth Regular Session of the MPR Central Committee, *Elima*, 16 March 1982, 8.

75. *Elima*, 2–3 September 1990, 8, cited and translated in FBIS-AFR-90-195-S, 9 October 1990, 8.

76. Cited in Young and Turner, *The Rise and Decline of the Zaïrian State*, 169.

77. Nairobi Domestic Radio Service, 1 June 1990, cited and translated in FBIS-AFR-90-108, 5. Phrases in quotation marks were spoken in English. On this controversy, see also "A Curious Encounter," *Weekly Review*, 8 June 1990, 20.

78. "Praise to the High Heavens," *Weekly Review*, 2 September 1994, 17.

79. "Mwangale Threatens to 'Crush' Moi's Critics," *Daily Nation*, 10 September 1990, 1–2, cited in FBIS-AFR-90-193, 4 October 1990, 9; and "Church Leaders Attacked," *Daily Nation*, 29 September 1990, 1–2, cited in FBIS-AFR-90-215, 6 November 1990, 9–10.

80. Jean-Mary Neossi, "Bertoua—Les militants descendent dans la rue," *Cameroon Tribune*, 7–8 April 1985, 5.

81. "Deux Nouveaux Évêques: NN. SS. Mandjo et Akichi sacrés en présence du Chef de l'État et de 23 évêques," *Fraternité Matin*, 20 September 1982, 1.

82. See, for example, Koba Bashibirira M., "Incidences magico-religieuses sur le pouvoir africain," *Cahiers des religions africaines* 19, no. 37 (January 1985): 44, 50.

83. Achille Mbembe, "Domaines de la nuit et autorité onirique dans le maquis du sud-Cameroun (1955–1958)," *Journal of African History* 31 (1991): 89–121.

84. Simon Bockie, *Death and the Invisible Powers: The World of Kongo Belief* (Bloomington: Indiana University Press, 1993), 16–18, 72.

85. Michel Martin, "Gabon's Animists Plump for Opposition Runner Ahead of Poll," Agence France Presse (via Clari-net), 4 December 1998, C-afp@clari.net. On the Bwiti cult, see James W. Fernandez, *Bwiti: An Ethnography of the Religious Imagination in Africa* (Princeton, N.J.: Princeton University Press, 1982).

86. David Lan, *Guns and Rain: Guerrillas and Spirit Mediums in Zimbabwe* (London, Berkeley, and Los Angeles: James Currey and University of California Press, 1985).

87. Sakombi Inongo, "Hommage posthume," *Elima*, 13 April 1984, 1, 8.

88. For the 1974 episode, see Thassinda uba Thassinda H., *Zaïre: Les princes de l'invisible: L'Afrique noire bâillonnée par le parti unique* (Caen, France: Editions C'est à Dire, 1992), 211–212; the later events are related in Kitemona N'Silu, "Les Léopards exorcisés par les chefs coutumiers batékés," *Elima*, 2 April 1987, 11.

89. Vangu Makuala, "Zamenga Batukezanga: 'Je me considère comme un écrivain villageois et non un intellectuel,'" *Elima*, 22 February 1984, 12. On Zamenga, see also Wyatt MacGaffey, "Zamenga of Zaïre: 'Novelist, Historian, Sociologist, Philosopher, and Moralist,'" *Research in African Literatures* 13, no. 2 (May 1982): 208–215.

90. Zamenga Batukezanga, *Bandoki (les sorciers)* (Kinshasa: Editions St. Paul-Afrique, n.d. [1973]), 13–14.

91. On the importance of food and eating in the invisible world, see the essays assembled in Arens and Karp, *Creativity of Power*, especially Bonnie L. Wright, "The Power of Articulation," 50; Michelle Gilbert, "Sources of Power in Akuropon-Akuapem: Ambiguity in Classification," 62, 78; and Alma Gottlieb, "Witches, Kings, and the Sacrifice of Identity or the Power of Paradox and the Paradox of Power among the Beng of Ivory

Coast," 249, 252. See, too, Peter Geschiere's work: Peter Geschiere, "Sorcery and the State: Popular Modes of Action among the Maka of Southeast Cameroon," *Critique of Anthropology* 8, no.1 (1988): 48; Cyprian F. Fisiy and Peter Geschiere, "Judges and Witches, or How Is the State to Deal with Witchcraft? Examples from Southeast Cameroon," *Cahiers d'études africaines* 30, no. 2 (1990): 139–140, 142; Cyprian F. Fisiy and Peter Geschiere, "Sorcery, Witchcraft, and Accumulation: Regional Variations in South and West Cameroon," *Critique of Anthropology* 11, no. 3 (1991): 259, 269; and Geschiere, *Sorcellerie et politique en Afrique.*

92. "Elections américaines," *Elima,* 7 August 1980, 1.

93. Zamenga Batukezanga, *Mille kilomètres à pied* (Kinshasa: Editions Saint Paul Afrique, October 1979), 80–81.

94. Zamenga Batukezanga, *Chérie Basso* (Kinshasa: Editions Saint Paul Afrique, 1983), 39–40.

95. Zamenga Batukezanga, *Mon mari en grève* (Kinshasa: ZABAT, 1986), 117.

96. Maillu, *kommon man,* 148.

97. David G. Maillu, *After 4:30* (Nairobi: Comb Books, 1974), 26.

98. "The MP and the Intestines," *Weekly Review,* 29 July 1994, 9–10.

99. Wilson Kaigarula, "Viewpoint: The 'Mumiani' Scare," Column, *Sunday News,* 23 March 1986, 3; Mamadou Kasse, "La résistance était vaine," *Le Soleil,* 8 November 1983, 20; and François Soudan, "La rumeur qui tue," *Jeune Afrique,* 19–25 March 1997, 12–15. For other examples, also see Mbaye Gueye, "Une ténébreuse affaire de sorcellerie," *Le Soleil,* 13 November 1984, 7; B. C. Menunga, "Lékié—Un groupe de sorciers dénoncé à Nkolossang," *Cameroon Tribune,* 2–3 February 1986, 7; and Zongia Mbali, "Zone de Kintambo: Un veillard lapidé pour sorcellerie," *Elima,* 1–2 September 1984, 3.

100. Johannes Fabian, *Power and Performance: Ethnographic Explorations through Proverbial Wisdom and Theater in Shaba, Zaire* (Madison: University of Wisconsin Press, 1990), 25.

101. Mobutu Sese Seko, "Le pouvoir et la démocratie en Afrique," *Elima,* 15 March 1980, 5; and Mobutu Sese Seko, "Le pouvoir et la démocratie en Afrique," continued, *Elima,* 17 March 1980, 12.

102. Mobutu Sese Seko, opening speech at the Fourth Regular Session of the MPR Central Committee, *Elima,* 16 March 1982, 8.

103. "Le mouvement populaire de la révolution reste l'unique institution du Zaïre," *Elima,* 8 October 1985, 5.

104. Basil Davidson, *The Black Man's Burden: Africa and the Curse of the Nation-State* (New York: Times Books, 1992), 250.

105. Gene Dauch and Denis Martin, *L'héritage de Kenyatta: La transition politique au Kenya (1975–1982)* (Paris: Presses Universitaires d'Aix-Marseilles and l'Harmattan, 1985), 145.

106. "Odinga: Detention and After," *Weekly Review,* 28 January 1994, 27; "Praise to the High Heavens," *Weekly Review,* 2 September 1994, 16; and "The Law and Party Titles," *Weekly Review,* 16 June 1995, 15.

107. "Magugu and Mzee's Picture," *Weekly Review,* 8 June 1990, 22; also see Charles Kimathi, "Moi's Stand on Kenyatta Portrait Explained," *Daily Nation,* 6 June 1990, 1–2, cited in FBIS-AFR-90-139, 19 July 1990, 15.

108. "States Indicted over Shehu's Portrait," *Daily Times,* 23 January 1980, 40; "Daily Times Opinion: The President's Portrait," *Daily Times,* 25 January 1980, 3; and Grape Vine, "President Shehu's Portrait," Column, *Daily Times,* 28 January 1980, 3.

109. "Assemblée Nationale: Bédié élu président par une large majorité (134 voix sur 146)," *Fraternité Matin,* 23 December 1980, 8–9.

110. Marcellin Abougnan, "A mon avis: Un chef, une nation," Column, *Fraternité Matin,* 30 April/1–3 May 1987, 2.

111. On the ethic of unity, see Bayart, *L'état au Cameroun;* and Jean-François Bayart, "One-Party Government and Political Development in Cameroon," in *An African Experiment in Nation-Building: The Bilingual Cameroon Republic since Reunification,* ed. Ndiva Kofele-Kale (Boulder, Colo.: Westview, 1980), 159–187.

112. Henri Bandolo, "Editorial: Le sens de la responsabilité," *Cameroon Tribune,* 30 August 1983, 1.

113. A chronology for the events of 1983–1984 may be found in Victor T. Le Vine, "Leadership and Regime Changes in Perspective," in Schatzberg and Zartman, *The Political Economy of Cameroon,* 37–39.

114. "Mwalimu Stresses Nationness," *Daily News,* 21 May 1981, 1.

115. Henri Bandolo, "Au terme de sa tournée provinciale, le Président Ahidjo se confie à Cameroon Tribune," *Cameroon Tribune,* 29 January 1983, 3.

116. "UNC: Vers un Congrès extraordinaire," *Cameroon Tribune,* 28–29 August 1983, 1; and "Le Président Paul Biya à la presse étrangère: Mieux vous informer des réalités camerounaises pour en rendre compte plus objectivement," *Cameroon Tribune,* 16 September 1983, 3.

117. Zephania Musendo, "Mwalimu Accepts Nomination," *Daily News,* 31 October 1987, 1; and "Debate on Party Systems Should Be Sustained . . ." *Daily News,* 3 June 1990, 5 (emphasis added).

118. Aly Kheury Ndaw, "Double héritage," *Le Soleil,* 16 January 1981, 1.

119. "Doe's Body Exhumed," *West Africa,* 4–10 May 1992, 768.

120. Kamje Teguia, "Religion—Consécration épiscopale de Mgr Gabriel Simo et Mgr Simon Victor Tonyè," *Cameroon Tribune,* 29 April 1987, 7.

121. "Consistoire E.P.C. du Mbam—Un nouveau pasteur sacré," *Cameroon Tribune,* 13–14 January 1985, 7. For other examples see "Ordination de l'Abbé Daniel Tchantchou," *Cameroon Tribune,* 2 August 1982, 4; and Edogue Fabien, "Mgr Christian Tumi, Nouvel Archévêque coadjuteur de Garoua a été présenté aux fidèles," *Cameroon Tribune,* 7 April 1983, 5.

122. Ibrahima Fall, "Célébration de la Tabaski: 'Retournons à Dieu' prêche l'Imam Ratib de Dakar," *Le Soleil,* 29 September 1982, 3. Also see Moustapha Mbodj, "Célébration de l'Aid El Fitr: Cohésion et concordance," *Le Soleil,* 23 July 1982, 3.

123. See, for example, "Saint-Louis—Communion entre le temporel et le spirituel," *Le Soleil,* 1 October 1982, 8.

124. "Abengourou—Pierre Nkruma nouveau prêtre du diocèse," *Fraternité Matin,* 9 August 1982, 1.

125. "Abengourou: Pierre Aka Nkruma 10è prêtre du diocèse ordonné demain," *Fraternité Matin,* 7–8 August 1982, 13; and Hien Solo, "Abengourou—L'Abbé Pierre Nkruma ordonné prêtre à Yakassé," *Fraternité Matin,* 18 August 1982, 11.

126. Bayart, *L'état en Afrique,* 193–226.

127. Adowa Van-Ess, "Rev. Stephens Made the Sixth President," *People's Daily Graphic,* 18 February 1985, 1.

128. "Anantahene for Kokofu," *Daily Graphic,* 10 January 1981, 5.

129. "Limann Honoured," *Daily Graphic,* 26 October 1981, 4–5.

130. Schatzberg, *Dialectics of Oppression in Zaïre,* 78.

131. "Le Président Biya élevé au grade de Fon Suprême des fons du Nord-Ouest," *Cameroon Tribune,* 16–17 December 1984, 3.

132. See, for example, "Queenmother to Be Buried on Sunday," *Daily Graphic,* 28 January 1981, 4–5; and Essolomwa Nkoy ea Linganga, "Malula, un grand patriote et un pasteur charismatique," *Elima,* 16–18 June 1989, 1, 6, 7.

133. Edward Said once noted that for him one of the most striking features of American social scientific work on the Middle East was "its singular avoidance of literature." See Edward W. Said, *Orientalism* (New York: Pantheon Books, 1978), 291.

134. Certeau, *L'invention du quotidien,* 151.

135. Martin, "A la quête des OPNI, 793–815.

136. V. Y. Mudimbé, *The Invention of Africa: Gnosis, Philosophy, and the Order of Knowledge* (Bloomington: Indiana University Press, 1988), x.

3. PARAMETERS OF THE POLITICAL

1. Dale F. Eickelman and James Piscatori, *Muslim Politics* (Princeton, N.J.: Princeton University Press, 1997), ix, 4, 55.

2. Jean-François Bayart, "La cité cultuelle en Afrique noire," in *Religion et modernité politique en Afrique noire: Dieu pour tous et chacun pour soi* (Paris: Karthala, 1993), 299–310. Also see Schatzberg, *Dialectics of Oppression in Zaire,* in which I avoided the first trap but probably fell into the second.

3. David Throup, "'Render unto Caesar the Things That Are Caesar's': The Politics of Church-State Conflict in Kenya 1978–1990," in *Religion and Politics in East Africa: The Period since Independence,* ed. Holger Bernt Hansen and Michael Twaddle (London: James Currey, 1995), 143–176. The essay's title underscores both of the illusions that Bayart mentions.

4. Throup, "Render unto Caesar," 172.

5. For an illuminating Rwandan example of the diversity of the "Church" at the local level, see Timothy P. Longman, "Christianity and Crisis in Rwanda: Religion, Civil Society, Democratization and Decline" (Ph.D. diss., University of Wisconsin-Madison, 1995).

6. G. P. Benson, "Ideological Politics versus Biblical Hermeneutics: Kenya's Protestant Churches and the *Nyayo* State," in Hansen and Twaddle, *Religion and Politics in East Africa,* 177–199.

7. Benson, "Ideological Politics," 194.

8. Benson, "Ideological Politics," 185.

9. For useful overviews of politics and religion, see Jeff Haynes, *Religion and Politics in Africa* (Nairobi and London: East African Educational Publishers and Zed Books, 1996); Paul Gifford, *African Christianity: Its Public Role* (Bloomington: Indiana University Press, 1998); and, more generally, Thomas Spear and Isaria N. Kimambo, eds., *East African Expressions of Christianity* (Oxford: James Currey, 1999).

10. Stephen Ellis and Gerrie Ter Haar, "Religion and Politics in Sub-Saharan Africa," *Journal of Modern African Studies* 36, no. 2 (June 1998): 175–201.

11. Theophilus Dosumu, "The Myth of Democratic Practice in Nigeria," *Daily Times,* 1 March 1984, 7.

12. "Task Before the Judges—Bishop Eneja," *Daily Times,* 26 January 1981, 22.

13. Kwabena Agyei-Arhin, "Politics Is for All," *People's Daily Graphic,* 2 November 1987, 5.

14. Luc Angoula Nanga, "A la cathédrale de Yaoundé—'Face à l'histoire, nous devons réengendrer un Cameroun nouveau' déclare Mgr Zoa," *Cameroon Tribune,* 21–22 May 1984, 2.

15. The importance of literal interpretation is suggested by Ellis and Ter Haar, "Religion and Politics in Sub-Saharan Africa," 179.

16. Henry Okullu, *Church and Politics in East Africa* (Nairobi: Uzima Press, 1974), 13.

17. Okullu, *Church and Politics,* 16 (emphasis added).

18. Okullu, *Church and Politics,* 40, 74; citation, 74.

19. "I Am Still Listening," *Weekly Review,* 18 November 1994, 7–8, citation, 8.

20. "Church-State Relations: Okullu's True Colors," *Weekly Review,* 12 April 1996, 13–14.

21. Abdou Diouf, "Des trésors que nous ne gaspillerons pas," *Le Soleil,* 8 November 1984, 12.

22. In March 2000 Diouf and the Parti Socialiste (PS) lost an election to Abdoulaye Wade and his Parti Démocratique Socialiste (PDS), thus ending four decades of PS rule.

23. For notions of congruence and congruence theory, see Harry Eckstein, "A Theory of Stable Democracy," in *Division and Cohesion in Democracy: A Study of Norway* (Princeton, N.J.: Princeton University Press, 1966), 223–288; Harry Eckstein and Ted Robert Gurr, *Patterns of Authority: A Structural Basis for Political Inquiry* (New York: John Wiley and Sons, 1975); Harry Eckstein, *The Natural History of Congruence Theory,* Monograph Series in World Affairs 18, no. 2 (Denver: University of Denver, 1980); Harry Eckstein, "Unfinished Business: Reflections on the Scope of Comparative Politics," *Comparative Political Studies* 31, no. 4 (August 1998): 505–534; and, for a critique, David D. Laitin, "Toward a Political Science Discipline: Authority Patterns Revisited," *Comparative Political Studies* 31, no. 4 (August 1998): 423–443.
John Paden's work on Northern Nigeria suggests a certain congruence of authority patterns in both political and formally religious domains. Similarly, Abdellah Hammoudi analyzes Moroccan politics in terms of the replication and projection of a model of authority between a religious figure and his disciples on to the realm of politics. See John N. Paden, *Religion and Political Culture in Kano* (Berkeley and Los Angeles: University of California Press, 1973); and Abdellah Hammoudi, *Master and Disciple: The Cultural Foundations of Moroccan Authoritarianism* (Chicago: University of Chicago Press, 1997).

24. "Serigne Abdoul Khadre 4è Khalife Général: Continuité," *Le Soleil,* 21 June 1989, 7.

25. Jean-Pierre Ayé, "Son Éminence le Cardinal Yago: Merci à vous tous," *Fraternité Matin,* 14 February 1983, 26–27.

26. "Église protestante méthodiste de Côte d'Ivoire—Le Pasteur Emmanuel Yando nouveau président," *Fraternité Matin,* 11 January 1982, 1. For a similar ceremony, also in the presence of Houphouet, much of his government, as well as religious leaders from the Catholic and Muslim communities, see Saliou Koné, "Bouaké—En présence du Chef de l'Etat: L'Église protestante CMA a célébré son cinquantenaire," *Fraternité Matin,* 13 December 1982, 10.

27. See, for example, "Tabaski—La fête de la soumission célébrée à Abidjan; La délégation du parti à Adjamé," *Fraternité Matin,* 7 September 1984, 3; "Tabaski: Des prières

pour la paix et la fraternité," *Fraternité Matin,* 19 September 1982, 1; and, in Senegal, "Tabaski: Le chef de l'Etat a prié à la grande mosquée," *Le Soleil,* 12 October 1981, 1.

28. For Muslim ceremonies in Cameroon, see "Fin de jeûne de Ramadan: 'Nous sommes les fils d'un même Cameroun' déclare le Président Paul Biya au Grand Imam qu'il a reçu en audience," *Cameroon Tribune,* 1–2 July 1984, 5; and Ibrahima Housseini, "Benoué: La fête de fin de Ramadan célébrée avec faste à Garoua," *Cameroon Tribune,* 18 July 1984, 5.

29. Pape Marcel Sene, "Ils ont été ordonnés samedi par le cardinal Hyacinthe Thiandoum—Quatre nouveaux prêtres pour Fadiouth," *Le Soleil,* 11 April 1983, 3.

30. "Municipales 82: Sérénité et discipline à Yaoundé," *Cameroon Tribune,* 24–25 October 1982, 4.

31. For other examples of the "political" presence at ordinations, see Vieux Doro Ndiaye, "Saint-Louis: L'Abbé Etienne Sarr ordonné 1er prêtre diocésain," *Le Soleil,* 14 April 1983, 10; Abdallah Faye, "Religion—Un nouveau prêtre à Kaolack: L'Abbé Ernest Diouf ordonné," *Le Soleil,* 16 April 1985, 6; "Le sacré de Mgr. Gapangwa, nouvel évêque d'Uvira," *Elima,* 9–10 November 1985, 9; "He Is Now a Priest," *Daily Graphic,* 5 August 1980, 4–5; "Ordination de l'Abbé Daniel Tchantchou," *Cameroon Tribune,* 2 August 1982, 4; Juliette Mbarga, "Deux nouveaux prêtres pour le diocèse de Mbalmayo," *Cameroon Tribune,* 23 November 1982, 6; Lambert Elate Mbassi, "Haut-Nyong—Un nouveau prêtre pour le diocèse de Doumé / Abong-Mbang," *Cameroon Tribune,* 22 January 1987, 10; Malongo Pamba Zola, "Présentation du nouvel évêque auxiliaire de Kikwit aux fidèles de Kinshasa," *Elima,* 11 July 1985, 3; Kongo Luzayamo Nzundu, "Célébration de la première messe de l'abbé Lubivila Nzanzu," *Elima,* 4–5 July 1987, 10; Nsamba Olangi Diatta, "Le diocèse de Luebo à l'heure de l'épiscopat de la charité 'Dinanga,'" *Elima,* 2 March 1988, 7; and "Le maréchal Mobutu assiste à l'intronisation du nouvel archévêque de Kisangani," *Elima,* 21 November 1988, 11.

32. For examples of the relatively weaker political presence in Nigeria and Ghana, see "Two Priests Ordained," *Daily Times,* 4 January 1980, 2; "Priest Ordained," *Daily Times,* 21 July 1981, 31; and "Four Are Consecrated," *Daily Graphic,* 19 October 1981, 1. For an example of political presence at a customary installation, see "Bale of Xtians Picked," *Daily Times,* 19 July 1982, 2.

33. Leonardo A. Villalón, *Islamic Society and State Power in Senegal: Disciples and Citizens in Fatick* (Cambridge: Cambridge University Press, 1995).

34. For example, "A l'occasion du gamou de Tivaouane—Soutien du Khalife général des Tidianes à Abdou Diouf," *Le Soleil,* 29 December 1982, 1; Babacar Dieng, "Louga: 33è anniversaire du magal de Darou Marnane," *Le Soleil,* 5–7 October 1984, 9; Abdallah FAYE, "Nioro: Des milliers de fidèles pour rendre grâce à Sokhna Diarra Bousso—Le Magal de Porokhane célébré dans la ferveur," *Le Soleil,* 13 March 1985, 10; and "Gamou de Pire—Des prières pour la paix dans la umma," *Le Soleil,* 7 January 1986, 10.

35. "Serigne Moustapha Bassirou Mbacké à Prophane—'Je ne me mêle pas de politique,'" *Le Soleil,* 19–20 February 1983, 8.

36. "Magal de Touba: L'administration prépare l'événement," *Le Soleil,* 2 November 1984, 10.

37. Young notes that the "true bequest" of the African colonial state was the "robust bureaucratic autocracy" that resulted. See Crawford Young, *The African Colonial State in Comparative Perspective* (New Haven, Conn.: Yale University Press, 1994), 286.

38. Abdallah Faye, "Accueil chalereux de Dagana à Habib Thiam," *Le Soleil,* 16 October 1981, 4.

39. See Schatzberg, *Dialectics of Oppression,* 119.

40. "Tambacounda a accueilli son nouveau préfet," *Le Soleil,* 16 August 1982, 7.

41. See, for example, "Le Khalife général des mourides hôte de la région," *Le Soleil,* 17 November 1981, 9.

42. Meke Mpembe Francis, "Religion—L'archidiocèse de Yaoundé dit au revoir à Mgr Ama," *Cameroon Tribune,* 16 November 1983, 5.

43. "Diocèse de Kenge: Malaise général au sein du clergé," *Elima,* 29 January 1986, 3.

44. "Palm Sunday Service Boycotted," *Daily Graphic,* 1 April 1980, 1, 5.

45. "Church-State Relations: A Tirade against the NCCK," *Weekly Review,* 13 September 1996, 11–12.

46. Kofi Akumanyi, "That's Life: Dilemma of a Priest," Column, *Daily Graphic,* 7 November 1981, 3.

47. Louis D. Edzimbe, "Toussaint—Mgr Jean Zoa recommande aux Chrétiens de concrétiser leur soutien à S.E. Paul Biya par leur ardeur au travail," *Cameroon Tribune,* 6–7 November 1983, 3; and "Mgr Jean Zoa hier face à la presse nationale—Le Pape nomme ses cardinaux dans un esprit de liberté totale, souligne le prélat," *Cameroon Tribune,* 6 June 1985, 3.

48. John C. Kamau, General Secretary, and Bishop David M. Gitari, Chairman, "Foreword," in National Christian Council of Kenya (NCCK), *A Christian View of Politics in Kenya: Love, Peace, and Unity* (Nairobi: Uzima Press, 1983), vi.

49. "The Church: A Partisan Role in Politics," *Weekly Review,* 22 May 1992, 12.

50. Mwai Kibaki, African Press Service, cited in Henry Okullu, *Church and State, in Nation Building and Human Development* (Nairobi: Uzima Press, 1984), 53.

51. "Discours du Mgr. L. Monsengwo Pasinya, Archévêque de Kisangani, à l'occasion de son doctorat Honoris Cause, Leuven, le 26 avril 1993," typescript dated 2 February 1993, 13–14 (CEDAF, Brussels, Eglise catholique, Dossier de presse, 05.04.04.VI, emphasis in original).

52. "Les Eglises et l'Etat sont au service d'une même cause," *Elima,* 5 August 1985, 1, 12, 15.

53. "Serve People, Says Nyerere," *Daily News,* 18 June 1981, 1.

54. Moses Kitururu, "Religion Should Serve Man—Wakil," *Daily News,* 3 March 1987, 1.

55. Breda Atta-Quayson, "The Church Urged to Awaken People's Minds," *People's Daily Graphic,* 30 December 1986, 1.

56. On the Presbyterians, see "Church, State Must Unite," *Daily Graphic,* 23 June 1982, 1, 4–5; on the Catholic bishops, see Breda Atta-Quayson, "'We Are Ready to Cooperate,'" *Daily Graphic,* 31 July 1982, 1, 4–5.

57. "Comment: A Task for the Church," Editorial, *People's Daily Graphic,* 26 September 1987, 2.

58. In addition to the works already cited, see Henry Okullu, "Church and Society in Africa," in *Alternative Development Strategies for Africa: 1: Coalition for Change,* ed. B. Onimode et al. (London: Institute for African Alternatives, 1990), 77–97; and Henry Okullu, *Church and Marriage in East Africa* (Nairobi: Uzima Press, 1976).

59. Henry Okullu, *Church and State, in Nation Building and Human Development* (Nairobi: Uzima Press, 1984) xii.

60. Okullu, *Church and State,* xiii.

61. Okullu, *Church and State,* 19–20.

62. Timothy Murere Njoya, "Dynamics of Change in African Christianity: African Theology through Historical and Socio-Political Change" (Ph.D. diss., Princeton Theological Seminary, 1976), iv.

63. Njoya, "Dynamics of Change in African Christianity," 67–68. For a somewhat different view of conversion, see Lamin Sanneh, *Translating the Message: The Missionary Impact on Culture* (Maryknoll, N.Y:. Orbis Books, 1989).

64. Njoya, "Dynamics of Change in African Christianity," 270–271.

65. Njoya, "Dynamics of Change in African Christianity," 355.

66. Njoya, "Dynamics of Change in African Christianity," 526.

67. See Timothy Njoya, *Out of Silence: A Collection of Sermons* (Nairobi: Beyond Magazine, 1987).

68. Njoya, "God's Justice Triumphs by Reason through Faith," text: Habakkuk, sermon given at PCEA St. Andrew's Church, Nairobi, 5 October 1986, 63–77, in *Out of Silence,* citation, 70–71.

69. Njoya, "God's Justice Triumphs by Reason Through Faith," 71.

70. Njoya, "What God Has Cleansed You Must Not Call Unclean," text: Acts 11:1–18, sermon given at PCEA St. Andrew's Church, Nairobi, 25 August 1985, 29–34, in *Out of Silence,* citation, 33.

71. Njoya, "This is My Body," text: Luke 22:1–23, sermon given at PCEA St. Andrew's Church, Nairobi, 11 March 1984, 7–13, in *Out of Silence,* 7–8, 12.

72. Also see Timothy Murere Njoya, *Human Dignity and National Identity: Essential for Social Ethics* (Nairobi: Jemisik Cultural Books, 1987), a rather lengthy and not always clear tract that maintains human dignity must always be at the base of the nation. There are also extended comparisons between family and nation.

73. David M. Gitari, "The Church's Witness to the Living God in Seeking Just Political, Social, and Economic Structures in Contemporary Africa," in *Witnessing to the Living God in Contemporary Africa: Findings and Papers of the Inaugural Meeting of Africa Theological Fraternity*, ed. David M. Gitari and G. P. Benson (Nairobi: Africa Theological Fraternity, Uzima Press, 1986), 119–120.

74. Gitari, "The Church's Witness to the Living God," 135.

75. David M. Gitari, "All Scripture Is Inspired by God," sermon given at Church of the Good Samaritan, Kathiga, 28 June 1987, text: 2 Timothy 3:14–4:7, in David M. Gitari, *Let the Bishop Speak* (Nairobi: Uzima Press, 1988), 51. The bishop in Parliament was Archbishop Stephen Oluoch Ondiek, of the Maria Legio Church, who was the incumbent MP for Ugenya and also an assistant minister in the Government.

76. David M. Gitari, "The Good Shepherd," text: Ezekiel 34, John 10, and Psalm 23, "NCCK Service of Worship on the Eve of Opening of the 7th Parliament, St. Andrew's P.C.E.A. Church, Monday 22 March 1993," in NCCK, *A New Parliamentary Agenda: Pastoral Letter and Prayers of Intercession* (Nairobi: NCCK, 1993), 9.

77. Mutegi Njau, "Njoya Counterattacks," *Daily Nation,* 5 June 1990, 1–2, cited in FBIS-AFR-90-139, 19 July 1990, 20.

78. For good overviews of some of these aspects of Senegalese politics, see Donal B. Cruise O'Brien, *The Mourides of Senegal: The Political and Economic Organization of an Islamic Brotherhood* (Oxford: Clarendon Press, 1971); Christian Coulon, *Le marabout et le prince: Islam et pouvoir au Senegal* (Paris: A. Pedone, 1981); Abdoulaye-Bara Diop, *La société Wolof; Tradition et changement: Les systèmes d'inégalité et de domination* (Paris: Karthala, 1981); and Momar Coumba Diop and Mamadou Diouf, *Le Sénégal sous Abdou Diouf: Etat et société* (Paris: Karthala, 1990).

79. Villalón, *Islamic Society and State Power in Senegal.*

80. Linda J. Beck, "'Patrimonial Democrats' in a Culturally Plural Society: Democratization and Political Accommodation in the Patronage Politics of Senegal" (Ph.D. diss., University of Wisconsin-Madison, 1996).

81. "Soutien à Abdou Diouf—recommande le Khalife Abdou Lahat Mbacké à la fin du grand Magal de Touba," *Le Soleil,* 7 December 1982, 1.

82. Abdoulaye Ba, "Djourbel: Tous les mourides suivront le 'ndigueul' du khalife," *Le Soleil,* 12–13 February 1983, 30.

83. Amadou Gaye, "Le Khalife général aux fidèles: 'Je vous invite à soutenir Abdou Diouf'," *Le Soleil,* 29 December 1982, 4. Also see, "Les 'Baye-Fall' de Serigne Modou Diouf soutiennent Abdou Diouf," *Le Soleil,* 27 January 1983, 11.

84. See *Le Soleil,* 2 March 1983, 1.

85. "Abdoul Ahad appelle les Mourides à voter Diouf: Un autre choix trahirait Bamba," *Le Soleil,* 14 October 1987, 1.

86. See *Le Soleil Urnes,* 4 March 1988, i. Abdou Diouf, 73.2 percent; Abdoulaye Wade, 25.8 percent. The PS won 103 seats in the assembly; the PDS had 17. Wade eventually received a one-year suspended sentence.

87. This is the impression I received from numerous informal conversations with Senegalese in Saint Louis and Dakar during the summer of 1994.

88. Isaac Asante, "Withdraw the Subsidy . . . On Feeding Students—Sarpong," *Daily Graphic,* 7 April 1981, 8.

89. Graphic Reporter, "Let Us Have Basic Needs . . . Churches Appeal to Government," *Daily Graphic,* 11 July 1980, 1, 4–5.

90. "Let Justice Now Prevail . . . In Labour Agreements," *Daily Graphic,* 12 January 1980, 4.

91. Graphic Reporter, "Churches," *People's Daily Graphic,* 26 January 1985, 5.

92. Faustina Ashirife, "Churches Urged to Assist Govt.," *People's Daily Graphic,* 27 February 1985, 4–5.

93. Frank Akinola, "Maintain Fair Play to All—Imam," *Daily Times,* 17 May 1988, 1, 8.

94. Cited in "The Church: Bishopric Missive," *Weekly Review,* 7 April 1995, 4. Also see "Roman Catholic Church: Another Hard-Hitting Statement," *Weekly Review,* 29 May 1992, 32–33, in reference to ethnic clashes; and "Causing Ripples: The Church Takes a Stand on Political Reforms," *Weekly Review,* 16 August 1996, 4–8.

95. Conférence épiscopale du Zaïre, 9 March 1990, reprinted in "Zaïre: Les évêques accusent," *Jeune Afrique,* no. 1527, 9 April 1990, 18–25. Also see "Lettre pastorale de Mgr. Pirigsha à propos des prochaines élections," *Zaïre-Afrique* no. 164 (April 1982): 247–249.

96. "Comment: The Churches Can Be More Positive," Editorial, *Daily Graphic,* 2 December 1982, 1. Also see "Comment: Intervention Through the Church Door," Editorial, *Daily Graphic,* 30 November 1982, 1.

97. "Cheats Have Infiltrated Churches . . . Says Col. Tehn-Addy," *Daily Graphic,* 29 December 1982, 1, 4–5.

98. Isaac Asante, "Relate Religion to People's Struggle . . . Churches Urged," *People's Daily Graphic,* 11 January 1983, 8.

99. George Amosah, "Stand Firmly Behind PNDC . . . Forces Urged," *People's Daily Graphic,* 6 June 1983, 1.

100. "Church Can Play Politics," *Daily Times,* 18 October 1982, 5.

101. Kayode Osifeso, "Recover All the Loots—Bishop," *Daily Times*, 1 May 1984, 24.

102. The portion of contemporary political discourse which inveighs against corruption and argues in favor of morality and moral regeneration is voluminous. For a sampling, see Mussa Lupalu, "Mwinyi Hails Church Role," *Daily News*, 9 November 1987, 1; "Mwinyi Tells Religious Leaders. . . . Impart Moral Values to Youth," *Sunday News*, 29 February 1988, 1; "Mwinyi Inaugurates Mosque," *Daily News*, 8 April 1988, 1; Jean-Claude Noubissie, "Douala—L'archidiocèse était de la fête," *Cameroon Tribune*, 11 November 1987, 5; "Rigging Is a Crime—Bishop," *Daily Times*, 2 August 1983, 18; Mavis Quaicoe, "Call on Cadres to Rid the Nation of Moral Decadence," *People's Daily Graphic*, 19 June 1986, 8–9; Ibrahima Fall, "Célébration de la Tabaski: 'Retournons à Dieu' prêche l'Imam ratib de Dakar," "Saint-Louis—Communion entre le temporel et le spirituel," *Le Soleil*, 1 October 1982, 8; and Pape Sédikh Mbodje, "103è anniversaire de l'appel Limamou—La communauté layène a prié pour le Sénégal," *Le Soleil*, 7 May 1984, 8.

103. "Embrace the Will of God—Buhari," *Daily Times*, 29 June 1984, 1.

104. Koja Olo, "The Woman Who Prayed for a Priest but Got a Politician," *Daily Times*, 15 February 1980, 16.

105. "I Wanted to Be a Priest—Says Rawlings," *Daily Graphic*, 27 May 1982, 3.

106. "Let Your Deeds Be Godly, Rawlings," *People's Daily Graphic*, 2 September 1985, 1.

107. J. J. Rawlings, "Rawlings Delivers Easter Message to the Nation," Accra Domestic [Radio] Service (in English), 31 March 1986, cited in FBIS-AFR, V. 2 April 1986, T1, T6.

108. Breda Atta-Quayson, "Revolution Meant to Make People Their Own Shepherds," *People's Daily Graphic*, 26 September 1987, 1.

109. At a time of deepening economic crisis during the 1980s, Houphouet constructed the Our Lady of Peace of Yamoussoukro Basilica, reportedly the world's largest Christian church, and offered it as a gift to the Vatican. The regime claimed that the funds came entirely from Houphouet's personal fortune, not from the state's coffers.

110. "Mosquée de Cocody-Riviera—Le Chef de l'Etat remet les clés de l'édifice aux dignitaires religieux," *Fraternité Matin*, 26 May 1987, 6.

111. "Camp de jeunesse de l'Église Évangélique de Réveil—Le Pasteur Monsia Étienne: 'La Côte d'Ivoire, un don d'Houphouet aux Ivoiriens,'" *Fraternité Matin*, 21 August 1986, 10–11.

112. "New Formula," *Weekly Review*, 13 December 1996, 4.

113. For a sampling, however, see the collection of essays in Donald Rothchild and Naomi Chazan, eds., *The Precarious Balance: State and Society in Africa* (Boulder, Colo.: Westview Press, 1988); Goran Hyden and Michael Bratton, eds., *Governance and Politics in Africa* (Boulder, Colo.: Lynne Rienner, 1992); John W. Harbeson, Donald Rothchild, and Naomi Chazan, eds., *Civil Society and the State in Africa* (Boulder, Colo.: Lynne Rienner, 1994); Joel D. Barkan, Michael McNulty, and M. A. Ayeni, "'Hometown' Voluntary Associations, Local Development, and the Emergence of Civil Society in Western Nigeria," *Journal of Modern African Studies* 29, no. 3 (1991): 457–480; Michael Bratton, "Beyond the State: Civil Society and Associational Life in Africa," *World Politics* 41, no. 3 (1989): 407–430; Stephen N. Ndegwa, *The Two Faces of Civil Society: NGO's and Politics in Africa* (West Hartford, Conn.: Kumarian Press, 1996); and Aili Mari Tripp, *Women and Politics in Uganda* (Madison, Oxford, and Kampala: University of Wisconsin Press, James Currey, and Fountain Press, 2000).

114. P. Sedikh Mbodj, "L'association des imams est née—Un pasteur d'âmes," *Le Soleil*, 5 March 1984, 2. Also see Mamadou Ndiaye, "'La fraternité selon l'Islam': Une conférence de Cheikh Tidjane Sy," *Le Soleil*, 7 April 1982, 9.

115. Nelson Duah, "Muslim Group Demonstrates," *People's Daily Graphic*, 25 April 1984, 8.

116. Meke Mpembe Francis, "La famille syndicale de Mfoundi rencontre le préfet et le président de la section RDPC," *Cameroon Tribune*, le 10 January 1986, 6.

117. Mulenga Kameta Lesa, Gécamines Musoni, Letter to the PDG at Lubumbashi, 3 August 1991 (CEDAF, Zaïre: Conditions de vie, Situation Sociale, Dossier de presse à partir de 1990, Zaïre-03.02.05 VI).

118. "Le dialogue entre la haute direction de la Banque du Zaïre et la délégation syndicale pour l'année 1987 a été très franche," *Elima*, 7 January 1988, 11.

119. "Communiqué: Sechoy et Cie: Fête de famille" (advertisement), *Le Soleil*, 16–17 April 1983, 8.

120. See, for example, the account of a ceremony at the Brasseries du Cameroun, "Remise de médailles d'honneur du travail au Brasseries: 'Les Brasseries du Cameroun à Garoua vibrent au diapason d'une évolution dynamique' déclare le Gouverneur du Nord," *Cameroon Tribune*, 22 February 1984, 7; "26 employés de la Société Hysacam récompensés pour leurs bons et loyaux services," *Cameroon Tribune*, 26–27 February 1984, 7; and "427 agents du groupe SCIBE-Zaïre et 40 planteurs décorés," *Elima*, le 8 et 9 February 1986, 9.

121. "Les pratiques fétichistes sont prohibées!" *Elima*, 7 January 1980, 15. On the use of a soccer team as a political springboard, see Docteur Kalonji-Kabasele Muboy-ayi, membre d'honneur de l'AJSZ/Kin [honorary member of the AJSZ, Kinshasa], "Football: archaïsmes, incivisme et irresponsabilité," *Elima*, 5 August 1985, 14–15.

122. "Football—Les Lions Indomptables ovationnés par le peuple camerounais et félicités par le Chef de l'Etat: Gloire aux ambassadeurs du renouveau national," *Cameroon Tribune*, 20–21 March 1984, 1.

123. Willie Chiwango, "Sports Defeats: Mwinyi Calls for Soul-searching," *Daily News*, 27 October 1988, 8.

124. Frederic C. Schaffer, *Democracy in Translation: Understanding Politics in an Unfamiliar Culture* (Ithaca, N.Y.: Cornell University Press, 1998).

125. See, for example, Haynes, *Religion and Politics in Africa;* and Gifford, *African Christianity.*

126. The universities were Harvard; University of California, Berkeley; Yale; Michigan; Stanford; Chicago; Princeton University of California, Los Angeles; University of California, San Diego; and University of Wisconsin-Madison. I am grateful to Lynda Kellam for her careful reading of the online catalogs, as well as for her compilation and tabulation of the relevant data.

127. In other words, I *exclude* from consideration elite newspapers such as the *New York Times, Washington Post, Wall Street Journal,* and *Christian Science Monitor.*

128. This is impressionistic. There is surprisingly little literature on the placement of articles in newspapers. For a very partial exception, however, see Herbert Gans, *Deciding What's News: A Study of CBS Evening News, NBC Nightly News, Newsweek, and Time* (New York: Random House, 1979). In commenting on the number and variety of "known" individuals in the news, Gans notes the small number of business and labor leaders presented in television news and news magazines. He suggests, however, that they do appear in the business sections of the magazines. Gans, *Deciding What's News,* 10, 12.

129. This, too, is largely impressionistic, and some of the evidence may, in fact, be mixed. The top ten British departments of political science and their respective universities, at least in 1997–1998, actually display a pattern that is not entirely dissimilar to the American one. Departments of politics ranked behind history, law, economics, and business, accounting for only slightly more than 8 percent of the total number of courses on the politics of labor in British universities. This may be due to the "Americanization" of political science in some quarters, but this is speculative. The universities in question were Oxford, Essex, King's College, the Institute of Commonwealth Studies, the London School of Economics, Sussex, Wales (Aberystwyth), Strathclyde, Glasgow, and Sheffield. Again, I am grateful to Lynda Kellam.

Some secondary sources on the organization of the British press, however, indicate that the close association of labor in Britain with the Labour Party may lead to treating certain labor-related subjects as being more "political" than they are in the United States. See, for example, Jeremy Tunstall, "The Problem of Industrial Relations News in the Press," in Oliver Boyd-Barrett, Colin Seymour-Ure, and Jeremy Tunstall, *Studies in the Press*, (London: Her Majesty's Stationery Office, 1977), 343–397.

130. Alasdair MacIntyre, "Is a Science of Comparative Politics Possible?" in Alasdair MacIntyre, *Against the Self-Images of the Age: Essays on Ideology and Philosophy* (London: Duckworth, 1971), 260–279.

131. Abraham Kaplan, *The Conduct of Inquiry: Methodology for Behavioral Science* (San Francisco: Chandler, 1964), 298.

132. MacIntyre, "Is a Science of Comparative Politics Possible?"

4. ALTERNATIVE CAUSALITIES

1. A mode of causality is simply an implicit conceptual template that privileges a specific causal factor such as the maximization of interests, divine intervention, sorcery, or the location and movement of the heavenly bodies.

2. "Discours de Mgr. Monsengwo, reprise solennelle des travaux de la CNS," 6 April 1992, mimeographed text, 5 (CEDAF [Brussels], Zaïre: Documents Relatifs à la Conférence Nationale, 2343 III, 1991).

3. Mvola Bita, "Football—Congrès annuel du comité provincial du Centre—M. Ndongo Aléga Martin reconduit à la tête du comité," *Cameroon Tribune,* 6–7 October 1985, 9.

4. Abbés Kinois, "Bâtir la nation, une tâche pour tous les chrétiens," text of 5 February 1992, 3 (CEDAF, Brussels, Dossier sur les évènements récents au Zaïre [January–February 1992], 2358 III 1992).

5. Cited in "Shagari Family Sees Coup as Divine Intervention," Agence France-Presse, Paris (in English), 9 January 1984, cited in FBIS-AFR, V. West Africa, 10 January 1984, T2.

6. "President Warns Against Subversive Activities," Nairobi Domestic Service, 24 August 1982, cited in FBIS-AFR, V. East Africa, 25 August 1982, R1.

7. Nsasse Ramazani, "Le fétichisme à l'honneur: De sang humain au stade Lumumba," *Elima,* 7 September 1984, 13.

8. Another site, at least in Congo/Zaïre, is popular music. See Tshonga-Onyumbe,

"Nkisi, nganga et ngangankisi dans la musique zaïroise moderne de 1960 à 1981," *Zaïre-Afrique* 22, no. 169 (1982): 555–566. Here, however, the role of sorcery in affairs of the heart is paramount.

9. "Le marabout avait la réputation de multiplier les billets be banque: Koumbaré a disparu avec près de 7 millions," *Fraternité Matin,* 10 February 1982, 4. For a similar case, also see "Faits Divers: Il disparaît dans une mosquée avec l'argent à multiplier," *Fraternité Matin,* 8 May 1981, 6.

10. John M. Janzen, *The Quest for Therapy in Lower Zaire* (Berkeley and Los Angeles: University of California Press, 1978), 3, 38, 57, 194–195, 215, 222. Also see Nancy Rose Hunt, *A Colonial Lexicon: Of Birth Ritual, Medicalization, and Mobility in the Congo* (Durham, N.C.: Duke University Press, 1999).

11. Bernard Hours, *L'état sorcier: Santé publique et société au Cameroun* (Paris: l'Harmattan, 1985), 54.

12. See Emmanuel Milingo, *The World in Between: Christian Healing and the Struggle for Spiritual Survival* (London and Maryknoll, N.Y.: C. Hurst and Orbis Books, 1984); Gerrie Ter Haar, *Spirit of Africa: The Healing Ministry of Archbishop Milingo of Zambia* (London: Hurst and Company, 1992); and Paul Gifford, *African Christianity: Its Public Role* (Bloomington: Indiana University Press, 1998), 227–228.

13. Donald T. Regan, *For the Record: From Wall Street to Washington* (San Diego, Calif.: Harcourt Brace Jovanovich, 1988), 3–4.

14. Regan, *For the Record,* 74.

15. Joan Quigley, *"What Does Joan Say?": My Seven Years as White House Astrologer to Nancy and Ronald Reagan* (New York: Carol Publishing Group, 1990), 12, 75; citation, 12.

16. Quigley also lays claim to a scientific mantle. She rejects the terms "seer" and "clairvoyant," noting instead that "I base my astrological analysis on the data provided by astronomers and charts calculated by computers. My conclusions are based on this accurate scientific material in the same way your doctor supports his diagnoses by the laboratory reports or an economist bases his predictions on statistics. I do not gaze into crystal balls. I study many different kinds of charts and come to well-thought-out conclusions." See Quigley, *"What Does Joan Say?,"* 13.

17. Lan, *Guns and Rain*; and Geschiere, *Sorcellerie et politique en Afrique.* Also see Harry G. West, "Sorcery of Construction and Sorcery of Ruin: Power and Ambivalence on the Mueda Plateau, Mozambique (1882–1994)" (Ph.D. diss., University of Wisconsin-Madison, 1997); K. B. Wilson, "Cults of Violence and Counter-Violence in Mozambique," *Journal of Southern African Studies* 18, no. 3 (September 1992): 528–582; and Florence Bernault, *Démocraties ambiguës en Afrique centrale—Congo-Brazzaville, Gabon: 1940–1965* (Paris: Karthala, 1996).

18. Achille Mbembe, *La naissance du maquis dans le Sud-Cameroun (1920–1960): Histoire des usages de la raison en colonie* (Paris: Karthala, 1996), 377–396; and Comi Toulabor, *Le Togo sous Eyadéma* (Paris: Karthala, 1986), 124–131. Also see the excellent collection of essays assembled by Diane Ciekawy and Peter Geschiere in *African Studies Review* 41, no. 3 (December 1999): 1–209.

19. The classic definition, of course, comes from Evans-Pritchard: "Azande believe that some people are witches and can injure them in virtue of an inherent quality. A witch performs no rite, utters no spell, and possesses no medicines. An act of witchcraft is a psychic act. They believe also that sorcerers may do them ill by performing magic rites with bad medicines. Azande distinguish clearly between witches and sor-

cerers. Against both they employ diviners, oracles, and medicines. . . ." See E. E. Evans-Pritchard, *Witchcraft, Oracles, and Magic among the Azande* (Oxford: Clarendon Press, 1937), 21.

20. O. K. Mutungi, *The Legal Aspects of Witchcraft in East Africa, with Particular Reference to Kenya* (Nairobi: East African Literature Bureau, Kenya, 1977), 9.

21. Jean-Mary Neossi, "La chasse aux sorciers recommandée au nouveau président du tribunal de Batouri," *Cameroon Tribune,* 28 February 1982, 6.

22. Mamounia Ngyambila, "Fait du jour—La sorcellerie: Une source de conflits," Column, *Elima,* 4 September 1984, 2.

23. Rev. Dr. Bayiga, "La sorcellerie: Son impact dans la vie de l'homme," *Cameroon Tribune,* 5 June 1986, 15 (emphasis in original).

24. Adam Lusekelo, "With a Light Touch: Jujulising," Column, *Sunday News,* 20 May 1984, 7, writes tongue in cheek about the larger problem of Tanzanians using sorcery for career advancement. "'Magic Winnings,'" *West Africa,* 27 June–3 July 1994, 1143, details the belief that a series of raffle winners had been using magic to win huge payoffs.

25. On the notion of organic intellectuals, see Antonio Gramsci, *Selections from the Prison Notebooks of Antonio Gramsci,* ed. and trans. Quintin Hoare and Geoffrey Newell Smith (New York: International Publishers, 1971); and on peasant intellectuals and their discourse, Steven Feierman, *Peasant Intellectuals: Anthropology and History in Tanzania* (Madison: University of Wisconsin Press, 1990).

26. "Trial by Ordeal," *Daily Graphic,* 21 March 1981, 1. For another account detailing the belief that the supernatural plays a role in traffic accidents, see "Gbagada Multiple Crash; Fetish Priests Appease the Gods," *Daily Times,* 24 October 1983, 5.

27. "Herbalist Convicted," *Daily Times,* 31 March 1980, 2. Also see "Witchcraft Used to Influence South African Court Case," Agence France-Presse (via Clari-net), 22 January 1998, C-afp@clari.net.

28. Ambroise Djidji, "Cinq sorciers de Bloléquin devant le tribunal," *Fraternité Matin,* 4 April 1984, 8.

29. "Une affaire de 'sorcellerie' . . . Ses neveux le bastonnent à mort," *Le Soleil,* 19 April 1984, 8. Also see Mbaye Gueye, "Une ténébreuse affaire de sorcellerie," *Le Soleil,* 13 November 1984, 7.

30. See Bogumil Jewsiewicki, *Naître et mourir au Zaïre: Un demi-siècle d'histoire au quotidien* (Paris: Karthala, 1993), 52. This remarkable collection of autobiographies underscores the ubiquity of sorcery during the mid-1980s.

31. "Brutal Murders Shake Shinyaga," *Sunday News,* 16 May 1982, 1; and "Twenty Suspected Witches Killed in North Tanzania Each Month," Agence France-Presse (via Clari-net), 30 September 1998, C-afp@clari.net.

32. See "Of Witches and Lynching," *Weekly Review,* 16 July 1993, 20; Edward Makori and Peter Makori, "Witchcraft in Parliament . . . Lynching of Witches in the Countryside," *Drum,* July 1993, 6–8; and, on the Mombasa violence, "Witchdoctor Charged in Mombasa Violence," Agence France-Presse (via Clari-net), 1 September 1997, C-afp@clari.net.

33. Elvis D. Aryeh, "I Prefer to Be Tried by the Fetish—Rawlings," *Daily Graphic,* 3 March 1980, 1.

34. Odafe Othihiwa, "Charms Scare at 1004 Flats," *Daily Times,* 14 October 1983, 1.

35. Of interest here as well is the fact that longtime Nigerian presidential hopeful, Obafemi Awolowo, also occasionally resorted to alternative understandings of causality. When he accepted the presidential nomination of the UPN in 1983, he

openly discussed removal of a "curse" he had placed on Nigerian politics in 1963—that "the twilight of democracy will change to utter darkness"—that he believed to be "inspired" by "Providence." See Obafemi Awolowo, *Awo Says Yes: Being His 1983 Presidential Election Acceptance Speech in Lagos on January 29, 1983 at Tafawa Balewa Square* (Lagos, Nigeria: Directorate of Research and Publicity, UPN National Secretariat, 1983), 7–8.

36. Monsa et Kitemona, "Qui a tué Bobo?" *Elima,* 16–17 June 1984, 8; and Kitemona N'Silu, "Bobutaka, le célèbre buteur de Vita Club, meurt en plein match contre Matonge!" *Elima,* 15 June 1984, 16.

37. "Les pratiques fétichistes sont prohibées!" *Elima,* 7 January 1980, 15.

38. Staff Correspondent, "AFC Warns against 'Juju' in Football," *Daily News,* 10 January 1980, 12; and "La lutte contre la superstition est engagée," *Elima,* 16 January 1980, 8.

39. "Nous pouvons prétendre à une finale exceptionnelle," interview with Amadou Abdoulaye Ba, *Le Soleil,* 1 August 1980, 24.

40. "'Le fétichisme en sport est un fléau,'" *Le Soleil,* 27 February 1980, 10.

41. "Just Fontaine, entraîneur du Maroc au 'Soleil,'" interview, *Le Soleil,* 24 June 1980, 10.

42. "Comment," Editorial, *Daily News,* 23 September 1988, 1.

43. Reuters, "Soccer—Democratic Congo Warns of Magic ahead of Key Match," 24 February 1998.

44. Mamadou Kasse, "La résistance était vaine," *Le Soleil,* 8 November 1983, 20.

45. Mukaku Lalabi-Muke, "Ces pratiques fétichistes qui avalisent le sport," *Elima,* 12 August 1983, 10.

46. "La vie dans nos clubs—Les dépenses: Snobisme ou nécessité?" *Fraternité Matin,* 28 October 1980, 12–13.

47. "Fétichisme: mythe, croyance ou réalité?," *Elima,* 26 February 1982, 10–11. In addition, during a 1985 court case in Tanzania in which several individuals were charged with treason for trying to stage a coup against President Nyerere's government, it eventually came out that one of those involved in trying to "protect" the authors of the attempted coup was a sorcerer who had once worked for the Tanga-based African Sports Club. See Mkumbwa Ally and Nasibu Mwanukuzi, "Treason Trial: Medicinemen Give Testimony," *Daily News,* 14 February 1985, 3.

48. "Commission de la médecine sportive: Combattre le fétichisme," *Fraternité Matin,* 15 June 1982, 16–17.

49. "Quel avenir pour les Éléphants?," *Fraternité Matin,* 28–30 April/1 May 1984, 12–13.

50. "Le Ministre Laurent Dona Fologo—Football ivoirien; fétichisme," *Fraternité Matin,* 6 January 1987, 28–29.

51. "Stella Club d'Abidjan—Amadou Djallo (président central): Chaque dirigeant a son féticheur, et tous les fétiches se neutralisent," *Fraternité Matin,* 21 July 1989, 14–15.

52. See Bwabwa Wa Kayembe, "Libre opinion: Et si nous parlions 'Léopards,'" Op-editorial, *Elima,* 3 August 1984, 12, who maintains that some Zaïrian players rely only on sorcerers.

53. Hégaud Ouattara, "Rencontre avec . . . Joseph Antoine Bell (Africa): Le football m'a fait beaucoup de mal," *Fraternité Matin,* 12 March 1982, 16–17.

54. Hégaud Ouattara, "Rencontre avec . . . Gbonké Martin (Entraîneur de l'Africa-Sports)," *Fraternité Matin,* 25 August 1983, 13.

55. Achike Okafo, "Lest We Forget: Away with Those Phoney Beliefs," Column, *Daily Times*, 30 December 1981, 7.

56. Zamenga Batukezanga, *Sept frères et une soeur* (Kinshasa: Editions St Paul-Afrique, December 1975), 20.

57. N. K., "Ces pratiques fétichistes qui 'tuent' le football kinois!: Qu'attend la Lifkin pour réprimer les auteurs?" *Elima*, 6 October 1983, 16.

58. M'Vuma Nkanga, "Les fétiches battus par le football," *Elima*, 4 June 1983, 8.

59. Lusadusu Basilwa, licencié en education physique et entraîneur de football [bachelor's degree in physical education and football coach], "Réflexion: Quel avenir pour le football zaïrois?" Op-Editorial, *Elima*, 2 August 1984, 15.

60. Koba Bashibirira M., "Incidences magico-religieuses sur le pouvoir africain," *Cahiers des religions africaines* 19, no. 37 (January 1985): 39–51, citation, 46.

61. For an account of sorcery in Cameroonian basketball, handball, and volleyball, see Mouelle Bissi, "Congrès annuels des Fédérations de basket, hand, et volleyball; 'Intensifier la lutte contre la violence, la corruption, l'indiscipline et la sorcellerie' recommande le ministre Ngongang Ouandji," *Cameroon Tribune*, 7–8 September 1980, 10.

62. Among the nobler efforts are Crawford Young, *Politics in the Congo: Decolonization and Independence* (Princeton, N.J.: Princeton University Press, 1965); Young and Turner, *The Rise and Decline of the Zairian State*; Herbert F. Weiss, *Political Protest in the Congo: The Parti Solidaire Africain during the Independence Struggle* (Princeton, N.J.: Princeton University Press, 1967); Thomas M. Callaghy, *The State-Society Struggle: Zaire in Comparative Perspective* (New York: Columbia University Press, 1984); Jean-Claude Willame, *Patrice Lumumba: La crise congolaise revisitée* (Paris: Karthala, 1990); Nzongola-Ntalaja, *Class Struggles and National Liberation in Africa: Essays on the Political Economy of Neocolonialism* (Roxbury, Mass.: Omenana, 1982); and the numerous works of Benoît Verhaegen and his collaborators, *Congo 1959–1967* (Brussels: CRISP, 1961–1969).

63. On Kabila's triumph, see Michael G. Schatzberg, "Beyond Mobutu: Kabila and the Congo," *Journal of Democracy* 8, no. 4 (October 1997): 70–84.

64. On the "transition" that never happened, see Michael G. Schatzberg, "Hijacking Change: Zaire's 'Transition' in Comparative Perspective," in *Democracy in Africa: The Hard Road Ahead*, ed. Marina Ottaway (Boulder, Colo.: Lynne Rienner, 1997), 113–134.

65. For a study of this first generation of Congolese physicians, see Willy de Craemer and Renée C. Fox, *The Emerging Physician* (Stanford, Calif.: Hoover Institution Press, 1968).

66. Most of the details of Sakombi's biography are drawn from Mabi Mulumba and Mutamba Makombo, *Cadres et dirigeants au Zaïre: Qui sont-ils? Dictionnaire biographique* (Kinshasa: Editions du Centre de Recherches Pédagogiques, 1986), 440. See, too, Isidore Ndaywel è Nziem, "La société zaïroise dans le miroir de son discours religieux (1990–1993)," *Cahiers africains* no. 6 (1993): 39; "Profonde restructuration du Conseil exécutif," *Elima*, 28 November 1988, 10; and "Profond remaniement au sein des organes du M.P.R.," *Elima*, 12 January 1990, 6, 8.

67. Sakombi Inongo, "L'État de la nation: A l'écoute du Zaïre," *Elima*, 19–20 January 1985, 1, 8.

68. Nguza Karl i Bond, *Mobutu ou l'incarnation du mal zaïrois* (London: Rex Collings, 1982), 29–30 and passim.

69. Sakombi Inongo, *Lettre ouverte à Nguza Karl i Bond* (n.p. [France], 1982), 69, 79; direct quotation, 79.

70. Fernand Bezy, Jean-Philippe Peemans, and Jean-Marie Wautelet, *Accumulation et sous-développement au Zaïre 1960–1980* (Louvain-la-Neuve, Belgium: Presses Universitaires de Louvain, 1981).

71. See Michael G. Schatzberg, "Explaining Zaire," *African Affairs* 82, no. 329 (October 1983): 569–573; quotations, 569, 571, 573.

72. Schatzberg, "Explaining Zaire," 571.

73. François Soudan, "Chronique d'une révolution," *Jeune Afrique*, no. 1928–1929, 16 December 1997–5 January 1998, 45.

74. "Confession publique d'un ancien baron du président Mobutu," *Elima*, 22 April 1992, 9.

75. Schatzberg, *Politics and Class in Zaire*, 86.

76. Michael G. Schatzberg, "Zaire," in *The Political Economy of African Foreign Policy: Comparative Analysis*, ed. Timothy M. Shaw and Olajide Aluko (Aldershot, Hants, England: Gower, 1984), 297.

77. See Bockie, *Death and the Invisible Powers*; and the magisterial work of Suzanne Preston Blier, *African Vodun: Art, Psychology, and Power* (Chicago: University of Chicago Press, 1995).

78. See Michael G. Schatzberg, "Field Log," Lisala, 28 April 1975, 72. A previous stint in Cameroon (1969–1971) had already sensitized me to the importance of this aspect of local life.

79. Scott, *Seeing Like a State*,highlights the importance of local knowledge.

80. Schatzberg, *Politics and Class in Zaïre,* 121–152.

81. Cited in Ndaywel è Nziem, "La société zaïroise," 41.

82. Michael G. Schatzberg, "*Fidélité au Guide:* The J.M.P.R. in Zairian Schools," *Journal of Modern African Studies* 16, no. 3 (1978): 426–427.

83. "Sakombi parle de Kabila et . . . de Mobutu," *Le Soft International,* no. 720, 12–18 December 1997, http://www.lesoftonline.net/05-03.articles.html, 1–2, 3, 5. I am grateful to René Lemarchand for calling this interview to my attention.

84. Ndaywel also reproduces part of the confession of Charles-Daniel Bofossa (W'amb'ea Nkoso), a former governor of the Bank of Zaïre. See Ndaywel è Nziem, "La société zaïroise," 33–39.

85. Letter from Nendaka Bika Victor to Mobutu, *Le Potentiel* (Kinshasa) 15 May 1991, 13.

86. "Extraits de la déclaration de la famille M'Polo à la CNS: Les assassins de M. M'Polo siègent au Palais du Peuple—Mme. Jacqueline M'Polo Ekonda (invitée de la CNS)," *Le Potentiel,* 28 May 1992, n.p.

87. Emmanuel Dungia, *Mobutu et l'argent du Zaïre: Révélations d'un diplomate, ex-agent des services secrets* (Paris: L'Harmattan, 1993), 42–49; and Emmanuel Dungia, *La pieuvre tropicale: Les tentacules de Mobutu* (Brussels: Emmanuel Dungia, n.d.).

88. Dungia, *Mobutu et l'argent du Zaïre,* 47–48.

89. Dungia, *Mobutu et l'argent du Zaïre,* 44.

90. Fortinant Mutubu, "Les militaires de Mobutu donnent raison à Tshisekedi," *"Umoja"* (Kinshasa), 2 March 1993, 2. The Prima Curia was Mobutu's quasi-religious organization, loosely inspired by certain Masonic rites. Many of the regime's barons belonged, and it was probably designed to ensure their political loyalty. Its precise role

remains an enigma, however. See Colette Braeckman, *Le dinosaure: Le Zaïre de Mobutu* (Paris: Fayard, 1992), 183–184.

91. Banza Kakese, "Le dernier billet à l'effigie de Mobutu," *La Semaine* (Kinshasa), 12 September 1991, n.p.

92. For a splendid treatment of Nuer understandings of money, see Sharon E. Hutchinson, *Nuer Dilemmas: Coping with Money, War, and the State* (Berkeley and Los Angeles: University of California Press, 1996), 56–102.

93. Schatzberg, *Dialectics of Oppression in Zaire*, 30–51.

94. Schatzberg, *Dialectics of Oppression in Zaire*, 130.

95. Charles O. Jones, "Mistrust but Verify: Memoirs of the Reagan Era," *American Political Science Review* 83, no. 3 (September 1989): 981–982.

96. It is possible that Museveni's remarks were quite cynical and taken out of context. Nevertheless, much of the readership probably would have believed the account. See "Museveni's Witchcraft," *Weekly Review,* 24 May 1991, 24.

97. "Ugandan Witchdoctor Arrested for Failing to Warn of Attack," Agence France-Presse (via Clari-net), 31 July 1998, C-afp@clari.net.

98. Jewsiewicki, *Naître et mourir au Zaïre,* 74.

99. Ben-Clet Kankonde Dambu, "Querelle autour de la débaptisation du Zaïre: Mobutu craint de perdre sa puissance magico-fétichiste," *Le Potentiel,* 6 August 1992, n.p.

5. MATRIX I—THE FATHER-CHIEF

1. "The Presidency '88: Consolidation of Power," *Weekly Review,* 6 January 1989, 18–19.

2. Schatzberg, *Dialectics of Oppression in Zaire,* 74–77.

3. Ngo Mohma Bénédicte, "Le rôle de l'homme dans la société camerounaise," Letter to the Editor, *Cameroon Tribune,* 1–2 February 1981, 11.

4. Peter Seitel, *See So That We May See: Performances and Interpretations of Traditional Tales from Tanzania* (Bloomington: Indiana University Press, 1980), 12–13.

5. "Le Point: Magnanimité présidentielle," Editorial, *Elima,* 4 November 1984, 1; and "Le message de dimanche: Performances et ardeur au travail," Editorial, *Elima,* 2 April 1984, 1.

6. Mobutu Sese Seko, "La pensée du jour: Notre préoccupation," *Elima,* 2 January 1984, 1.

7. "Moi Denies Odinga Detained," Nairobi Domestic Service (in English), 4 January 1983, cited in FBIS-AFR-83-003, 5 January 1983, East Africa, V., R2; and "An Enormous Pay Increase," *Weekly Review,* 25 November 1994, 14 (emphasis added).

8. Kalubi Kalonji Menda, "Des produits pharmaceutiques et du matériel de diagnostic remis aux centres de santé de Bulungu," *Elima,* 27–28 June 1987, 9. Also see "Dons du Président de la République à la sous-région de la Mongala," *Elima,* 28 October 1980, 1.

9. Kwame Penni, "Jerry's Gifts to Ekwe Hospital," *People's Daily Graphic,* 31 May 1984, 1; and for the retraction, see "Ekwe Hospital," *People's Daily Graphic,* 1 June 1984, 1.

10. Nicholas Opera Sumba, Kenyan African Students Association, Bombay, India, "Students in India," Letter to the Editor, *Weekly Review,* 7 December 1990, 3.

11. Meke Mepembi Francis, "Inauguration du restaurant universitaire hier—'Un joyau du gouvernement du renouveau à la jeunesse' souligne le Pr Joseph Owona," *Cameroon Tribune,* 16 January 1985, 3.

12. "Le Point: La sollicitude présidentielle," Editorial, *Elima,* 24 January 1985, 1, 8.

13. "Université: instructions spécifiques en matière d'aides et de bourses," *Cameroon Tribune,* 27–28 April 1980, 1.

14. Amadou Vamoulke, "'Nation: Le Point': Le père et le guide," Column, *Cameroon Tribune,* 13 February 1982, 8.

15. "Le Président aux Éléphants: Vous devez nourir la volonté de gagner," *Fraternité Matin,* 5 September 1985, 25.

16. "A Boost for the Stars," *Weekly Review,* 9 May 1997, 29; and, on the salary figure, see "An Enormous Pay Increase," *Weekly Review,* 25 November 1994, 14.

17. "Un encouragement aux paysans," *Cameroon Tribune,* 21 August 1982, 1; "Dans tous les secteurs publics et privés, LE PRESIDENT PAUL BIYA AUGMENTE LES SALAIRES; C'est la plus forte augmentation de ces dernières années," *Cameroon Tribune,* 18 November 1982, 1 (emphasis in original headline); and "A la veille du premier anniversaire de son accession au Pouvoir—Le Président Biya décide d'importantes mesures de revalorisation des salaires," *Cameroon Tribune,* 5 November 1983, 1.

18. Jean-Mary Neossi, "La pluie de la bénédiction," *Cameroon Tribune,* 27 May 1983, 2.

19. For a pre-colonial example among the Bashu Nande (Central Africa), see Randall M. Packard, *Chiefship and Cosmology: An Historical Study of Political Competition* (Bloomington: Indiana University Press, 1981), 68–70, 193–196.

20. *Elima,* 27 February 1980, 1, 7.

21. A. O. Matutta, Dar es Salaam, "Mwalimu Ndiyo Mwenye Kazi Ngumu," *Uhuru* (Dar es Salaam), 25 November 1970, 4. I am grateful to Gilbert Khadiagala for his assistance in translating and analyzing these Swahili language materials.

22. James Butty, "Africa's First Woman 'President,'" *West Africa,* 2–8 September 1996, 1395 and 1395–1396.

23. "Le Point: Réconfort paternel," Column, *Elima,* 29 August 1985, 1, 8. On the role of Mobutu's spouse and her place in the symbolism as the "mother" of the nation, see Schatzberg, *Dialectics of Oppression in Zaire,* 77–78.

24. "Yamoussoukro capitale: La déclaration du Comité Exécutif," *Fraternité Matin,* 21 January 1983, 14–15. Yamoussoukro is still the official capital, but Abidjan remains that nation's primary administrative and economic center. Most embassies have remained in Abidjan.

25. "Le message du dimanche: Les militants du MPR face au terrorisme," Editorial, *Elima,* le 17 June 1985, 1, 14.

26. "Le Chef de de l'Etat a largement récompensé notre héros," *Fraternité Matin,* 27 August 1984, 14–15.

27. "Le Chef de l'Etat a reçu une délégation de 'Kake la Mbenza,'" *Elima,* 12 November 1980, 1, 7.

28. Halima Shariff, "You Are Pillars of the Nation, Elders Told," *Sunday News,* 11 January 1987, 1.

29. The Nigerian *Daily Times* published on average thirty-six photographs of chiefs per year during the period 1980–1989. The total of 358 far exceeded the other newspapers for which I have partial data on this (Ghana, Côte d'Ivoire, and Cameroon). Ghana's *People's Daily Graphic* had 130 photos of chiefs from 1981 through 1989; *Fraternité Matin* (Côte d'Ivoire) had 85 from 1982 through 1989; Cameroon (*Cameroon Tribune*) had 22 from 1985 through 1989. Many of the photographs indicate chiefs mingling and mixing with other personalities from both the state and the formal religious sector. Complete citations to them are available on request.

30. Nana Fredua-Agyeman, "Focus: Treachery at Palace," Column, *Daily Graphic,* 16 January 1981, 3.

31. Breda Atta-Quayson and Mavis Quaicoe, "Chairman Rawlings Is Back from Tour," *People's Daily Graphic,* 3 August 1984, 1.

32. Chief Olu Akaraogun, "Sijuwade—The Torch-Bearer of Yoruba Cultural Heritage," *Daily Times,* 6 December 1980, 7.

33. "Daily Times Opinion: Respect for Natural Rulers," Editorial, *Daily Times,* 7 January 1982, 3. For another statement on the desirability of neutrality among Nigeria's customary rulers who are "fathers to all," see "Daily Times Opinion: Role of Traditional Rulers," *Daily Times,* Editorial, 20 April 1985, 3.

34. "Keep Peace, Politicians Told," *Daily Times,* 11 May 1983, 2.

35. "SDP Presidential Candidate Laments Ethnic Strife," *Daily Times,* 24 June 1992, 7 cited in FBIS-AFR-92-139, 20 July 1992, 44.

36. "Royal Fathers Take Plea to IBB," *Daily Times,* 8 July 1989, 1, 10.

37. Ibrahim Babangida, "June 12 and Its Aftermath," excerpts from Babangida's farewell address, 26 August 1993, in *West Africa,* 6–12 September 1993, 1579.

38. On indirect rule, see Frederick Lugard, *The Dual Mandate in British Tropical Africa,* with a new introduction by Margery Perham, 5th ed. (Hamden, Conn.: Archon Books, 1965). For a comprehensive overview of the various sorts of administrative arrangements that colonial states employed, see Young, *The African Colonial State in Comparative Perspective.*

39. "Noun: Femme élu chef de village à Njindaré," *Cameroon Tribune,* 1–2 September 1985, 5.

40. Auguste Miremont, "Un pacte d'amour," *Fraternité Matin,* 11 July 1985, 1, 24, citation, 24.

41. "Election présidentielle du 14 January 1984," *Cameroon Tribune,* 20 January 1984, 3.

42. Celestin Monga, "An Open Letter to Paul Biya," *Le Nouvel Horizon,* 18 February 1991, 7, cited in FBIS-AFR-91-040, 28 February 1991, 4.

43. Elvis D. Aryeh, "Warning to Users of Govt Cars," *Daily Graphic,* 15 January 1980, 1.

44. For an application of the same point in relation to the Cameroonian police, see Jacqueline Abena Nlomo, "Ecole Nationale Supérieure de Police: 12 commissaires, 21 officiers ont reçu leur diplôme hier," *Cameroon Tribune,* 1 July 1981, 3.

45. Ibrahima Ndiaye, "Lycée Commercial de Kaolack: Renforcer l'autorité sur l'enfant," *Le Soleil,* 15 July 1983, 11.

46. Soppi M., "Témoignage—Autorisations maritales: Les 'malheurs' de Mme Soppi M.," *Cameroon Tribune,* 7 March 1989, 7.

47. "President Mobutu's Address to Parliament 28 Apr [sic]," Kinshasa Domestic Service (in French), 28 April 1981, cited in FBIS-AFR-81-082, 29 April 1981, V. S3.

48. "Le maréchal Mobutu annonce les grandes options du nouveau septennat," *Elima*, 6 December 1984, 5.

49. "Le maréchal Mobutu: 'Tout doit changer, tout va changer,'" *Elima*, 21–22 May 1988, 4–5.

50. "Paix, unité et cohésion," *Le Soleil*, 20 April 1984, 3.

51. "L'adresse du chef de l'Etat," *Le Soleil*, 7 April 1986, 3.

52. "Message du Chef de l'Etat—'Je ne saurai tolérer un état dans l'Etat,'" *Fraternité Matin*, 22 April 1983, 14–15.

53. Matthew Tostevin, "New Woman Leader Says She Is 'Hard as Steel,'" Reuters, 18 August 1996.

54. Wole Soyinka saw this in his drama about the perils of government after independence. Kongi, a prototypical dictator and "benevolent father," would have to "have his submission in full view of the people. The wayward child admits his errors and begs his father's forgiveness." See Wole Soyinka, *Kongi's Harvest* (London: Oxford University Press, 1967), 18–19.

55. "Condamné à mort pour crime crapuleux et grâcié par le Chef de l'État . . . ," *Fraternité Matin*, 28 April 1983, 20–21.

56. "Houphouet Reinstates Dismissed Public Workers," *Fraternité Matin*, 16 September 1985, 6–7 (in French), cited in FBIS-AFR-85-181, 18 September 1985, V., T2–T3. For other Ivoirian cases of the magnanimous, paternal pardon, see Michel Kouamé, "Le Chef de l'Etat recevant hier les membres de l'ancien bureau du SYNESCI: 'Rejoignez vos frères'," *Fraternité Matin*, 16 September 1988, 4; and "Houphouet-Boigny Urges Amnesty for Detainees," Abidjan Radio Côte d'Ivoire Chaine Nationale-Une (in French), 24 June 1992, cited in FBIS-AFR-92-143, 24 July 1992, 21–22.

57. Eugénie Douayéré, "Laurent Gbagbo au Président Houphouet-Boigny: 'Je vous présente mes excuses'," *Fraternité Matin*, 30 September 1988, 4.

58. For an analysis that attempts to explain various features of Houphouet's rule and style of leadership by reference to Akan-style features of government, see Jeanne Maddox Toungara, "The Apotheosis of Côte d'Ivoire's Nana Houphouet-Boigny," *Journal of Modern African Studies* 28, no. 1 (March 1990): 23–54.

59. "Democratic Party Said Planning to Rejoin KANU," Nairobi, Kenya News Agency (KNA) (in English), 13 January 1992, cited in FBIS-AFR-92-010, 15 January 1992, 7.

60. "Africa This Week," *West Africa*, 16–22 September 1996, 1460.

61. Angelo-Mobateli, "Bénéficiares de la magnaminité présidentielle—100 fils égarés réinsérés dans la société zaïroise," *Elima*, 1 July 1986, 9.

62. "Le Point: Une nouvelle preuve de magnanimité," Editorial, *Elima*, 16–17 March 1989, 1, 8. For other examples of Mobutu's penchant for paternal pardons, see Monsa Iyaka Duku, "Hier à Kinkole, à l'occasion de la journée du Poisson—Le Chef de l'Etat s'est adressé à la Nation," *Elima*, le 25 June 1987, 9; and "Mobutu Gives Address to Rally on Current Issues," Kinshasa, Association Zairoise de Presse (AZAP) (in French), 24 June 1987, cited in FBIS-AFR-87-123, 26 June 1987, VIII, A1.

63. "Pari optimiste sur la sagesse," *Le Soleil*, 19 May 1988, 2.

64. See Timamo Chrétien, "Bienvenue à ceux qui viennent de bénéficier des mesures de grâce," Column, *Cameroon Tribune*, 1–2 June, 1980, 6; "Le Président Biya a accordé des remises de peines aux prisonniers," *Cameroon Tribune*, 19 November 1982, 4; and "D'importantes remises de peines décidées par le chef de l'Etat: LE PARDON," *Cameroon Tribune*, 17 June 1988, 1.

65. See "Shagari Gives Account of His 100 Days Stewardship," *Daily Times,* 11 January 1980, 13–15; and "Gowon, 14 Others Pardoned," *Daily Times,* 2 October 1981, 1.

66. Prince Akweke Abyesinia Nwafor Orizu, *Insight into Nigeria,* 274.

67. See Staff Reporter, "Nyerere Pardons 1,900 Inmates," *Daily News,* 6 November 1980, 1; Attilio Tagalile, "Nyerere Pardons 2,494 Inmates," *Daily News,* 10 December 1983, 1; and "Mwinyi Pardons 835 Prisoners," *Daily News,* 9 December 1987, 1.

68. For other examples tending toward the more bureaucratic end of the continuum, see "Amnesty for Prisoners," *Daily Graphic,* 8 March 1982, 8; and "175 détenus grâciés," *Le Soleil,* 7 April 1986, 2.

69. "Senghor: Méthode et mesure," Interview, *Le Soleil,* 4–5 July 1981, 4.

70. "Limann Grants Amnesties . . . to Mark 1st Anniversary," *Daily Graphic,* 24 September 1980, 1.

71. "Le Président Biya accorde sa grâce aux condamnés à mort," *Cameroon Tribune,* 15 March 1984, 1.

72. An incomplete sampling of these works would include David J. Gould, *Bureaucratic Corruption and Underdevelopment in the Third World: The Case of Zaire* (Elmsford, N.Y.: Pergamon Press, 1980); Pierre Péan, *Affaires africaines* (Paris: Fayard, 1983); Young and Turner, *The Rise and Decline of the Zairian State;* Joseph, *Democracy and Prebendal Politics in Nigeria;* Bayart, *L'état en Afrique;* Robert E. Klitgaard, *Tropical Gangsters* (New York: Basic Books, 1990); Braeckman, *Le dinosaure;* Jean-Claude Willame, *L'automne d'un despotisme: Pouvoir, argent, et obéissance dans le Zaïre des années quatre-vingt* (Paris: Karthala, 1992); William Reno, *Corruption and State Politics in Sierra Leone* (Cambridge: Cambridge University Press, 1995); and Jean-François Bayart, Stephen Ellis, and Beatrice Hibou, *La criminalisation de l'état an Afrique* (Brussels: Editions Complexes, 1997).

73. Conférence épiscopale du Zaïre, 9 March 1990, reprinted in "Zaïre: Les évêques accusent," 21.

74. Joe Bradford Nyinah, "Lest We Forget," *People's Daily Graphic,* 15 May 1989, 1, 9; citation, 9.

75. Odafe Othihiwa, "We Mustn't Lose Hope—Bishop's Christmas Day Plea to Nigerians," *Daily Times,* 26 December 1983, 1.

76. "Nigeria: Going on Down," *Economist,* 8 June 1996, 48.

77. "Le Point: Des cadres gloutons," Editorial, *Elima,* 24 March 1981, 1, 7.

78. Ndongabi Masamuna, "A mon avis—Au nom des intérêts égoistes," Column, *Elima,* 25 March 1981, 5.

79. N'Zinga N'Singi, "Fait du jour: Les mains sales," Column, *Elima,* 18 February 1983, 2. Also see N'Zinga N'Singi, "Fait du jour: Procès contre l'égoisme et l'individualisme des Kinois," Column, *Elima,* 4 December 1982, 2.

80. Keme Ceesay, London, "Jammeh's Coup," Letter to the Editor, *West Africa,* 22–28 August 1994, 1457.

81. Oduori Radoli, Maseno, "Kenya's Image," Letter to the Editor, *Weekly Review,* 24 May 1991, 5.

82. See Tripp, *Changing the Rules.*

83. Estom A. Mongi, Dar es Salaam, "We Still Need Mwalimu," Letter to the Editor, *Daily News,* 13 October 1980, 5.

84. A. M. Mwakyembe, Mwere, Unguja, "Kama Wako, Nyerere Nambari Wani," *Uhuru* (Dar es Salaam), 31 May 1971.

85. Wilson Kaigarula, "Spearhead Socialist Revolution—Nyerere," *Daily News,* 23 November 1981, 1. Also see Fili Karashani, "War on Corruption Continues—Nyerere," *Daily News,* 6 February 1981, 1; "Juwata Raps Corruption," *Daily News,* 15 June 1981, 3; Isaac Mruma, "Nepotism Is Rampant—MP," *Daily News,* 27 June 1981, 3; Mkumbwa Ally, "Combating Sabotage: Mwalimu Reveals Shocking Rackets," *Daily News,* 6 April 1983, 1; and Yohana Kalengela, Iringa, "Corruption," Letter to the Editor, *Daily News,* 10 May 1983, 5.

86. "Comment: Pajero Politics," Editorial, *People's Daily Graphic,* 15 February 1986, 2.

87. "Le Point: Du respect des biens publics," Editorial, *Elima,* 29 October 1982, 1.

88. Lambert Mende Omalanga (rapporteur) and Tshilengi wa Kabamba (président) et al., "Rapport de la Commission des Biens Mal Acquis" (République du Zaïre, Conférence Nationale Souveraine, Commission des Biens Mal Acquis, Palais du Peuple, September 1992), 118 (CEDAF, Brussels, 2492—III).

89. "People Speak Their Minds on Corruption," *Daily News,* 2 March 1990, 1. On automobiles, also see "Millions Spent on Car Hires," *Daily News,* 22 January 1981, 1.

90. "Let Us Resist Greed, Power—Okogie," *Daily Times,* 1 January 1980, 5.

91. "Rigging Is a Crime—Bishop," *Daily Times,* 2 August 1983, 18.

92. "Saint-Louis—Communion entre le temporel et le spirituel," *Le Soleil,* 1 October 1982, 8.

93. "Daily Times Opinion: Memoranda for Ethical Committee," Editorial, *Daily Times,* 8 January 1983, 3.

94. "Daily Times Opinion: Nigeria's Ethical Reconstruction," Editorial, *Daily Times,* 1 November 1983, 3. In the Ghanaian context, also see Ntiamoah-Mafoh, "Corruption: Is It Just [a] Question of Degrading Morals?" *People's Daily Graphic,* 24 June 1985, 3. And for an outpouring of sentiment about the Jawara government's corrupt ministers, see the letters to the editor in *West Africa,* 8–14 August 1994, 1376.

95. "Comment: Creating Anti-Corruption Consciousness (1)," Editorial, *People's Daily Graphic,* 16 September 1983, 2.

96. See the now classic article by Peter Ekeh, "Colonialism and the Two Publics in Africa: A Theoretical Statement," *Comparative Studies in Society and History* 17, no. 1 (1975): 91–112; for a novelist's perception, see Chinua Achebe, *No Longer at Ease* (London: Heinemann, 1960).

97. Mobutu Sese Seko, "Discours devant le 2ième Congrès Ordinaire du MPR," November 1977, 12.

98. Lambert Mende Omalanga (rapporteur) and Tshilengi wa Kabamba (président) et al., "Rapport de la Commission des Biens Mal Acquis," 209. For a reasonably typical, and ineffectual, declaration of the MRP Central Committee against corruption, see "Déclaration N° 9/CC du 29 October 1986," *Elima,* 30 October 1986, 5–7.

99. Aliou Barry, "Linguere: Pas de place pour les magouilleurs," *Le Soleil,* 20–21 March 1982, 4.

100. "Le message du chef de l'Etat," *Le Soleil,* 5 April 1982, 1, 4; citation, 4.

101. Ibrahima Gaye, "Le sursaut par l'exemple," *Le Soleil,* 14 December 1983, 1, 5. For Nigerian instances of the same phenomenon (i.e., the voluntary renunciation of a portion of one's salary), see "₦5,000 Gift for Charity," *Daily Times,* 2 January 1981, 1; and "Twelve Legislators Accept Pay Cut," *Daily Times,* 20 May 1982, 40.

102. "Graphic View—Picking up the Pieces," Editorial, *Daily Graphic,* 5 January 1980, 2.

103. "PNDC Members Face Same Economic Hardships—Ndebugre," *People's Daily Graphic,* 20 May 1983, 1.

6. MATRIX II—GENDER AND GENERATION

1. My thinking on the position of women in the polity, gender, and related questions has been influenced by a variety of disparate scholarship. For stimulating treatments see, among others, Gerda Lerner, *The Creation of Patriarchy* (New York: Oxford University Press, 1986); Maurice Godelier, *The Making of Great Men: Male Domination and Power among the New Guinea Baruya,* trans. Rupert Swyer (Cambridge and Paris: Cambridge University Press and Editions de la Maison des Sciences de l'Homme, 1986); Virginia Sapiro, *A Vindication of Political Virtue: The Political Theory of Mary Wollstonecraft* (Chicago: University of Chicago Press, 1992), 166–185; and Oyeronke Oyewumi, *The Invention of Women: Making an African Sense of Western Gender Discourses* (Minneapolis: University of Minnesota Press, 1997).

For studies pertaining to middle Africa, see Janet MacGaffey, *Entrepreneurs and Parasites: The Struggle for Indigenous Capitalism in Zaïre* (Cambridge: Cambridge University Press, 1987), 165–183; Janet MacGaffey et al., *The Real Economy of Zaïre: The Contribution of Smuggling and Other Unofficial Activities to National Wealth* (Philadelphia: University of Pennsylvania Press, 1991), 26–40; Benoît Verhaegen, *Femmes de Kisangani: Combats pour la survie* (Louvain-la-Neuve and Paris: Centre d'Histoire de l'Afrique and L'Harmattan, 1990); Thérèse Verheust, "Portrait des femmes: Les intellectuelles zaïroises," *Les Cahiers du CEDAF,* no. 6 (October 1985): 1–150; Claire C. Robertson, *Sharing the Same Bowl: A Socioeconomic History of Women and Class in Accra, Ghana* (Bloomington: Indiana University Press, 1984); Ajoa Yeboah-Afari, *A Decade of Thoughts of a Native Daughter,* vol. 1 (Accra, Ghana: Graphic Corporation, 1988); Linda J. Beck, "Democratization and the 'Hidden Public': The Impact of Patronage Networks on the Political Participation of Senegalese Women," *Comparative Politics,* forthcoming; Regina Smith Oboler, *Women, Power, and Economic Change: The Nandi of Kenya* (Stanford, Calif.: Stanford University Press, 1985); David William Cohen and E. S. Atieno-Odhiambo, *Burying SM: The Politics of Knowledge and the Sociology of Power in Africa* (Portsmouth and London: Heinemann and James Currey, 1992); Luise White, *The Comforts of Home: Prostitution in Colonial Nairobi* (Chicago: University of Chicago Press, 1990); Margaret Strobel, *Muslim Women of Mombasa, 1890–1975* (New Haven, Conn.: Yale University Press, 1979); Christine Obbo, *African Women: Their Struggle for Economic Independence* (London: Zed Press, 1980); Tripp, *Changing the Rules*; and Mulligan-Hansel, "The Political Economy of Contemporary Women's Organizations in Tanzania."

2. Although not a country I am directly concerned with in this study, Uganda has become a major exception. See Tripp, *Women and Politics in Uganda.*

3. During fieldwork in Zaïre in 1975, I noticed that illiterate barmaids in Lisala were quite aware of *mbula ya basi,* or the United Nations Year of the Woman.

4. The comparative literature on the social construction of gender is large and growing. See, for example, Roger N. Lancaster, *Life Is Hard: Machismo, Danger, and the Intimacy of Power in Nicaragua* (Berkeley and Los Angeles: University of California Press, 1992); Matthew C. Gutmann, *The Meanings of Macho: Being a Man in Mexico City* (Berke-

ley and Los Angeles: University of California Press, 1996); Dorinne K. Kondo, *Crafting Selves: Power, Gender, and Discourses of Identity in a Japanese Workplace* (Chicago: University of Chicago Press, 1990); Robin M. LeBlanc, *Bicycle Citizens: The Political World of the Japanese Housewife* (Berkeley and Los Angeles: University of California, 1999); Rosabeth Moss Kanter, *Men and Women of the Corporation* (New York: Basic Books, 1977); and Judith Hicks Stiehm, *Bring Me Men and Women: Mandated Change at the U. S. Air Force Academy* (Berkeley and Los Angeles: University of California Press, 1981).

5. Mariama Diop (née Bâ), "'Il nous appartient de faire d'une porte un véritable portail,'" *Le Soleil*, 30 March 1979, 4. Consulted at the Archives Nationales, Dakar, Senegal, "Femmes II—Dossier." Her literary output includes Mariama Bâ, *So Long a Letter*, trans. Modupe Bode-Thomas (London: Heinemann, 1981), which adopts the voice of a woman caught in a polygamous marriage after her husband takes a second wife without consulting her. Also see Mariama Bâ, *Un chant écarlate* (Dakar, Senegal: Nouvelles Editions Africaines, 1984).

6. "Daily Times Opinion: Improving Women's Image," Editorial, *Daily Times,* 1 April 1985, 3.

7. For other comparable treatments, see "Le Point: Une compagne fidèle et une mère exemplaire," Editorial, *Elima,* 4 September 1984, 1, 7; Essolomwa Nkoy ea Linganga, "Cinq ans d'une union exemplaire," *Elima,* 1 May 1985, 1, 8; and Ifoly-Insilo, "La citoyenne Présidente Bobi Ladawa fait un don de vivres à l'hôpital général de Basankusu," *Elima,* 1 March 1989, 8.

8. Essolomwa Nkoy ea Linganga, "Heureux anniversaire, citoyenne Présidente," *Elima,* 4–5 September 1982, 1, 15. Also see "Mama Bobi Ladawa à l'Institut Mama Mobutu pour aveugles," *Elima,* 6 May 1984, 1.

9. For more on the role of Mama Bobi, as well as on the related cult of Mobutu's mother, Mama Yemo, see Schatzberg, *Dialectics of Oppression in Zaire,* 77–78.

10. "Abdou Diouf: 'Un seul impératif: la cohésion,'" *Le Soleil,* 2 August 1982, 7–8.

11. Dwamena Bekoe, "Free Yourselves From Reliance on Men . . . Nana Agyeman-Rawlings Advises Women," *People's Daily Graphic,* 4 July 1988, 1.

12. Casimir Datchoua Soupa, "'La femme camerounaise veut s'occuper des affaires de son pays': Déclare la présidente OFUNC du Ntem," interview, *Cameroon Tribune,* 20 April 1982, 4.

13. Patrice Etoundi Mbala, "Un mois au Cameroun—Mars 1989: Société—Femme," special monthly section, *Cameroon Tribune,* 9–10 April 1989, iv.

14. Zephania Musendo, "Kate Kamba: A Profile," *Sunday News,* 23 February 1983, 6.

15. "We Won't Overstay—IBB," *Daily Times,* 20 March 1986, 13. On this point, also see "Planners 'Leave Out Women,'" *Daily News,* 20 January 1990, 3.

16. "Un défi aux femmes," *Le Soleil,* 8 September 1983, 5.

17. "L'adresse du chef de l'Etat," *Le Soleil,* 7 April 1986, 3.

18. "Quinzaine de la femme," *Le Soleil,* 13 March 1986, 8 (emphasis added).

19. "Ideal Womanhood' Show," *People's Daily Graphic,* 25 August 1984, 8.

20. Rosemary Ardayfio, "Women's Participation in National Economy," *People's Daily Graphic,* 17 December 1984, 1.

21. For more on the coverage that blamed the market women for certain aspects of Ghana's economic crisis, see "Graphic View—Less than Equal Half," Editorial, *Daily Graphic,* 15 July 1980, 2; Bamfo-Darkwah, Cape Coast, "Will Our Women Be Sincere Now," Letter to Editor, *Daily Graphic,* 23 September 1980, 3; "Comment: Our Women

and Society," Editorial, *People's Daily Graphic,* 8 March 1983, 2; and Nelson Duah, "'Change Apathy to Revolution,'" *People's Daily Graphic,* 10 January 1984, 1.

22. "Queen '80: They Have Come a Long Way," *Daily Times,* 1 November 1980, 32.

23. "'Our Women Need to Improve their Reading Habit' Says a Librarian," *Daily Times,* 19 September 1980, 16.

24. Badjang ba Nken, "Des voeux à Mme Jeanne Irène Biya," *Cameroon Tribune,* 2–3 January 1989, 2.

25. See, for example, Ibrahima Gaye, "Que les femmes s'organisent et se mettent à la tâche," *Le Soleil,* 15–16 March 1980, 4; N'Zinga Nsingi, "Fait du jour: L'ANAPEZa pour qui?," *Elima,* 6 October 1982, 2; and Zenobia Ofori-Dankwa and Moureen Chidom, "'Women Must Make Their Impact Felt,'" *People's Daily Graphic,* 4 August 1984, 1, 4–5.

26. "Fatoumata Ka Présidente," *Le Soleil,* 29 November 1982, 4–5.

27. Theresa Ogbuibe, "A Beginning for Nigerian Women," *Daily Times,* 12 July 1985, 18.

28. "Women Urged to Assert Themselves in Political Dev.," *People's Daily Graphic,* 8 October 1987, 8–9.

29. For an enlightening treatment of this and related issues, see Lynn S. Khadiagala, "Law, Power, and Justice: The Adjudication of Women's Property Rights in Uganda" (Ph.D. diss., University of Wisconsin-Madison, 1999), 113 and passim.

30. Koja Olo, "The Woman Who Prayed for a Priest but Got a Politician," *Daily Times,* 15 February 1980, 16.

31. For other examples of the woman-as-adviser phenomenon, see Rose Hayford, "Mrs Rawlings Advises Youth," *People's Daily Graphic,* 29 October 1984, 1; Seke-Nsimba, "Bilan et perspectives de la politique de la femme 21 ans après l'existence du MPR," *Elima,* 16 May 1988, 18; and "Women Appeal to Govt," *Daily Times,* 18 April 1985, 2.

32. Timothy Njoya, "God's Policy on Marriage," text: Ephesians 5:21–33, sermon given at Nairobi University service, January 1984, in Njoya, *Out of Silence,* 17–18.

33. Michael G. Schatzberg, "Field Log," Lisala, Zaïre, 10 June 1975, 85.

34. "Few Debating the Issue of Political Inheritance," *The Weekly Nation,* 17 November 1989, 7–8, cited in FBIS-AFR-90-011-S, 17 January 1990, 3–4.

35. Hilary Ng'weno, "Letter from the Editor," *Weekly Review,* 19 July 1991, 1. On St. Kizito, also see "The Meru Tragedy," *Weekly Review,* 19 July 1991, 5–13; "Manslaughter Charges in Kizito Case," *Weekly Review,* 2 August 1991, 8; "St. Kizito's—A Year Later: Taking Stock," *Weekly Review,* 17 July 1992, 23–24; and H. Leslie Steeves, *Gender Violence and the Press: The St. Kizito Story* (Athens: Ohio University Center for International Studies, Africa Series no. 67, 1997).

36. "Sexism in Kenya," *Weekly Review,* 9 August 1991, 4–20, citation, 5.

37. Carlos Moore, *Fela, Fela: This Bitch of a Life* (London: Allison and Busby, 1982), 234, 235, 162, 235, cited in Iyorcha D. Ayu, *Essays in Popular Struggle* (Oguta, Nigeria: Zim Pan African Publishers, 1986), 39–40.

38. "Shun Equality Drive with Men, Women Advised," *Daily Times,* 20 February 1987, 13.

39. Amu-Nnadi, Chijioke, "Presidency to the Women," Column, *Daily Times,* 5 September 1987, 5.

40. Tola Ijituyi, "Vote for a Woman-President," *Daily Times,* 20 January 1988, 11.

41. Also see the essay by Olufunmilayo Fashola, "Towards a Woman President for Nigeria," *Daily Times,* 18 May 1988, 11.

42. Marshal Kebby, "Woman President in Nigeria?" *Daily Times,* 13 April 1989, 15.

43. Abramakeh Ologoh Lazarus, "Let's Try a Woman," Letter to the Editor, *Weekly Review,* 10 August 1990, 3.

44. Under Muslim law and custom, Ahidjo had four wives. Generally only the youngest appeared in public. See, A. Z. B., "Voeux à la présidence pour Mme Ahidjo," *Cameroon Tribune,* 15 January 1981, 3. On Mme. Biya, see, for example, "Noël dans 4 jours: Mme Biya distribue des cadeaux aux enfants," *Cameroon Tribune,* 21 December 1982, 1; Jacqueline Abena Nlomo, "Voeux à Mme Biya, dans un climat de symapthie," *Cameroon Tribune,* 6 January 1983, 3; Prosper Roger Effemba, "Fête spéciale de l'arbre de Noël à Ebang I—Mme Jeanne Biya apporte plus de 460 cadeaux aux enfants de l'école publique," *Cameroon Tribune,* 16 December 1983, 3; "Les enfants de Mvomeka'a en liesse." *Cameroon Tribune,* le 20 December 1983, 3; and "Des voeux de Nouvel An à Mme Biya—Une atmosphère de famille très sympathique," *Cameroon Tribune,* 6 January 1984, 1.

45. "Mme Aka Anghui au nom de l'AFI: Mme Houphouet-Boigny, mère spirituelle des femmes," *Fraternité Matin,* 6 January 1988, 6; and "600 layettes offertes à 52 maternités," *Fraternité Matin,* 3 January 1984, 3. Also see, "100 and Out: Ivory Coast's 'Mother of Mothers' Dies," Agence France-Presse (via Clari-net), 19 January 1998, C-afp@clari.net.

46. "Mme Abdou Diouf a inauguré le dispensaire de Darou Wahab," *Le Soleil,* 24 November 1981, 1; "Mme Abdou Diouf remet des moulins aux femmes de Djilor," *Le Soleil,* 17 March 1981, 1; and Aliou Barry, "Trois moulins à mil aux femmes de Djilor," *Le Soleil,* 17 March 1981, 3.

47. "Fête patronale de l'Eglise de Joal," *Le Soleil,* 4 February 1991, 6.

48. Papa Boubacar Samb, "Mme Elisabeth Diouf: Le social en bandoulière," *Le Soleil,* 25 February 1992, 9.

49. Ibrahim Babangida, *Quotes of a General: Selected Quotes of Major General Ibrahim Babangida, Chief of Army Staff (Nigeria) 01 Jan 1984–27 August 1985* (Surulere, Nigeria: Terry Publishers, 1987), 32, 48–49. Also see Maryam Babangida, *The Home Front: Nigerian Army Officers and Their Wives* (Ibadan, Nigeria: Fountain Publications, 1988). This short book is a guide for wives of army officers and adopts a tenor of subordination to the husband's military career throughout.

50. *Eze Onu Egwunwoke—His Vision and Mission* (n.p., 1980), 8–10.

51. "Wife Beating Deplored," *Daily News,* 12 October 1981, 3; and "Comment," Editorial, *Daily News,* 7 December 1983, 1.

52. Subira Kumbuka, "Jumbe Tells UWT: Women Rights Assured," *Daily News,* 11 March 1980, 1.

53. Ichikaeli Maro, "Mwinyi States Hurdles to Women's Progress," *Daily News,* 10 May 1988, 1.

54. B. C. Menunga, "Un mariage renvoyé pour mésentente sur l'option matrimoniale," *Cameroon Tribune,* 20 April 1982, 6.

55. Rose Mensah-Kutin, "Women for Change, A Woman's Real Place," Column, *People's Daily Graphic,* 3 March 1988, 7. On the same theme, also see "Why the 'Kalabule,'" *Daily Graphic,* 22 February 1982, 1, 4–5; "Law on Bereaved Spouse Signed," *People's Daily Graphic,* 16 June 1984, 5; and Akwele Ajavon, "Liberating the Woman in U. Volta—From Outmoded Customs and Prejudices," *People's Daily Graphic,* 18 June 1984, 3.

56. "Let's Direct Our Own Destiny—First Lady," *Daily Times,* 15 July 1987, 32.

57. For a sampling, see "Motion de soutien et de fidélité des mamans zaïroises au Président-Fondateur du MPR," *Elima,* 29 July 1986, 5; Elima, "Message du dimanche:

Un hommage mérité," Column, *Elima,* 18–19 May 1987, 1; and Lucie Mboto Fouda, "Le RDPC et l'intégration des femmes à la vie nationale—Exploiter l'immense capital de compétences et de générosité," *Cameroon Tribune,* 12 April 1985, 5.

58. "Pregnant Women Invade National Assembly," *Daily Times,* 27 August 1980, 1. Also see "200 Women Arrested by Police," *Daily Times,* 1 June 1982, 2, concerning a protest against an illegal acquisition of land.

59. "Women Marchers Defy Police," *Daily Times,* 28 January 1987, 24.

60. Lutumba Basunda, "S.O.S.: Les épouses des fonctionnaires et des enseignants menaceraient d'aller en grève contre leurs maris?" *Elima,* 6–7 May 1991.

61. See "Dailies on Need to Curtail 'Police Brutality,'" Nairobi, KTN Television (in English), 5 March 1992, cited in FBIS-AFR-92-044, 5 March 1992, 9; "People Express Solidarity with Political Prisoners," Nairobi, KTN Television (in English), 6 March 1992, cited in FBIS-AFR-92-046, 9 March 1992, 5; "A Strike for Freedom," *Weekly Review,* 6 March 1992, 3–6; and "Editorial Blames Strikers for Uhuru Park Unrest," Nairobi, Kenya Broadcasting Corporation Network (in English), 9 March 1992, cited in FBIS-AFR-92-047, 10 March 1992, 7–8.

62. Kwaku A. Danso, California, U.S., "Poor Leadership," Letter to the Editor, *West Africa,* 26 July–1 August 1993, 1288.

63. Nfansu Jaata, Kanifing, the Gambia, "Jammeh's Gambia," Letter to the Editor, *West Africa,* 17–23 June 1996, 936.

64. Ebenezer Williams, "The Love of Power," Op-Ed Column [?], *Daily Times,* 2 January 1981, 3. Also see, "Abiola: Ogunsanya Greets," *Daily Times,* 17 July 1982, 32.

65. Bara Diouf, " Face à nous-mêmes," Editorial, *Le Soleil,* 4 December 1980, 1.

66. Yahya Diallo, "La Retraite de Senghor: Un acte inédit," *Le Soleil,* 8 December 1980, 1, 3. For additional commentary, see Christian Valentin, Député de l'Assemblé Nationale [member, National Assembly], "Le départ," *Le Soleil,* 11 December 1980, 1, 3; and Bara Diouf, "Continuité," *Le Soleil,* 12 December 1980, 1.

67. L. S. Senghor, "Message à la nation de Senghor, chef de l'État," *Le Soleil,* 2 January 1981, 6. On the theme of generational change, also see "Senghor: Méthodes et mesure," interview, *Le Soleil,* 4 et 5 July 1981, 4.

68. For an excellent analysis of the economic context of the resignation, see Diop and Diouf, *Le Sénégal sous Abdou Diouf.*

69. "Présentation des vœux de la Cour Suprême: Allocution de M. le Premier Président de la Cour Suprême," 30 December 1980, typescript (Archives Nationales, Dakar, Senegal, "Dossier Politique—Senghor 1980").

70. Mamadou Gaye Dioumacor, "Quand démission et ouverture démocratique riment . . . ," Letter to the Editor, *Le Soleil,* 11 February 1981, 4.

71. Aly Kheury Ndaw, "Double héritage," *Le Soleil,* 16 January 1981, 1.

72. Abdelwaheb Abdallah, "De Senghor à Diouf: Une transition réussie," interview, *Le Soleil,* 24–25 April 1982, 9.

73. "Abdou Diouf: 'La démocratie sénégalaise n'est pas bipolaire elle est plurielle et pluraliste,'" *Le Soleil,* 29 June 1987, 7–8.

74. "Opposition Leader on Politics, Elections," BBC World Service (in English), 14 September 1987, cited in FBIS-AFR-87-179, 16 September 1987, 22.

75. Onomo Metala, "'Je ne m'éterniserai pas au pouvoir' avait déclaré le Président Ahidjo," *Cameroon Tribune,* 6 November 1982, 2.

76. Henri Bandolo, "Au terme de sa tournée provinciale, le Président Ahidjo se confie à Cameroon Tribune," interview, *Cameroon Tribune,* 29 January 1983, 2–3. For the ac-

tual resignation speech, see "Le Président Ahidjo annonce sa démission: Le Premier Ministre Paul Biya lui succède," *Cameroon Tribune,* 5 November 1982, 1.

77. Henri Bandolo, " De la scène au trône," Editorial, *Cameroon Tribune,* 6 November 1982, 1.

78. Mkumbwa Ally, "Think of New President," *Daily News,* 29 March 1984, 1; and "Crucial Political Developments," *Daily News,* 1 January 1985, 4.

79. Alex Mwita, Faculty of Medicine, Muhimbili, Dar es Salaam, "Mwalimu Talented," Letter to the Editor, *Daily News,* 9 January 1984, 9.

80. K. L. Kaboko, Dar es Salaam,"No Leader Is Indispensable," Letter to the Editor, *Daily News,* 29 December 1983, 5.

81. Bites Ruhata, Ministry of Water and Energy, Dar es Salaam,"There Will Always Be Someone," Letter to the Editor, *Daily News,* 2 January 1984, 7. Also see N. M. Kasaka, Dar es Salaam,"We Need New Leaders for New Ideas," Letter to the Editor, *Daily News,* 9 January 1984, 9.

82. Msema Kweli, Dar es Salaam, "Let's Uphold True Democracy," Letter to the Editor, *Daily News,* 12 January 1984, 11.

83. "Nyerere Comments on Retirement, Economy," BBC World Service (in English), 21 March 1985, cited in FBIS-AFR-85-057, 25 March 1985, R1.

84. "Nyerere Recommends Ali Hassan Mwinyi Succeed Him," Dar es Salaam Domestic Service (in Swahili), 15 August 1985, cited in FBIS-AFR-85-168, 19 August 1985, R3.

85. "Nyerere Explains Reasons for Retirement," Dar es Salaam Domestic Service (in Swahili), 21 June 1985, cited in FBIS-AFR-85-121, 24 June 1985, R1. On the general theme of generational rotation in a Tanzanian ethnic group, see Otto Bischofberger, *The Generation Classes of the Zanaki (Tanzania)* (Fribourg, Switzerland: University Press, 1972).

86. Mkumbwa Ally, "Mwalimu Meets Dar Leaders and Says . . . 'I Am Retiring in Sound Mental Health,'" *Daily News,* 7 June 1990, 1.

87. John Kulekana, "Mwalimu Praises Zanzibar Leaders," *Daily News,* 16 August 1990, 1.

88. Speech of Philippe Yacé, President of the National Assembly and Secretary-General of the PDCI-RDA, at the opening of the first legislative session of 1980, *Fraternité Matin,* 2 May 1980, 11.

89. "Political Bureau Meets; Future Reshuffle Announced," *Fraternité Matin,* 6 June 1986, 32 (in French), cited in FBIS-AFR-86-111, 10 June 1986, T3.

90. Gnagne Agnéro Lasme, "Passation de pouvoir à Orbaff—Les Abremans aux commandes," *Fraternité Matin,* 20–21 May 1989, 17.

7. DEMOCRACY AND THE LOGIC OF LEGITIMACY

1. Wyatt MacGaffey, *Kongo Political Culture: The Conceptual Challenge of the Particular* (Bloomington: Indiana University Press, 2000), 7.

2. J. D. Y. Peel, *Ijeshas and Nigerians: The Incorporation of a Yoruba Kingdom, 1890s–1970s* (Cambridge: Cambridge University Press, 1983).

3. Jan Vansina, *Paths in the Rainforest: Toward a History of Political Tradition in Equatorial Africa* (Madison: University of Wisconsin Press, 1990), 258, 259–260; citation, 259–260.

4. The next several paragraphs are in part drawn from Schatzberg, *Dialectics of Oppression in Zaire*, 82–89.

5. Bayart, *L'état en Afrique*.

6. See Robert O. Crummey, *The Formation of Muscovy, 1304–1613* (London and New York: Longman: 1987), 106–107; and David MacKenzie and Michael W. Curran, *A History of Russia, the Soviet Union, and Beyond,* 4th ed. (Belmont, Calif.: Wadsworth Publishing Co., 1993), 143. I am grateful to Edward Schatz for his clarification of this point.

7. Anne Norton, *Republic of Signs: Liberal Theory and American Popular Culture* (Chicago: University of Chicago Press, 1993), 97 (emphasis in original).

8. Even a small sampling of the voluminous literature on sorcery elsewhere in the world would be tedious. Nevertheless, see, among others, Bronislaw Malinowski, *Magic, Science, and Religion and Other Essays* (Glencoe, Ill.: Free Press, 1948); Paul Boyer and Stephen Nissenbaum, *Salem Possessed: The Social Origins of Witchcraft* (Cambridge, Mass.: Harvard University Press, 1974); Zora Hurston, "Hoodoo in America," *Journal of American Folklore* 44, no 174 (October–December 1931): 317–417; and Michael Taussig, *The Magic of the State* (New York: Routledge, 1997). On the political importance of astrology in India, see Mohan Ram, "The Power and Persuasion of India's Stargazers," *Far Eastern Economic Review* 126 (6 December 1984): 59–60; R. Dev Raj, "India-Culture: Astrologers Thrive in Political Uncertainty," Inter Press Service, New Delhi, 2 March 1998; and Harinder Baweja, "Stooping to Conquer," *India Today,* 31 May 1997.

9. Sills and Merton, "Social Science Quotations," 3.

10. Oyeronke Oyewumi, *The Invention of Women: Making an African Sense of Western Gender Discourses* (Minneapolis: University of Minnesota Press, 1997).

11. "President Moi Comments on Koigi wa Wamwere," Nairobi Domestic Service (in Swahili), 15 October 1990, cited in FBIS-AFR-90-200, 16 October 1990, 5.

12. "Rawlings Explains," *Daily Graphic,* 6 January 1982, 1, 3, 4–5.

13. Farida Ayari, "Radio France Talks to Rawlings," interview, *People's Daily Graphic,* 6 May 1985, 3.

14. An influential example has been Samuel P. Huntington, *The Third Wave: Democratization in the Late Twentieth Century* (Norman: University of Oklahoma Press, 1991).

15. Michael Bratton and Nicolas van de Walle, *Democratic Experiments in Africa: Regime Transitions in Comparative Perspective* (Cambridge: Cambridge University Press, 1997), 12–13.

16. Bratton and van de Walle, *Democratic Experiments in Africa, 13.*

17. For a somewhat skeptical view of elections in Africa, see Said Adejumobi, "Elections in Africa: A Fading Shadow of Democracy," *International Political Science Review* 21, no. 1 (2000): 59–73.

18. Schaffer, *Democracy in Translation,* 53–65 and passim.

19. Schaffer, *Democracy in Translation,* 75.

20. Schaffer, *Democracy in Translation,* 95–98, 115; citation, 115.

21. Weber, *Economy and Society.*

22. Rodney Barker, *Political Legitimacy and the State* (Oxford: Clarendon Press, 1990), 11.

23. Richard M. Merelman, "On Legitimalaise in the United States: A Weberian Analysis," *Sociological Quarterly* 39, no. 3 (1998): 351–368, citation, 351.

24. "Comment: Jerry Explains the Human Factor," Editorial, *People's Daily Graphic*, 20 January 1984, 2 (emphasis added).

25. David Beetham, *The Legitimation of Power* (Atlantic Highlands, N.J.: Humanities Press International, 1991), 19–20.

26. On the question of emotion in image and metaphor, see Harold Scheub, *Story* (Madison: University of Wisconsin Press, 1998), 14, 21 and passim.

27. Frantz Fanon, *Les damnés de la terre,* preface by Jean-Paul Sartre, 2d ed. (Paris: François Maspero, 1961); and W. Arthur Lewis, *Politics in West Africa* (New York: Oxford University Press, 1965).

28. Here I part company with Guiseppe di Palma, who argues that "political democratization should not rightfully be seen as a prolonged affair." He also, mistakenly, sees political legitimacy as "behavioral compliance." See Guiseppe di Palma, *To Craft Democracies: An Essay on Democratic Transitions* (Berkeley and Los Angeles: University of California Press, 1990), 153, 12.

29. On this point, see Chinua Achebe, *The Trouble with Nigeria* (Enugu, Nigeria: Fourth Dimension Publishers, 1983).

30. Kwame Nkrumah, *Ghana: The Autobiography of Kwame Nkrumah* (1957, New York: International Publishers, 1971).

31. Kaye Whiteman, "The Gallic Paradox," *Africa Report* (January–February 1991): 17–20, citation, 18.

32. On Kabila, see Schatzberg, "Beyond Mobutu: Kabila and the Congo," 70–84.

33. Excellent collections of essays on recent Nigerian politics may be found in Paul A. Beckett and Crawford Young, eds., *Dilemmas of Democracy in Nigeria* (Rochester, N.Y.: University of Rochester Press, 1997); and Larry Diamond, Anthony Kirk-Greene, and Oyelele Oyediran, eds., *Transition without End: Nigerian Politics and Civil Society under Babangida* (Boulder, Colo.: Lynne Rienner, 1997).

34. See Bratton and van de Walle, *Democratic Experiments in Africa,* 10. Aili Tripp usefully notes that in much of Africa "the process has not moved much beyond the holding of elections. The patterns of neopatrimonial rule, personal rule, and state-based clientelism remain intact and are simply manifesting themselves in a multiparty context." See Aili Mari Tripp, "Political Reform in Tanzania: The Struggle for Associational Autonomy," *Comparative Politics* 32, no. 2 (January 2000): 191–214; citation, 212.

35. The experience of Haiti also demonstrates this point.

SELECTED BIBLIOGRAPHY

NEWSPAPERS AND NEWSMAGAZINES

Cameroon Tribune. Yaoundé, Cameroon. 1980–1989.
Daily Graphic and *People's Daily Graphic.* Accra, Ghana. 1980–1989.
Daily News and *Sunday News.* Dar es Salaam, Tanzania. 1980–1990.
Daily Times. Lagos, Nigeria. 1980–1989.
Elima. Kinshasa, Zaïre. 1980–1990.
Foreign Broadcast Information Service (FBIS). *Daily Report: Sub-Saharan Africa.* Washington,
    D.C. 1980–1994.
Fraternité Matin. Abidjan, Côte d'Ivoire. 1980–1989.
Le Soleil. Dakar, Senegal. 1980–1989, 1991.
Weekly Review. Nairobi, Kenya. 1983–1996.
West Africa. London. 1983–1996.

BOOKS, ARTICLES, AND MISCELLANEOUS

"Discours de Mgr. Monsengwo, reprise solennelle des travaux de la CNS," 6 April 1992.
    Mimeographed text. CEDAF (Brussels). Zaïre: Documents Relatifs à la Conférence
    Nationale. 2343 III, 1991.
"Lettre pastorale de Mgr. Pirigsha à propos des prochaines élections." *Zaïre-Afrique,* no. 164
    (April 1982): 247–249.
"Présentation des voeux de la Cour Suprême: Allocution de M. le Premier Président de la
    Cour Suprême," 30 December 1980, typescript. Archives Nationales, Dakar, Senegal,
    "Dossier Politique—Senghor 1980."
"Sakombi parle de Kabila et . . . de Mobutu," *Le Soft International,* no. 720, 12–18 Decem-
    ber 1997. In http://www.lesoftonline.net/05–03.articles.html.

Selected Bibliography

Abbés Kinois. "Bâtir la nation, une tâche pour tous les chrétiens," text of 5 February 1992. CEDAF (Brussels). Dossier sur les évènements récents au Zaïre (January–February 1992). 2358 III 1992.

Achebe, Chinua. *No Longer at Ease.* London: Heinemann, 1960.

———. *The Trouble with Nigeria.* Enugu, Nigeria: Fourth Dimension Publishers, 1983.

Adejumobi, Said. "Elections in Africa: A Fading Shadow of Democracy." *International Political Science Review* 21, no. 1 (2000): 59–73.

Adiaffi, Jean-Marie. *La carte d'identité.* Abidjan: CEDA, 1980.

Afigo, A. E. (Commissioner for Education, Imo State). "The Development of Improved Work Ethic among Nigerian Workers." In Imo State, Nigeria, Establishment and Training Department, Cabinet Office, Owerri, "Report of the Public Seminars on the Objective, Policies, and Programmes of the Military Administration, 23–24 August and 24–25 September, 1984." Owerri, Nigeria: Government Printer, 1984.

Allan, Maina. *One by One.* With a touch by David G. Maillu. Nairobi: Comb Books, 1975.

Amon d'Aby, F. J. *Proverbes populaires de Côte d'Ivoire.* Abidjan: CEDA, 1984.

Anderson, Benedict R. O'G. "The Idea of Power in Javanese Culture." In *Language and Power: Exploring Political Cultures in Indonesia,* compiled by Benedict R. O'G. Anderson, 17–78. Ithaca, N.Y.: Cornell University Press, 1990.

Appiah, Kwame Anthony. *In My Father's House: Africa in the Philosophy of Culture.* Oxford: Oxford University Press, 1992.

Arens, W., and Ivan Karp, "Introduction." In *Creativity of Power: Cosmology and Action in African Societies,* edited by W. Arens and Ivan Karp, xi–xxix. Washington, D.C.: Smithsonian Institution Press, 1989.

Ashforth, Adam. *The Politics of Official Discourse in Twentieth-Century South Africa.* Oxford: Clarendon Press, 1990.

Atieno-Odhiambo, E. S. "Democracy and the Ideology of Order in Kenya." In *The Political Economy of Kenya,* edited by Michael G. Schatzberg, 177–201. New York: Praeger, 1987.

Awolowo, Obafemi. "I Have Brought Back with Me a Big Cargo of Satisfaction." In *Voice of Wisdom: Selected Speeches of Chief Obafemi Awolowo,* vol. 3. Compiled by Chief Obafemi Awolowo. Akure, Nigeria: Fagbamigbe Publishers, 1981.

———. *Awo Says Yes: Being His 1983 Presidential Election Acceptance Speech in Lagos on January 29, 1983 at Tafawa Balewa Square.* Lagos, Nigeria: Directorate of Research and Publicity, UPN National Secretariat, 1983.

Ayu, Iyorcha D. *Essays in Popular Struggle.* Oguta, Nigeria: Zim Pan African Publishers, 1986.

Bâ, Mariama. *So Long a Letter.* Translated by Modupe Bode-Thomas. London: Heinemann, 1981.

———. *Un chant écarlate.* Dakar: Nouvelles Editions Africaines, 1984.

Babangida, Ibrahim. *Quotes of a General: Selected Quotes of Major General Ibrahim Babangida, Chief of Army Staff (Nigeria) 01 Jan 1984–27 August 1985.* Surulere, Nigeria: Terry Publishers, 1987.

Babangida, Maryam. *The Home Front: Nigerian Army Officers and Their Wives.* Ibadan, Nigeria: Fountain Publications, 1988.

Bachrach, Peter, and Morton S. Baratz. *Power and Poverty: Theory and Practice.* New York: Oxford University Press, 1970.

Barkan, Joel D., Michael McNulty, and M. A. Ayeni. "'Hometown' Voluntary Associations, Local Development, and the Emergence of Civil Society in Western Nigeria." *Journal of Modern African Studies* 29, no. 3 (1991): 457–480.

Selected Bibliography

Barker, Rodney. *Political Legitimacy and the State.* Oxford: Clarendon Press, 1990.

Baweja, Harinder. "Stooping to Conquer." *India Today,* 31 May 1997.

Bayart, Jean-François. *L'état au Cameroun.* Paris: Presses de la Fondation Nationale des Sciences Politiques, 1979.

———. "One-Party Government and Political Development in Cameroon." In *An African Experiment in Nation-Building: The Bilingual Cameroon Republic since Reunification,* edited by Ndiva Kofele-Kale, 159–187. Boulder, Colo.: Westview, 1980.

———. *L'état en Afrique: La politique du ventre.* Paris: Fayard, 1989.

———. "La cité cultuelle en Afrique noire." In *Religion et modernité politique en Afrique noire: Dieu pour tous et chacun pour soi,* edited by Jean-François Bayart, 299–310. Paris: Karthala, 1993.

Bayart, Jean-François, Stephen Ellis, and Beatrice Hibou. *La Criminalisation de l'état an Afrique.* Brussels: Editions Complexes, 1997.

Beck, Linda J. "'Patrimonial Democrats' in a Culturally Plural Society: Democratization and Political Accommodation in the Patronage Politics of Senegal." Ph.D. diss., University of Wisconsin-Madison, 1996.

———. "Democratization and the 'Hidden Public': The Impact of Patronage Networks on the Political Participation of Senegalese Women." *Comparative Politics* (forthcoming).

Beckett, Paul A., and Crawford Young, eds. *Dilemmas of Democracy in Nigeria.* Rochester, N.Y.: University of Rochester Press, 1997.

Beetham, David. *The Legitimation of Power.* Atlantic Highlands, N.J.: Humanities Press International, 1991.

Benson, G. P. "Ideological Politics versus Biblical Hermeneutics: Kenya's Protestant Churches and the *Nyayo* State." In *Religion and Politics in East Africa,* edited by Holger Bernt Hansen and Michael Twaddle, 177–199. London: James Currey, 1995.

Berger, Peter L., and Thomas Luckmann. *The Social Construction of Reality: A Treatise in the Sociology of Knowledge.* Garden City, N.Y.: Doubleday-Anchor, 1966.

Bernault, Florence. *Démocraties ambiguës en Afrique centrale—Congo-Brazzaville, Gabon: 1940–1965.* Paris: Karthala, 1996.

Bezy, Fernand, Jean-Philippe Peemans, and Jean-Marie Wautelet. *Accumulation et sous-développement au Zaïre 1960–1980.* Louvain-la-Neuve, Belgium: Presses Universitaires de Louvain, 1981.

Bischofberger, Otto. *The Generation Classes of the Zanaki (Tanzania).* Fribourg, Switzerland: University Press, 1972.

Blier, Suzanne Preston. *African Vodun: Art, Psychology, and Power.* Chicago: University of Chicago Press, 1995.

Bockie, Simon. *Death and the Invisible Powers: The World of Kongo Belief.* Bloomington: Indiana University Press, 1993.

Boulding, Kenneth E. *Three Faces of Power.* Newbury Park, Calif.: Sage, 1989.

Boyer, Paul, and Stephen Nissenbaum. *Salem Possessed: The Social Origins of Witchcraft.* Cambridge, Mass.: Harvard University Press, 1974.

Braeckman, Colette. *Le dinosaure: Le Zaïre de Mobutu.* Paris: Fayard, 1992.

Bratton, Michael. "Beyond the State: Civil Society and Associational Life in Africa." *World Politics* 41, no. 3 (1989): 407–430.

Bratton, Michael, and Nicolas van de Walle. *Democratic Experiments in Africa: Regime Transitions in Comparative Perspective.* Cambridge: Cambridge University Press, 1997.

Bruner, Jerome. *Actual Minds, Possible Worlds.* Cambridge, Mass.: Harvard University Press, 1986.

Selected Bibliography

Burke, Kenneth. *A Grammar of Motives.* New York: Prentice-Hall, 1945.

Callaghy, Thomas M. *The State-Society Struggle: Zaire in Comparative Perspective.* New York: Columbia University Press, 1984.

Ciekawy, Diane, and Peter Geschiere, eds. *African Studies Review* 41, no. 3 (December 1999): 1–209.

Cohen, Abner. *Two-Dimensional Man: An Essay on the Anthropology of Power and Symbolism in Complex Society.* Berkeley: University of California Press, 1974.

Cohen, David William, and E. S. Atieno-Odhiambo. *Siaya: The Historical Anthropology of an African Landscape.* London: James Currey, 1989.

———. *Burying SM: The Politics of Knowledge and the Sociology of Power in Africa.* Portsmouth and London: Heinemann and James Currey, 1992.

Conférence épiscopale du Zaïre. "Zaïre: Les évêques accusent." *Jeune Afrique,* no. 1527, 9 April 1990, 18–25.

Coulon, Christian. *Le marabout et le prince: Islam et pouvoir au Senegal.* Paris: A. Pedone, 1981.

Cruise O'Brien, Donal B. *The Mourides of Senegal: The Political and Economic Organization of an Islamic Brotherhood.* Oxford: Clarendon Press, 1971.

Crummey, Robert O. *The Formation of Muscovy, 1304–1613.* London and New York: Longman: 1987.

Dadié, Bernard B. *Les vois dans le vent (tragédie).* Abidjan: Nouvelles Editions Africaines, 1982. [Original edition by Editions Clés, Yaoundé, 1970].

Dahl, Robert A. *Modern Political Analysis.* Englewood Cliffs, N.J.: Prentice-Hall, 1963.

———. "Power." In *International Encyclopedia of the Social Sciences,* vol. 12: 405–415. New York: Macmillan and Free Press, 1968.

Dauch, Gene, and Denis Martin. *L'héritage de Kenyatta: La transition politique au Kenya (1975–1982).* Paris: Presses Universitaires d'Aix-Marseilles and L'Harmattan, 1985.

Davidson, Basil. *The Black Man's Burden: Africa and the Curse of the Nation-State.* New York: Times Books, 1992.

de Certeau, Michel. *L'invention du quotidien, 1: Arts de faire.* Paris: Union Générale d'Editions, 1980.

de Craemer, Willy, and Renée C. Fox. *The Emerging Physician.* Stanford, Calif.: Hoover Institution Press, 1968.

Decalo, Samuel. "Modalities of Civil-Military Stability in Africa." *Journal of Modern African Studies* 27, no. 4 (1989): 547–578.

di Palma, Giuseppe. *To Craft Democracies: An Essay on Democratic Transitions.* Berkeley and Los Angeles: University of California Press, 1990.

Diamond, Larry, Anthony Kirk-Greene, and Oyelele Oyediran, eds. *Transition without End: Nigerian Politics and Civil Society under Babangida.* Boulder, Colo.: Lynne Rienner, 1997.

Diop, Abdoulaye-Bara. *La société Wolof; Tradition et changement: Les systèmes d'inégalité et de domination.* Paris: Karthala, 1981.

Diop [née Bâ], Mariama. "'Il nous appartient de faire d'une porte un véritable portail.'" *Le Soleil,* 30 March 1979, 4. Consulted at the Archives Nationales, Dakar, Senegal, "Femmes II—Dossier."

Diop, Momar Coumba, et Mamadou Diouf. *Le Sénégal sous Abdou Diouf: Etat et société.* Paris: Karthala, 1990.

Douglas, Mary. *Purity and Danger: An Analysis of Concepts of Pollution and Taboo.* Harmondsworth: Penguin, 1970 [1966].

Dungia, Emmanuel. *Mobutu et l'argent du Zaïre: Révélations d'un diplomate, ex-agent des services secrets.* Paris: L'Harmattan, 1993.

Selected Bibliography

———. *La pieuvre tropicale: Les tentacules de Mobutu.* Brussels: Emmanuel Dungia, n.d.

Eckstein, Harry. "A Theory of Stable Democracy." In *Division and Cohesion in Democracy: A Study of Norway,* 223–288. Princeton, N.J.: Princeton University Press, 1966.

———. *The Natural History of Congruence Theory* (Monograph Series in World Affairs 18, no. 2). Denver: University of Denver, 1980.

———. "Unfinished Business: Reflections on the Scope of Comparative Politics. *Comparative Political Studies* 3, no. 4 (August 1998): 505–534.

Eckstein, Harry, and Ted Robert Gurr. *Patterns of Authority: A Structural Basis for Political Inquiry.* New York: John Wiley and Sons, 1975.

Edelman, Murray. *Constructing the Political Spectacle.* Chicago: University of Chicago Press, 1988.

———. *From Art to Politics: How Artistic Creations Shape Political Conceptions.* Chicago: University of Chicago Press, 1995.

Eickelman Dale F., and James Piscatori. *Muslim Politics.* Princeton, N.J.: Princeton University Press, 1997.

Ekeh, Peter. "Colonialism and the Two Publics in Africa: A Theoretical Statement." *Comparative Studies in Society and History* 17, no. 1 (1975): 91–112.

Ellis, Richard J. *American Political Cultures.* New York: Oxford University Press, 1993.

Ellis, Stephen, and Gerrie Ter Haar. "Religion and Politics in Sub-Saharan Africa." *Journal of Modern African Studies* 36, no. 2 (June 1998): 175–201.

Evans-Pritchard, E. E. *Witchcraft, Oracles, and Magic among the Azande.* Oxford: Clarendon Press, 1937.

Eze Onu Egwunwoke—His Vision and Mission. N.p., 1980.

Fabian, Johannes. *Power and Performance: Ethnographic Explorations through Proverbial Wisdom and Theater in Shaba, Zaire.* Madison: University of Wisconsin Press, 1990.

———. *Remembering the Present: Painting and Popular History in Zaire.* Berkeley: University of California Press, 1996.

Fanon, Frantz. *Les damnés de la terre.* Preface by Jean-Paul Sartre. 2nd ed. Paris: François Maspero, 1961.

Farah, Nuruddin. *Secrets.* New York: Arcade Publishing, 1998.

Feierman, Steven. *Peasant Intellectuals: Anthropology and History in Tanzania.* Madison: University of Wisconsin Press, 1990.

Fernandez, James W. *Bwiti: An Ethnography of the Religious Imagination in Africa.* Princeton, N.J.: Princeton University Press, 1982.

Fisiy, Cyprian F., and Peter Geschiere. "Judges and Witches, or How Is the State to Deal with Witchcraft? Examples from Southeast Cameroon." *Cahiers d'études africaines* 30, no. 2 (1990): 135–156.

———. "Sorcery, Witchcraft, and Accumulation: Regional Variations in South and West Cameroon." *Critique of Anthropology* 11, no. 3 (1991): 251–278.

Foucault, Michel. *The Archaeology of Knowledge and the Discourse on Language.* Translated by A. M. Sheridan Smith. New York: Pantheon, 1972.

———. *The Order of Things: An Archaeology of the Human Sciences.* New York: Vintage, 1973.

———. *Discipline and Punish: The Birth of the Prison.* Translated by Alan Sheridan. New York: Pantheon, 1977.

———. "The Subject and Power." In *Art after Modernism: Rethinking Representation,* edited by Brian Wallis, 417–442. Boston and New York: David R. Godine and New Museum of Contemporary Art, 1984.

————. *Power/Knowledge: Selected Interviews and Other Writings, 1972–1977.* Edited and translated by Colin Gordon. New York: Pantheon, 1984.

Gans, Herbert. *Deciding What's News: A Study of CBS Evening News, NBC Nightly News, Newsweek, and Time.* New York: Random House, 1979.

Geertz, Clifford. *The Interpretation of Cultures: Selected Essays.* New York: Basic Books, 1973.

————. *Local Knowledge: Further Essays in Interpretive Anthropology.* New York: Basic Books, 1983.

Geschiere, Peter. "Sorcery and the State: Popular Modes of Action among the Maka of Southeast Cameroon." *Critique of Anthropology* 8, no. 1 (1988): 35–63.

————. *Sorcellerie et politique en Afrique: La viande des autres.* Paris: Karthala, 1995.

Gifford, Paul. *African Christianity: Its Public Role.* Bloomington: Indiana University Press, 1998.

Gilbert, Michelle. "Sources of Power in Akuropon-Akuapem: Ambiguity in Classification." In *Creativity of Power: Cosmology and Action in African Societies,* edited by W. Arens and Ivan Karp, 59–90. Washington, D.C.: Smithsonian Institution Press, 1989.

Gilroy, Paul. *The Black Atlantic: Modernity and Double Consciousness.* Cambridge, Mass.: Harvard University Press, 1993.

Gitari, David M. "The Church's Witness to the Living God in Seeking Just Political, Social, and Economic Structures in Contemporary Africa." In *Witnessing to the Living God in Contemporary Africa: Findings and Papers of the Inaugural Meeting of Africa Theological Fraternity,* edited by David M. Gitari and G. P. Benson, 119–140. Nairobi: Africa Theological Fraternity, Uzima Press, 1986.

————. *Let the Bishop Speak.* Nairobi: Uzima Press, 1988.

Githinji, Sam. *Struggling for Survival.* Nairobi: Kenya Literature Bureau, 1983.

Godelier, Maurice. *The Making of Great Men: Male Domination and Power among the New Guinea Baruya.* Translated by Rupert Swyer. Cambridge and Paris: Cambridge University Press and Editions de la Maison des Sciences de l'Homme, 1986.

Goodman, Nelson. *Ways of Worldmaking.* Indianapolis: Hackett, 1978.

————. *Of Mind and Other Matters.* Cambridge, Mass.: Harvard University Press, 1984.

Gottlieb, Alma. "Witches, Kings, and the Sacrifice of Identity or the Power of Paradox and the Paradox of Power among the Beng of Ivory Coast." In *Creativity of Power: Cosmology and Action in African Societies,* edited by W. Arens and Ivan Karp, 245–272. Washington, D.C.: Smithsonian Institution Press, 1989.

Gould, David J. *Bureaucratic Corruption and Underdevelopment in the Third World: The Case of Zaire.* Elmsford, N.Y.: Pergamon Press, 1980.

Gramsci, Antonio. *Selections from the Prison Notebooks of Antonio Gramsci.* Edited and translated by Quintin Hoare and Geoffrey Newell Smith. New York: International Publishers, 1971.

Gugler, Josef. "African Literary Comment on Dictators: Wole Soyinka's Plays and Nuruddin Farah's Novels." *Journal of Modern African Studies* 26, no. 1 (March 1988): 171–177.

Gutmann, Matthew C. *The Meanings of Macho: Being a Man in Mexico City.* Berkeley and Los Angeles: University of California Press, 1996.

Hammoudi, Abdellah. *Master and Disciple: The Cultural Foundations of Moroccan Authoritarianism.* Chicago: University of Chicago Press, 1997.

Harbeson, John W., Donald Rothchild, and Naomi Chazan, eds. *Civil Society and the State in Africa.* Boulder, Colo.: Lynne Rienner, 1994.

Haugerud, Angelique. *The Culture of Politics in Modern Kenya.* Cambridge: Cambridge University Press, 1995.

Selected Bibliography

Haynes, Jeff. *Religion and Politics in Africa.* Nairobi and London: East African Educational Publishers and Zed Books, 1996.

Holland, Dorothy, and Naomi Quinn, eds. *Cultural Models in Language and Thought.* Cambridge: Cambridge University Press, 1987.

Hours, Bernard. *L'état sorcier: Santé publique et société au Cameroun.* Paris: L'Harmattan, 1985.

Hunt, Nancy Rose. *A Colonial Lexicon: Of Birth Ritual, Medicalization, and Mobility in the Congo.* Durham, N.C.: Duke University Press, 1999.

Huntington, Samuel P. *The Third Wave: Democratization in the Late Twentieth Century.* Norman: University of Oklahoma Press, 1991.

Hurston, Zora. "Hoodoo in America." *Journal of American Folklore* 44, no. 174 (October–December 1931): 317–417.

Hutchinson, Sharon E. *Nuer Dilemmas: Coping with Money, War, and the State.* Berkeley and Los Angeles: University of California Press, 1996.

Hyden, Goran, and Michael Bratton, eds. *Governance and Politics in Africa.* Boulder, Colo.: Lynne Rienner, 1992.

Ilunga Kabongo. "Déroutante Afrique ou la syncope d'un discours." *Canadian Journal of African Studies* 18, no. 1 (1984): 13–22.

Inglehart, Ronald. "The Renaissance of Political Culture." *American Political Science Review* 82, no. 4 (1988): 1203–1230.

———. *Culture Shift in Advanced Industrial Society.* Princeton, N.J.: Princeton University Press, 1990.

———. *Modernization and Postmodernization: Cultural, Economic, and Political Change in Forty-three Societies.* Princeton, N.J.: Princeton University Press, 1997.

Janzen, John M. *The Quest for Therapy in Lower Zaire.* Berkeley and Los Angeles: University of California Press, 1978.

Jewsiewicki, Bogumil. *Naître et mourir au Zaïre: Un demi-siècle d'histoire au quotidien.* Paris: Karthala, 1993.

Jones, Charles O. "Mistrust but Verify: Memoirs of the Reagan Era." *American Political Science Review* 83, no. 3 (September 1989): 981–988.

Joseph, Richard A. *Democracy and Prebendal Politics in Nigeria: The Rise and Fall of the Second Republic.* Cambridge: Cambridge University Press, 1987.

July, Robert W. *The Origins of Modern African Thought: Its Development in West Africa during the Nineteenth and Twentieth Centuries.* London: Faber and Faber, 1968.

Kamau, John C. (General Secretary), and David M. Gitari (Bishop, Chairman). "Foreword." In *A Christian View of Politics in Kenya: Love, Peace and Unity.* By National Christian Council of Kenya (NCCK). Nairobi: Uzima Press, 1983.

Kanter, Rosabeth Moss. *Men and Women of the Corporation.* New York: Basic Books, 1977.

Kaplan, Abraham. *The Conduct of Inquiry: Methodology for Behavioral Science.* San Francisco: Chandler, 1964.

Khadiagala, Lynn S. "Law, Power, and Justice: The Adjudication of Women's Property Rights in Uganda." Ph.D. diss., University of Wisconsin-Madison, 1999.

Kirk-Greene, A. H. M. *'Stay by Your Radios': Documentation for a Study of Military Government in Tropical Africa.* Africa Social Research Documents, vol. 12. Leiden and Cambridge: Afrika-Studiecentrum and African Studies Centre, 1981.

Klitgaard, Robert E. *Tropical Gangsters.* New York: Basic Books, 1990.

Koba Bashibirira M. "Incidences magico-religieuses sur le pouvoir africain." *Cahiers des religions africaines* 19, no. 37 (January 1985): 39–51.

Kondo, Dorinne K. *Crafting Selves: Power, Gender, and Discourses of Identity in a Japanese Workplace*. Chicago: University of Chicago Press, 1990.

Kourouma, Ahmadou. *Les soleils des indépendances*. Paris: Editions du Seuil, 1970.

Laitin, David D. *Hegemony and Culture: Politics and Religious Change among the Yoruba*. Chicago and London: University of Chicago Press, 1986.

———. "Toward a Political Science Discipline: Authority Patterns Revisited." *Comparative Political Studies* 31, no. 4 (1998): 423–443.

Lakoff, George. *Moral Politics: What Conservatives Know That Liberals Don't*. Chicago: University of Chicago Press, 1996.

Lakoff, George, and Mark Johnson. *Metaphors We Live By*. Chicago: University of Chicago Press, 1980.

Lan, David. *Guns and Rain: Guerrillas and Spirit Mediums in Zimbabwe*. London, Berkeley, and Los Angeles: James Currey and University of California Press, 1985.

Lancaster, Roger N. *Life Is Hard: Machismo, Danger, and the Intimacy of Power in Nicaragua*. Berkeley and Los Angeles: University of California Press, 1992.

Lane, Christel. *Rites of Rulers: Ritual in Industrial Society—The Soviet Case*. Cambridge: Cambridge University Press, 1981.

Le Vine, Victor T. "Leadership and Regime Changes in Perspective." In *The Political Economy of Cameroon,* edited by Michael G. Schatzberg and I. William Zartman, 20–52. New York: Praeger, 1986.

LeBlanc, Robin M. *Bicycle Citizens: The Political World of the Japanese Housewife*. Berkeley and Los Angeles: University of California, 1999.

Lentz, Carola. "The Chief, the Mine Captain, and the Politician: Legitimating Power in Northern Ghana." *Africa* 68, no. 1 (1998): 46–67.

Lerner, Gerda. *The Creation of Patriarchy*. New York: Oxford University Press, 1986.

Lewis, W. Arthur. *Politics in West Africa*. New York: Oxford University Press, 1965.

Lindfors, Bernth. *Popular Literatures in Africa*. Trenton: Africa World Press, 1991.

Longman, Timothy P. "Christianity and Crisis in Rwanda: Religion, Civil Society, Democratization and Decline." Ph.D. diss., University of Wisconsin-Madison, 1995.

Lugard, Frederick. *The Dual Mandate in British Tropical Africa,* with a new introduction by Margery Perham, 5th ed. Hamden, Conn.: Archon Books, 1965.

Lukes, Steven. *Power: A Radical View*. London: Macmillan, 1974.

Lutz, Catherine A., and Jane A. Collins. *Reading National Geographic*. Chicago: University of Chicago Press, 1993.

Mabi Mulumba and Mutamba Makombo. *Cadres et dirigeants au Zaïre: Qui sont-ils? Dictionnaire biographique*. Kinshasa: Editions du Centre de Recherches Pédagogiques, 1986.

MacGaffey, Wyatt. "Zamenga of Zaïre: 'Novelist, Historian, Sociologist, Philosopher, and Moralist.'" *Research in African Literatures* 13, no. 2 (May 1982): 208–215.

———. *Kongo Political Culture: The Conceptual Challenge of the Particular*. Bloomington: Indiana University Press, 2000.

MacGaffey, Janet. *Entrepreneurs and Parasites: The Struggle for Indigenous Capitalism in Zaïre*. Cambridge: Cambridge University Press, 1987.

MacGaffey, Janet, et al. *The Real Economy of Zaïre: The Contribution of Smuggling and Other Unofficial Activities to National Wealth*. Philadelphia: University of Pennsylvania Press, 1991.

MacIntyre, Alasdair. "Is a Science of Comparative Politics Possible?" In *Against the Self-Images of the Age: Essays on Ideology and Philosophy,* compiled by Alasdair MacIntyre, 260–79. London: Duckworth, 1971.

Selected Bibliography

MacKenzie, David, and Michael W. Curran. *A History of Russia, the Soviet Union, and Beyond*, 4th ed. Belmont, Calif.: Wadsworth Publishing Co., 1993.

Maillu, David G. *My Dear Bottle*. Nairobi: Comb Books, 1973.

———. *Unfit for Human Consumption*. Nairobi: Comb Books, 1973.

———. *After 4:30*. Nairobi: Comb Books, 1974.

———. *the kommon man–part one*. Nairobi: Comb Books, 1975.

———. *No!* Nairobi: Comb Books, 1976.

———. *The Ayah*. Nairobi: Heinemann, 1986.

Malinowski, Bronislaw. *Magic, Science, and Religion and Other Essays*. Glencoe, Ill.: Free Press, 1948.

March, James G. "The Power of Power." In *Varieties of Political Theory*, edited by David Easton, 39–70. Englewood Cliffs, N.J.: Prentice-Hall, 1966.

Markovitz, Irving Leonard. *Léopold Sédar Senghor and the Politics of Negritude*. New York: Atheneum, 1969.

Martin, Denis-Constant. *Tanzanie: L'invention d'une culture politique*. Paris: Presses de la Fondation Nationale des Sciences Politiques and Karthala, 1988.

———. "A la quête des OPNI: Comment traiter l'invention du politique?" *Revue française de sciences politiques* 39, no. 6 (December 1989): 793–815.

———, ed. *Nouveaux langages du politique en Afrique orientale*. Paris and Nairobi: Karthala and IFRA, 1998.

Maughan-Brown, David. *Land, Freedom, and Fiction: History and Ideology in Kenya*. London: Zed Books, 1985.

Mbembe, Achille. "La palabre de l'indépendance: Les ordres du discours nationalistes au Cameroun (1948–1958)." *Revue française de science politique* 35, no. 3 (June 1985): 459–487.

———. *Afriques indociles: Christianisme, pouvoir et état en société postcoloniale*. Paris: Karthala, 1988.

———. "Domaines de la nuit et autorité onirique dans le maquis du sud-Cameroun (1955–1958)." *Journal of African History* 31 (1991): 89–121.

———. "Provisional Notes on the Postcolony." *Africa* 62:1 (1992): 3–37.

———. *La naissance du maquis dans le Sud-Cameroun (1920–1960): Histoire des usages de la raison en colonie*. Paris: Karthala, 1996.

Meillassoux, Claude. "The Social Organization of the Peasantry: The Economic Basis of Kinship." *Journal of Peasant Studies* 1, no. 1 (1973): 81–90.

———. *Maidens, Meal, and Money: Capitalism and the Domestic Community*. Cambridge: Cambridge University Press, 1981.

Mende Omalanga, Lambert (rapporteur), and Tshilengi wa Kabamba (président) et al. "Rapport de la Commission des Biens Mal Acquis," September 1992. République du Zaïre, Conférence Nationale Souveraine, Commission des Biens Mal Acquis, Palais du Peuple. CEDAF (Brussels) / 2492—III.

Merelman, Richard M. "On Legitimalaise in the United States: A Weberian Analysis." *Sociological Quarterly* 39, no. 3 (1998): 351–368.

Metz, Steven. "In Lieu of Orthodoxy: The Socialist Theories of Nkrumah and Nyerere." *Journal of Modern African Studies* 20, no. 3 (1982): 377–392.

Milingo, Emmanuel. *The World in Between: Christian Healing and the Struggle for Spiritual Survival*. London and Maryknoll, N.Y.: C. Hurst and Orbis Books, 1984.

Miller, Christopher L. *Blank Darkness: Africanist Discourse in French*. Chicago: University of Chicago Press, 1985.

———. *Theories of Africans: Francophone Literature and Anthropology in Africa.* Chicago: University of Chicago Press, 1990.

Mitchell, W. J. T. *Picture Theory: Essays on Verbal and Visual Representation.* Chicago: University of Chicago Press, 1994.

Monsengwo Pasinya, L. "Discours du Mgr. L. Monsengwo Pasinya, Archévêque de Kisangani, à l'occasion de son doctorat Honoris Cause, Leuven, le 26 avril 1993." Typescript dated 2 February 1993. CEDAF (Brussels). Eglise catholique. Dossier de presse. 05.04.04.VI.

Mote, Jasinta. *The Flesh.* Produced by David G. Maillu. Nairobi: Comb Books, 1975.

Mudimbé, V. Y. *The Invention of Africa: Gnosis, Philosophy, and the Order of Knowledge.* Bloomington: Indiana University Press, 1988.

Mulligan-Hansel, Kathleen. "The Political Economy of Contemporary Women's Organizations in Tanzania: Socialism, Liberalization and Gendered Fields of Power." Ph.D. diss., University of Wisconsin-Madison, 1999.

Mutungi, O. K. *The Legal Aspects of Witchcraft in East Africa, with Particular Reference to Kenya.* Nairobi: East African Literature Bureau, Kenya, 1977.

Mwangi, Meja. *Striving for the Wind.* London: Heinemann, 1990.

National Council of Churches of Kenya (NCCK). *A New Parliamentary Agenda: Pastoral Letter and Prayers of Intercession.* Nairobi: NCCK, 1993.

Ndao, Cheik Aliou. *Excellence, vos épouses!* Dakar, Senegal: Les Nouvelles Editions Africaines Africaines and SEPIA, 1993.

Ndaywel è Nziem, Isidore. "La société zaïroise dans le miroir de son discours religieux (1990–1993)." *Cahiers africains,* no. 6 (1993).

Ndegwa, Stephen N. *The Two Faces of Civil Society: NGO's and Politics in Africa.* West Hartford, Conn.: Kumarian Press, 1996.

Ngugi wa Thiong'o. *Matigari.* Translated by Wangui wa Goro. Oxford: Heinemann, 1987.

Nguza Karl i Bond. *Mobutu ou l'incarnation du mal zaïrois.* London: Rex Collings, 1982.

Njoya, Timothy Murere. "Dynamics of Change in African Christianity: African Theology through Historical and Socio-Political Change." Ph.D. diss., Princeton Theological Seminary, 1976.

———. *Human Dignity and National Identity: Essential for Social Ethics.* Nairobi: Jemisik Cultural Books, 1987.

———. *Out of Silence: A Collection of Sermons.* Nairobi: Beyond Magazine, 1987.

Nkrumah, Kwame. *Ghana: The Autobiography of Kwame Nkrumah.* New York: International Publishers, 1971 [1957].

Norton, Anne. *Republic of Signs: Liberal Theory and American Popular Culture.* Chicago: University of Chicago Press, 1993.

Norval, Aletta J. *Deconstructing Apartheid Discourse.* London: Verso, 1996.

Nwankwo, Arthur A. *Thoughts on Nigeria.* Enugu, Nigeria: Fourth Dimension Publishing Company Ltd., 1986.

Nyerere, Julius K. *Ujamaa: Essays on Socialism.* Oxford: Oxford University Press, 1968.

Nzongola-Ntalaja. *Class Struggles and National Liberation in Africa: Essays on the Political Economy of Neocolonialism.* Roxbury, Mass.: Omenana, 1982.

Obbo, Christine. *African Women: Their Struggle for Economic Independence.* London: Zed Press, 1980.

Oboler, Regina Smith. *Women, Power, and Economic Change: The Nandi of Kenya.* Stanford, Calif.: Stanford University Press, 1985.

Okri, Ben. *The Famished Road.* New York: Anchor Doubleday, 1992.

Okullu, Henry. *Church and Politics in East Africa.* Nairobi: Uzima Press, 1974.

———. *Church and Marriage in East Africa.* Nairobi: Uzima Press, 1976.

———. *Church and State, in Nation Building and Human Development.* Nairobi: Uzima Press, 1984.

———. "Church and Society in Africa." In *Alternative Development Strategies for Africa: 1: Coalition for Change,* edited by B. Onimode et al., 77–97. London: Institute for African Alternatives, 1990.

Omotoso, Kole. *Just Before Dawn.* Ibadan, Nigeria: Spectrum Books, 1988.

Oniororo, Niyi. *Letters to Nigerian Society.* Ibadan, Nigeria: Ororo Publications, 1990.

Orizu, Akweke Abyesinia Nwafor (The Rt. Hon. Prince). *Insight into Nigeria: The Shehu Shagari Era.* Ibadan, Nigeria: Evans Brothers, 1983.

Orwell, George. "Politics and the English Language." In *In Front of Your Nose, 1945–1950,* vol. 4: *The Collected Essays, Journalism, and Letters of George Orwell,* edited by Sonia Orwell and Ian Angus, 127–40. New York: Harcourt Brace Jovanovich, 1968 [1946].

Ottaway, David, and Marina Ottaway. *Afrocommunism.* New York: Holmes and Meier, 1981.

Oyewumi, Oyeronke. *The Invention of Women: Making an African Sense of Western Gender Discourses.* Minneapolis: University of Minnesota Press, 1997.

Packard, Randall M. *Chiefship and Cosmology: An Historical Study of Political Competition.* Bloomington: Indiana University Press, 1981.

Paden, John N. *Religion and Political Culture in Kano.* Berkeley and Los Angeles: University of California Press, 1973.

Pasquinelli, Carla. "Power without the State." *Telos* 68 (1986): 79–92.

Péan, Pierre. *Affaires africaines.* Paris: Fayard, 1983.

Peel, J. D. Y. *Ijeshas and Nigerians: The Incorporation of a Yoruba Kingdom, 1890s–1970s.* Cambridge: Cambridge University Press, 1983.

Pye, Lucian W. *Asian Power and Politics: The Cultural Dimensions of Authority.* Cambridge, Mass.: Belknap Press of Harvard University Press, 1985.

Quigley, Joan. *"What Does Joan Say?": My Seven Years as White House Astrologer to Nancy and Ronald Reagan.* New York: Carol Publishing Group, 1990.

Raj, R. Dev. "India-Culture: Astrologers Thrive in Political Uncertainty." Inter Press Service, New Delhi, 2 March 1998.

Ram, Mohan. "The Power and Persuasion of India's Stargazers." *Far Eastern Economic Review* 126 (6 December 1984): 59–60.

Regan, Donald T. *For the Record: From Wall Street to Washington.* San Diego, Calif.: Harcourt Brace Jovanovich, 1988.

Reno, William. *Corruption and State Politics in Sierra Leone.* Cambridge: Cambridge University Press, 1995.

Robertson, Claire C. *Sharing the Same Bowl: A Socioeconomic History of Women and Class in Accra, Ghana.* Bloomington: Indiana University Press, 1984.

Rothchild, Donald, and Naomi Chazan, eds. *The Precarious Balance: State and Society in Africa.* Boulder, Colo.: Westview Press, 1988.

Rotimi, Ola. "Of PPA Presidential Choice and the Nation." *Punch,* 30 December 1982. Reprinted in Ola Rotimi, *Statements: Towards August '83. . . .* Lagos, Nigeria: Kurunmi Adventures Ltd, 1983.

Russell, Bertrand. *Power: A New Social Analysis.* London: George Allen and Unwin, 1938.

Said, Edward W. *Orientalism.* New York: Pantheon Books, 1978.

Sakombi Inongo. *Lettre ouverte à Nguza Karl i Bond.* N.p. [France], 1982.

Selected Bibliography

Sanneh, Lamin. *Translating the Message: The Missionary Impact on Culture.* Maryknoll, N.Y.: Orbis Books, 1989.

Sapiro, Virginia. *A Vindication of Political Virtue: The Political Theory of Mary Wollstonecraft.* Chicago: University of Chicago Press, 1992.

Schaffer, Frederic C. *Democracy in Translation: Understanding Politics in an Unfamiliar Culture.* Ithaca, N.Y.: Cornell University Press, 1998.

Schatzberg, Michael G. "*Fidélité au Guide:* The J.M.P.R. in Zairian Schools." *Journal of Modern African Studies* 16, no. 3 (1978): 417–431.

———. *Politics and Class in Zaire: Bureaucracy, Business, and Beer in Lisala.* New York: Africana, 1980.

———. "Explaining Zaire." *African Affairs* 82, no. 329 (October 1983): 569–573.

———. "Zaire." In *The Political Economy of African Foreign Policy: Comparative Analysis,* edited by Timothy M. Shaw and Olajide Aluko, 283–318. Aldershot, Hants, England: Gower, 1984.

———. "The Metaphors of Father and Family." In *The Political Economy of Cameroon,* edited by Michael G. Schatzberg and I. William Zartman, 1–19. New York: Praeger, 1986.

———. "Two Faces of Kenya: The Researcher and the State." *African Studies Review* 29, no. 4 (December 1986): 1–15.

———. *The Dialectics of Oppression in Zaire.* Bloomington: Indiana University Press, 1988.

———. "Power, Legitimacy, and 'Democratisation' in Africa." *Africa* 63, no. 4 (1993): 445–461.

———. "Hijacking Change: Zaire's 'Transition' in Comparative Perspective." In *Democracy in Africa: The Hard Road Ahead,* edited by Marina Ottaway, 113–134. Boulder, Colo.: Lynne Rienner, 1997.

———. "Beyond Mobutu: Kabila and the Congo." *Journal of Democracy* 8, no. 4 (October 1997): 70–84.

Scheub, Harold. *Story.* Madison: University of Wisconsin Press, 1998.

Schochet, Gordon J. *Patriarchalism in Political Thought: The Authoritarian Family and Political Speculation and Attitudes Especially in Seventeenth-Century England.* Oxford: Basil Blackwell, 1975.

Schutz, Alfred. *The Phenomenology of the Social World.* Translated by George Walsh and Frederic Lehnert. Evanston, Ill.: Northwestern University Press, 1967.

Schwartz, Barry. *George Washington: The Making of an American Symbol.* New York: Free Press, 1987.

Scott, James C. *Domination and the Arts of Resistance: Hidden Transcripts.* New Haven, Conn.: Yale University Press, 1990.

———. *Seeing Like a State: How Certain Schemes to Improve the Human Condition Have Failed.* New Haven, Conn.: Yale University Press, 1998.

Seitel, Peter. *See So That We May See: Performances and Interpretations of Traditional Tales from Tanzania.* Bloomington: Indiana University Press, 1980.

Sills, David L., and Robert K. Merton. "Social Science Quotations: Who Said What, When, and Where." *Items* 45, no. 1 (March 1991): 1–3.

Soyinka, Wole. *Kongi's Harvest.* London: Oxford University Press, 1967.

———. *AKE: The Years of Childhood.* New York: Random House, 1981.

Spear, Thomas, and Isaria N. Kimambo, eds. *East African Expressions of Christianity.* Oxford: James Currey, 1999.

Selected Bibliography

Steeves, H. Leslie. *Gender Violence and the Press: The St. Kizito Story.* Athens: Ohio University Center for International Studies, Africa Series no. 67, 1997.

Stiehm, Judith Hicks. *Bring Me Men and Women: Mandated Change at the U. S. Air Force Academy.* Berkeley and Los Angeles: University of California Press, 1981.

Strobel, Margaret. *Muslim Women of Mombasa, 1890–1975.* New Haven, Conn.: Yale University Press, 1979.

Taussig, Michael. *The Magic of the State.* New York: Routledge, 1997.

Ter Haar, Gerrie. *Spirit of Africa: The Healing Ministry of Archbishop Milingo of Zambia.* London: Hurst and Company, 1992.

Thassinda uba Thassinda H. *Zaïre: Les princes de l'invisible: L'Afrique noire bâillonnée par le parti unique.* Caen, France: Editions C'est à Dire, 1992.

Throup, David. "'Render unto Caesar the Things That Are Caesar's': The Politics of Church-State Conflict in Kenya 1978–1990." In *Religion and Politics in East Africa: The Period Since Independence,* edited by Holger Bernt Hansen and Michael Twaddle, 143–176. London: James Currey, 1995.

Toulabor, Comi M. *Le Togo sous Eyadéma.* Paris: Karthala, 1986.

Toungara, Jeanne Maddox. "The Apotheosis of Côte d'Ivoire's Nana Houphouet-Boigny." *Journal of Modern African Studies* 28, no. 1 (March 1990): 23–54.

Tripp, Aili Mari. *Changing the Rules: The Politics of Liberalization and the Urban Informal Economy in Tanzania.* Berkeley and Los Angeles: University of California Press, 1997.

———. *Women and Politics in Uganda.* Madison, Oxford, and Kampala: University of Wisconsin Press, James Currey, and Fountain Press, 2000.

———. "Political Reform in Tanzania: The Struggle for Associational Autonomy." *Comparative Politics* 32, no. 2 (January 2000): 191–214.

Tshonga-Onyumbe. "Nkisi, nganga et ngangankisi dans la musique zaïroise moderne de 1960 à 1981." *Zaïre-Afrique* 22, no 169 (1982): 555–566.

Tunstall, Jeremy. "The Problem of Industrial Relations News in the Press." In *Studies in the Press,* edited by Oliver Boyd-Barrett, Colin Seymour-Ure, and Jeremy Tunstall, 343–97. London: Her Majesty's Stationery Office, 1977.

Turner, Victor. *Dramas, Fields, and Metaphors: Symbolic Action in Human Society.* Ithaca, N.Y.: Cornell University Press, 1974.

Umezinwa, Willy A. "The African Novel, the African Politician, and the Metaphor of Size." *Imprévu* 1 (1990): 25–42.

Vansina, Jan. *Oral Tradition as History.* Madison: University of Wisconsin Press, 1985.

———. *Paths in the Rainforest: Toward a History of Political Tradition in Equatorial Africa.* Madison: University of Wisconsin Press, 1990.

Verdery, Katherine. *National Ideology under Socialism: Identity and Cultural Politics in Ceausescu's Romania.* Berkeley and Los Angeles: University of California Press, 1991.

Verhaegen, Benoît, et al. *Congo 1959–1967.* Brussels: CRISP, 1961–1969.

———. *Femmes de Kisangani: Combats pour la survie.* Louvain-la-Neuve and Paris: Centre d'Histoire de l'Afrique and L'Harmattan, 1990.

Verheust, Thérèse. "Portrait des femmes: Les intellectuelles zaïroises." *Les Cahiers du CEDAF,* no. 6 (October 1985): 1–150.

Villalón, Leonardo A. *Islamic Society and State Power in Senegal: Disciples and Citizens in Fatick.* Cambridge: Cambridge University Press, 1995.

Weber, Max. *Economy and Society.* Edited by Guenther Roth and Claus Wittich. 2 vols. Berkeley and Los Angeles: University of California Press, 1978.

Weiss, Herbert F. *Political Protest in the Congo: The Parti Solidaire Africain during the Independence Struggle.* Princeton, N.J.: Princeton University Press, 1967.

West, Harry G. "Sorcery of Construction and Sorcery of Ruin: Power and Ambivalence on the Mueda Plateau, Mozambique (1882–1994)." Ph.D. diss., University of Wisconsin-Madison, 1997.

White, Luise. *The Comforts of Home: Prostitution in Colonial Nairobi.* Chicago: University of Chicago Press, 1990.

Whiteman, Kaye. "The Gallic Paradox." *Africa Report* (January–February 1991): 17–20.

Wiebe, Robert H. *Self-Rule: A Cultural History of American Democracy.* Chicago: University of Chicago Press, 1995.

Willame, Jean-Claude. *Patrice Lumumba: La crise congolaise revisitée.* Paris: Karthala, 1990.

———. *L'automne d'un despotisme: Pouvoir, argent, et obéissance dans le Zaïre des années quatre-vingt.* Paris: Karthala, 1992.

Wilson, K. B. "Cults of Violence and Counter-Violence in Mozambique." *Journal of Southern African Studies* 18, no. 3 (September 1992): 528–582.

Wolf, Eric. R. "Distinguished Lecture: Facing Power—Old Insights, New Questions." *American Anthropologist* 92, no. 3 (September 1990): 586–596.

World Bank. *World Development Report 1997: The State in a Changing World.* Oxford: Oxford University Press, 1997.

Wright, Bonnie L. "The Power of Articulation." In *Creativity of Power: Cosmology and Action in African Societies,* edited by W. Arens and Ivan Karp, 39–57. Washington, D.C.: Smithsonian Institution Press, 1989.

Wrong, Dennis H. *Power: Its Forms, Bases, and Uses.* New York: Harper and Row, 1979.

Yazawa, Melvin. *From Colonies to Commonwealth: Familial Ideology and the Beginnings of the American Republic.* Baltimore: Johns Hopkins University Press, 1985.

Yeboah-Afari, Ajoa. *A Decade of Thoughts of a Native Daughter,* vol. 1. Accra, Ghana: Graphic Corporation, 1988.

Yoka, Lye M. *Lettre d'un Kinois à l'oncle du village.* Brussels and Paris: Institut Africain–CEDAF and L'Harmattan, 1995.

Young, Crawford, *Politics in the Congo: Decolonization and Independence.* Princeton, N.J.: Princeton University Press, 1965.

———. *Ideology and Development in Africa.* New Haven, Conn.: Yale University Press, 1982.

———. *The African Colonial State in Comparative Perspective.* New Haven, Conn.: Yale University Press, 1994.

Young, Crawford and Thomas Turner, *The Rise and Decline of the Zairian State.* Madison: University of Wisconsin Press, 1985.

Zamenga Batukezanga. *Bandoki (les sorciers).* Kinshasa: Editions St Paul-Afrique, n.d. [1973].

———. *Sept frères et une soeur.* Kinshasa: Editions St Paul-Afrique, December 1975.

———. *Mille kilomètres à pied.* Kinshasa: Editions Saint Paul Afrique, October 1979.

———. *Chérie Basso.* Kinshasa: Editions Saint Paul Afrique, 1983.

———. *Mon mari en grève.* Kinshasa: ZABAT, 1986.

INDEX

Index

Bandolo, Henri, 61
Bangla people, 67
Bantu languages, 202
Baratz, Morton, 38, 39
Barker, Rodney, 211
Barre, Mohammed Said, 218
Batéké people, 55
Bathily, Abdoulaye, 195
Batukezanga, Zamenga, 37
Bayart, Jean-François, 2, 40, 61, 66; on colonial period, 204; on politics and religion, 72–73
"beautiful people," 57
beauty pageants, 181
Beck, Linda, 93
Bédié, Henri Konan, 16, 60, 219
Beetham, David, 214
Bell, Joseph Antoine, 126
Bell Luc René, 111–112
Bénin, 218
Benson, G. P., 73
Berger, Peter, 3
Biafran secession, 60, 166
big people/big men, 44, 45, 46, 50, 203, 217
binary oppositions, 72, 101, 103, 108
Biya, Jeanne, 22, 182
Biya, Paul, 11, 17, 219; alternation of power and, 196, 214; chiefly authority and, 67–68; church-state relations and, 74–75; decline in legitimacy, 27; as father-chief, 151, 152, 153–154, 159, 213; indivisibility of power and, 61; punishment/pardon and, 25, 166, 167–168; religious symbolism and, 53; soccer and, 105–106
Blair, Tony, 110
Bobutaka (soccer player), 121–122
Bockie, Simon, 54
Bokassa, Emperor Jean-Bedel, 218
Boley, George, 154
Bongo, Omar, 54, 218
Boulding, Kenneth, 38
Bratton, Michael, 209, 219
bribery, 26
Britain (United Kingdom), 32, 110, 248n129
Bruner, Jerome, 3
Buhari, General Muhammadu, 30, 44, 74, 98–99, 112
bureaucracy, 90, 110
Burke, Kenneth, 4
Burundi, 32, 155
Bush, George H. W., 34
business, 21, 71, 103–105, 109
Bwiti cult, 54

Cameroon, 2, 5, 21, 115, 213; alternation of power in, 196–197, 214; church and state in, 74–75, 79, 81–82; civil society in, 103; corruption in, 213; "eating" (consumption) in, 40–41; ethnic divisions in, 20; family festivals/photographs in, 22; father-chief in, 10, 11, 148–149, 152; formal religion in, 53, 64, 66, 67; indivisibility and unity of power in, 61, 62; nation as family, 17; political transition in, 31, 219; punishment and pardon in, 166, 167–168; soccer in, 105–106, 111–112; sorcery in, 118; women in, 178–179, 182, 190, 214
Cameroon Tribune (newspaper), 6, 64, 159
capitalism, 88, 204
cartoons, 7
Catholicism, 5, 53, 66; in Cameroon, 75; in Ghana, 82–83, 85, 95; in Kenya, 97; in Nigeria, 74, 171; political skill of popes, 72; press coverage of, 65–66; in Senegal, 78; Vatican II, 75; in Zaïre, 80–81, 85, 112, 168. *See also* Christianity
causality, 1, 7, 35, 110, 112; alternative modes of, 111–118, 139–144, 205–206; democracy and, 221; Mobutu's "liberalization" and, 129–139; sorcery and, 118–129, 140–142
Central African Republic, 218
Certeau, Michel de, 4, 69
Chama Cha Mapinduzi (CCM) (Tanzania), 12, 43, 62, 170; alternation of power and, 198; elections and, 219; women and, 189
Chérie Basso (Zamenga), 57
Chesanga, John, 165
chiefs, 67–68, 156–157, 203
"children," citizens as, 8–9, 25, 29, 106, 159–160; alternation of power and, 192, 194, 198–199; father-chief and, 149–150; First Lady as mother to, 177; paternal generosity and, 152–155; punishment and pardon of, 160–168
Chiluba, Frederick, 218
Christianity, 37, 73, 75, 92, 99; colonialism and, 88; political use of, 51–52, 55; sorcery and, 117; in the United States, 113. *See also* Catholicism; Protestantism
civil society, 72, 101–107, 206
Clark, Robert, 33
Clinton, Bill, 34
Cohen, David William, 42
colonialism, 5, 15, 67, 204; church and state under, 73; end of, 216; missionary Christianity and, 88

Index

communalism/community, 31, 210

Conférence Nationale Souveraine (CNS) (Zaïre), 136, 170, 172

Congo-Brazzaville, 57, 202, 218

Congo-Kinshasa (Congo/Zaïre). *See* Democratic Republic of the Congo; Zaïre

consumption, 26–27, 53, 90, 205. *See also* "eating"; food

contract, sanctity of, 32, 34

"Contract with America," 32

Convention People's Party (CPP) (Ghana), 16–17

corruption, 26, 95, 99, 132, 213–214; food metaphor and, 41; limits of, 168–173; military coups and, 30; women and, 186

Côte d'Ivoire, 5, 17, 21; alternation of power in, 199–200; alternative causality in, 113–114; church and state in, 79, 101; corruption in, 213; "eating" (consumption) in, 50; father-chief in, 8–9, 155, 213; formal religion in, 53, 65–66; indivisibility and unity of power in, 60–61; political transition in, 219; punishment and pardon in, 162, 163–164; soccer in, 124, 125–126, 153; sorcery in, 119, 124, 125–126; state-party in, 16; women in, 181, 187, 214

courtesy visits, 79, 81

cult of personality, 2, 10, 11, 12, 23; African independence and, 204; apogee of, 25; religion and, 112

Dahl, Robert, 38, 207

Daily Graphic (Accra), 6, 67, 180

Daily News (Dar es Salaam), 6, 189

Daily Times (Lagos), 6, 30, 60; on public morals, 171; on women, 181–182, 186

data, 139

Davidson, Basil, 59

debt, 218

democracy, 62, 76, 108, 174, 200; alternation of power and, 197; end of colonial rule and, 216; family metaphor and, 13; formal religion and, 66; logic of legitimacy and, 2, 35, 201–221; religion and, 89. *See also* elections

Democratic Republic of the Congo, 5, 123, 129–139, 142–143, 219. *See also* Zaïre

"democratization," 2, 101, 201, 215–221

Diallo, El Hadj Oumar, 171

Diola ethnic group, 93

Diouf, Abdou, 12, 18, 115; alternation of power and, 30–31, 193, 195, 214, 219; church-

state relations and, 76–78, 79–80, 92, 93–94; civil society and, 102; consumption limits and, 26; corruption and, 172, 214; father-chief role and, 151; indivisibility of power and, 63; international relations and, 17; Islam and, 20; punishment/pardon and, 162, 165–166; wife of, 187–188; women and, 178, 180, 182

Diouf, Elisabeth, 188, 214

Doe, Samuel, 41–42, 63, 218

Dungia, Emmanuel, 136–137, 139

"Dynamics of Change in African Christianity" (Njoya), 88

"eating," 108, 180, 203, 205, 220; corruption and, 214; as face of power, 40–50; father-chief as provider, 150; sorcery and, 57–58; "tribalism" and, 90. *See also* consumption; corruption; food

"Eating the Country" (Tanzanian short story), 47

economics, 3, 26, 73, 138; church-state relations and, 87, 96; single-party regimes and, 216; sorcery and, 140

Edelman, Murray, 4

education, 160, 168, 181–182, 210

Eickelman, Dale, 72

Ekonda, Jacqueline M'Polo, 136

Elders, Joycelyn, 33–34

elections: in Bénin, 218; in Cameroon, 159; in Côte d'Ivoire, 9, 50, 219; in Gabon, 54; in Gambia, 30; in Ghana, 218; in Kenya, 21, 208; in Nigeria, 41, 46, 158–159, 218, 219; in Senegal, 20, 79, 93–94; in South Africa, 218; in the United States, 32, 34, 56, 114. *See also* democracy

Elima (newspaper), 6, 56, 113, 170

Ellis, Stephen, 73

Eneja, Michael, 74

England. *See* Britain (United Kingdom)

English language, 5

Engulu, Léon, 52

Enin, Aanaa, 27

Episcopal Conference of Zaïre (CEZ), 85

Equatorial Guinea, 218

essentialism, 31, 38, 205–206

Essolomwa Nkoy ea Linganga, 176

Ethiopia, 123, 218

ethnicity, 62, 68, 93; alternation of power and, 199–200; church-state relations and, 75; ethnic divisions, 20–21; ethnic identities, 13; ethnic violence, 120–121; national unity and, 148

Index

Europe (western), 110
Eyadéma, Gnassingbé, 29, 118

fables, 3
Fahmy, Mourad, 122
Fall, Abdul Kader, 102
Fall, Amady, 160
family, 3, 147, 189; festivals and photographs, 21–23, 104, 156; idealized, 1; ideology of kinship and, 203; moral matrix of political governance and, 23–24, 147; nation as, 12–15; state as, 16–19
Fanon, Frantz, 216
Farah, Nuruddin, 49
father-chiefs, 145–150; alternation of power and, 192–200; corruption and, 168–173, 171–172; nurture/nourishment and, 150–160, 212; political legitimacy of, 203, 204; punishment/pardon and, 160–168. *See also* paternalism
Fela (Nigerian singer), 186
Fellowship of the Ghana Christian Women, 180
feminism, 188
fetishes, 121, 123, 126, 128. *See also* sorcery; witchcraft
"First Ladyism," 214
Fologo, Dona, 125–126
Fontaine, Just, 123
food, 24–25, 26, 180, 209, 210. *See also* consumption; "eating"
football. *See* soccer
Foreign Broadcast Information Service (FBIS), 6
Foucault, Michel, 4, 7, 39
France, 9, 61, 131, 137, 153
Fraternité Matin (newspaper), 6, 8, 50, 187, 199
French language, 5, 17, 40, 210

Ga people, 67
Gabon, 54, 202, 218
Gambia, 30, 169, 192
Ganaka, Gabriel, 171
Gaulle, Charles de, 9
Gbagbo, Laurent, 164, 219
Geertz, Clifford, 3, 4
gender, 207
geography, 5, 6
Germany, 210
Geschiere, Peter, 118
Ghana, 5, 16–17, 26, 213; church and state in, 82–83, 86, 95–96, 97–98, 99–100; civil society in, 102; corruption in, 170, 172–173, 213; "eating" (consumption) in, 42;

father-chief in, 151, 157; formal religion in, 66–67; military coups in, 30, 208, 219; nation as family, 13–14; Organization of African Unity (OAU) and, 17–18; political transition in, 219; punishment and pardon in, 167; soccer in, 124; sorcery in, 119, 121, 124; women in, 178, 180–181, 183, 190
Ghana: The Autobiography of Kwame Nkrumah (Nkrumah), 217
Ghana Muslim Representative Council (GMRC), 102
Gingrich, Newt, 32
Gitari, Bishop David M., 73, 90–92
Goodman, Nelson, 3
government. *See* state, the
gris-gris (charms), 123
Gueï, Gen. Robert, 219
Guinea, 18

Habyarimana, Juvénal, 218
Harouna, Sar, 113–114
Haruna, Right Rev. Herbert, 98
Haya ethnic group, 147, 150
health care, 191
hegemony, 23, 230–231n95
Houphouet-Boigny, Félix, 8–9, 16, 66; alternation of power and, 199; church-state relations and, 78, 101; decline in legitimacy, 26–27; family festival and, 156; as father-chief, 60–61, 159, 213; international relations and, 18; punishment/pardon and, 162, 163–164; religious symbolism and, 53; soccer and, 125, 152–153
Hutu ethnic group, 32

Ibrahim, Alhaji Liadi, 97
Ibrahim, Alhaji Sanni, 96
identity, 68
ideology, 3
Idowu, Bolaji, 98
Igbo ethnic group, 21
Imanyara, Gitobu, 18
India, 206
individualism, 32
Inglehart, Ronald, 4
Inongo, Sakombi, 54
intellectuals, 159–160
International Monetary Fund, 218
international relations, 17–18, 137
interviews, 5, 30
Iran, 218
Islam, 5, 12, 19, 37; civil society and, 102; in

Index

Index

MICHAEL G. SCHATZBERG is Professor of Political Science and a member of the African Studies Program at the University of Wisconsin–Madison. He is the author of *Politics and Class in Zaïre* (1980), *The Dialectics of Oppression in Zaïre* (Indiana University Press, 1988), and *Mobutu or Chaos?* (1991). He is also the editor of *The Political Economy of Zimbabwe* (1984), *The Political Economy of Kenya* (1987), and co-editor (with I. William Zartman) of *The Political Economy of Cameroon* (1986).